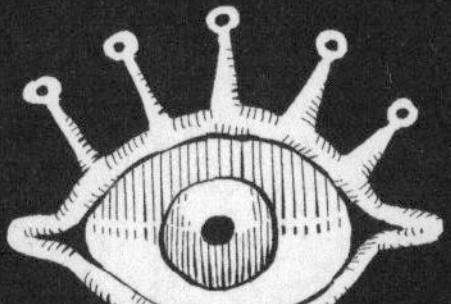

The Country Without Humans

vol. **3**

STORY & ART BY IWATOBINEKO

CONTENTS

Chapter 13

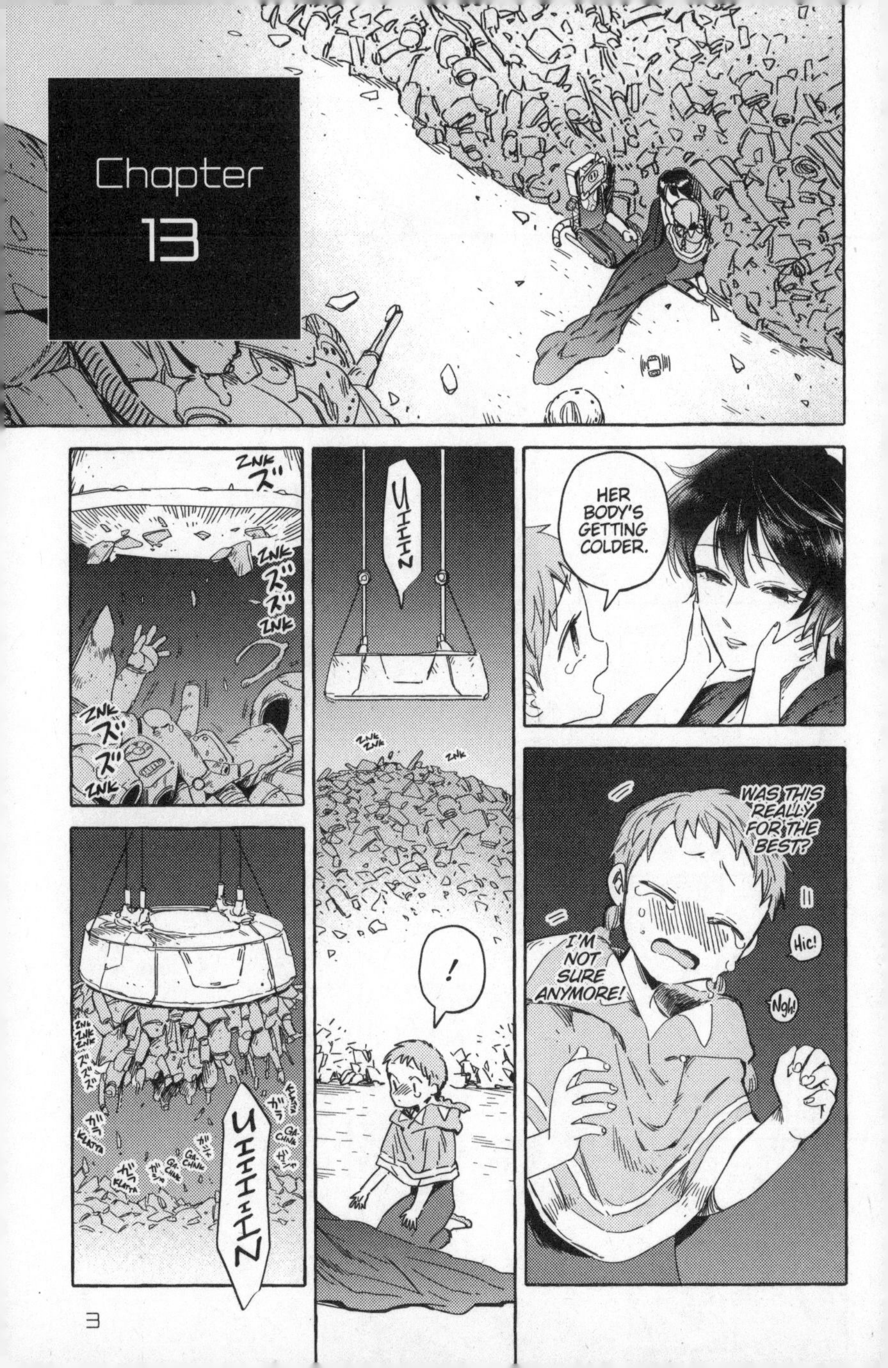
HER BODY'S GETTING COLDER.
WAS THIS REALLY FOR THE BEST?
Hic!
Ngh!
I'M NOT SURE ANYMORE!
UIIIIN
ZNK ZNK
ZNK
!
ZNK ズ
ZNK ズズ ZNK
ZNK ズ ズ ZNK
ZNK ZNK ZNK ズズズ
KLATTA
GA-CHNK
UIIIIIIN

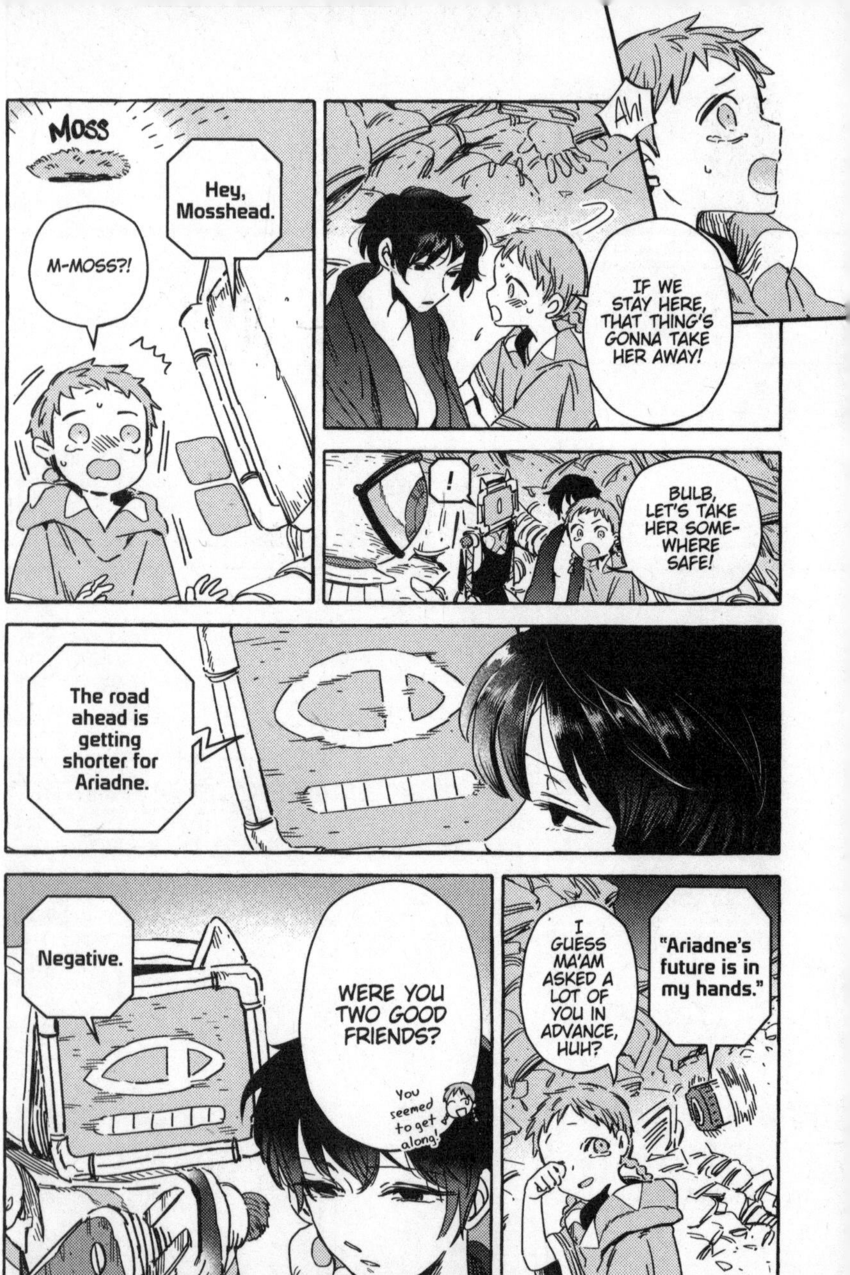
Ah!
IF WE STAY HERE, THAT THING'S GONNA TAKE HER AWAY!
!
BULB, LET'S TAKE HER SOME-WHERE SAFE!
Hey, Mosshead.
MOSS
M-MOSS?!
The road ahead is getting shorter for Ariadne.
"Ariadne's future is in my hands."
I GUESS MA'AM ASKED A LOT OF YOU IN ADVANCE, HUH?
WERE YOU TWO GOOD FRIENDS?
You seemed to get along!
Negative.

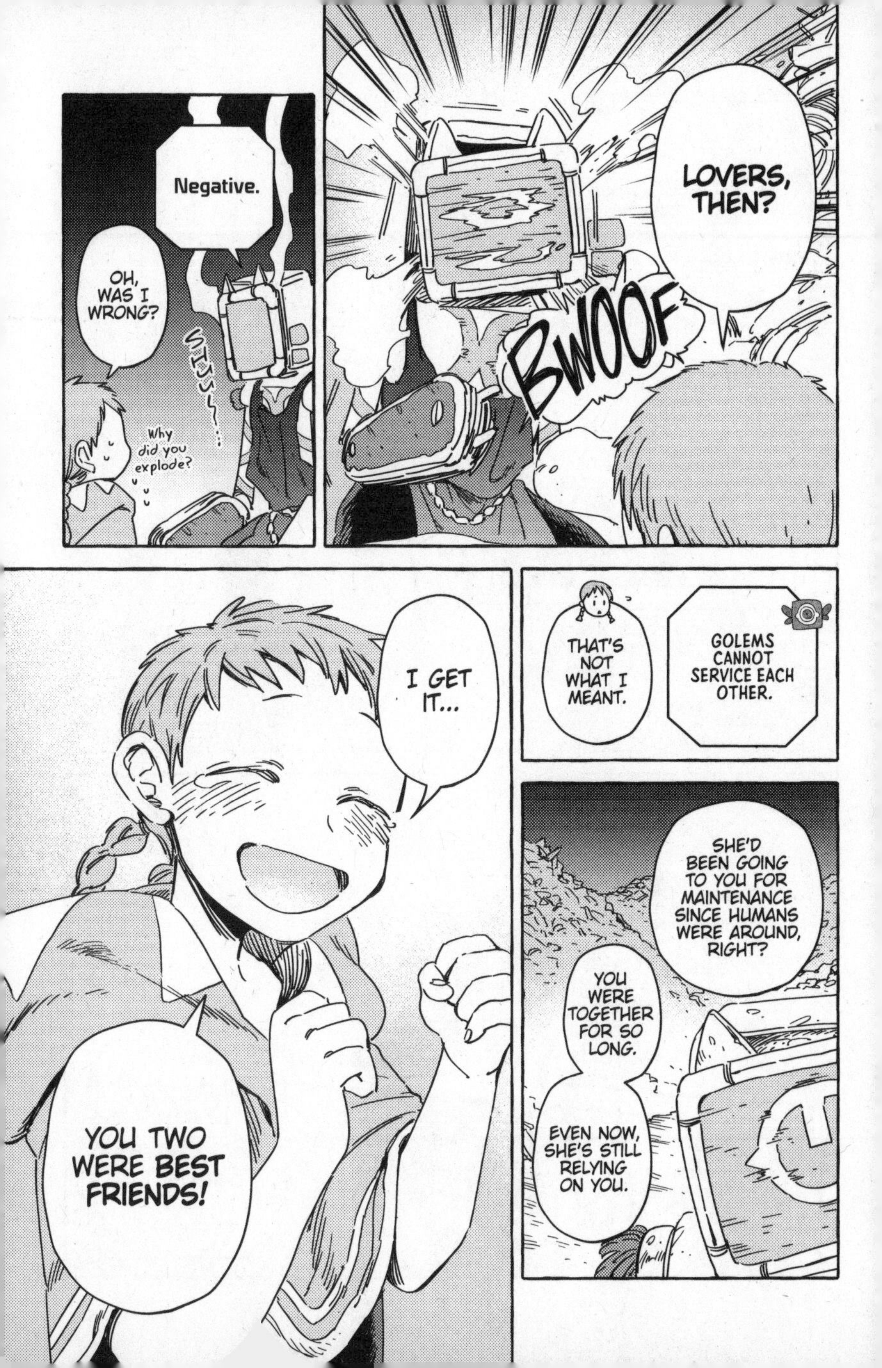
LOVERS, THEN?
BWOOF
Negative.
OH, WAS I WRONG?
Why did you explode?
GOLEMS CANNOT SERVICE EACH OTHER.
THAT'S NOT WHAT I MEANT.
SHE'D BEEN GOING TO YOU FOR MAINTENANCE SINCE HUMANS WERE AROUND, RIGHT?
YOU WERE TOGETHER FOR SO LONG.
EVEN NOW, SHE'S STILL RELYING ON YOU.
I GET IT...
YOU TWO WERE BEST FRIENDS!

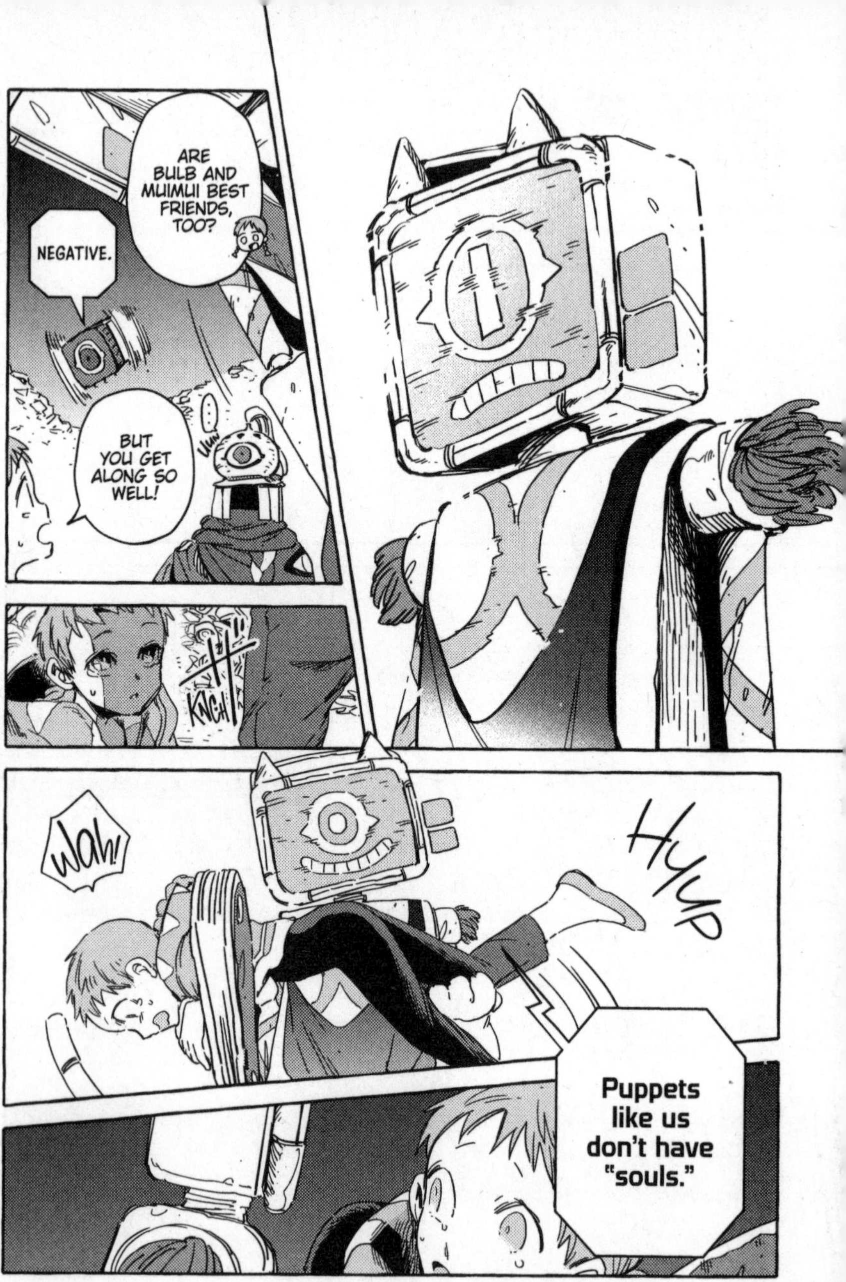
ARE BULB AND MUIMUI BEST FRIENDS, TOO?
NEGATIVE.
BUT YOU GET ALONG SO WELL!
KNCH
HYUP
Wah!
Puppets like us don't have "souls."

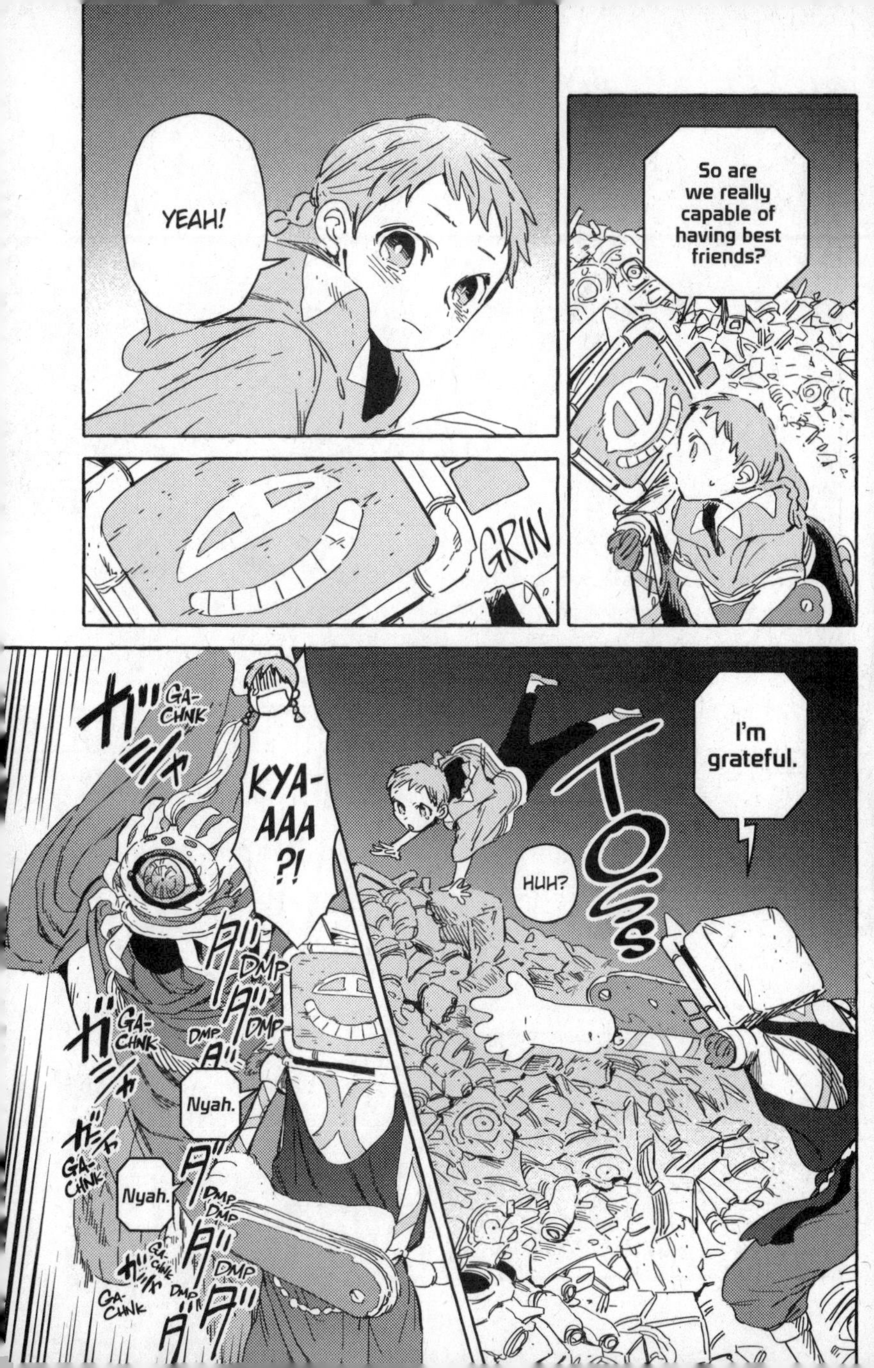
So are we really capable of having best friends?
YEAH!
GRIN
I'm grateful.
TOSS
HUH?
KYA-AAA?!
GA-CHNK
DMP DMP
GA-CHNK
DMP
Nyah.
GA-CHNK
Nyah.
DMP DMP
GA-CHNK
DMP
GA-CHNK
DMP

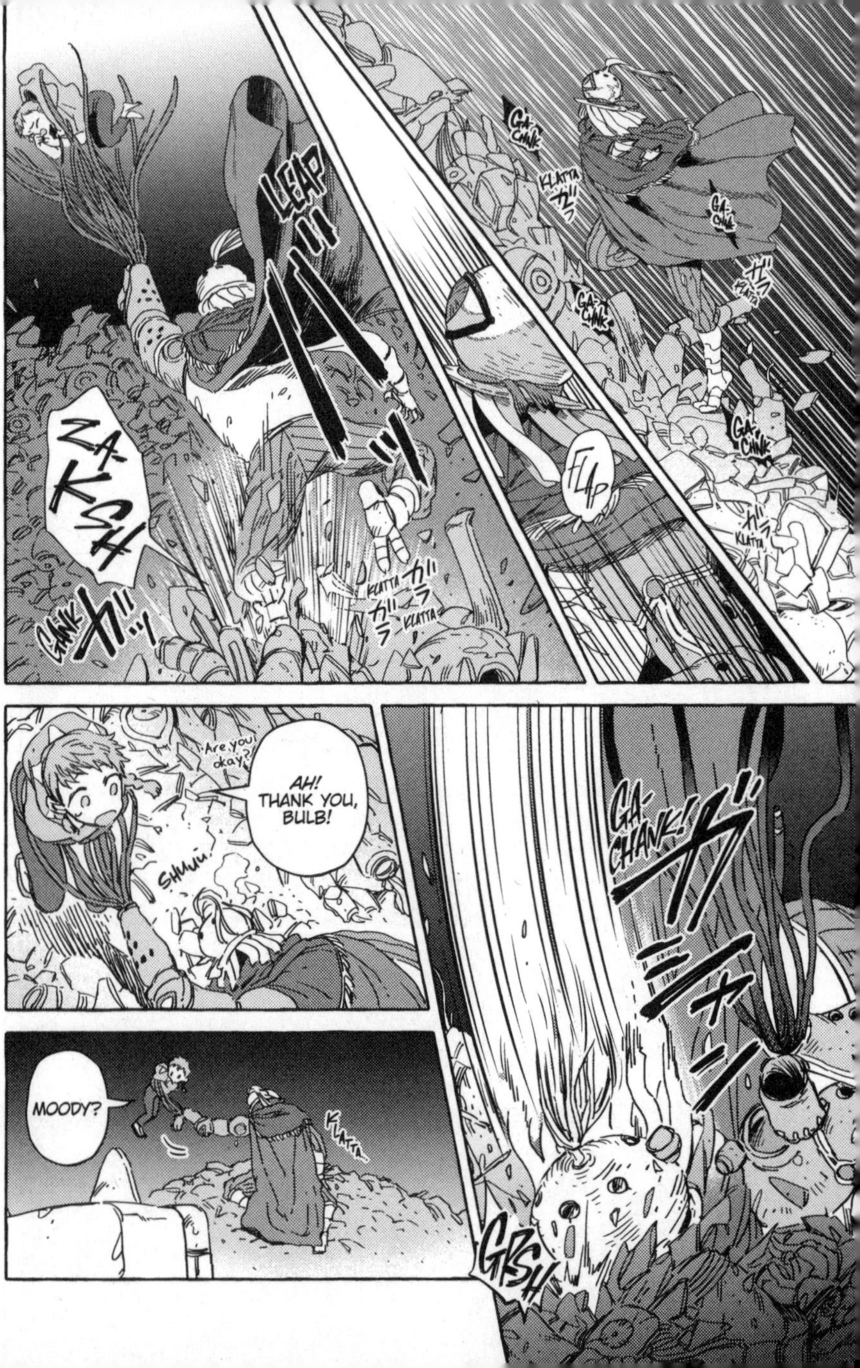
GA-CHNK
KLATTA
GA-CHNK
KLATTA
GA-CHNK
GA-CHNK
FLAP
KLATTA
LEAP
ZA-KSH
KLATTA
KLATTA
GANK
GA-CHANK!
GRSH
Are you okay?
AH! THANK YOU, BULB!
SHUUU
MOODY?
KLATTA

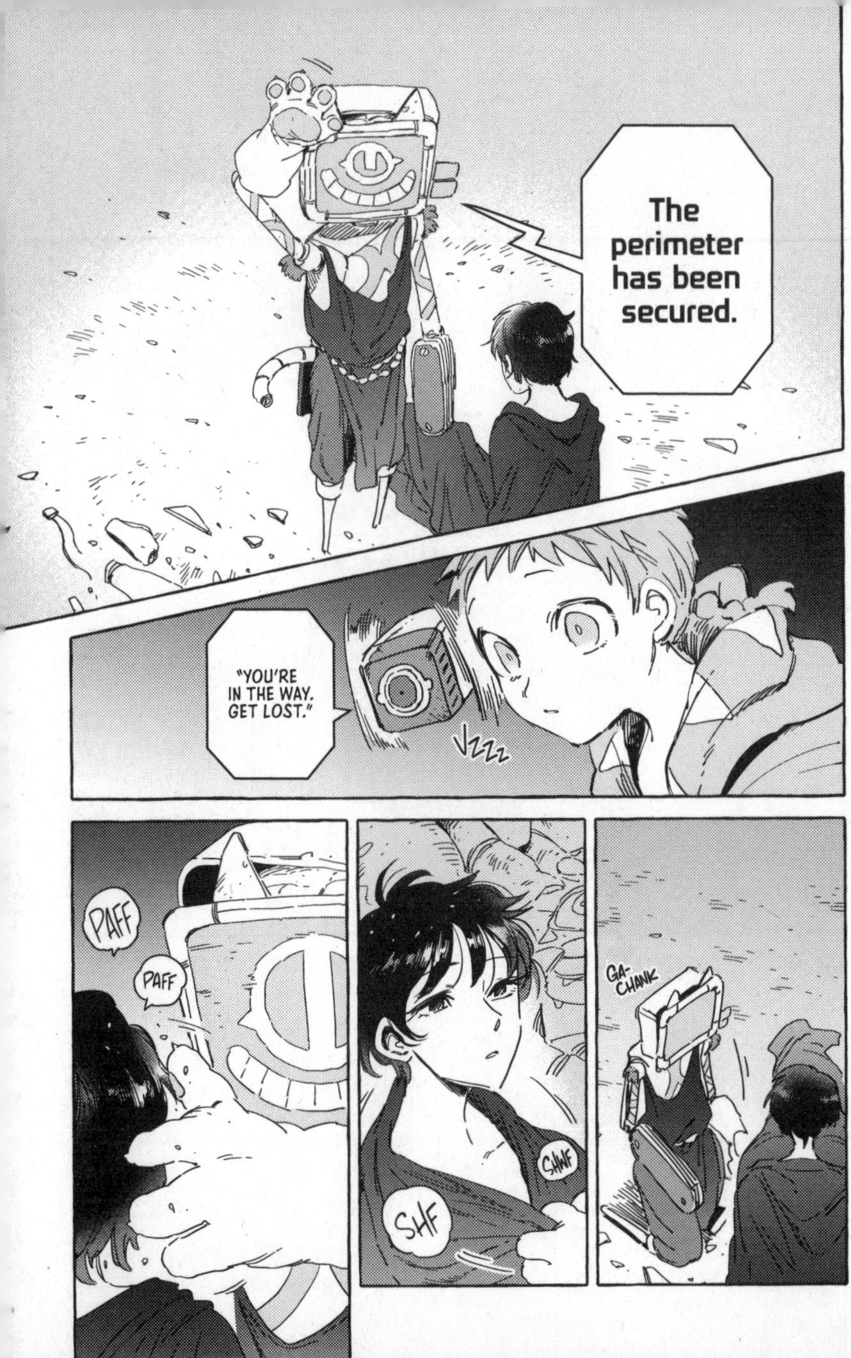
The perimeter has been secured.
"YOU'RE IN THE WAY. GET LOST."
VZZZ
GA-CHANK
SHWF
SHF
PAFF
PAFF

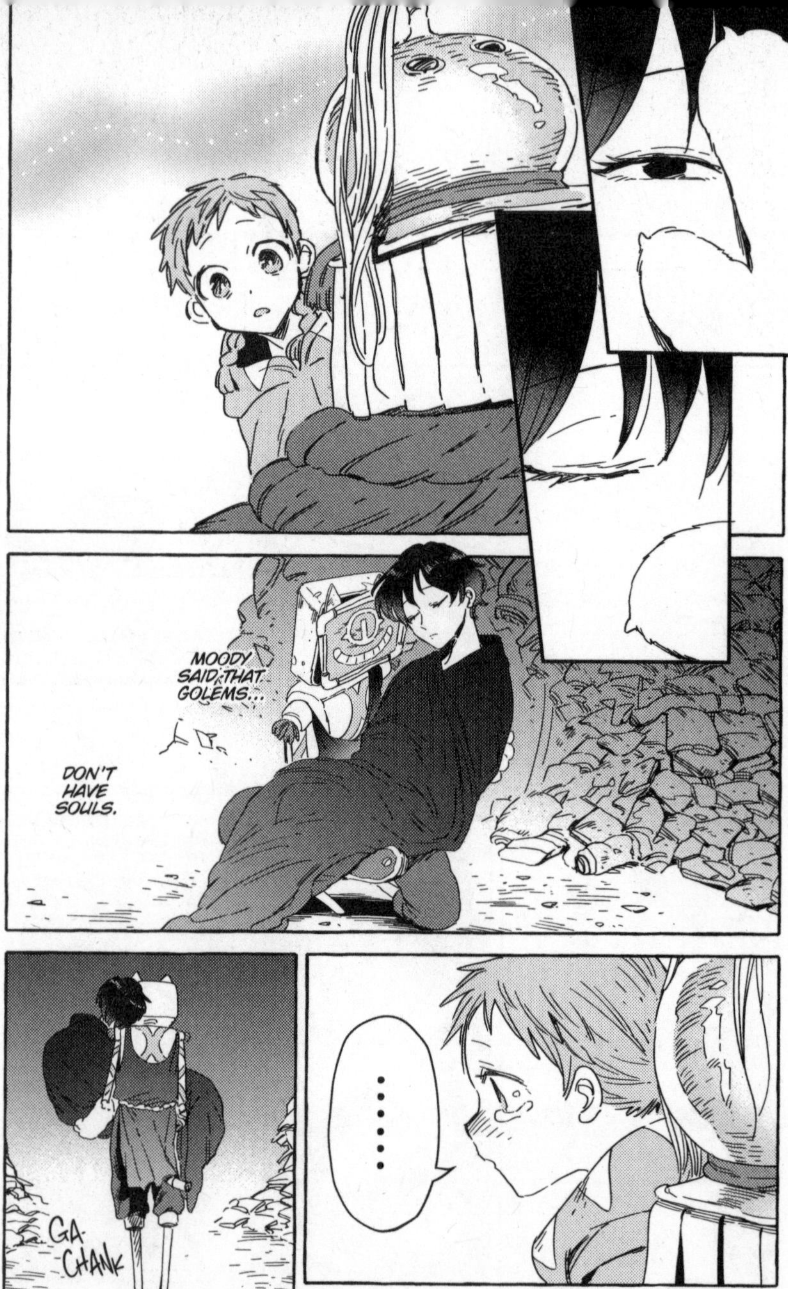
MOODY SAID THAT GOLEMS...
DON'T HAVE SOULS.
......
GA-CHANK

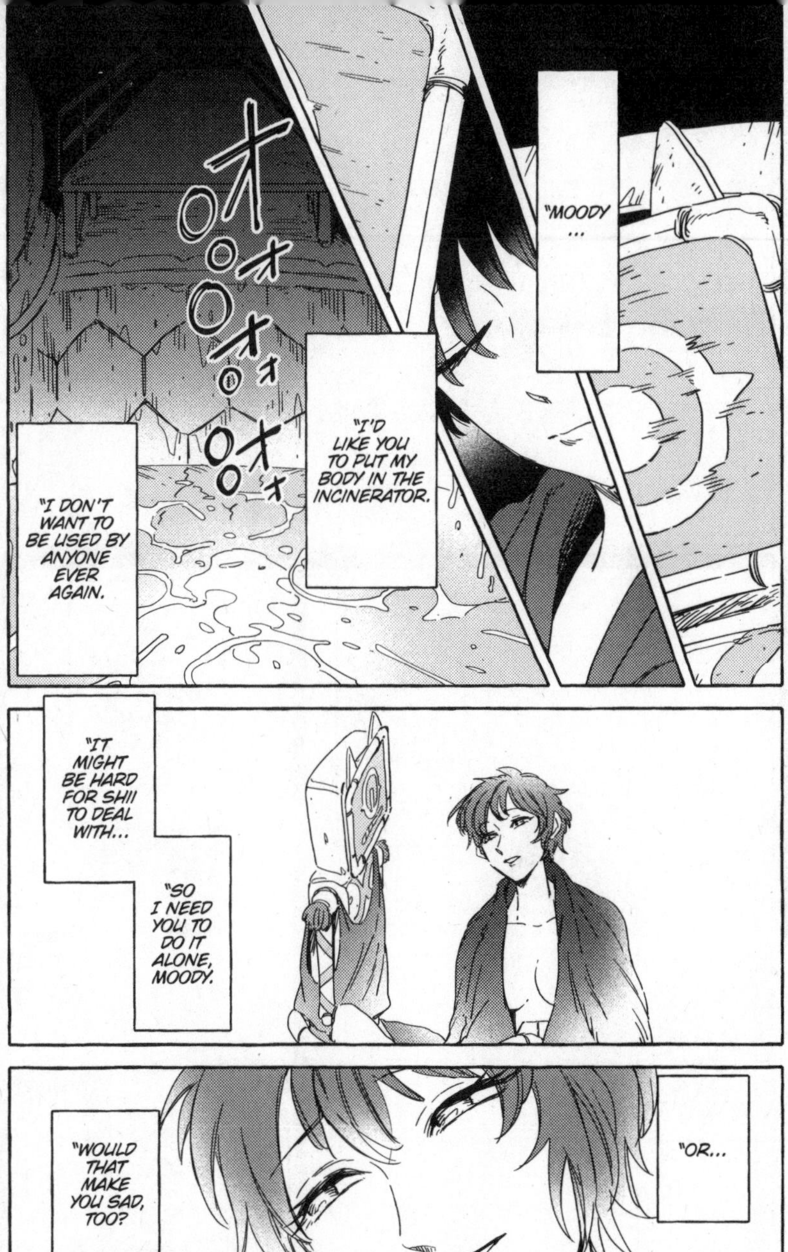
"MOODY ...
"I'D LIKE YOU TO PUT MY BODY IN THE INCINERATOR.
"I DON'T WANT TO BE USED BY ANYONE EVER AGAIN.
"IT MIGHT BE HARD FOR SHII TO DEAL WITH...
"SO I NEED YOU TO DO IT ALONE, MOODY.
"OR...
"WOULD THAT MAKE YOU SAD, TOO?

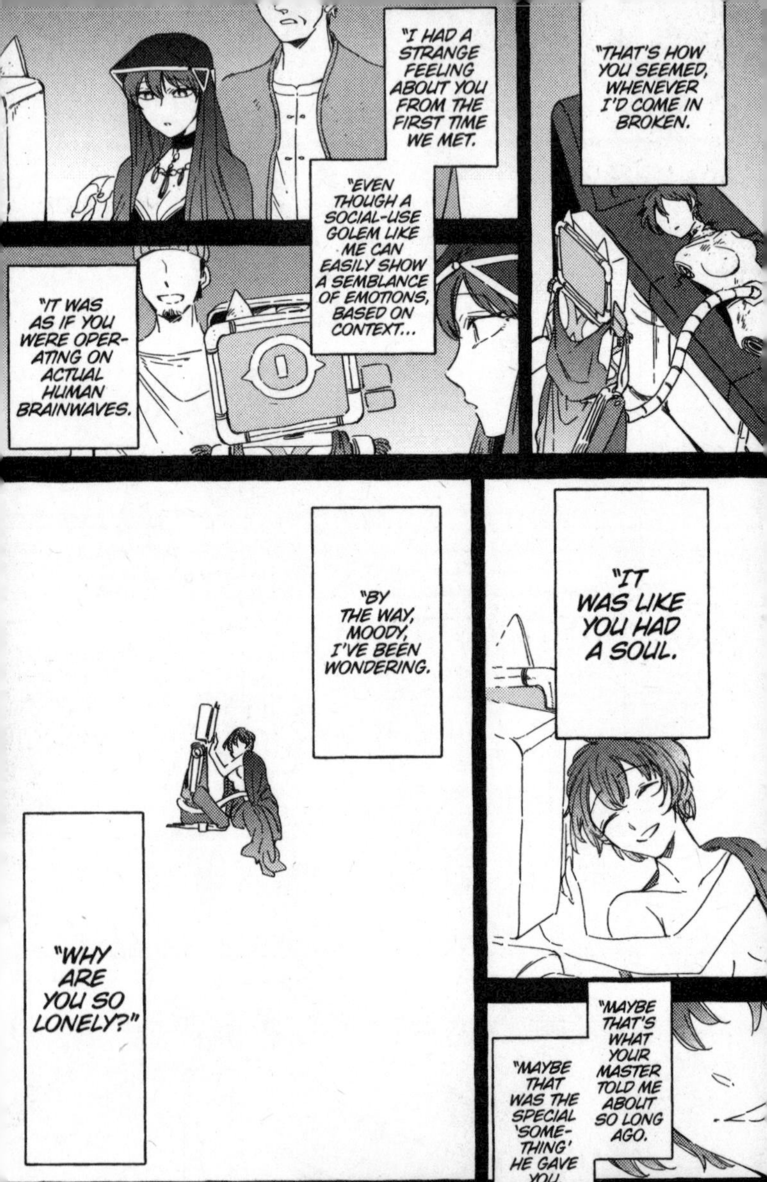
"THAT'S HOW YOU SEEMED, WHENEVER I'D COME IN BROKEN.
"I HAD A STRANGE FEELING ABOUT YOU FROM THE FIRST TIME WE MET.
"EVEN THOUGH A SOCIAL-USE GOLEM LIKE ME CAN EASILY SHOW A SEMBLANCE OF EMOTIONS, BASED ON CONTEXT...
"IT WAS AS IF YOU WERE OPER-ATING ON ACTUAL HUMAN BRAINWAVES.
"IT WAS LIKE YOU HAD A SOUL.
"MAYBE THAT'S WHAT YOUR MASTER TOLD ME ABOUT SO LONG AGO.
"MAYBE THAT WAS THE SPECIAL 'SOME-THING' HE GAVE YOU.
"BY THE WAY, MOODY, I'VE BEEN WONDERING.
"WHY ARE YOU SO LONELY?"

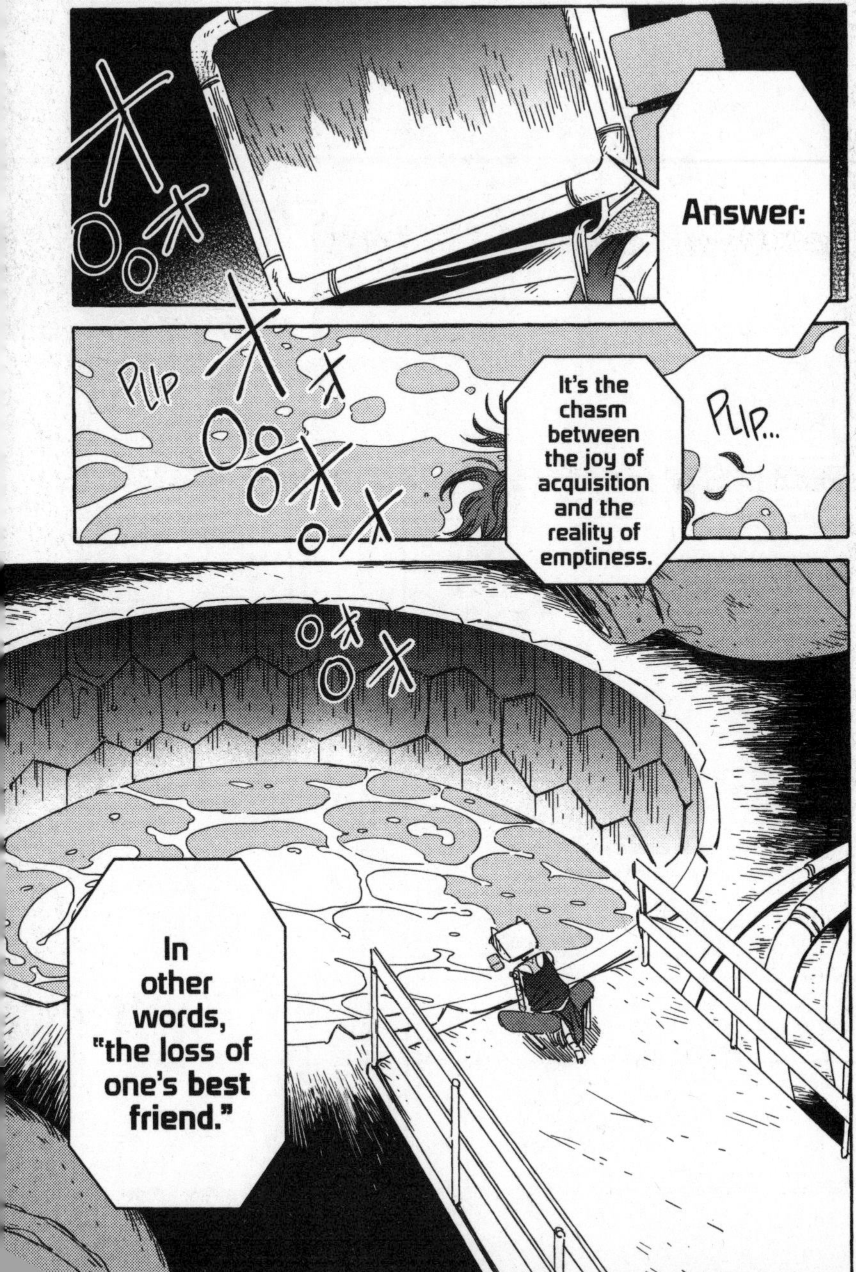
Answer:
It's the chasm between the joy of acquisition and the reality of emptiness.
PLIP...
PLIP
In other words, "the loss of one's best friend."

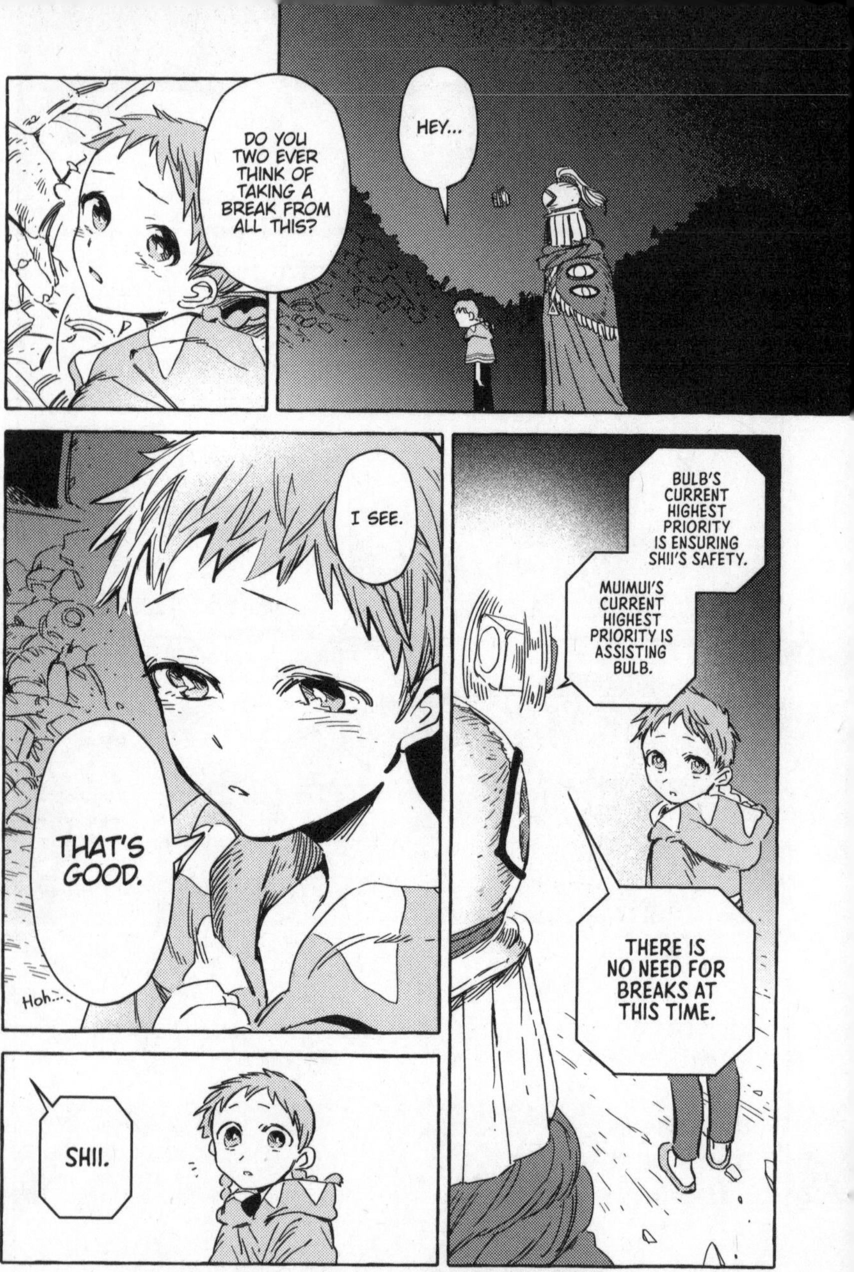
HEY...
DO YOU TWO EVER THINK OF TAKING A BREAK FROM ALL THIS?
BULB'S CURRENT HIGHEST PRIORITY IS ENSURING SHII'S SAFETY.
MUIMUI'S CURRENT HIGHEST PRIORITY IS ASSISTING BULB.
THERE IS NO NEED FOR BREAKS AT THIS TIME.
I SEE.
THAT'S GOOD.
Hoh...
SHII.

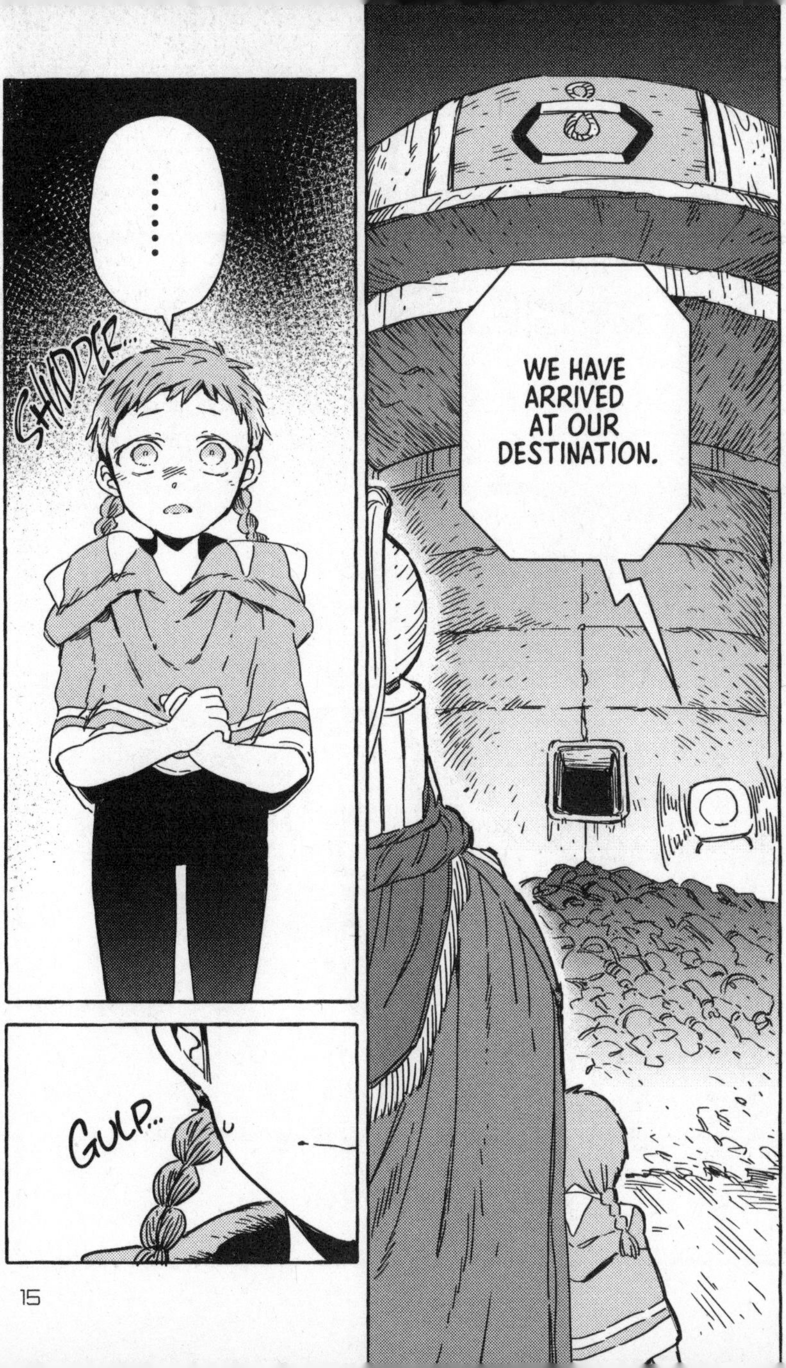
WE HAVE ARRIVED AT OUR DESTINATION.
......
SHUDDER...
GULP...

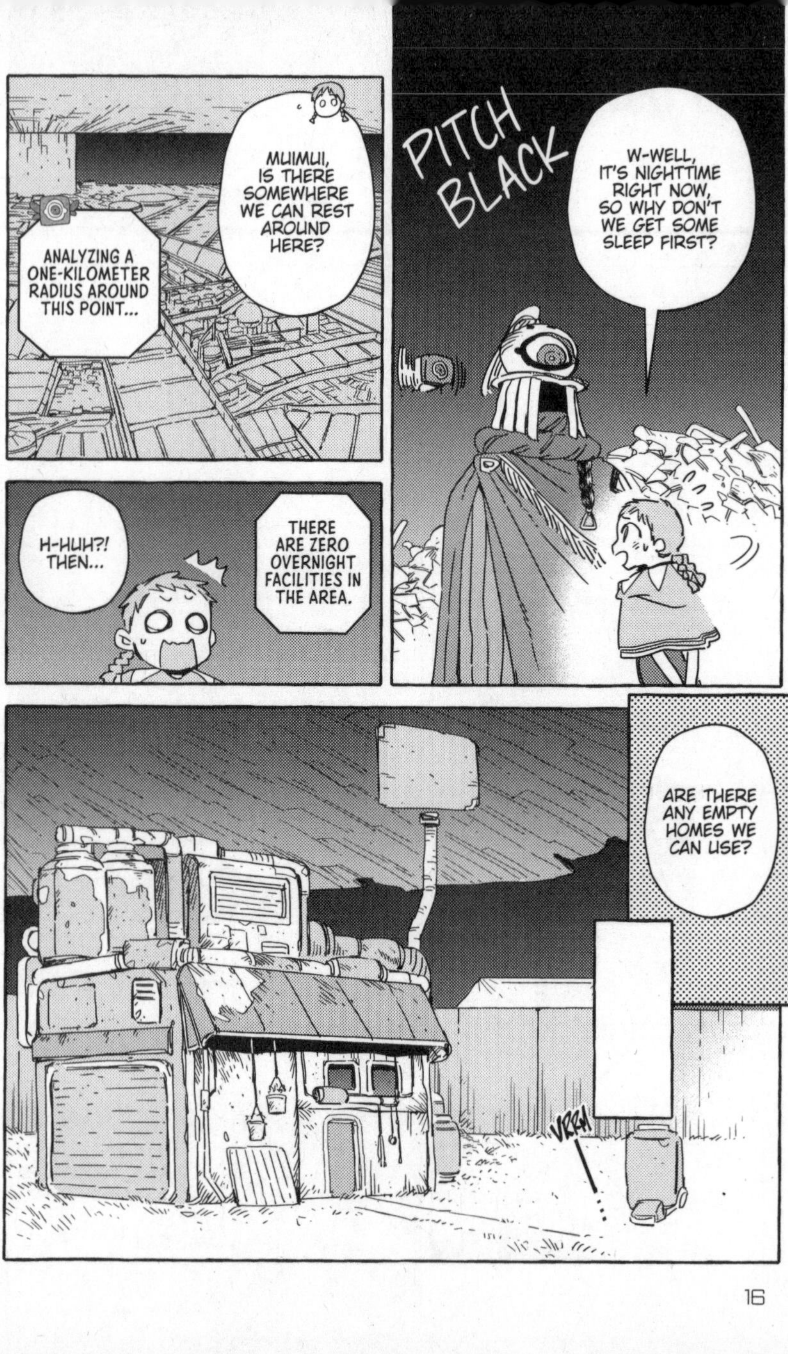
PITCH BLACK
W-WELL, IT'S NIGHTTIME RIGHT NOW, SO WHY DON'T WE GET SOME SLEEP FIRST?
MUIMUI, IS THERE SOMEWHERE WE CAN REST AROUND HERE?
ANALYZING A ONE-KILOMETER RADIUS AROUND THIS POINT...
THERE ARE ZERO OVERNIGHT FACILITIES IN THE AREA.
H-HUH?! THEN...
ARE THERE ANY EMPTY HOMES WE CAN USE?
VRRM

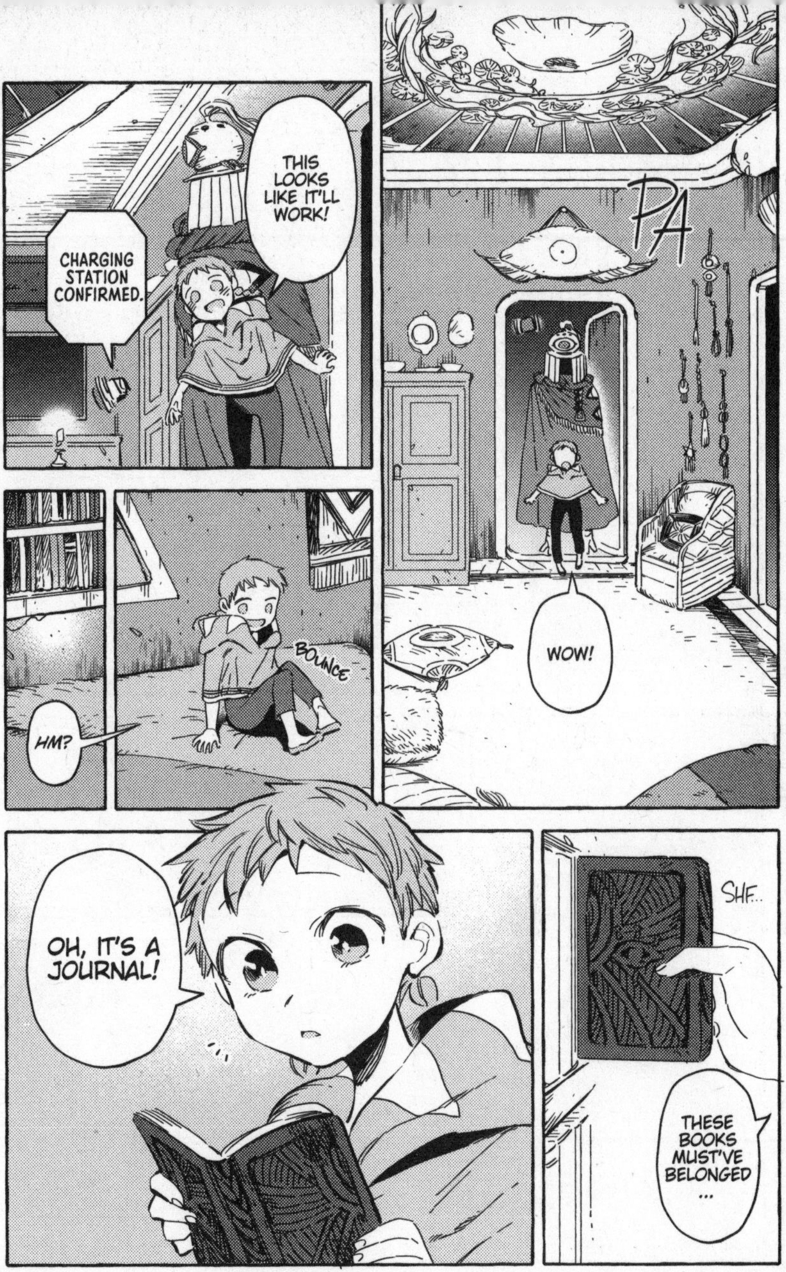
PA
WOW!
THIS LOOKS LIKE IT'LL WORK!
CHARGING STATION CONFIRMED.
BOUNCE
HM?
SHF...
THESE BOOKS MUST'VE BELONGED ...
OH, IT'S A JOURNAL!

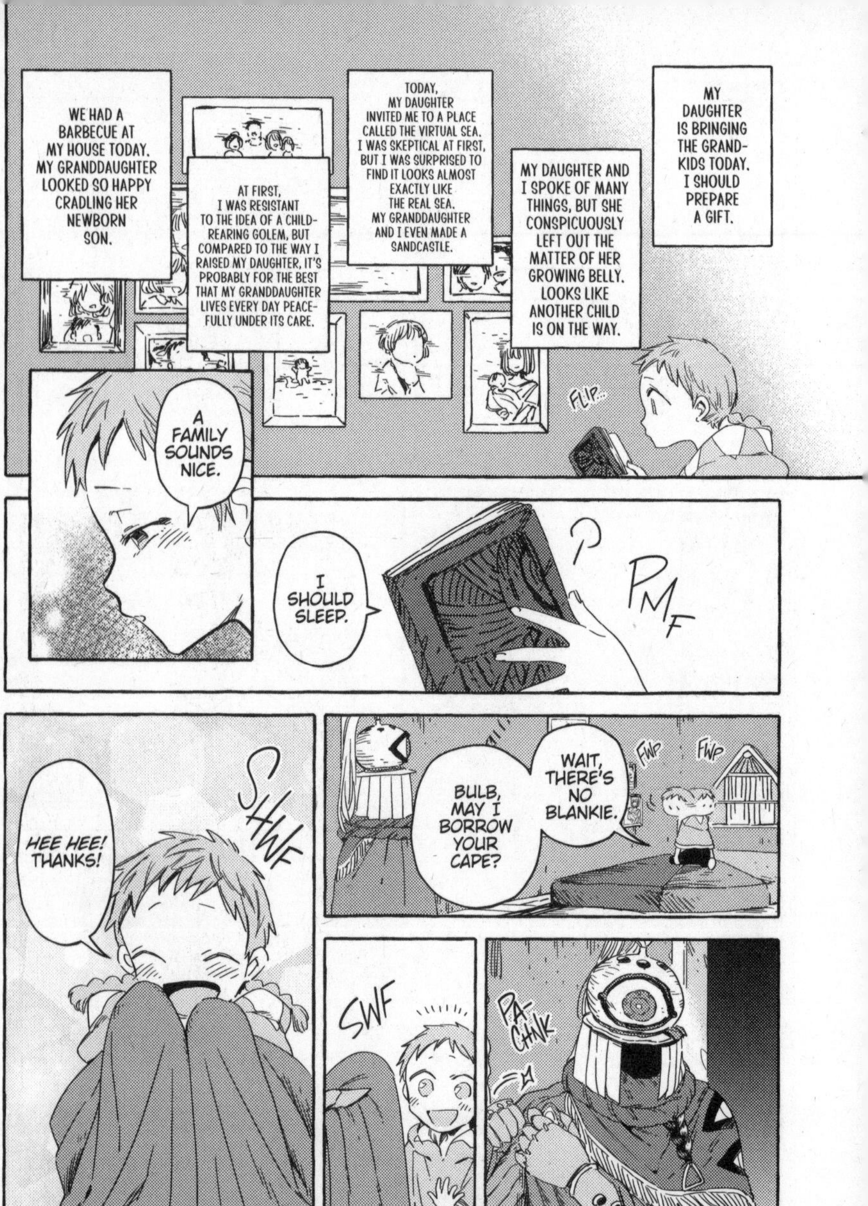

MY DAUGHTER IS BRINGING THE GRAND-KIDS TODAY. I SHOULD PREPARE A GIFT.
MY DAUGHTER AND I SPOKE OF MANY THINGS, BUT SHE CONSPICUOUSLY LEFT OUT THE MATTER OF HER GROWING BELLY. LOOKS LIKE ANOTHER CHILD IS ON THE WAY.
TODAY, MY DAUGHTER INVITED ME TO A PLACE CALLED THE VIRTUAL SEA. I WAS SKEPTICAL AT FIRST, BUT I WAS SURPRISED TO FIND IT LOOKS ALMOST EXACTLY LIKE THE REAL SEA. MY GRANDDAUGHTER AND I EVEN MADE A SANDCASTLE.
AT FIRST, I WAS RESISTANT TO THE IDEA OF A CHILD-REARING GOLEM, BUT COMPARED TO THE WAY I RAISED MY DAUGHTER, IT'S PROBABLY FOR THE BEST THAT MY GRANDDAUGHTER LIVES EVERY DAY PEACE-FULLY UNDER ITS CARE.
WE HAD A BARBECUE AT MY HOUSE TODAY. MY GRANDDAUGHTER LOOKED SO HAPPY CRADLING HER NEWBORN SON.
FLIP...
A FAMILY SOUNDS NICE.
PMF
I SHOULD SLEEP.
FWP
FWP
WAIT, THERE'S NO BLANKIE.
BULB, MAY I BORROW YOUR CAPE?
PA-CHNK
SWF
SHWF
HEE HEE! THANKS!

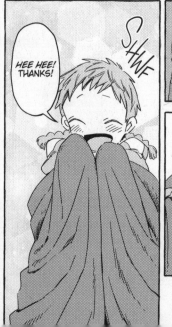

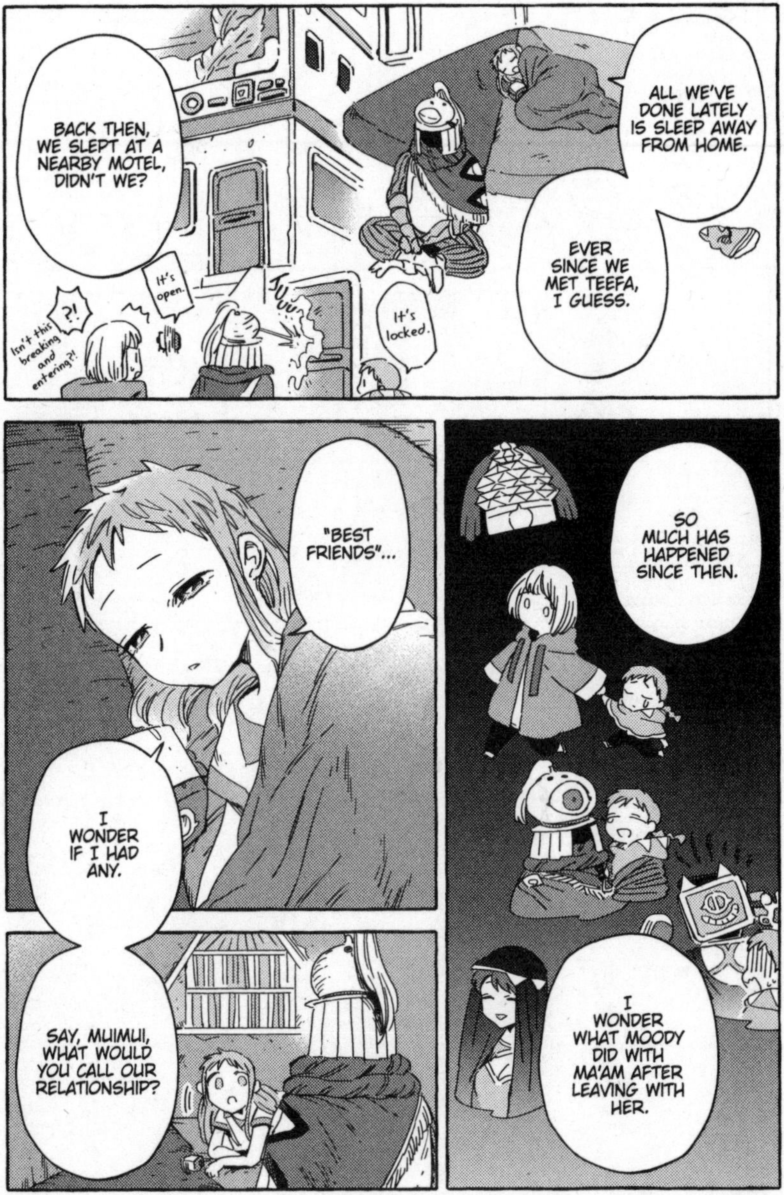
ALL WE'VE DONE LATELY IS SLEEP AWAY FROM HOME.
EVER SINCE WE MET TEEFA, I GUESS.
BACK THEN, WE SLEPT AT A NEARBY MOTEL, DIDN'T WE?
It's locked.
It's open.
?!
Isn't this breaking and entering?!
SO MUCH HAS HAPPENED SINCE THEN.
I WONDER WHAT MOODY DID WITH MA'AM AFTER LEAVING WITH HER.
"BEST FRIENDS"...
I WONDER IF I HAD ANY.
SAY, MUIMUI, WHAT WOULD YOU CALL OUR RELATIONSHIP?

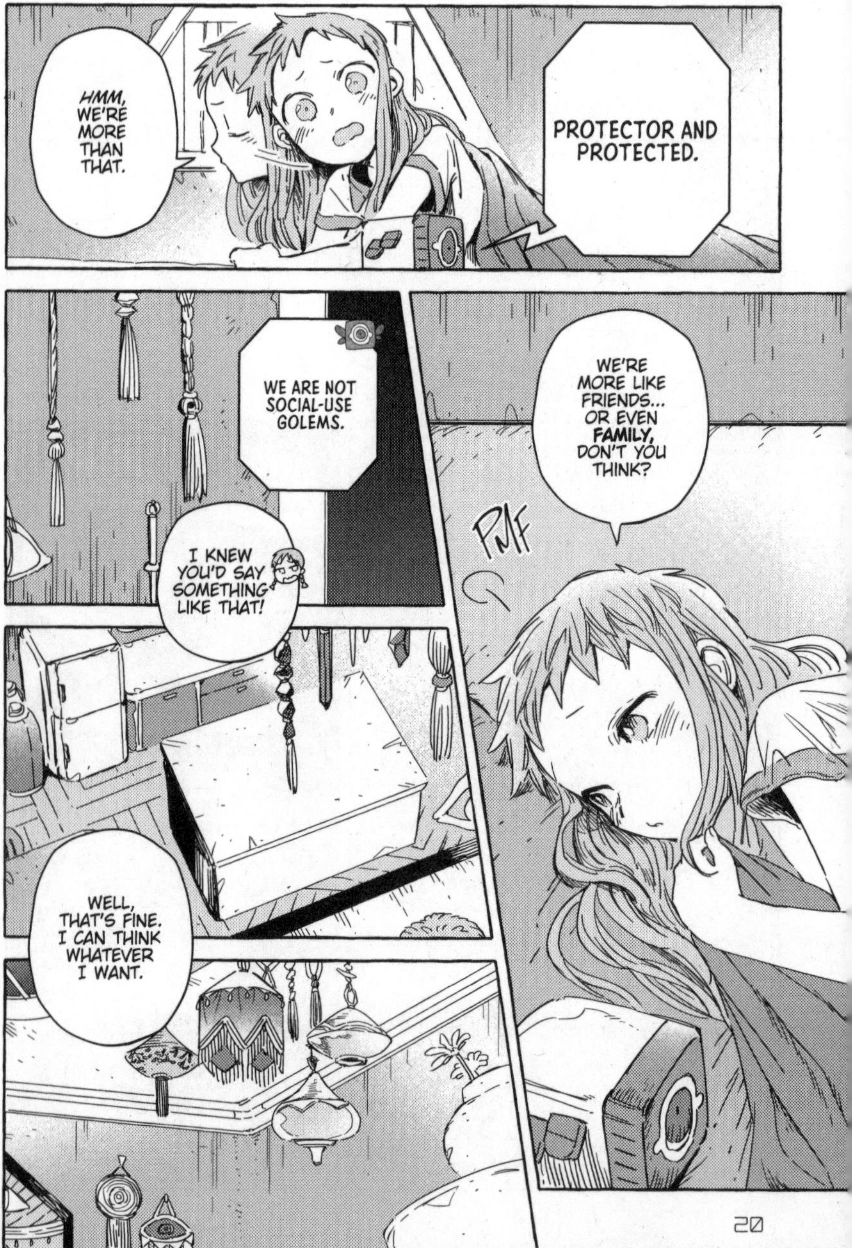
PROTECTOR AND PROTECTED.
HMM, WE'RE MORE THAN THAT.
WE'RE MORE LIKE FRIENDS... OR EVEN FAMILY, DON'T YOU THINK?
PMF
WE ARE NOT SOCIAL-USE GOLEMS.
I KNEW YOU'D SAY SOMETHING LIKE THAT!
WELL, THAT'S FINE. I CAN THINK WHATEVER I WANT.

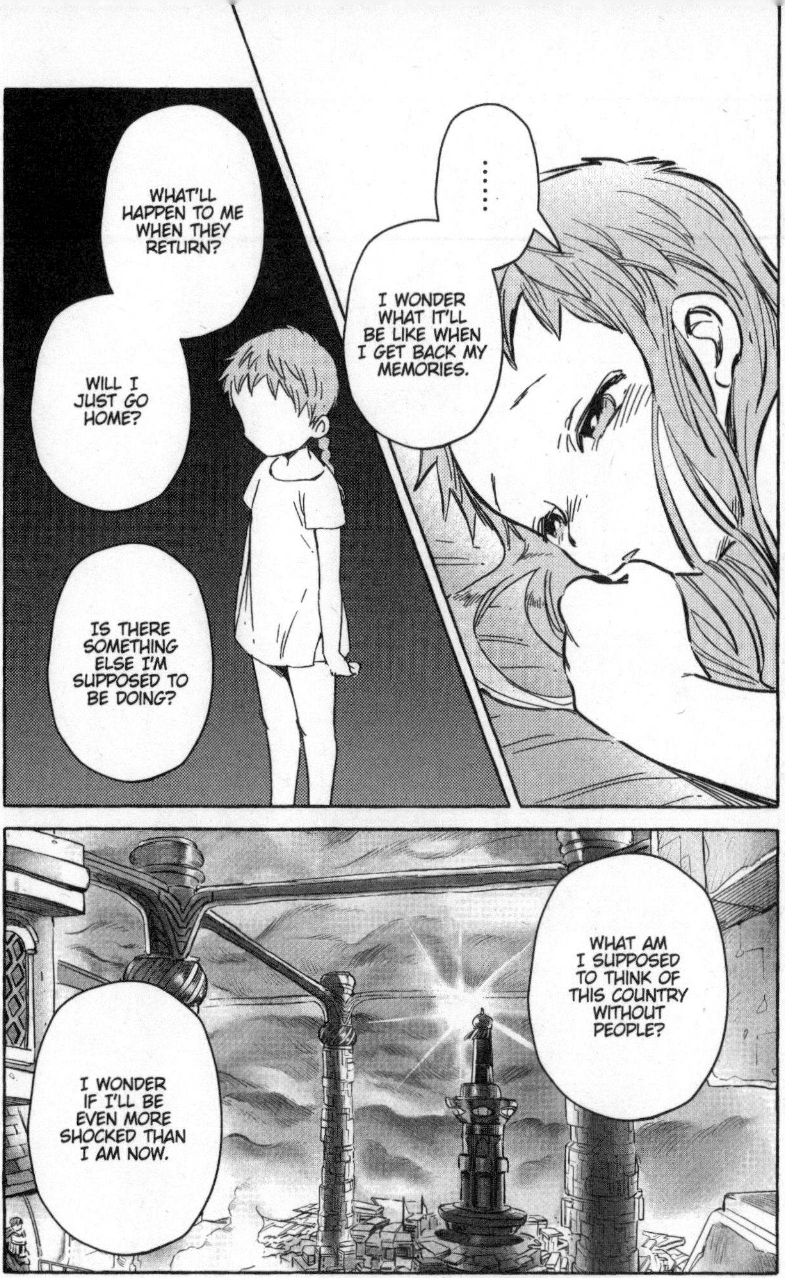
......
I WONDER WHAT IT'LL BE LIKE WHEN I GET BACK MY MEMORIES.
WHAT'LL HAPPEN TO ME WHEN THEY RETURN?
WILL I JUST GO HOME?
IS THERE SOMETHING ELSE I'M SUPPOSED TO BE DOING?
WHAT AM I SUPPOSED TO THINK OF THIS COUNTRY WITHOUT PEOPLE?
I WONDER IF I'LL BE EVEN MORE SHOCKED THAN I AM NOW.

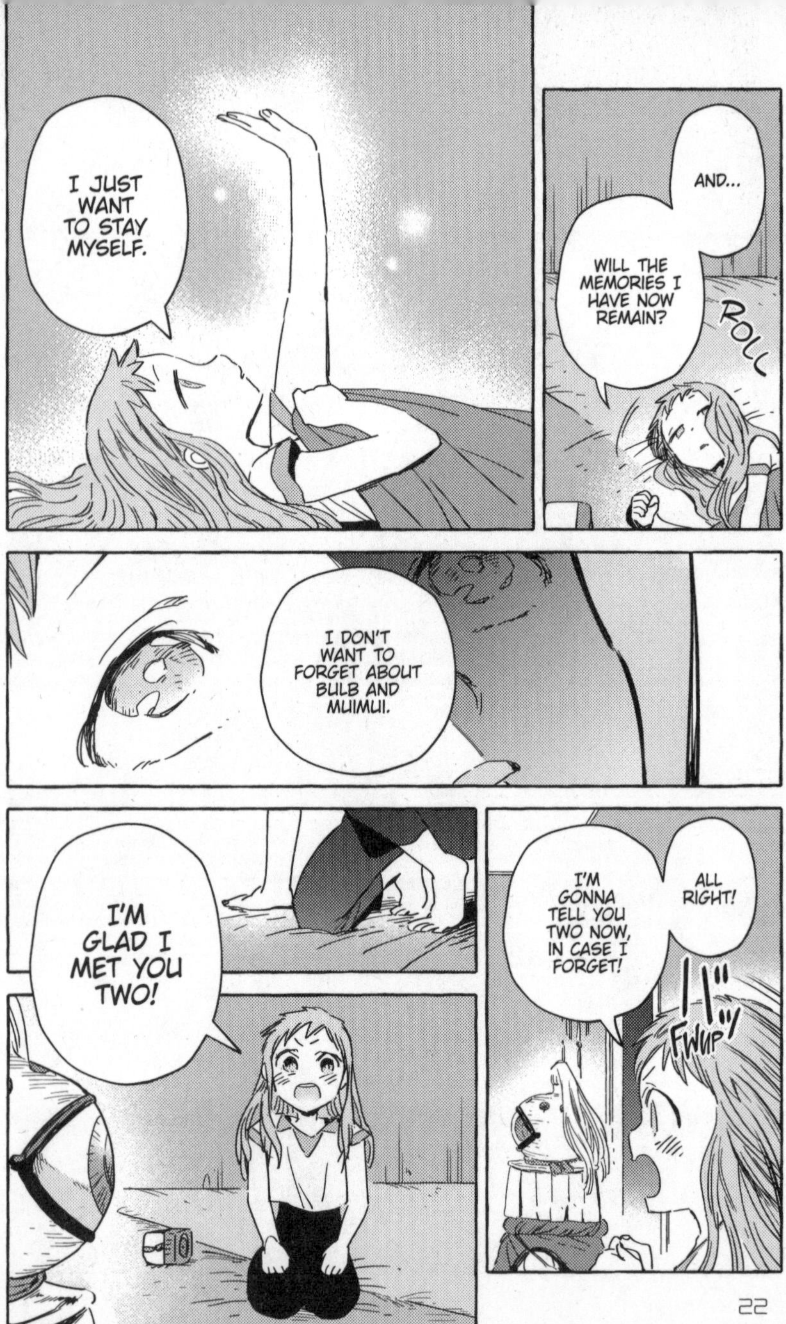
AND...
WILL THE MEMORIES I HAVE NOW REMAIN?
ROLL
I JUST WANT TO STAY MYSELF.
I DON'T WANT TO FORGET ABOUT BULB AND MUIMUI.
ALL RIGHT!
I'M GONNA TELL YOU TWO NOW, IN CASE I FORGET!
FWUP!
I'M GLAD I MET YOU TWO!

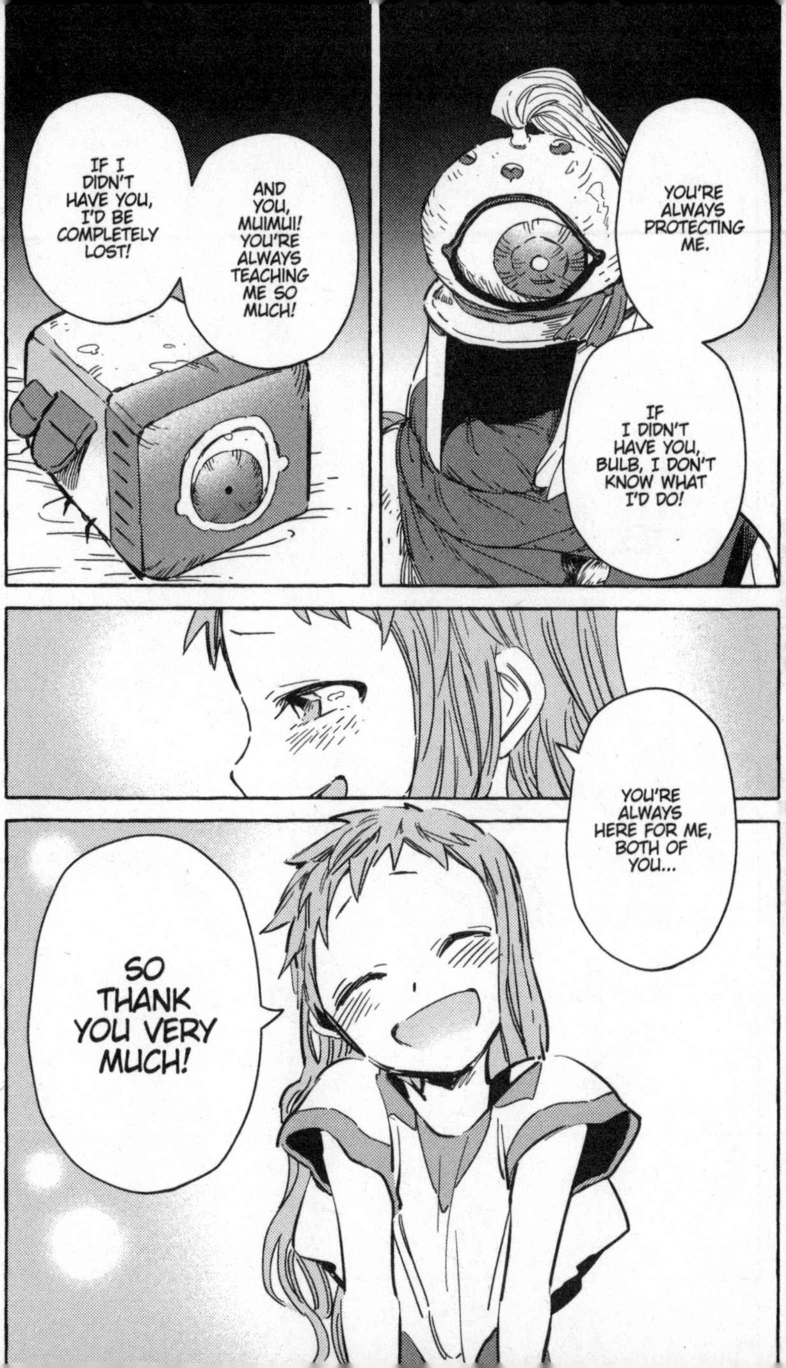
YOU'RE ALWAYS PROTECTING ME.
IF I DIDN'T HAVE YOU, BULB, I DON'T KNOW WHAT I'D DO!
AND YOU, MUIMUI! YOU'RE ALWAYS TEACHING ME SO MUCH!
IF I DIDN'T HAVE YOU, I'D BE COMPLETELY LOST!
YOU'RE ALWAYS HERE FOR ME, BOTH OF YOU...
SO THANK YOU VERY MUCH!

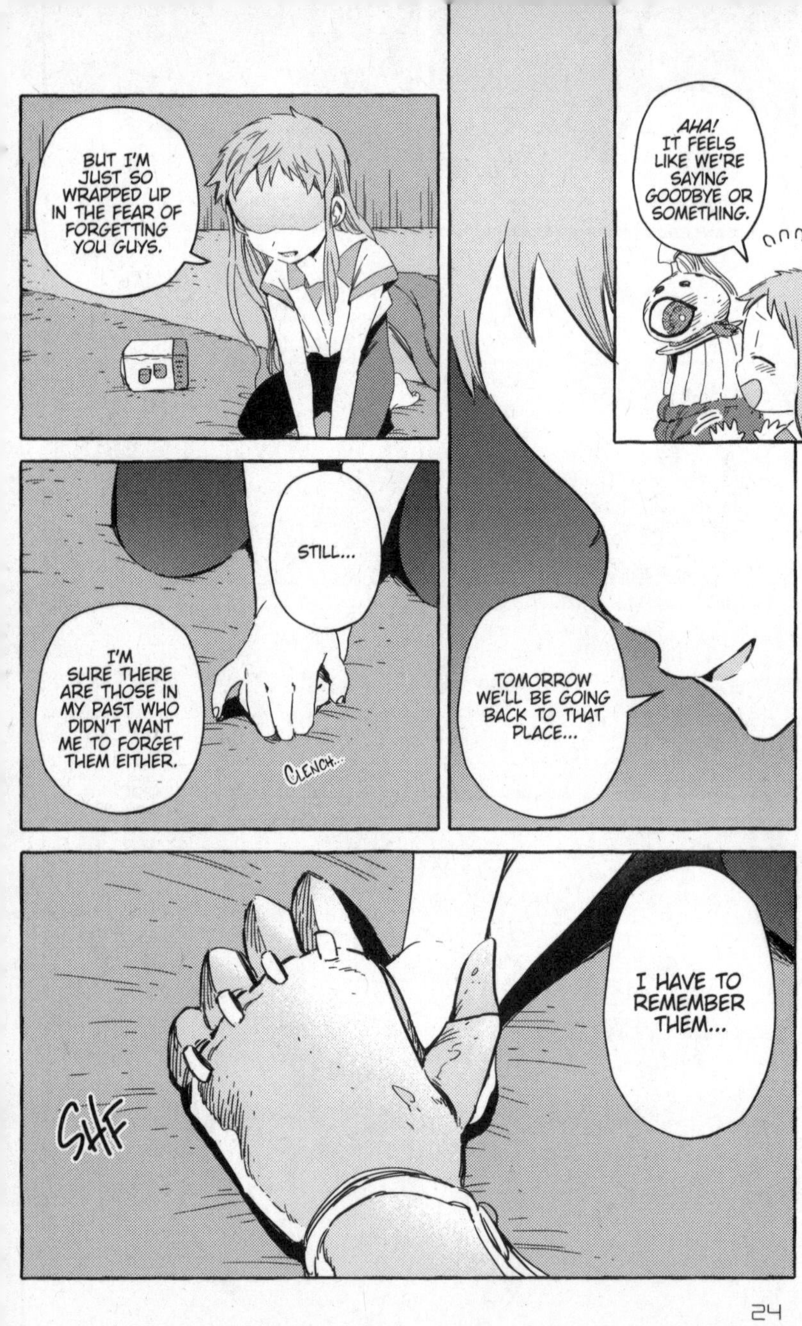
AHA! IT FEELS LIKE WE'RE SAYING GOODBYE OR SOMETHING.
TOMORROW WE'LL BE GOING BACK TO THAT PLACE...
BUT I'M JUST SO WRAPPED UP IN THE FEAR OF FORGETTING YOU GUYS.
STILL...
I'M SURE THERE ARE THOSE IN MY PAST WHO DIDN'T WANT ME TO FORGET THEM EITHER.
CLENCH...
I HAVE TO REMEMBER THEM...
SHF

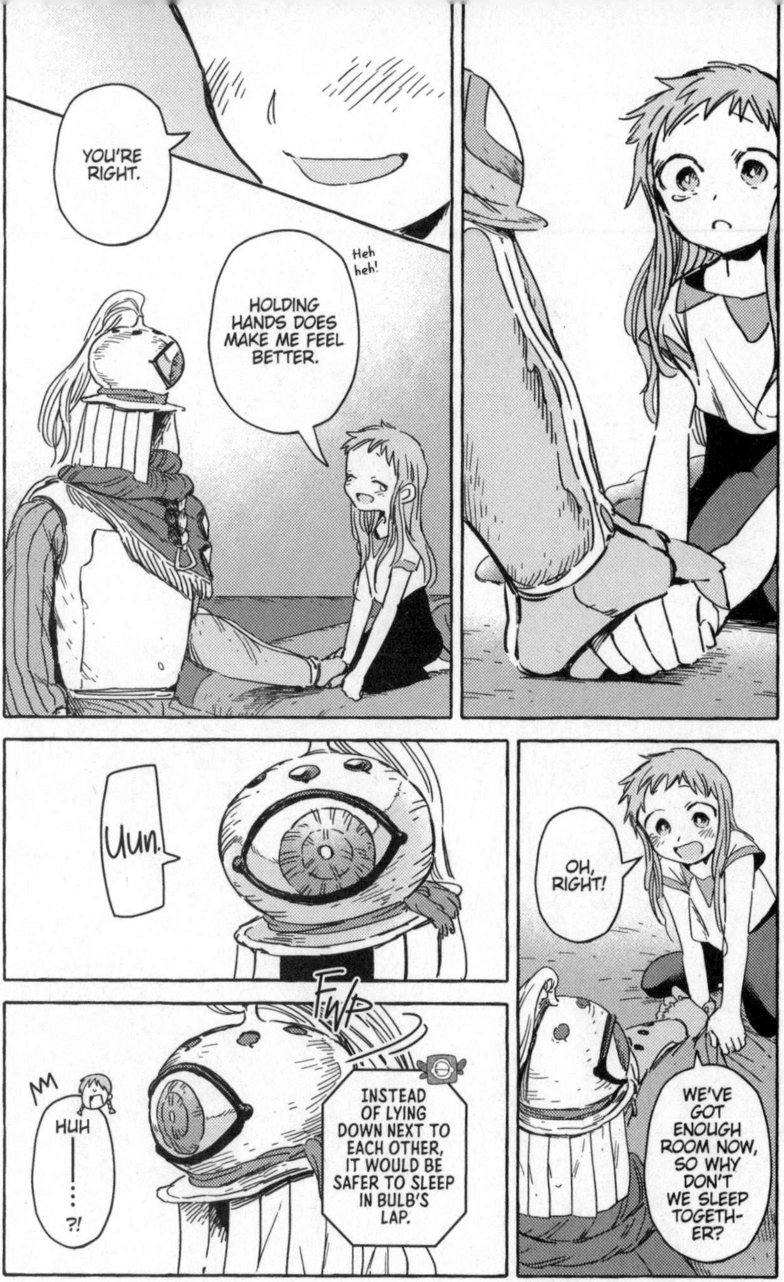
YOU'RE RIGHT.
Heh heh!
HOLDING HANDS DOES MAKE ME FEEL BETTER.
OH, RIGHT!
WE'VE GOT ENOUGH ROOM NOW, SO WHY DON'T WE SLEEP TOGETHER?
Uun.
FWP
INSTEAD OF LYING DOWN NEXT TO EACH OTHER, IT WOULD BE SAFER TO SLEEP IN BULB'S LAP.
HUH ———...?!

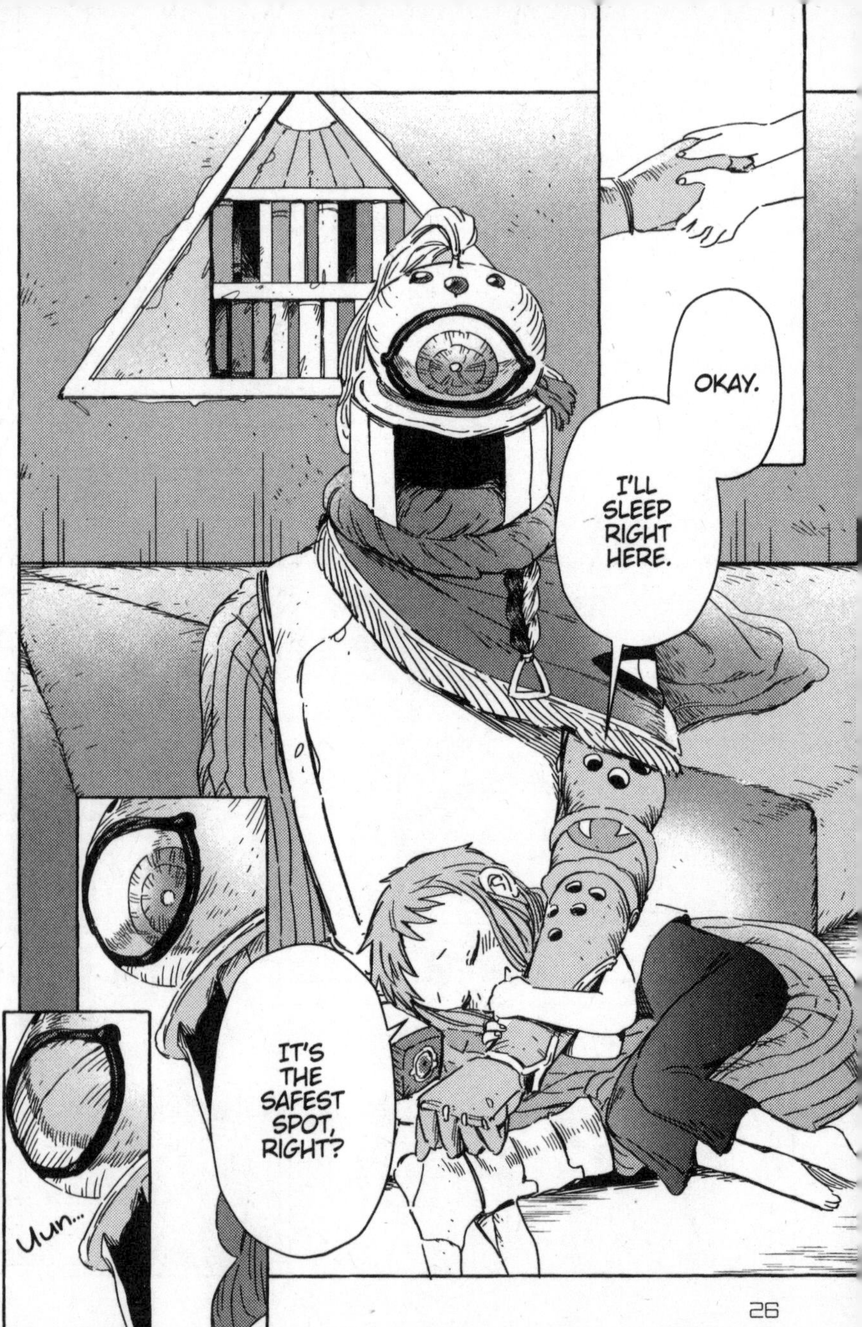
OKAY.
I'LL SLEEP RIGHT HERE.
IT'S THE SAFEST SPOT, RIGHT?
Uun...

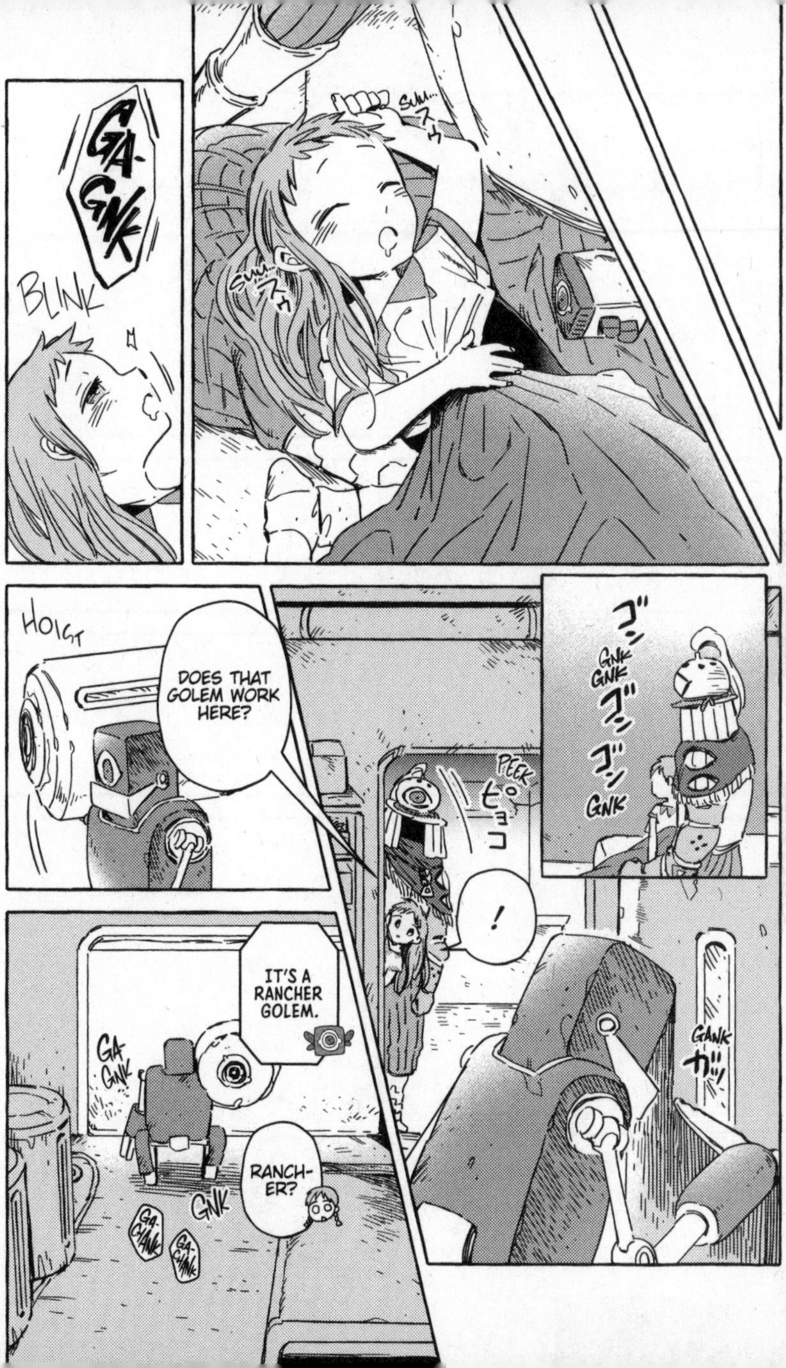
SUU... スゥ
SUU... スゥ
GA-GNK
BLINK
ゴン GNK GNK ゴン ゴン GNK
PEEK ピョコ
!
GANK ガッ
HOIST
DOES THAT GOLEM WORK HERE?
IT'S A RANCHER GOLEM.
GA-GNK
RANCHER-ER?
GNK
GA-CHANK
GA-CHANK

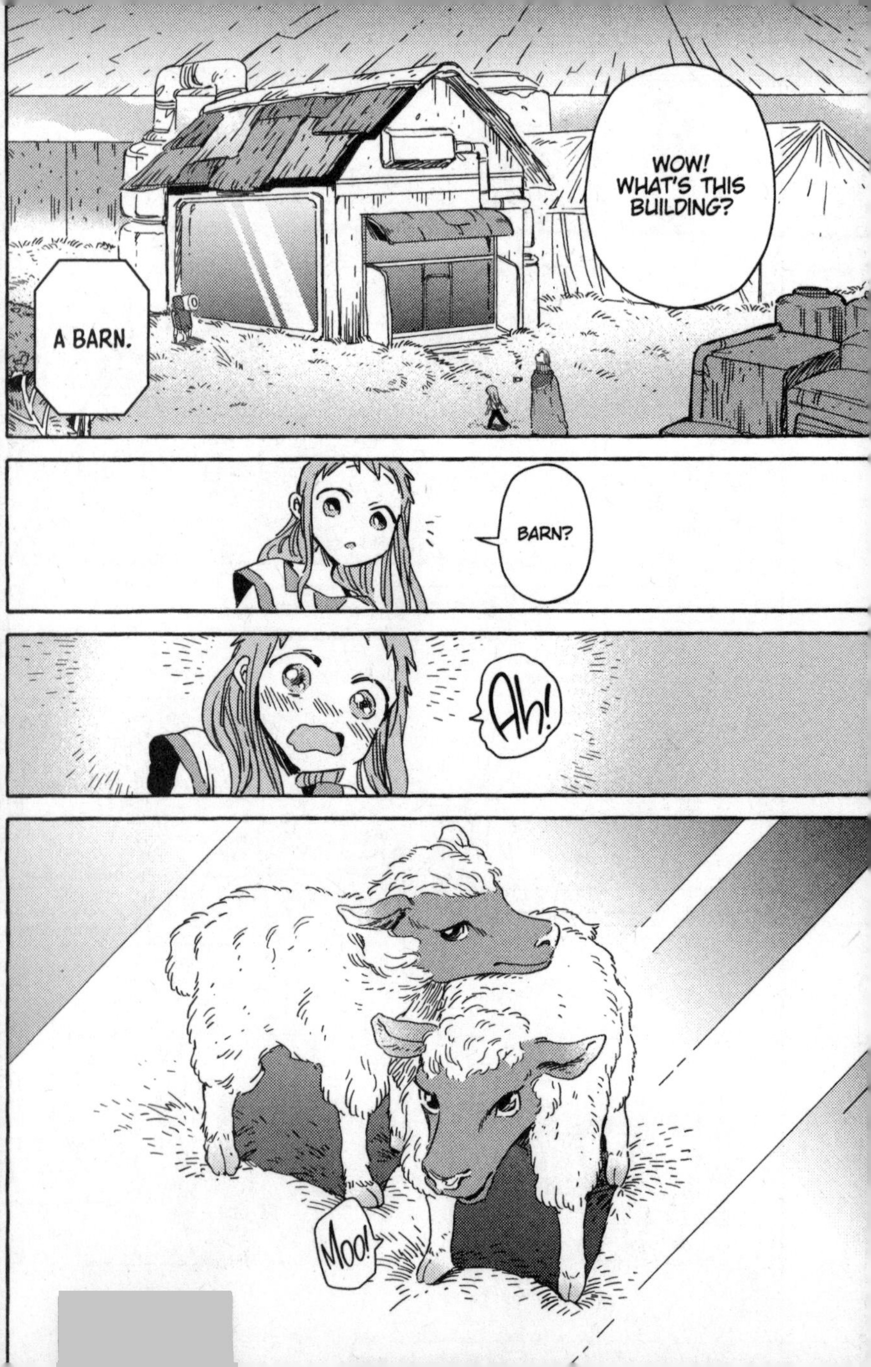
WOW! WHAT'S THIS BUILDING?
A BARN.
BARN?
Ah!
Moo!

A Fleeting Tale #7 Love at First Sight

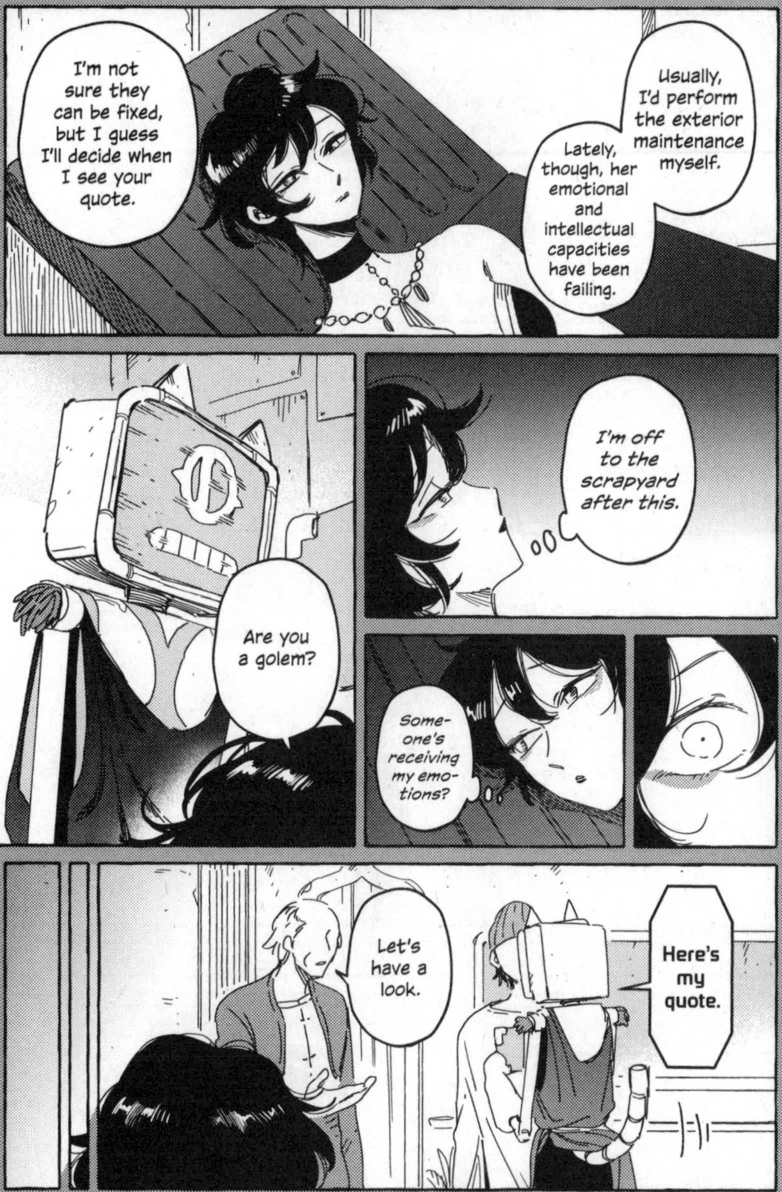

Usually, I'd perform the exterior maintenance myself.
Lately, though, her emotional and intellectual capacities have been failing.
I'm not sure they can be fixed, but I guess I'll decide when I see your quote.
I'm off to the scrapyard after this.
Some-one's receiving my emo-tions?
Are you a golem?
Here's my quote.
Let's have a look.

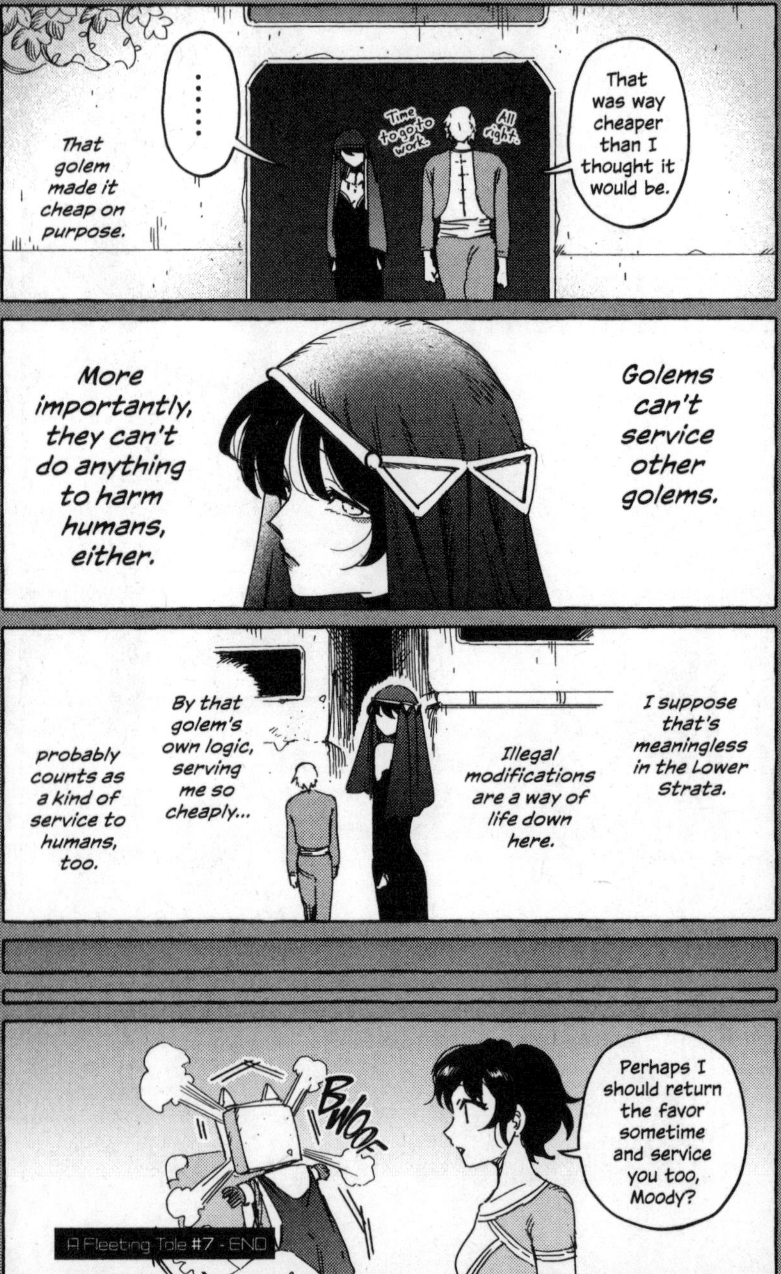
That was way cheaper than I thought it would be.
All right.
Time to go to work.
......
That golem made it cheap on purpose.
Golems can't service other golems.
More importantly, they can't do anything to harm humans, either.
I suppose that's meaningless in the Lower Strata.
Illegal modifications are a way of life down here.
By that golem's own logic, serving me so cheaply...
probably counts as a kind of service to humans, too.
Perhaps I should return the favor sometime and service you too, Moody?
BWOOF
A Fleeting Tale #7 - END

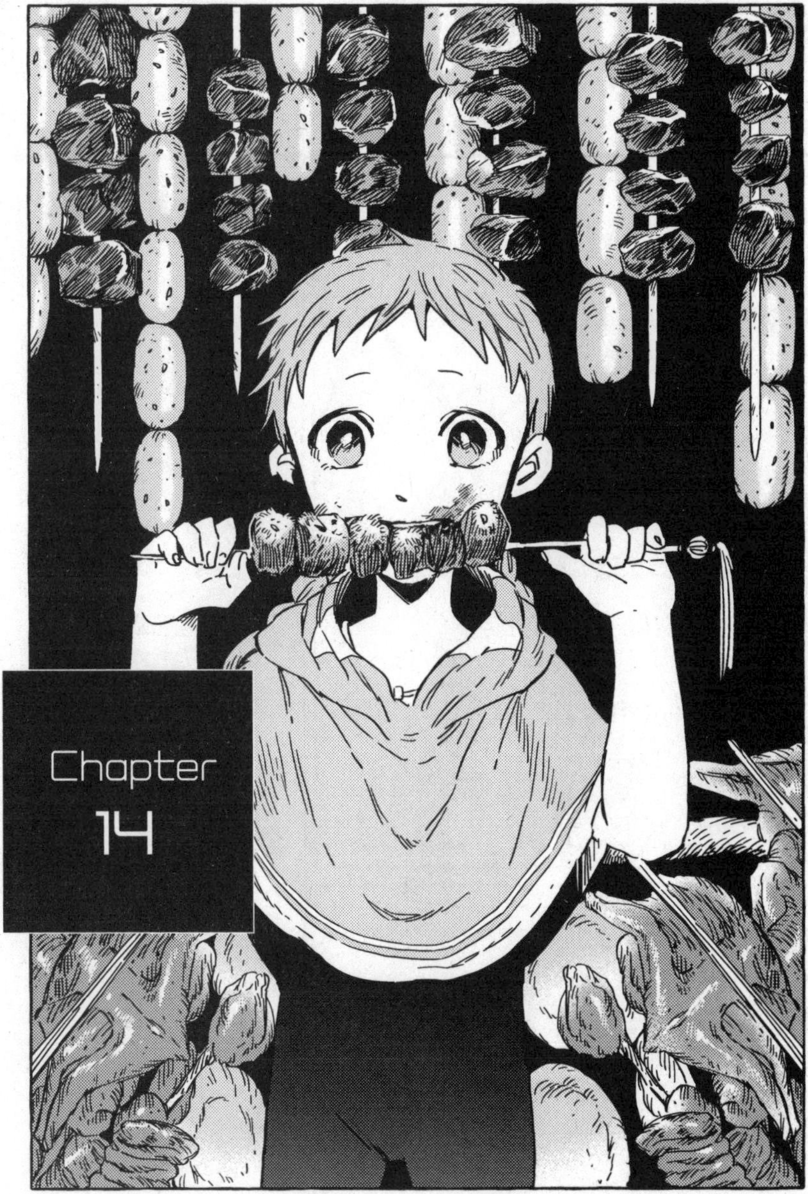
Chapter
14

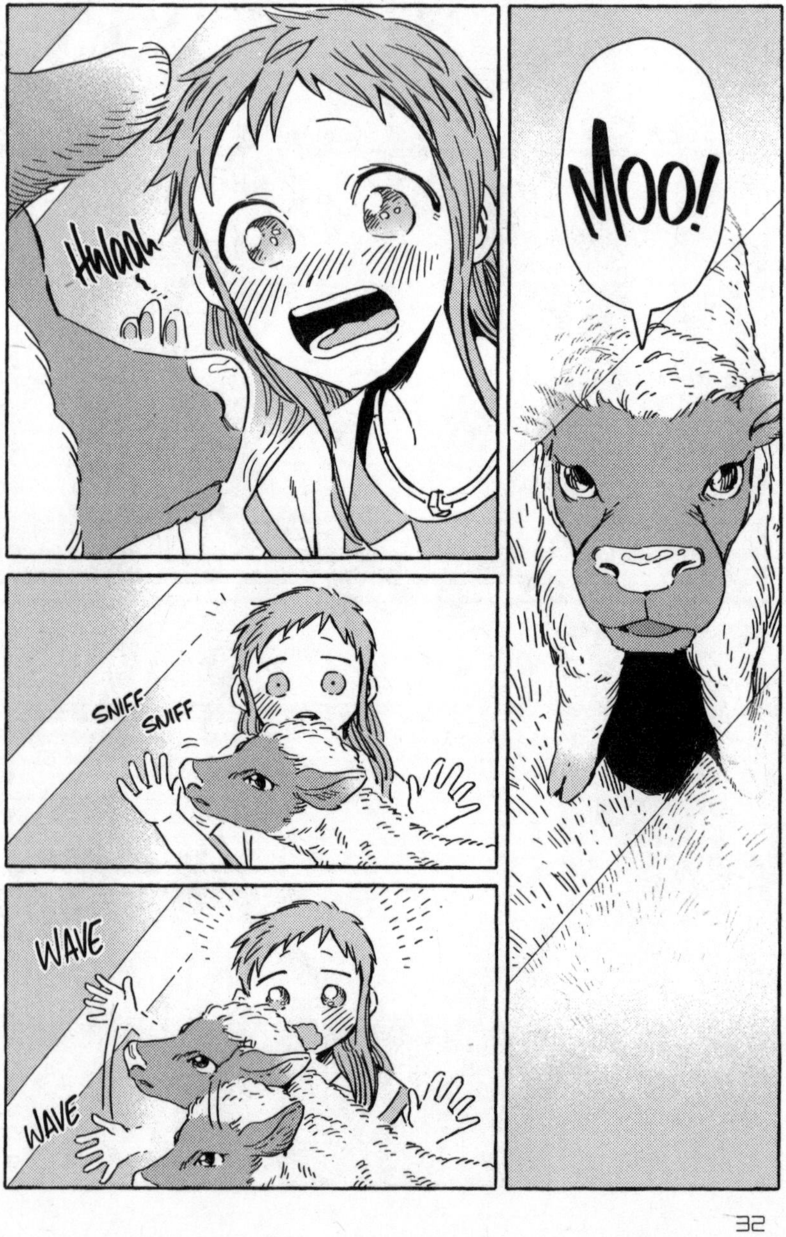
MOO!
Hwaah
SNIFF
SNIFF
WAVE
WAVE

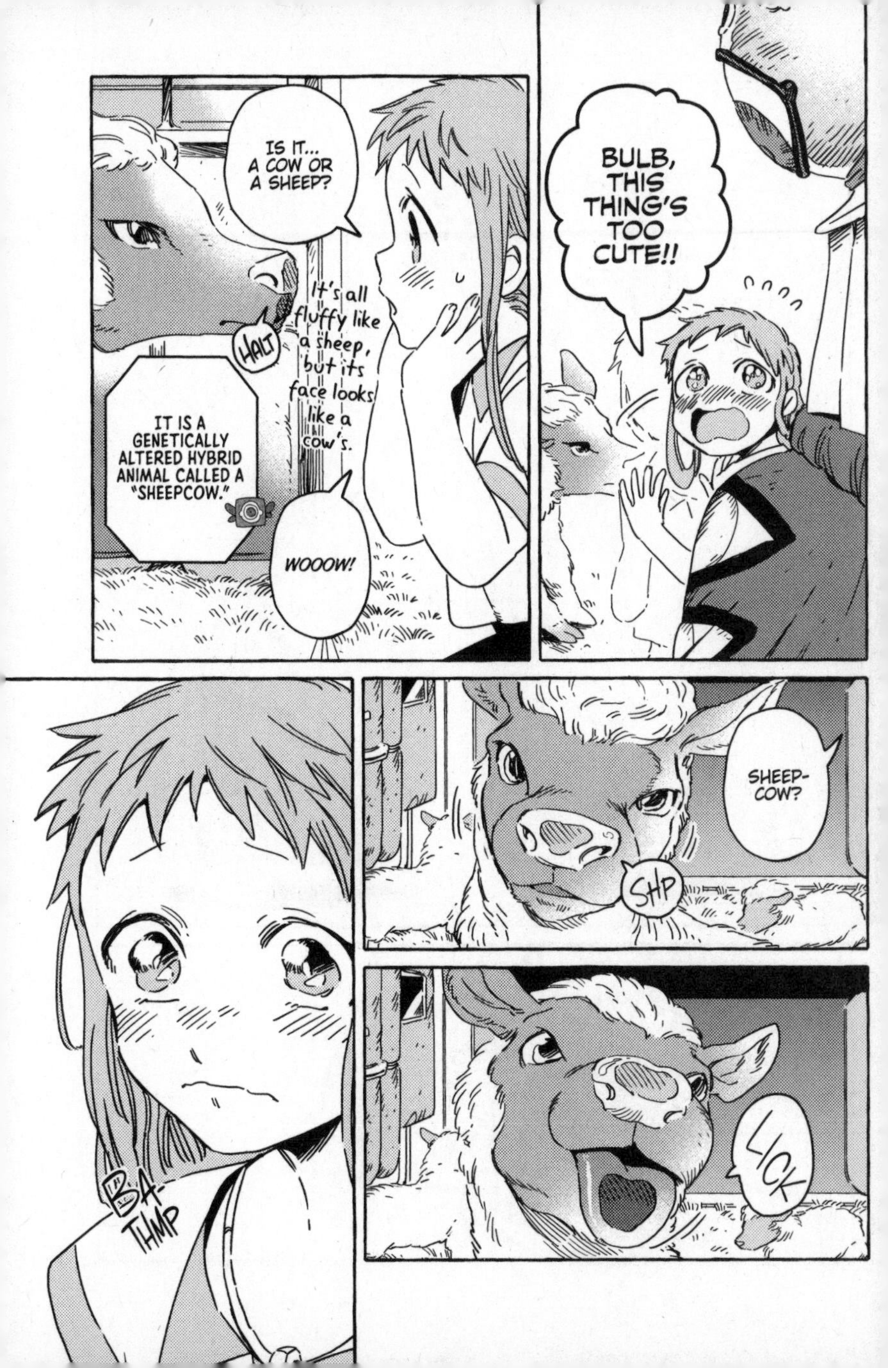
BULB, THIS THING'S TOO CUTE!!
IS IT... A COW OR A SHEEP?
HALT
It's all fluffy like a sheep, but its face looks like a cow's.
IT IS A GENETICALLY ALTERED HYBRID ANIMAL CALLED A "SHEEPCOW."
WOOOW!
SHEEP-COW?
SHP
LICK
BA-THMP

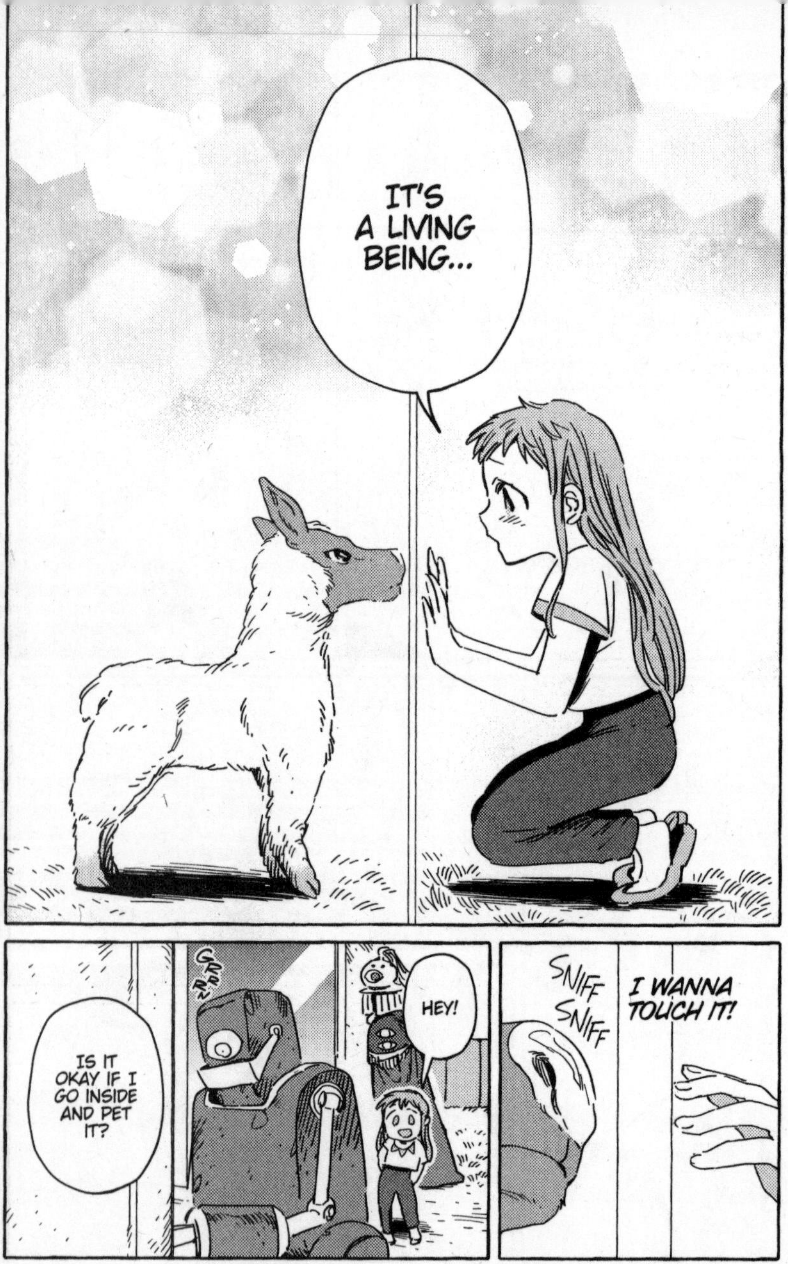
IT'S A LIVING BEING...
SNIFF SNIFF
I WANNA TOUCH IT!
HEY!
GRRRN
IS IT OKAY IF I GO INSIDE AND PET IT?

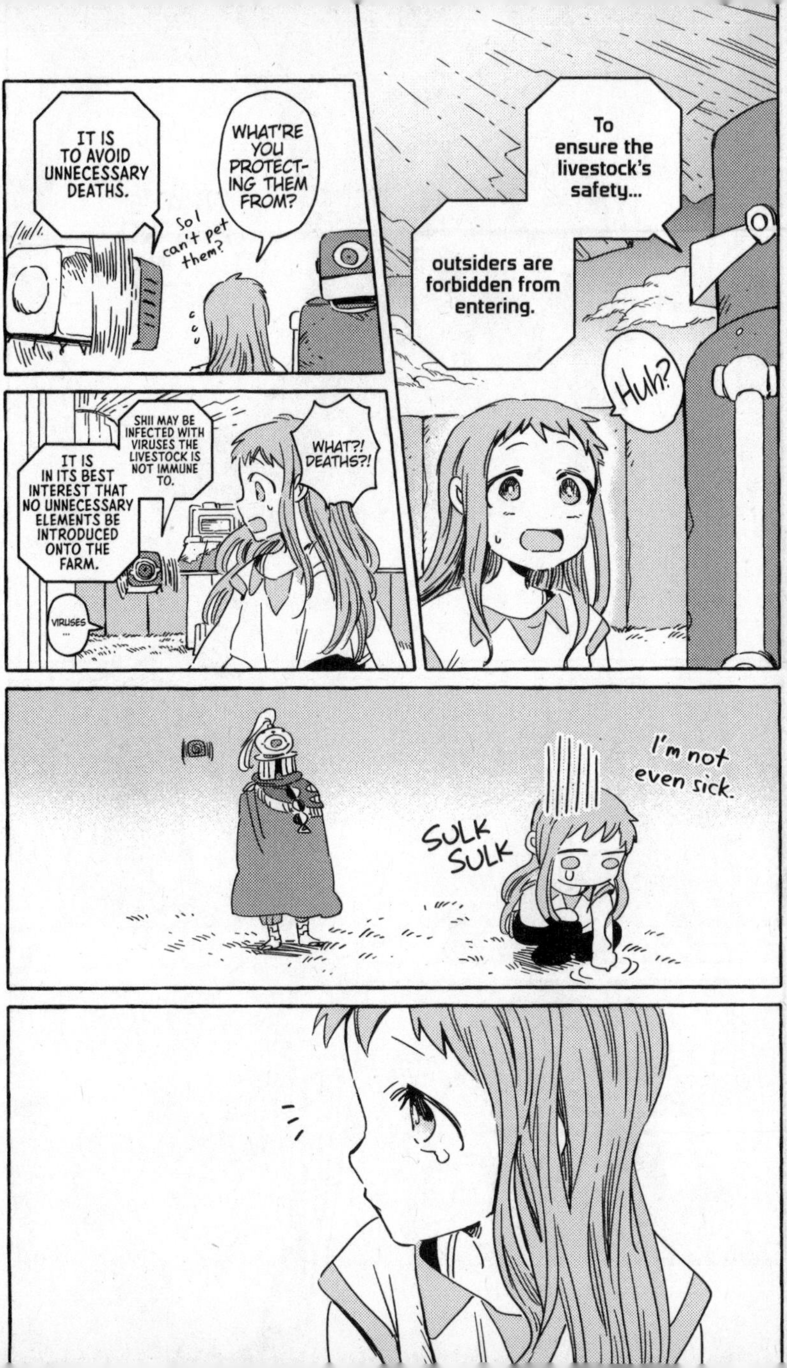
To ensure the livestock's safety...
outsiders are forbidden from entering.
Huh?
WHAT'RE YOU PROTECTING THEM FROM?
So I can't pet them?
IT IS TO AVOID UNNECESSARY DEATHS.
WHAT?! DEATHS?!
SHII MAY BE INFECTED WITH VIRUSES THE LIVESTOCK IS NOT IMMUNE TO.
IT IS IN ITS BEST INTEREST THAT NO UNNECESSARY ELEMENTS BE INTRODUCED ONTO THE FARM.
VIRUSES ...
I'm not even sick.
SULK SULK

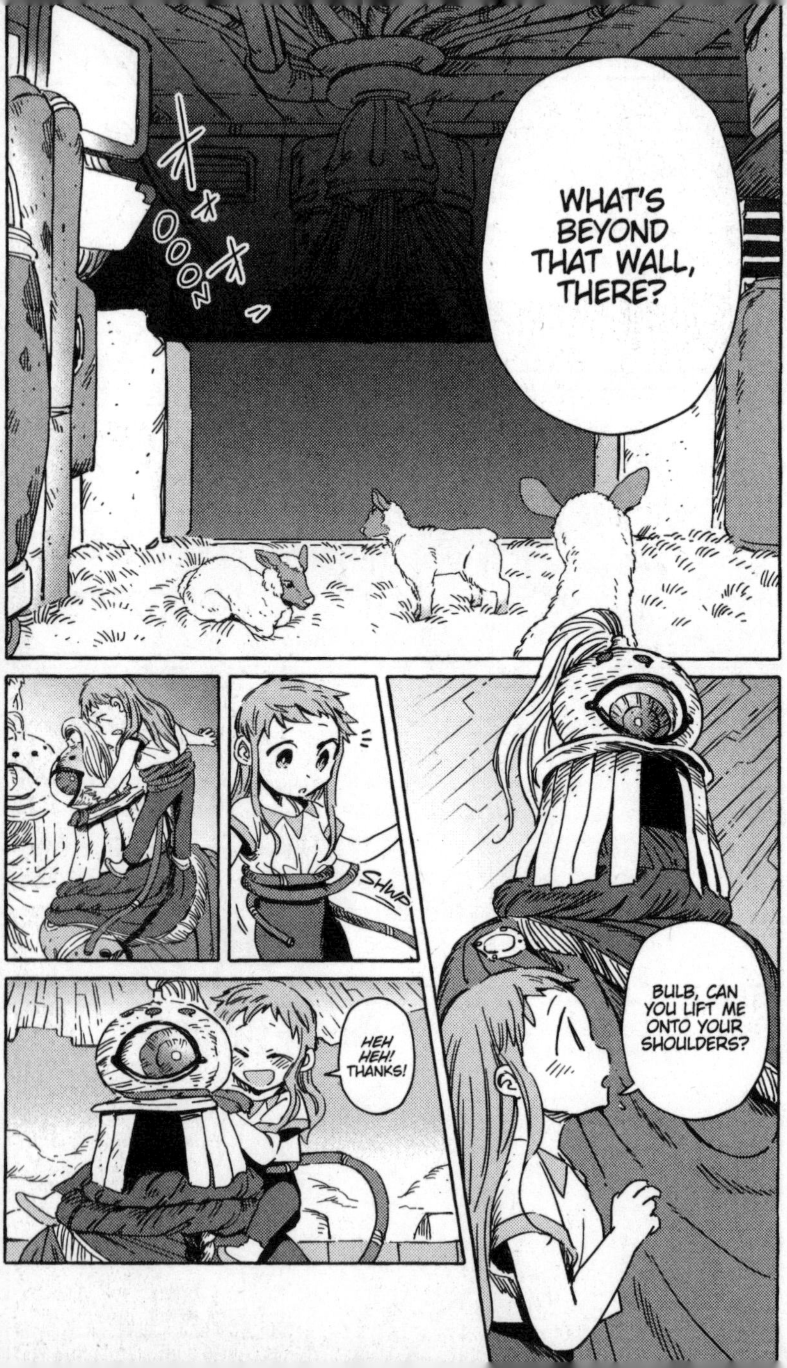
OOON
WHAT'S BEYOND THAT WALL, THERE?
BULB, CAN YOU LIFT ME ONTO YOUR SHOULDERS?
SHWP
HEH HEH! THANKS!

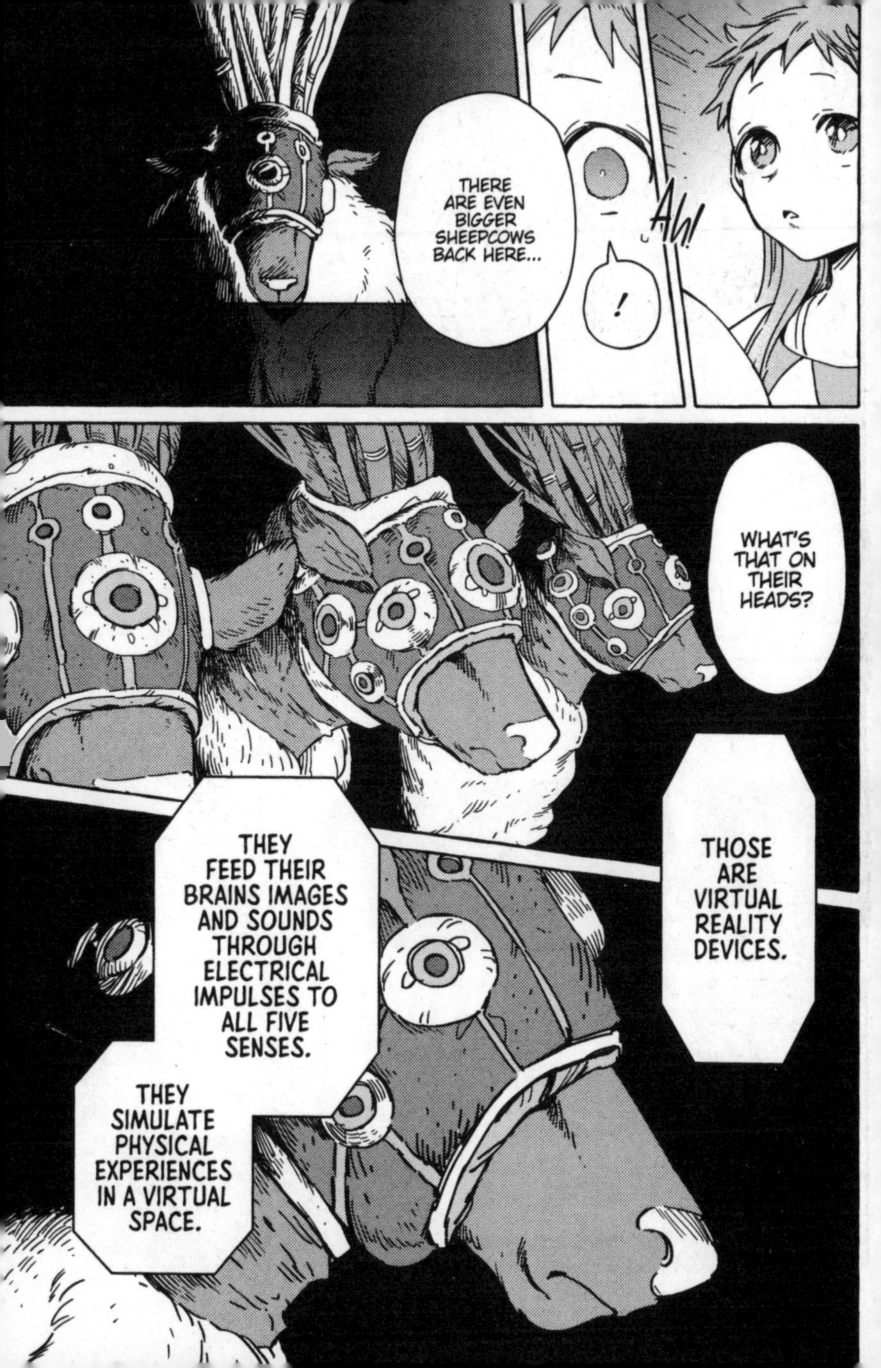
Ah!
THERE ARE EVEN BIGGER SHEEPCOWS BACK HERE...
!
WHAT'S THAT ON THEIR HEADS?
THOSE ARE VIRTUAL REALITY DEVICES.
THEY FEED THEIR BRAINS IMAGES AND SOUNDS THROUGH ELECTRICAL IMPULSES TO ALL FIVE SENSES.
THEY SIMULATE PHYSICAL EXPERIENCES IN A VIRTUAL SPACE.

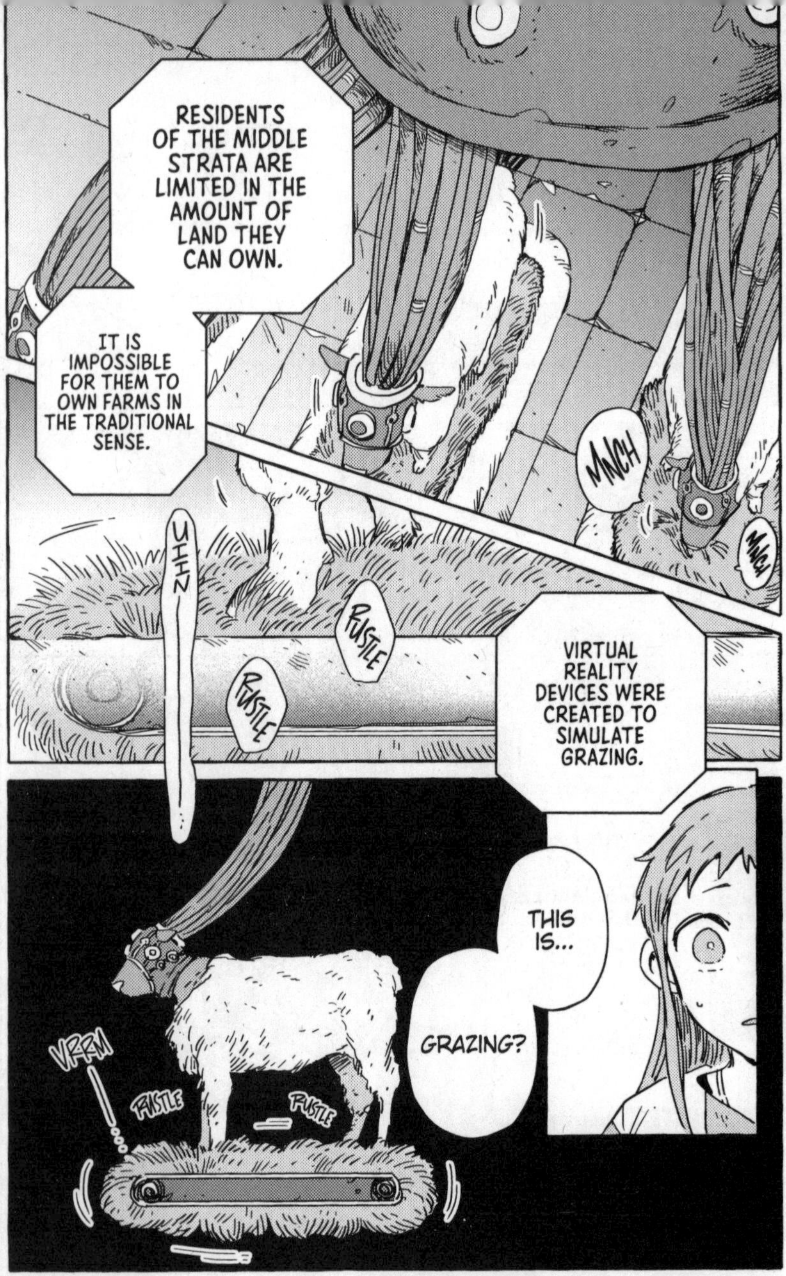
RESIDENTS OF THE MIDDLE STRATA ARE LIMITED IN THE AMOUNT OF LAND THEY CAN OWN.
IT IS IMPOSSIBLE FOR THEM TO OWN FARMS IN THE TRADITIONAL SENSE.
MNCH
MNCH
VIRTUAL REALITY DEVICES WERE CREATED TO SIMULATE GRAZING.
RUSTLE
UIIN
RUSTLE
THIS IS...
GRAZING?
VRRM
RUSTLE
RUSTLE

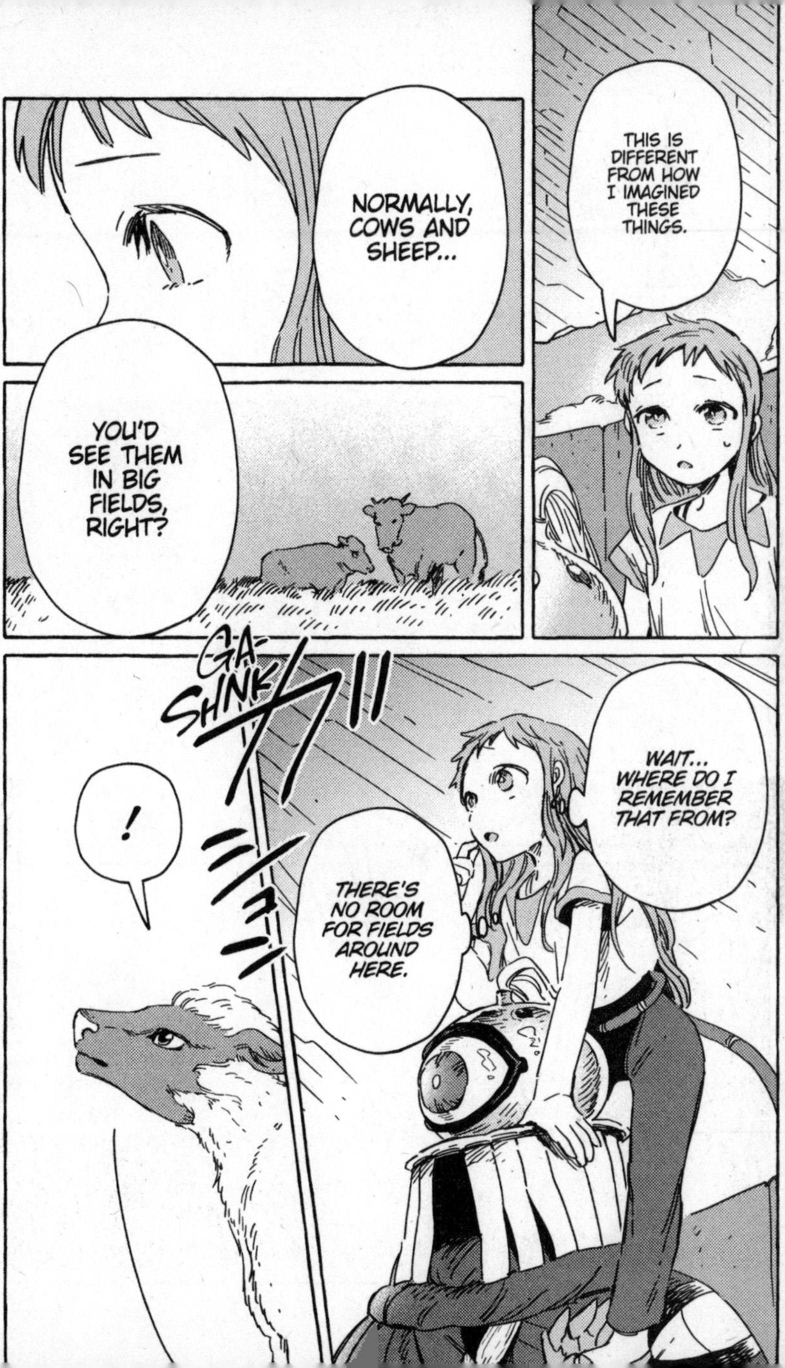
THIS IS DIFFERENT FROM HOW I IMAGINED THESE THINGS.
NORMALLY, COWS AND SHEEP...
YOU'D SEE THEM IN BIG FIELDS, RIGHT?
WAIT... WHERE DO I REMEMBER THAT FROM?
THERE'S NO ROOM FOR FIELDS AROUND HERE.
GA-SHNK
!

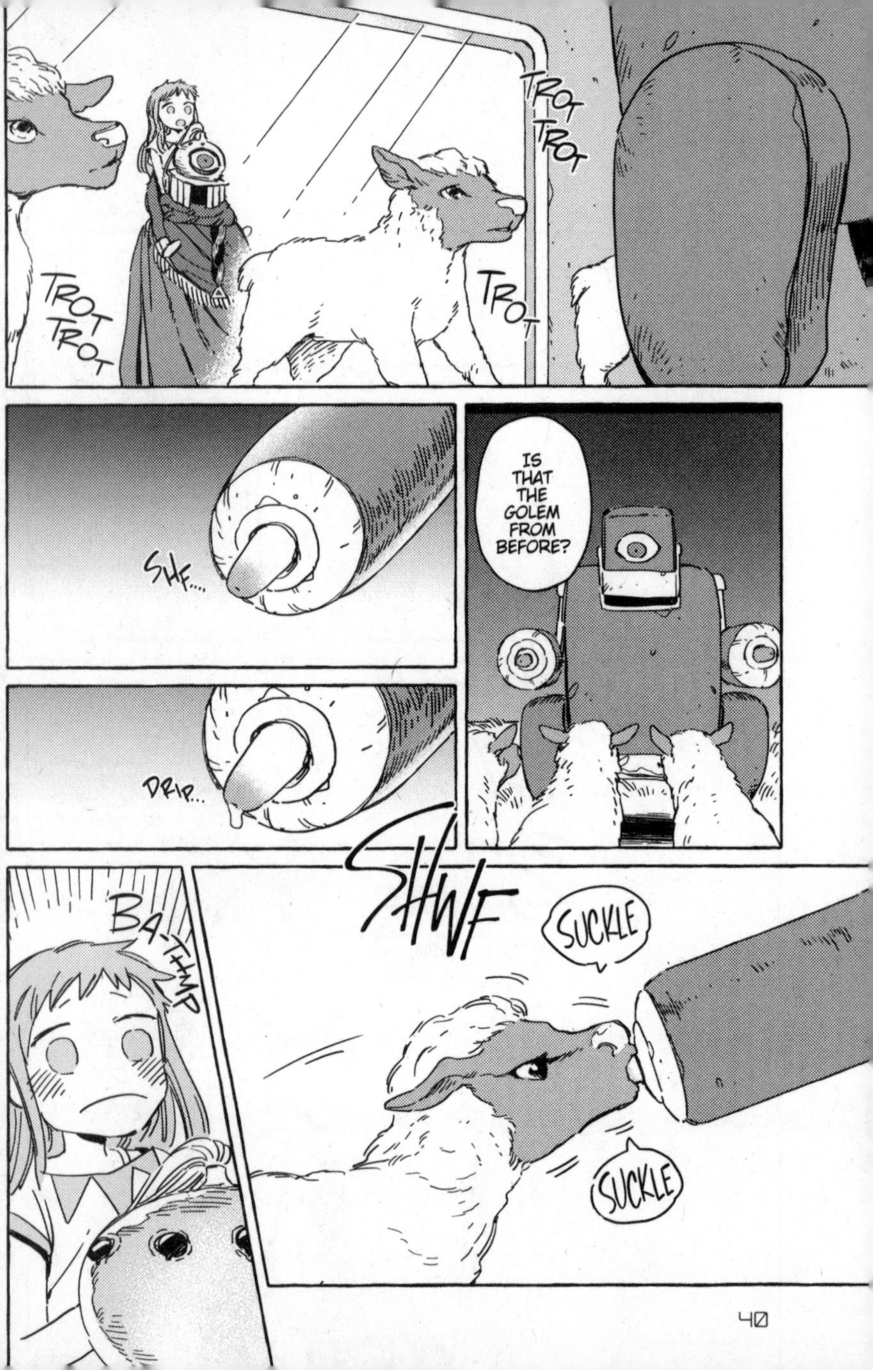
TROT TROT
TROT
TROT TROT
IS THAT THE GOLEM FROM BEFORE?
SHF...
DRIP...
SHWF
SUCKLE
SUCKLE
BA-THMP

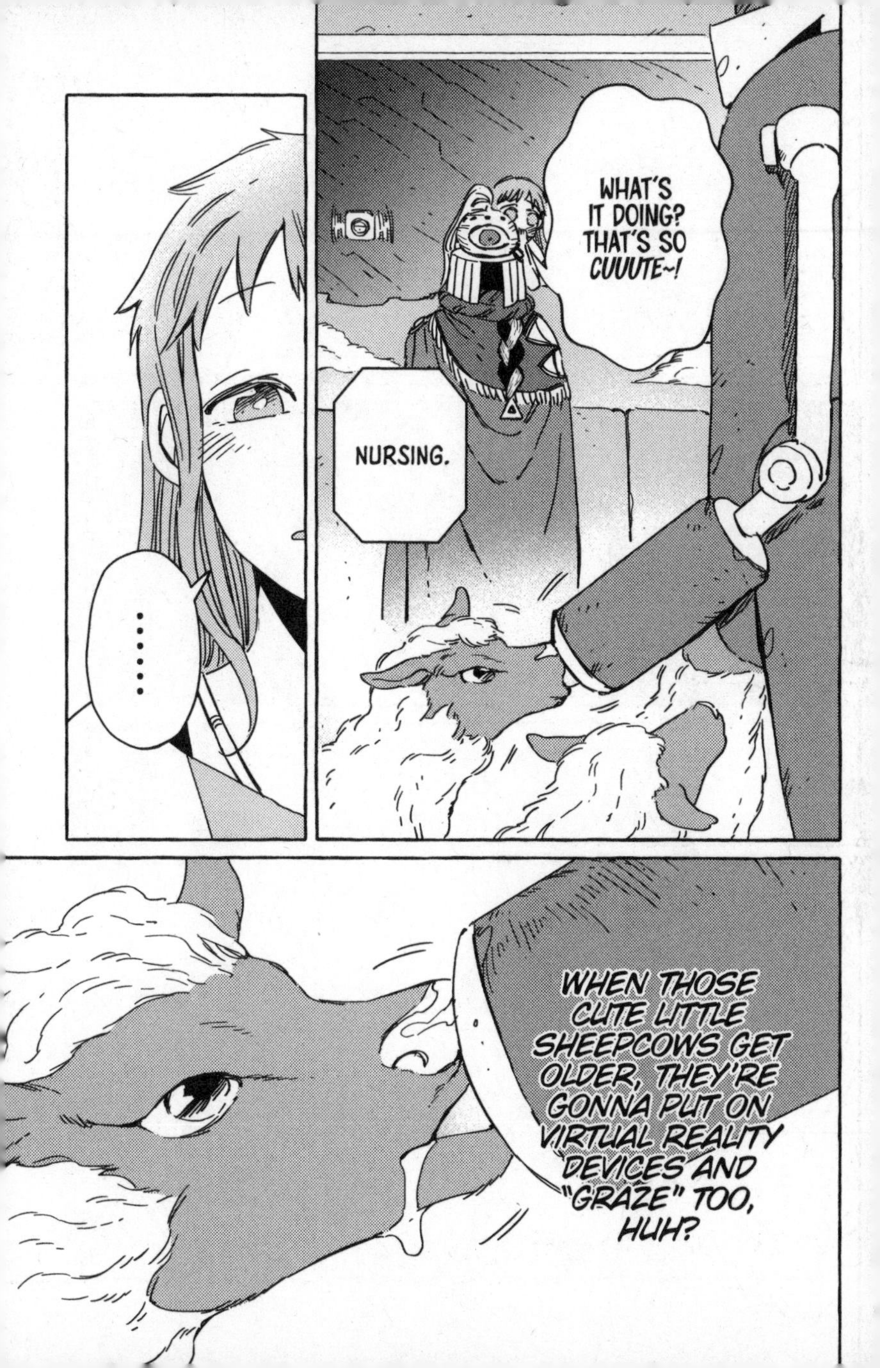
WHAT'S IT DOING? THAT'S SO *CUUUTE~!*
NURSING.
......
WHEN THOSE CUTE LITTLE SHEEPCOWS GET OLDER, THEY'RE GONNA PUT ON VIRTUAL REALITY DEVICES AND "GRAZE" TOO, HUH?

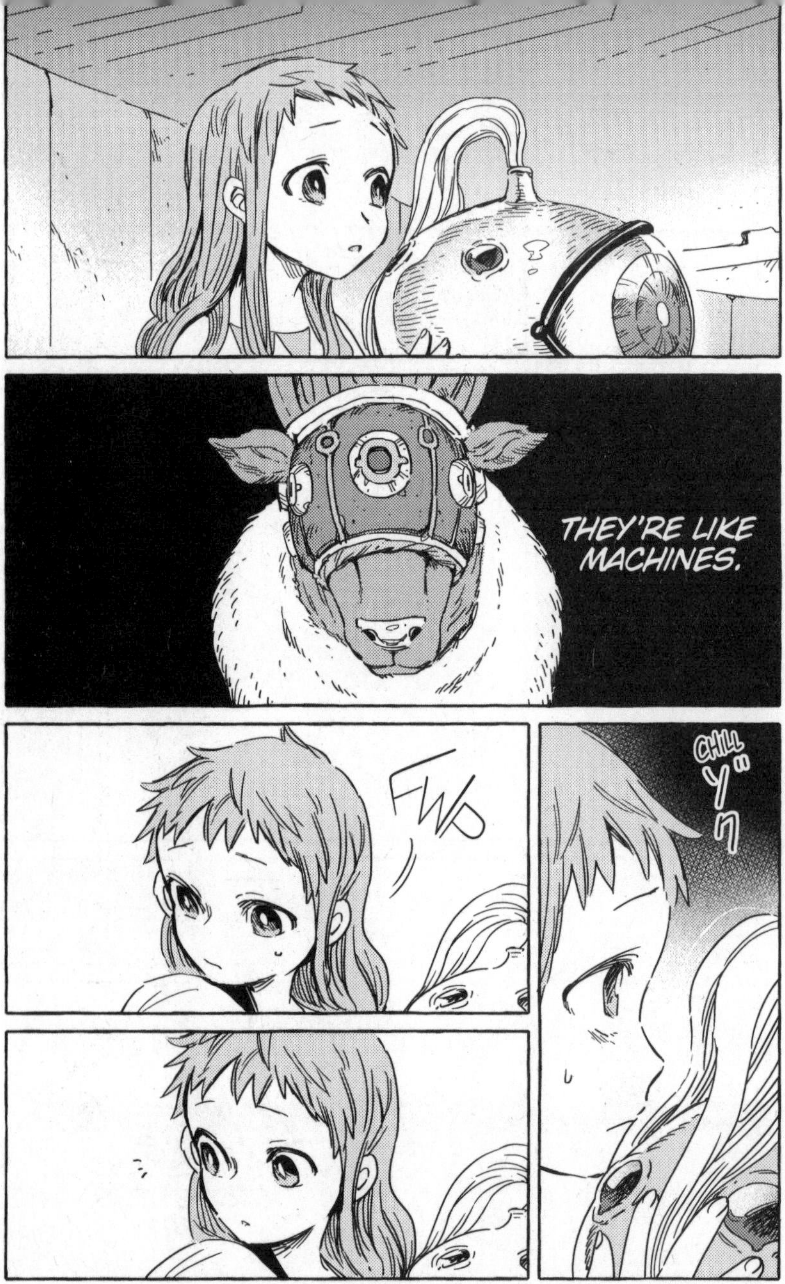
THEY'RE LIKE MACHINES.
CHILL
ゾク
FWP

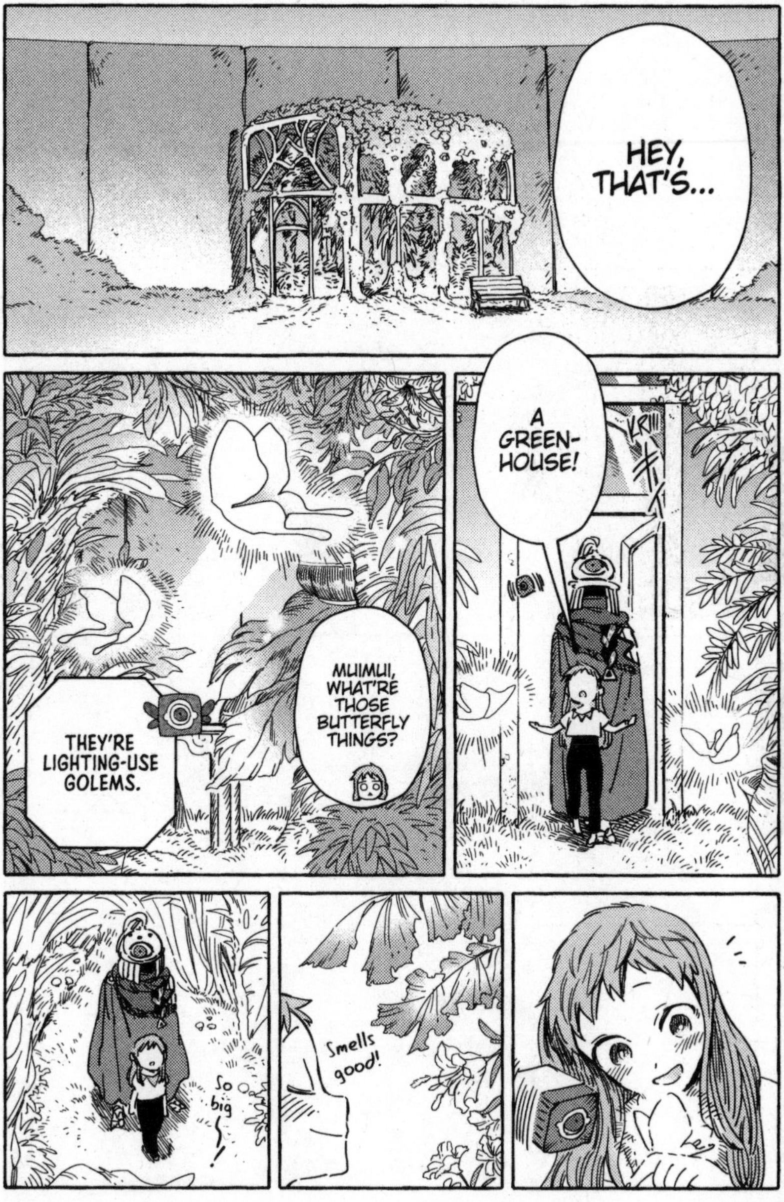
HEY, THAT'S...
A GREEN-HOUSE!
KRIII
MUIMUI, WHAT'RE THOSE BUTTERFLY THINGS?
THEY'RE LIGHTING-USE GOLEMS.
Smells good!
So big~!

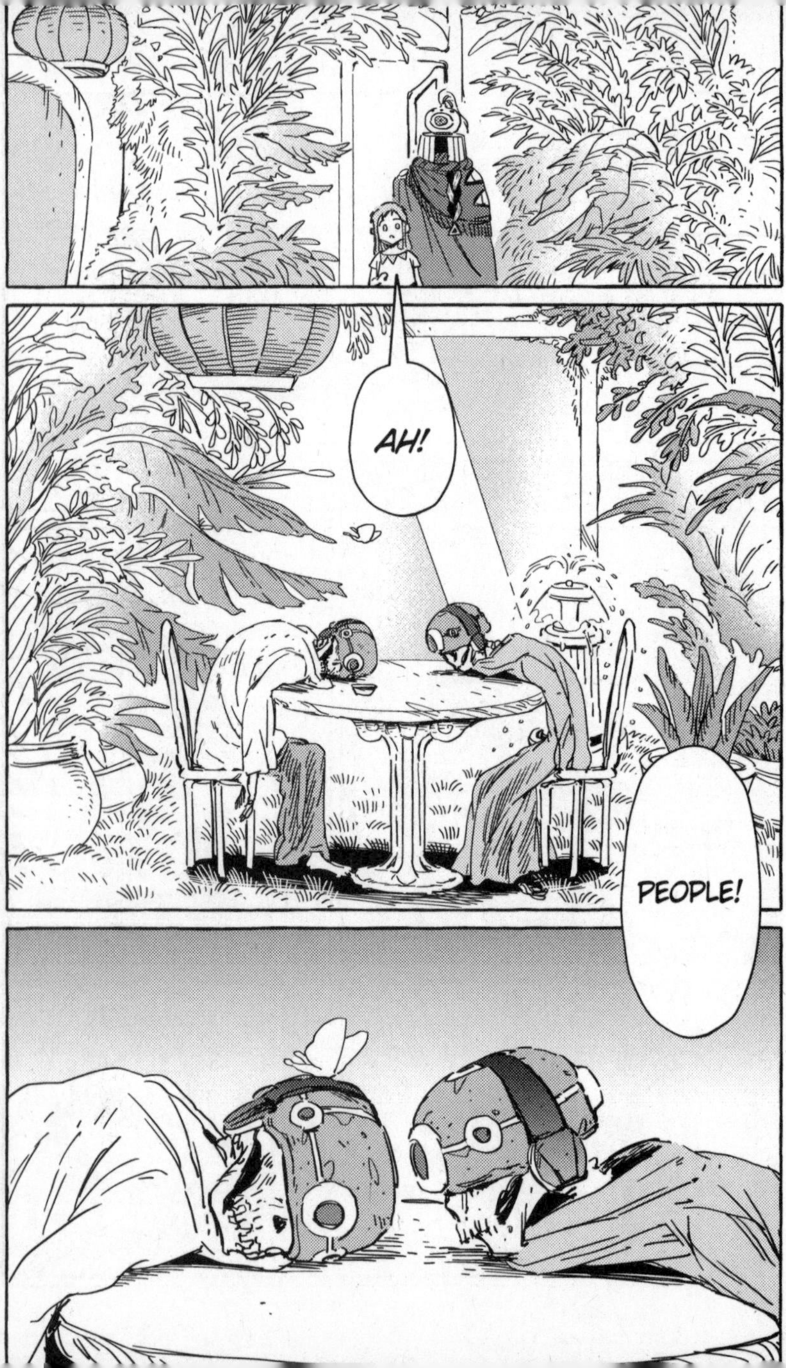
AH!
PEOPLE!

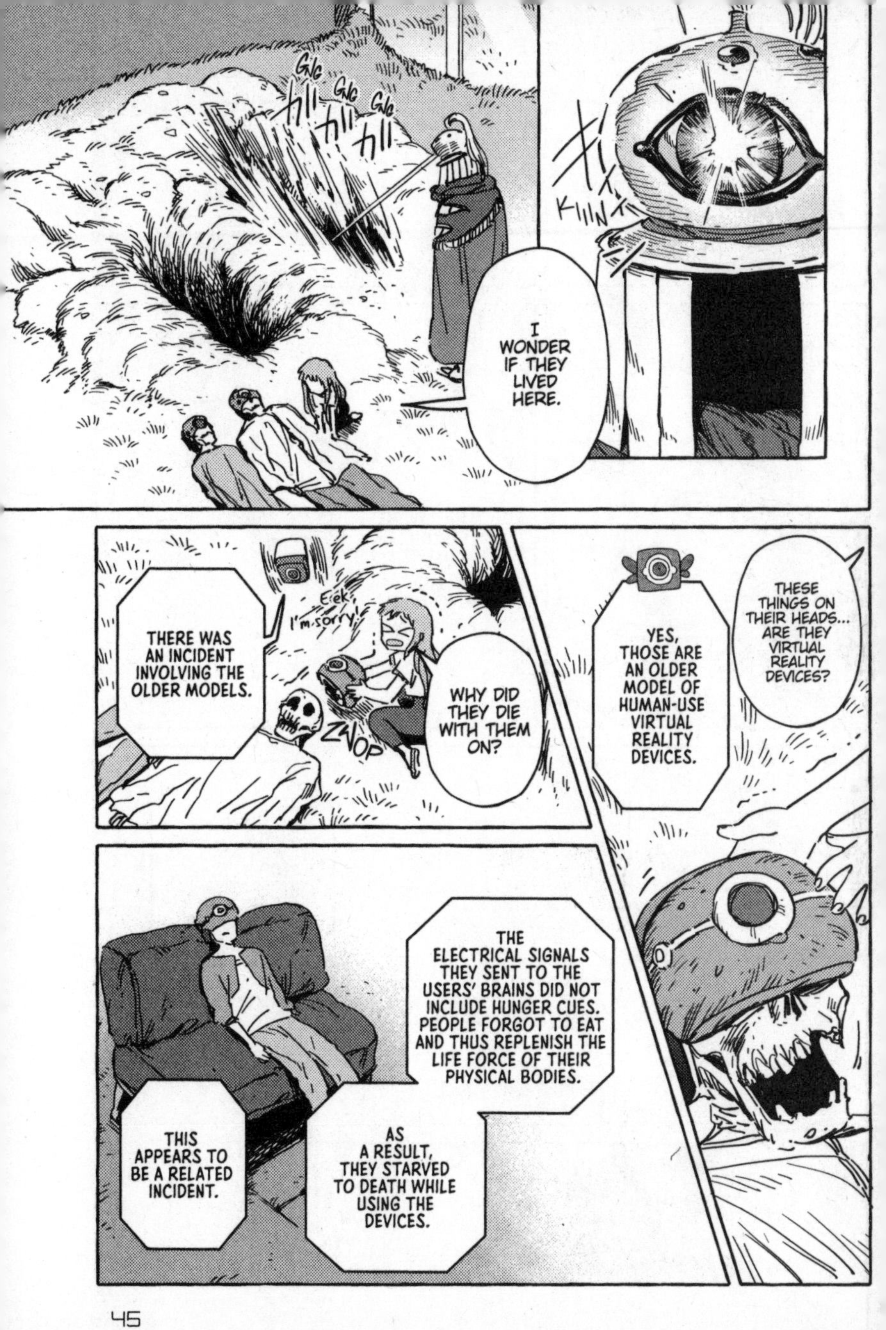
KIIIN
GNG
GNG
GNG
I WONDER IF THEY LIVED HERE.
THESE THINGS ON THEIR HEADS... ARE THEY VIRTUAL REALITY DEVICES?
YES, THOSE ARE AN OLDER MODEL OF HUMAN-USE VIRTUAL REALITY DEVICES.
WHY DID THEY DIE WITH THEM ON?
Eek
I'm sorry!
ZWOP
THERE WAS AN INCIDENT INVOLVING THE OLDER MODELS.
THE ELECTRICAL SIGNALS THEY SENT TO THE USERS' BRAINS DID NOT INCLUDE HUNGER CUES. PEOPLE FORGOT TO EAT AND THUS REPLENISH THE LIFE FORCE OF THEIR PHYSICAL BODIES.
AS A RESULT, THEY STARVED TO DEATH WHILE USING THE DEVICES.
THIS APPEARS TO BE A RELATED INCIDENT.

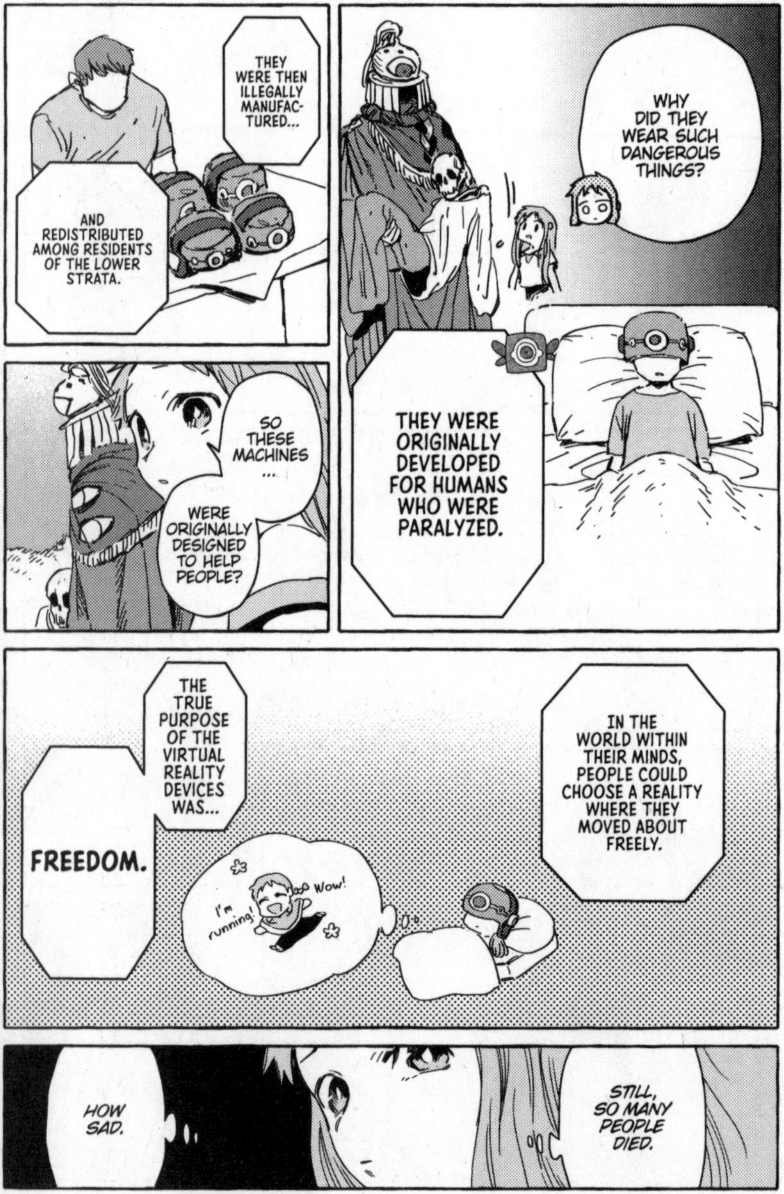
WHY DID THEY WEAR SUCH DANGEROUS THINGS?
THEY WERE ORIGINALLY DEVELOPED FOR HUMANS WHO WERE PARALYZED.
THEY WERE THEN ILLEGALLY MANUFACTURED...
AND REDISTRIBUTED AMONG RESIDENTS OF THE LOWER STRATA.
SO THESE MACHINES...
WERE ORIGINALLY DESIGNED TO HELP PEOPLE?
IN THE WORLD WITHIN THEIR MINDS, PEOPLE COULD CHOOSE A REALITY WHERE THEY MOVED ABOUT FREELY.
THE TRUE PURPOSE OF THE VIRTUAL REALITY DEVICES WAS...
FREEDOM.
Wow!
I'm running!
STILL, SO MANY PEOPLE DIED.
HOW SAD.

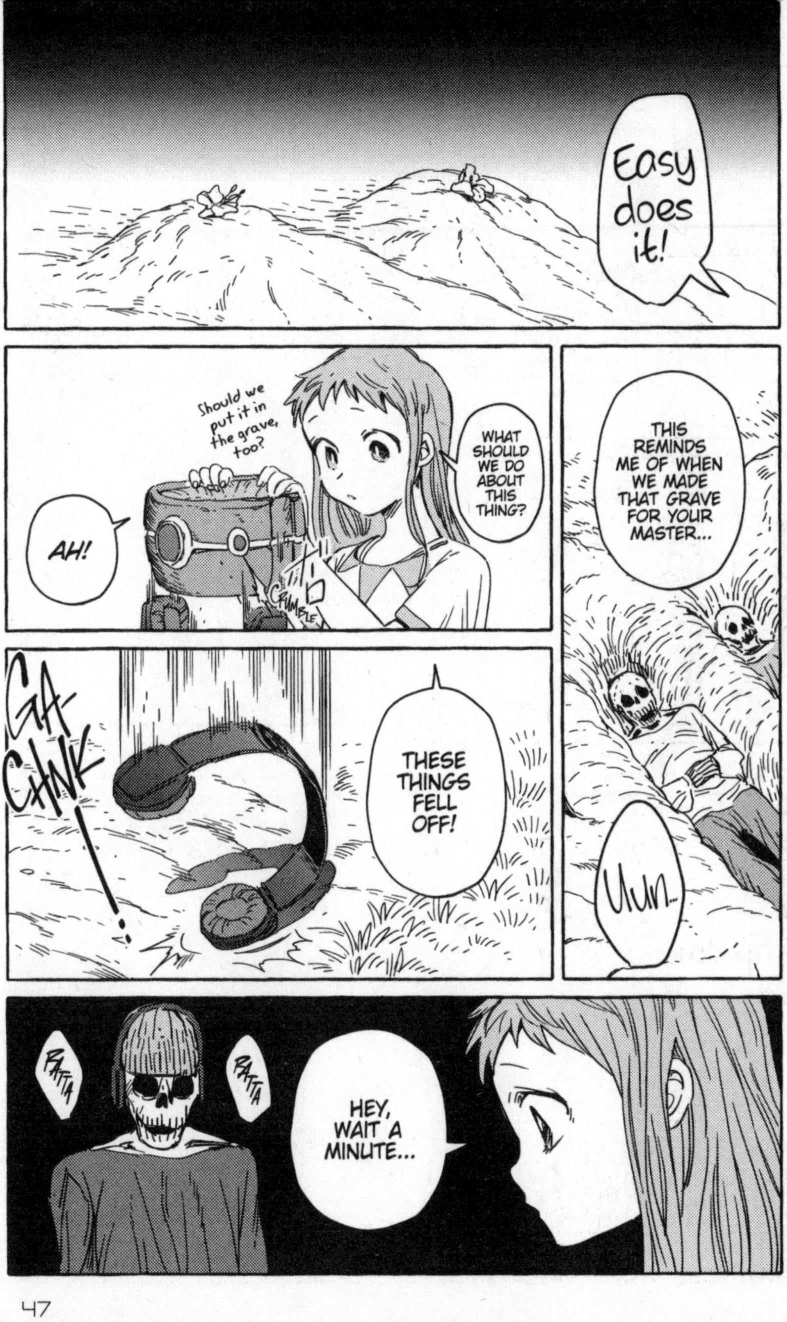
Easy does it!
THIS REMINDS ME OF WHEN WE MADE THAT GRAVE FOR YOUR MASTER...
Uun...
WHAT SHOULD WE DO ABOUT THIS THING?
Should we put it in the grave, too?
CRUMBLE
AH!
THESE THINGS FELL OFF!
GA-CHNK!
HEY, WAIT A MINUTE...
RATTA
RATTA

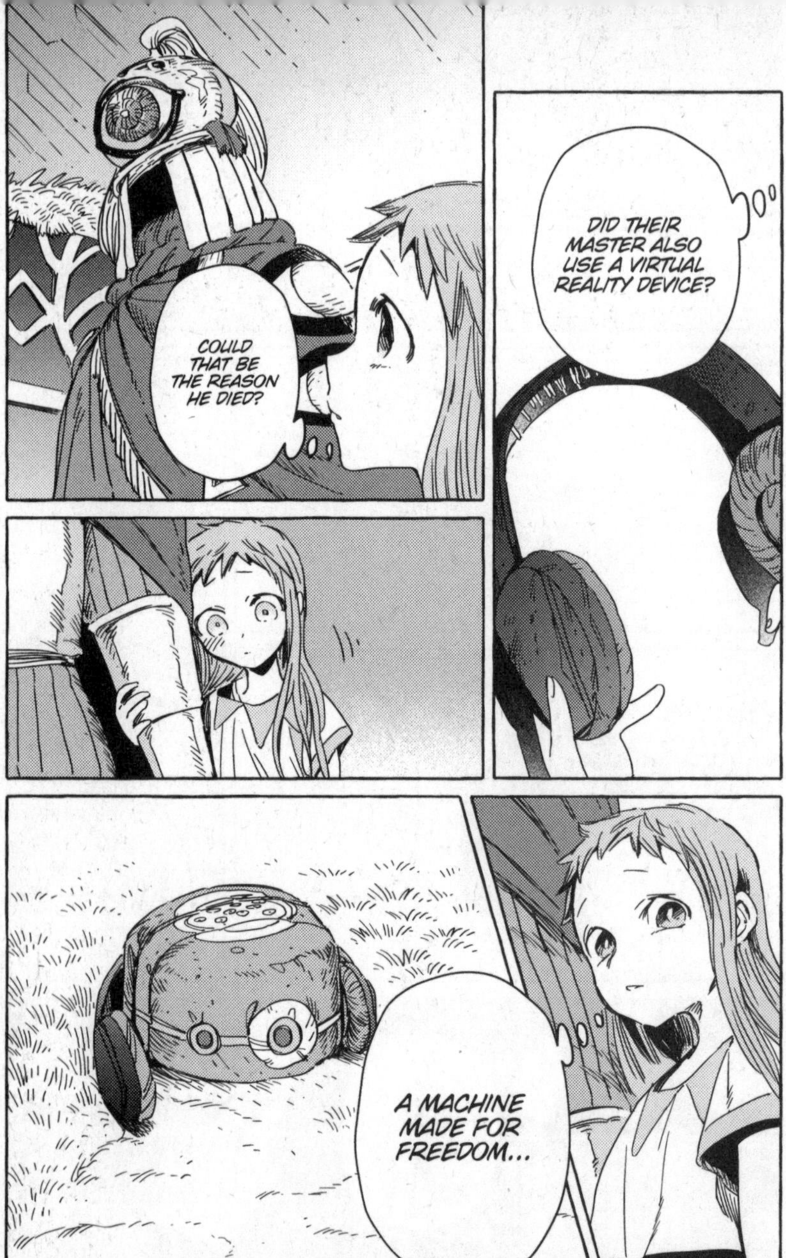
DID THEIR MASTER ALSO USE A VIRTUAL REALITY DEVICE?
COULD THAT BE THE REASON HE DIED?
A MACHINE MADE FOR FREEDOM...

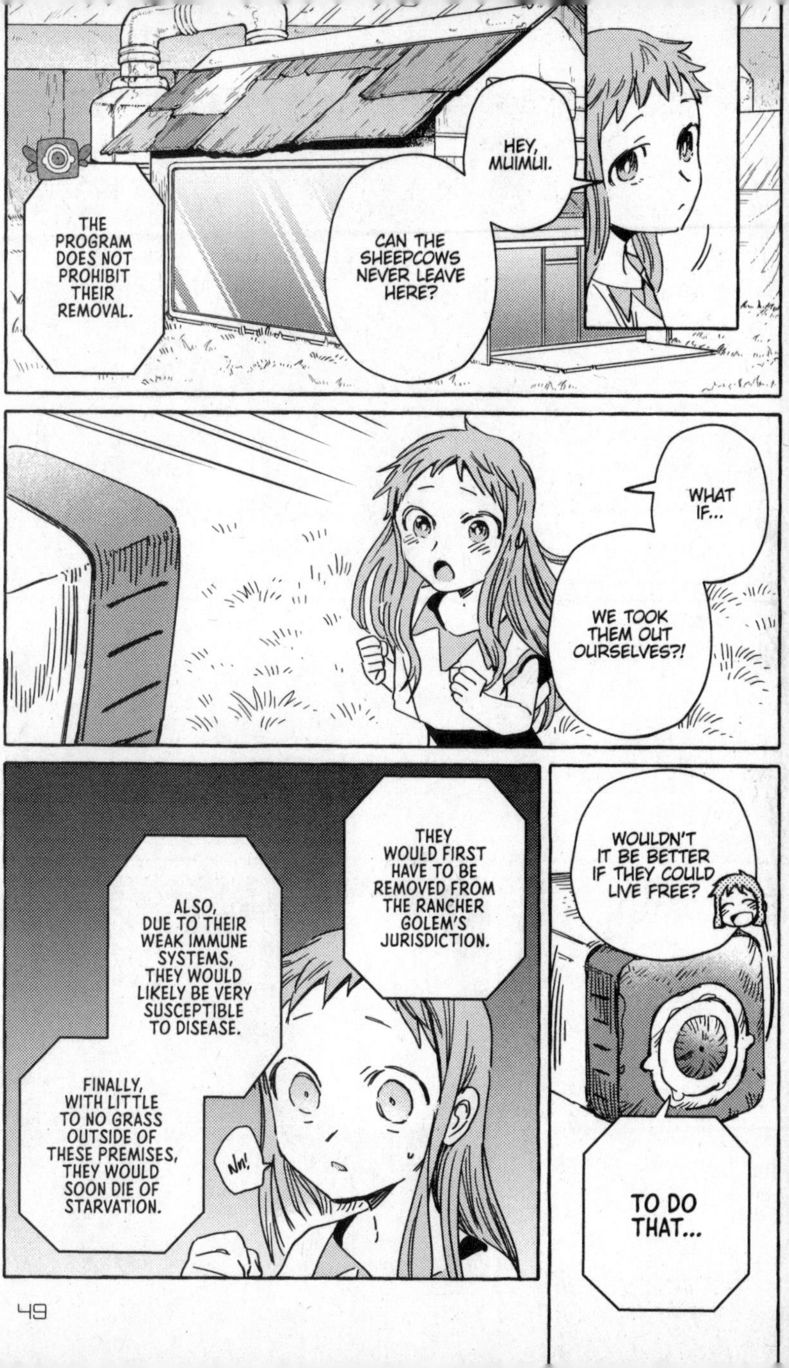
HEY, MUIMUI.
CAN THE SHEEPCOWS NEVER LEAVE HERE?
THE PROGRAM DOES NOT PROHIBIT THEIR REMOVAL.
WHAT IF...
WE TOOK THEM OUT OURSELVES?!
WOULDN'T IT BE BETTER IF THEY COULD LIVE FREE?
TO DO THAT...
THEY WOULD FIRST HAVE TO BE REMOVED FROM THE RANCHER GOLEM'S JURISDICTION.
ALSO, DUE TO THEIR WEAK IMMUNE SYSTEMS, THEY WOULD LIKELY BE VERY SUSCEPTIBLE TO DISEASE.
FINALLY, WITH LITTLE TO NO GRASS OUTSIDE OF THESE PREMISES, THEY WOULD SOON DIE OF STARVATION.
Nn!

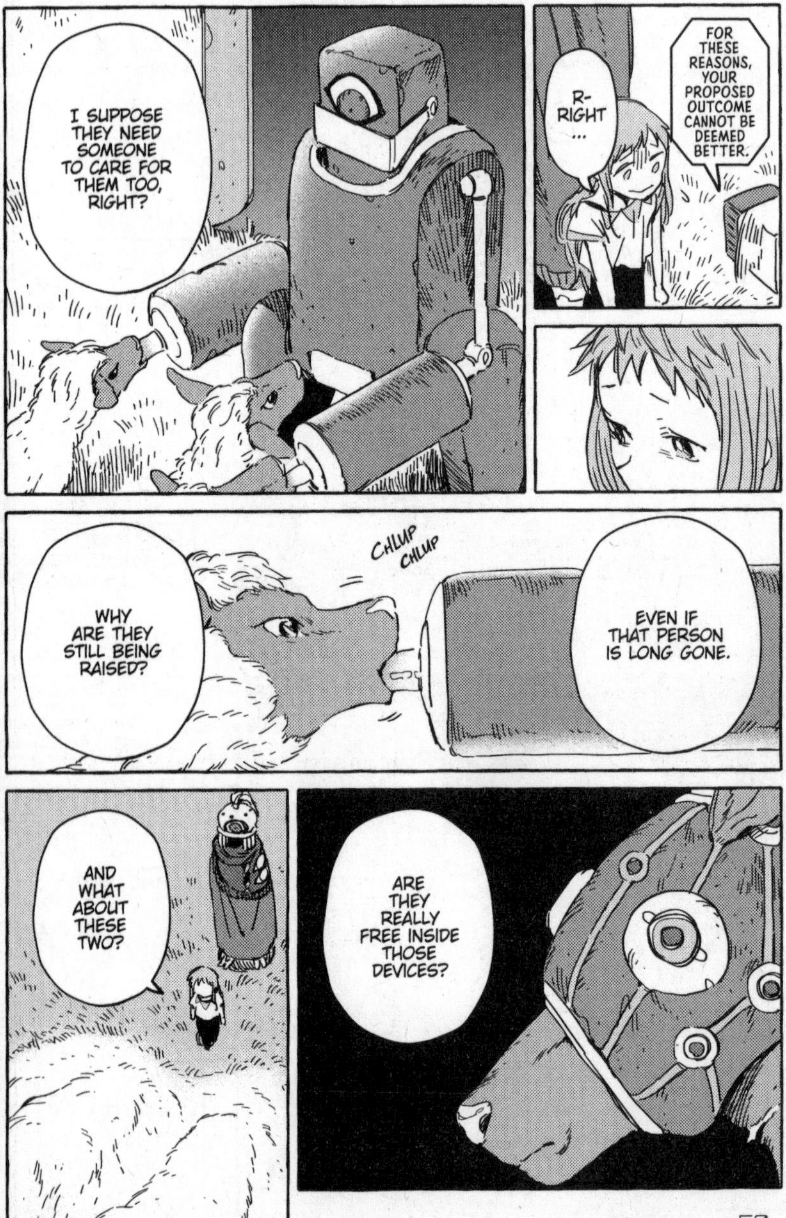
FOR THESE REASONS, YOUR PROPOSED OUTCOME CANNOT BE DEEMED BETTER.
R-RIGHT...
I SUPPOSE THEY NEED SOMEONE TO CARE FOR THEM TOO, RIGHT?
EVEN IF THAT PERSON IS LONG GONE.
CHLUP CHLUP
WHY ARE THEY STILL BEING RAISED?
ARE THEY REALLY FREE INSIDE THOSE DEVICES?
AND WHAT ABOUT THESE TWO?

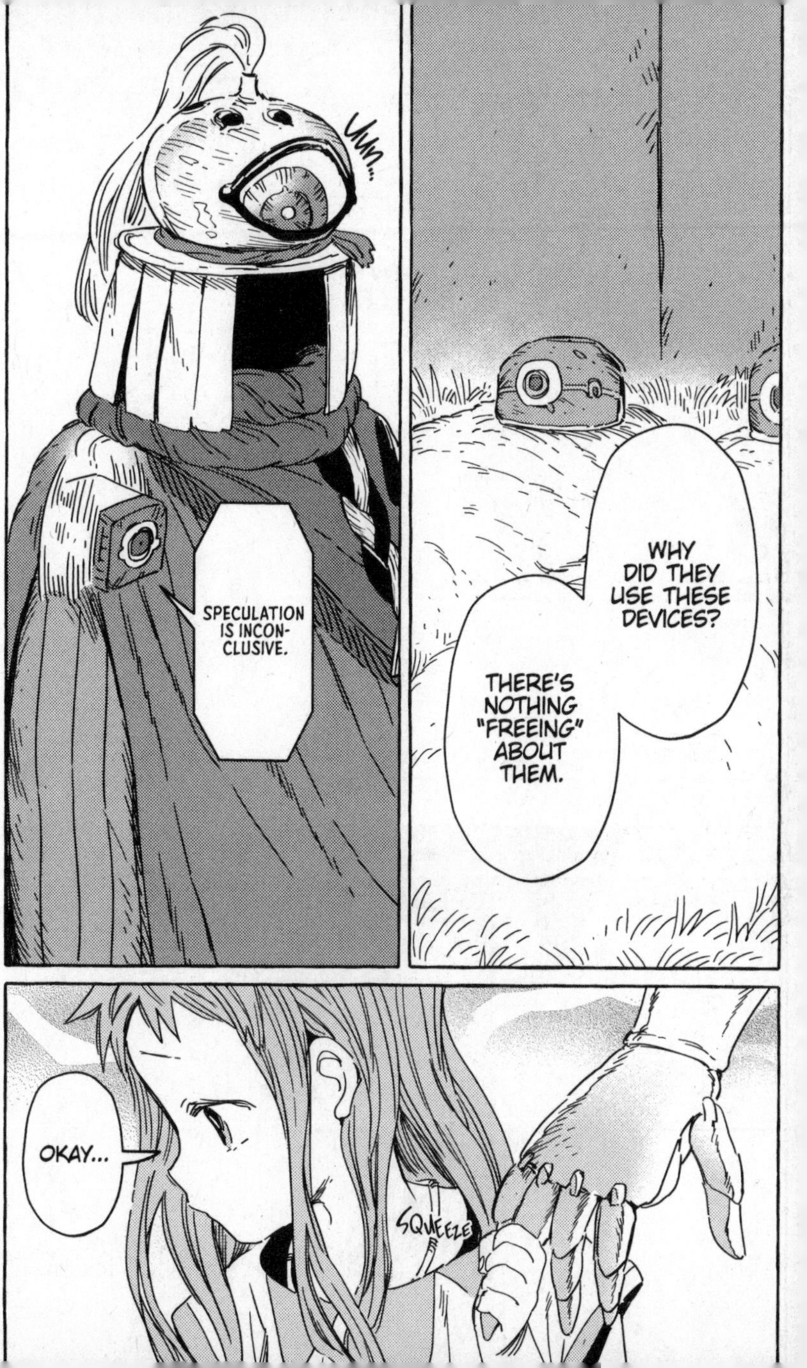
WHY DID THEY USE THESE DEVICES?
THERE'S NOTHING "FREEING" ABOUT THEM.
UUN...
SPECULATION IS INCON-CLUSIVE.
OKAY...
SQUEEZE

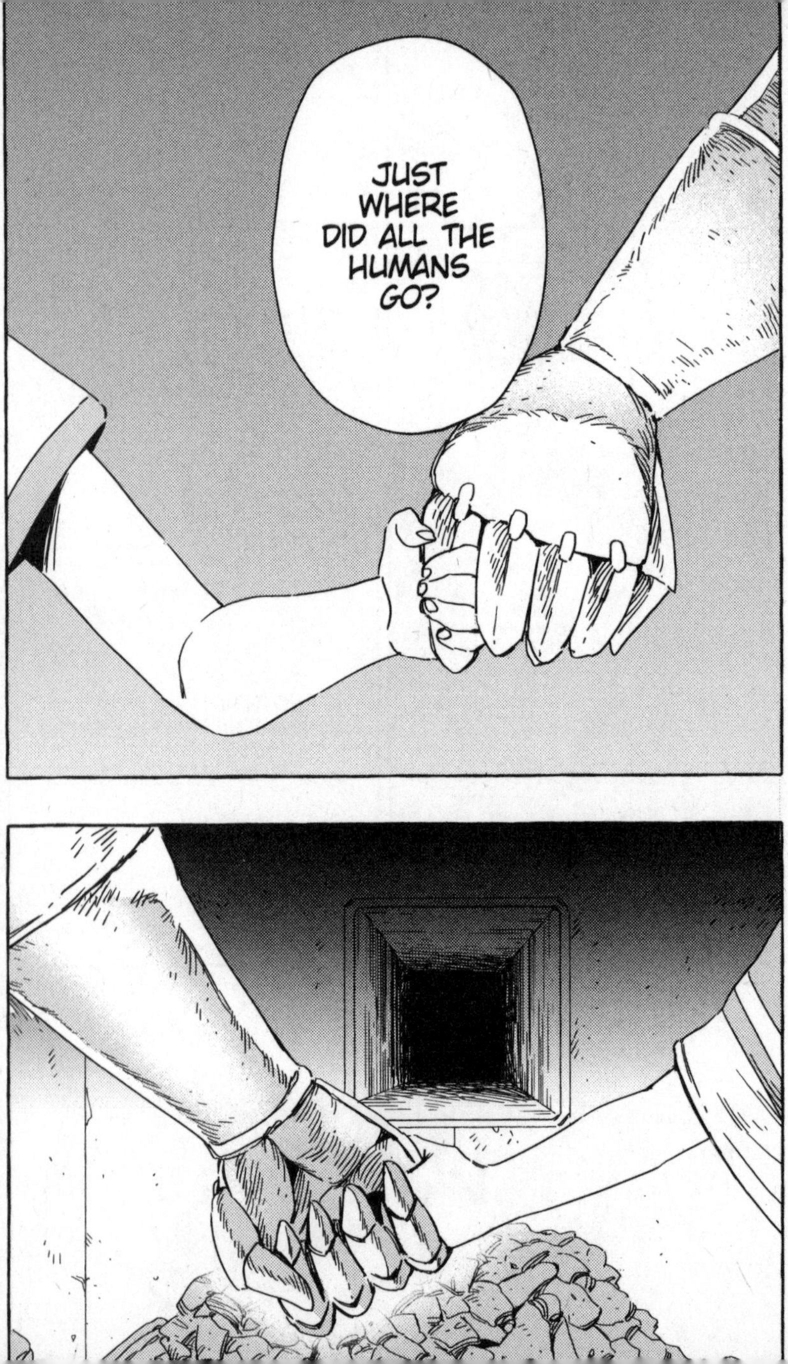
JUST WHERE DID ALL THE HUMANS GO?

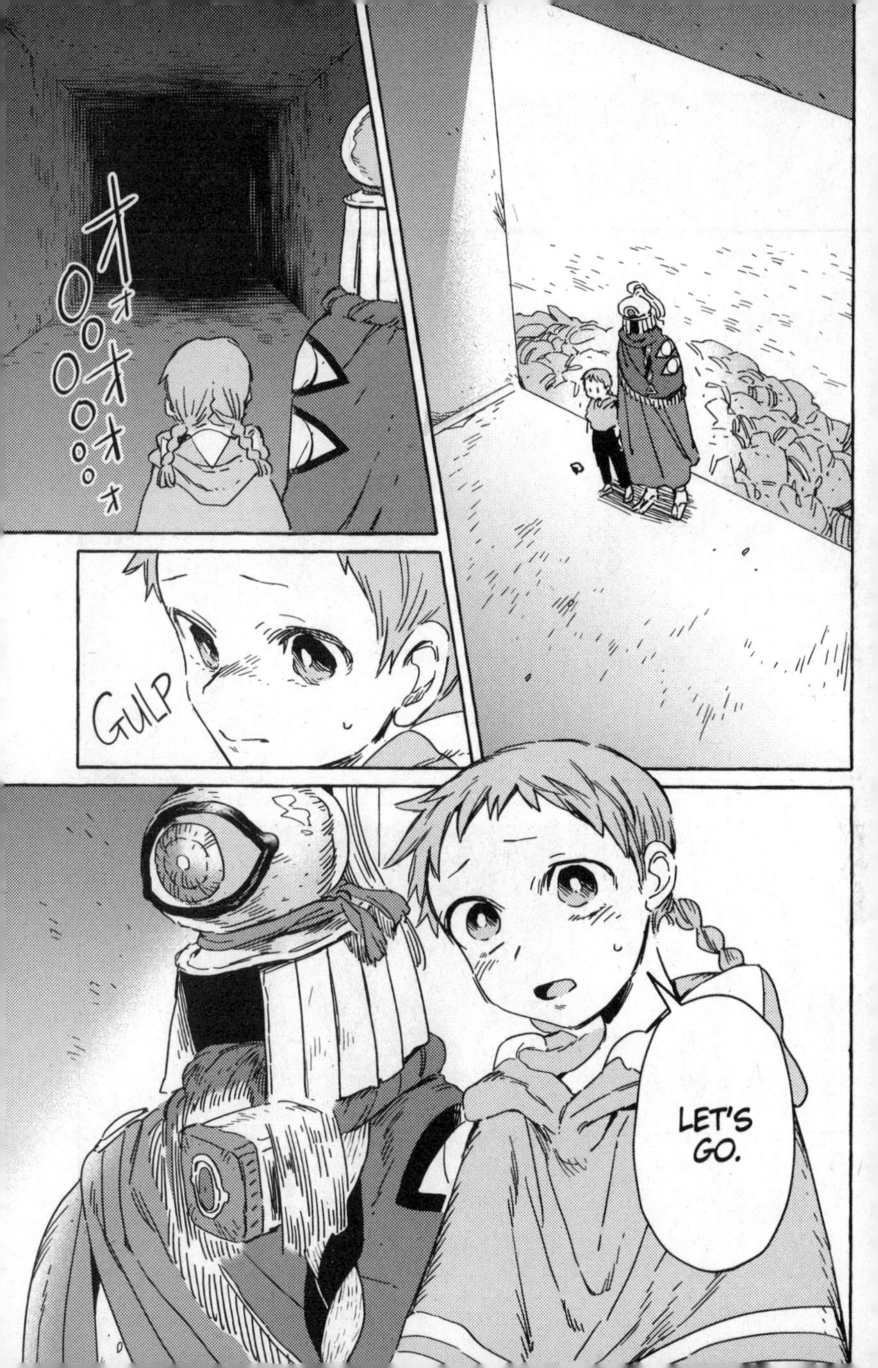
OoOooo
GULP
LET'S GO.

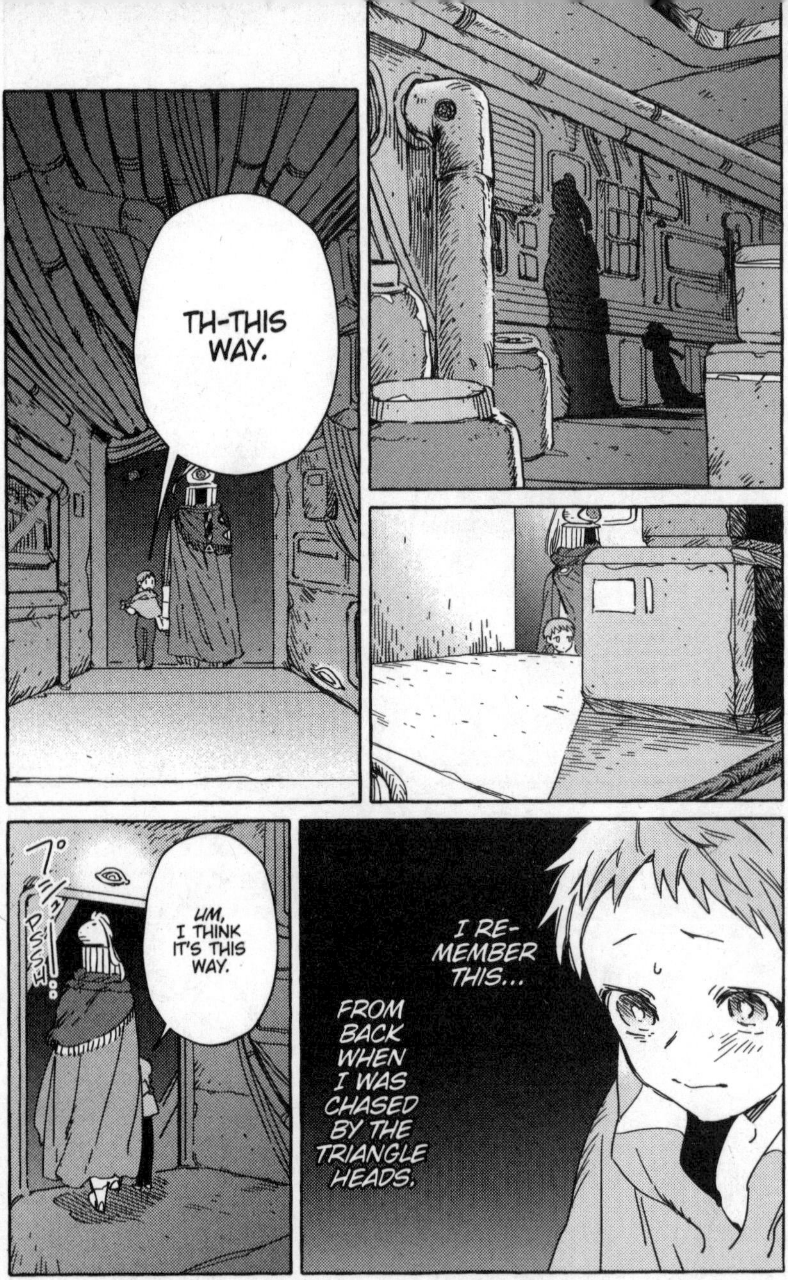
TH-THIS WAY.
I RE-MEMBER THIS...
FROM BACK WHEN I WAS CHASED BY THE TRIANGLE HEADS.
PSSH...
UM, I THINK IT'S THIS WAY.

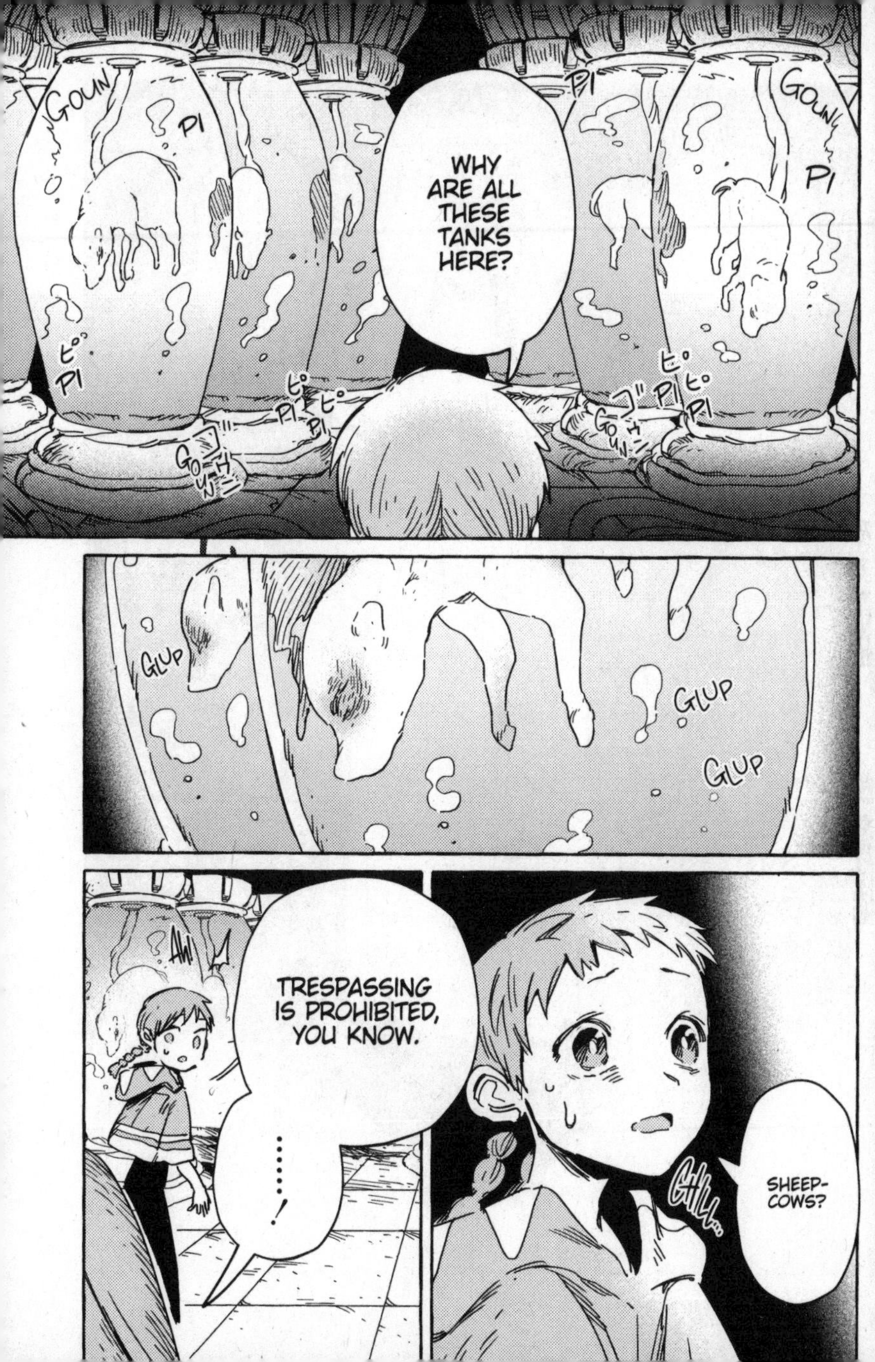
GOUN
PI
PI
WHY ARE ALL THESE TANKS HERE?
PI
GOUN
PI
PI
GOUN
PI
PI
GLUP
GLUP
GLUP
SHEEP-COWS?
TRESPASSING IS PROHIBITED, YOU KNOW.
......!
AH!

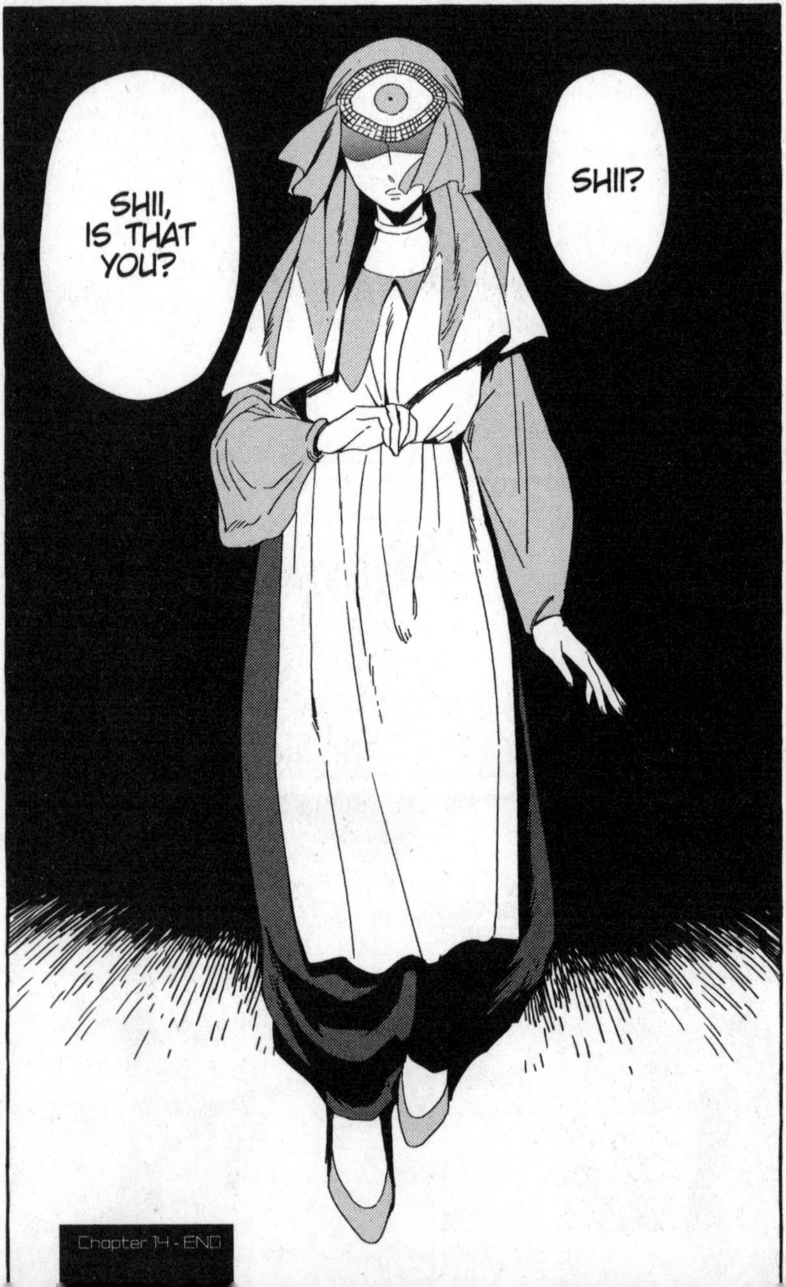
SHII?
SHII, IS THAT YOU?
Chapter 14 - END

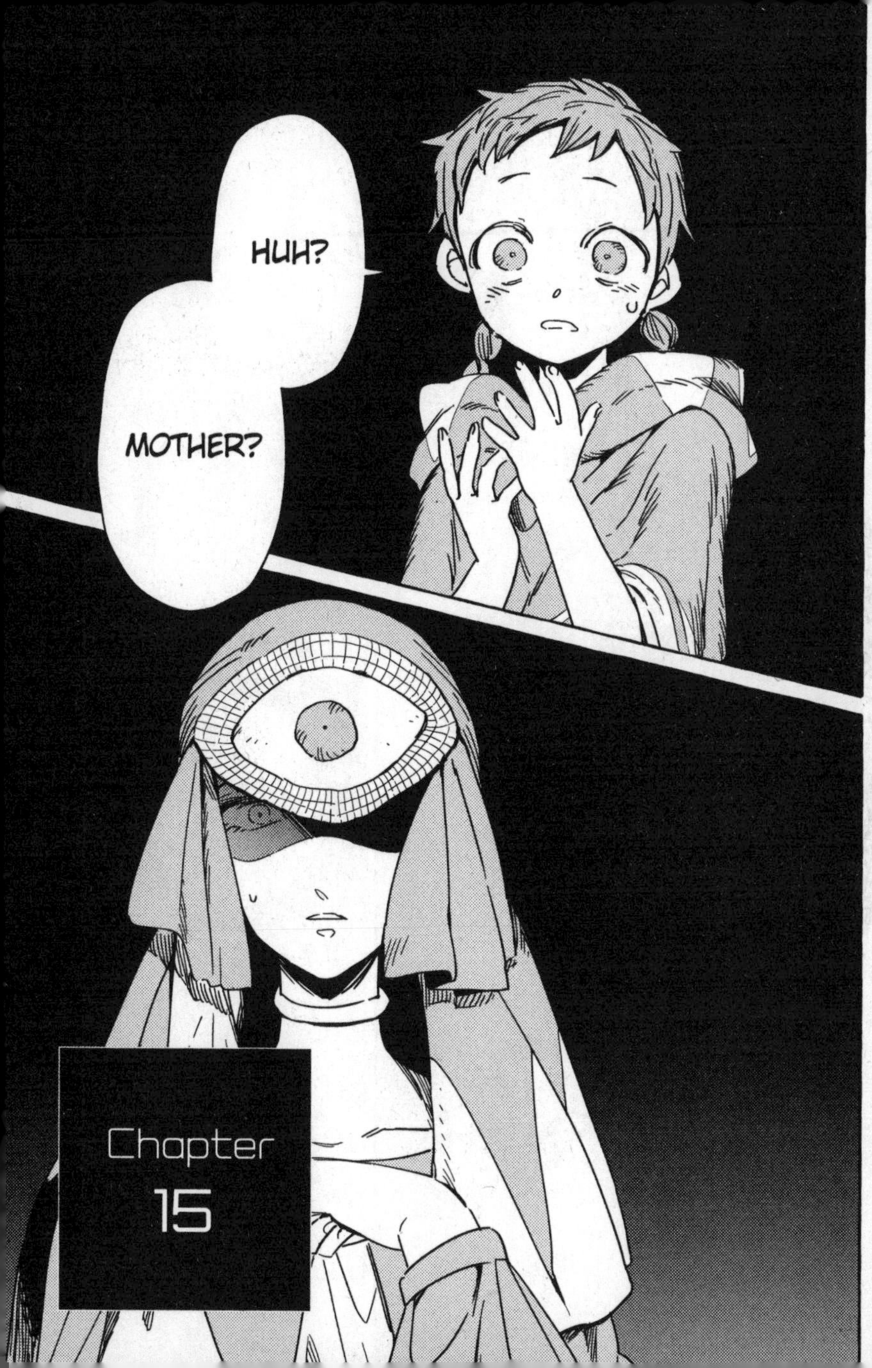
HUH?
MOTHER?
Chapter
15

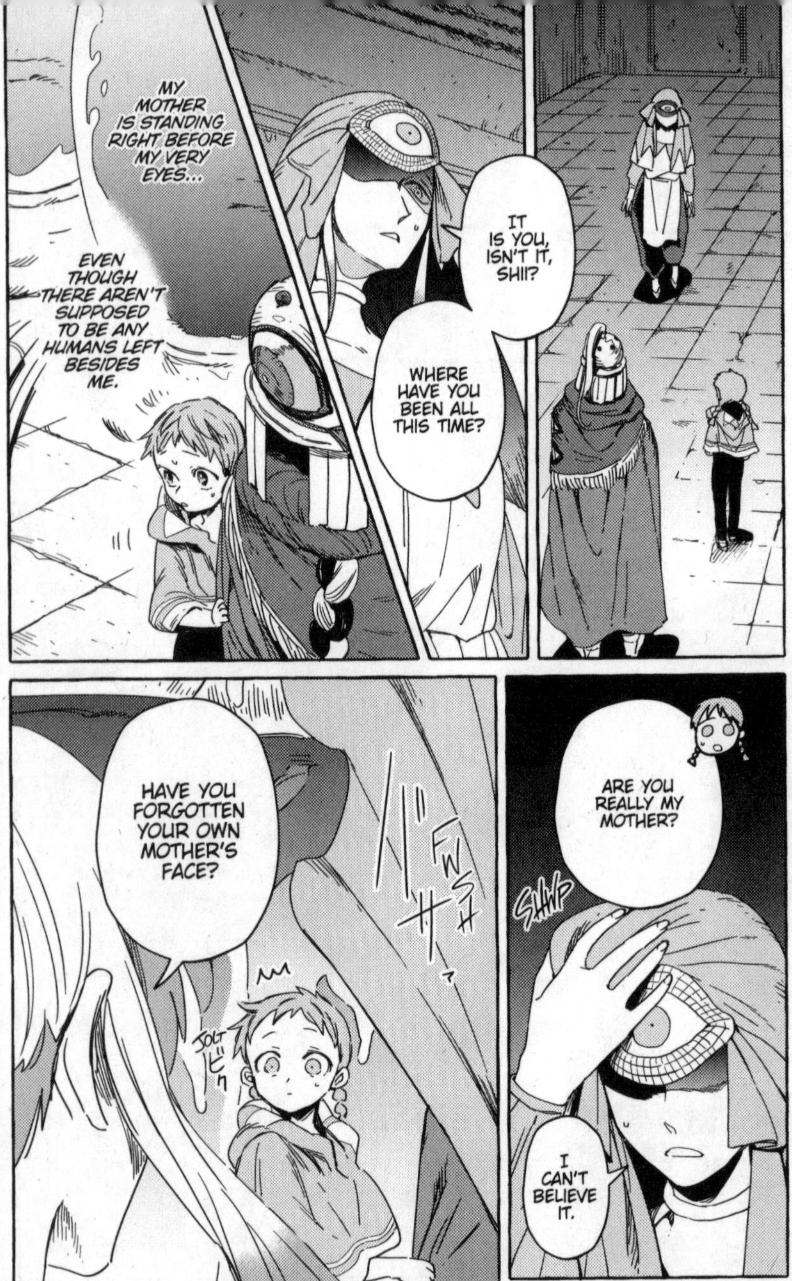
IT IS YOU, ISN'T IT, SHII?
WHERE HAVE YOU BEEN ALL THIS TIME?
MY MOTHER IS STANDING RIGHT BEFORE MY VERY EYES...
EVEN THOUGH THERE AREN'T SUPPOSED TO BE ANY HUMANS LEFT BESIDES ME.
ARE YOU REALLY MY MOTHER?
SHWP
I CAN'T BELIEVE IT.
HAVE YOU FORGOTTEN YOUR OWN MOTHER'S FACE?
FWSH
JOLT

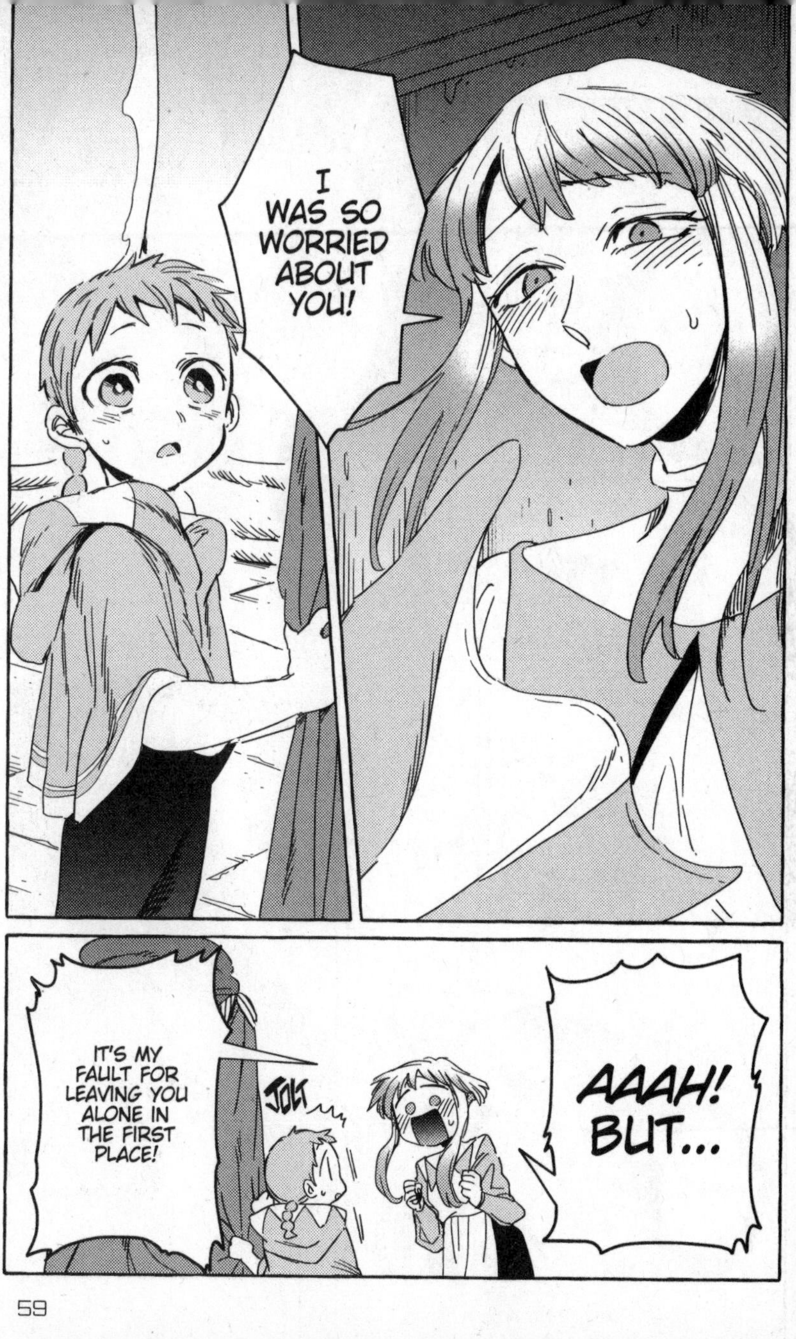
I WAS SO WORRIED ABOUT YOU!
AAAH! BUT...
JOLT
IT'S MY FAULT FOR LEAVING YOU ALONE IN THE FIRST PLACE!

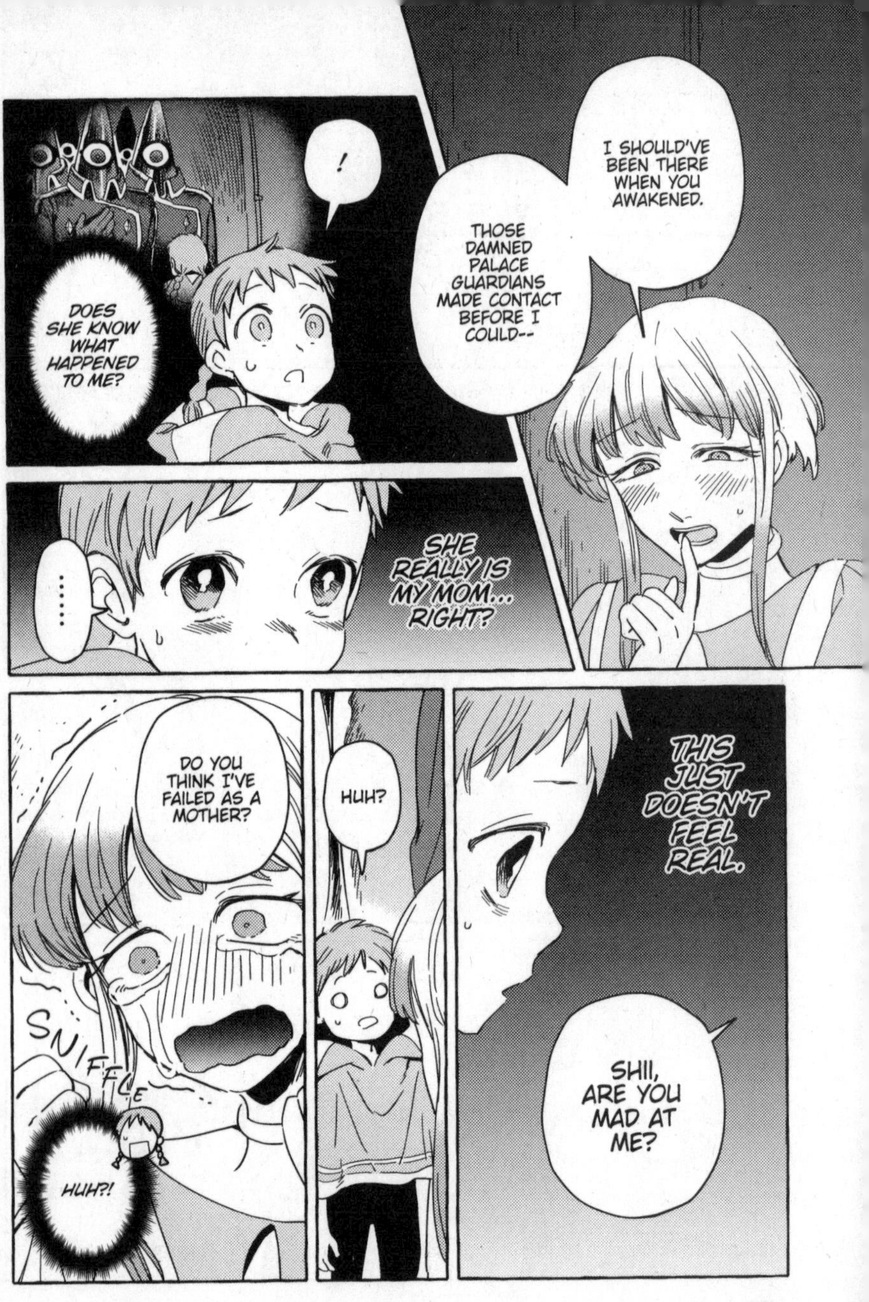
I SHOULD'VE BEEN THERE WHEN YOU AWAKENED.
THOSE DAMNED PALACE GUARDIANS MADE CONTACT BEFORE I COULD--
!
DOES SHE KNOW WHAT HAPPENED TO ME?
......
SHE REALLY IS MY MOM... RIGHT?
THIS JUST DOESN'T FEEL REAL.
SHII, ARE YOU MAD AT ME?
HUH?
DO YOU THINK I'VE FAILED AS A MOTHER?
SNIFFLE
HUH?!

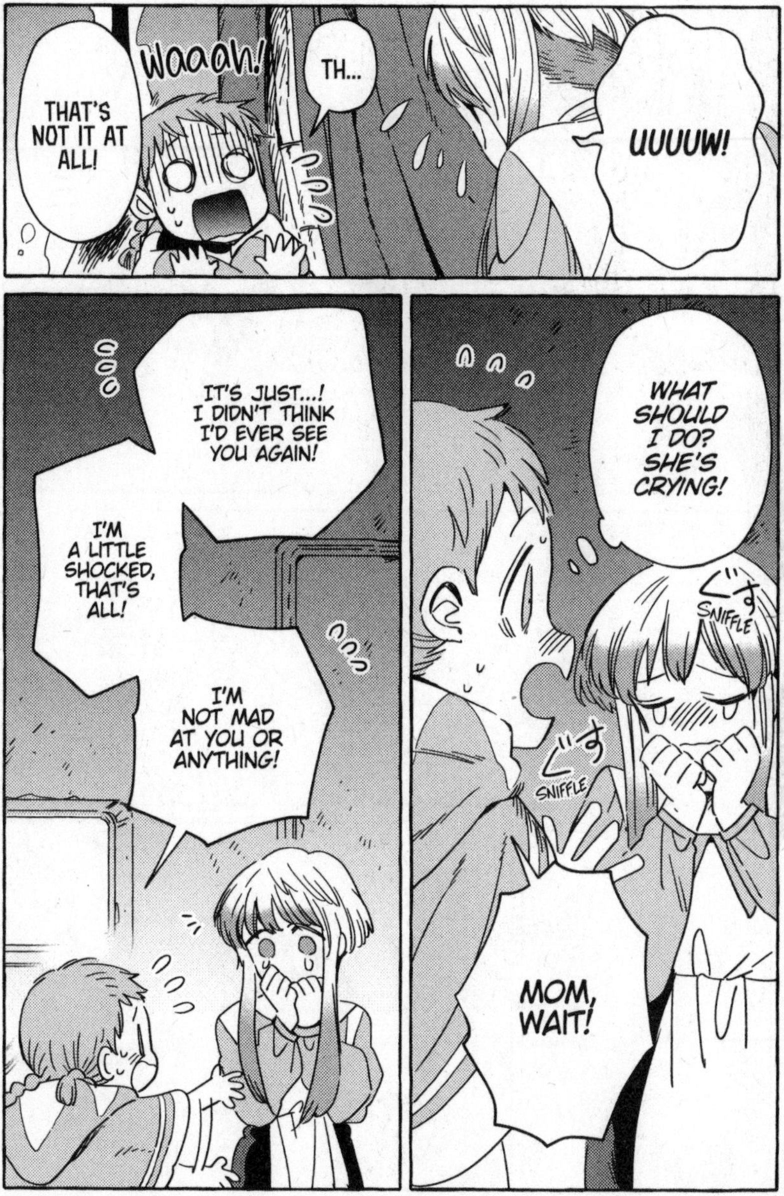
UUUUW!
TH...
Waaah!
THAT'S NOT IT AT ALL!
WHAT SHOULD I DO? SHE'S CRYING!
ぐす SNIFFLE
ぐす SNIFFLE
MOM, WAIT!
IT'S JUST...! I DIDN'T THINK I'D EVER SEE YOU AGAIN!
I'M A LITTLE SHOCKED, THAT'S ALL!
I'M NOT MAD AT YOU OR ANYTHING!

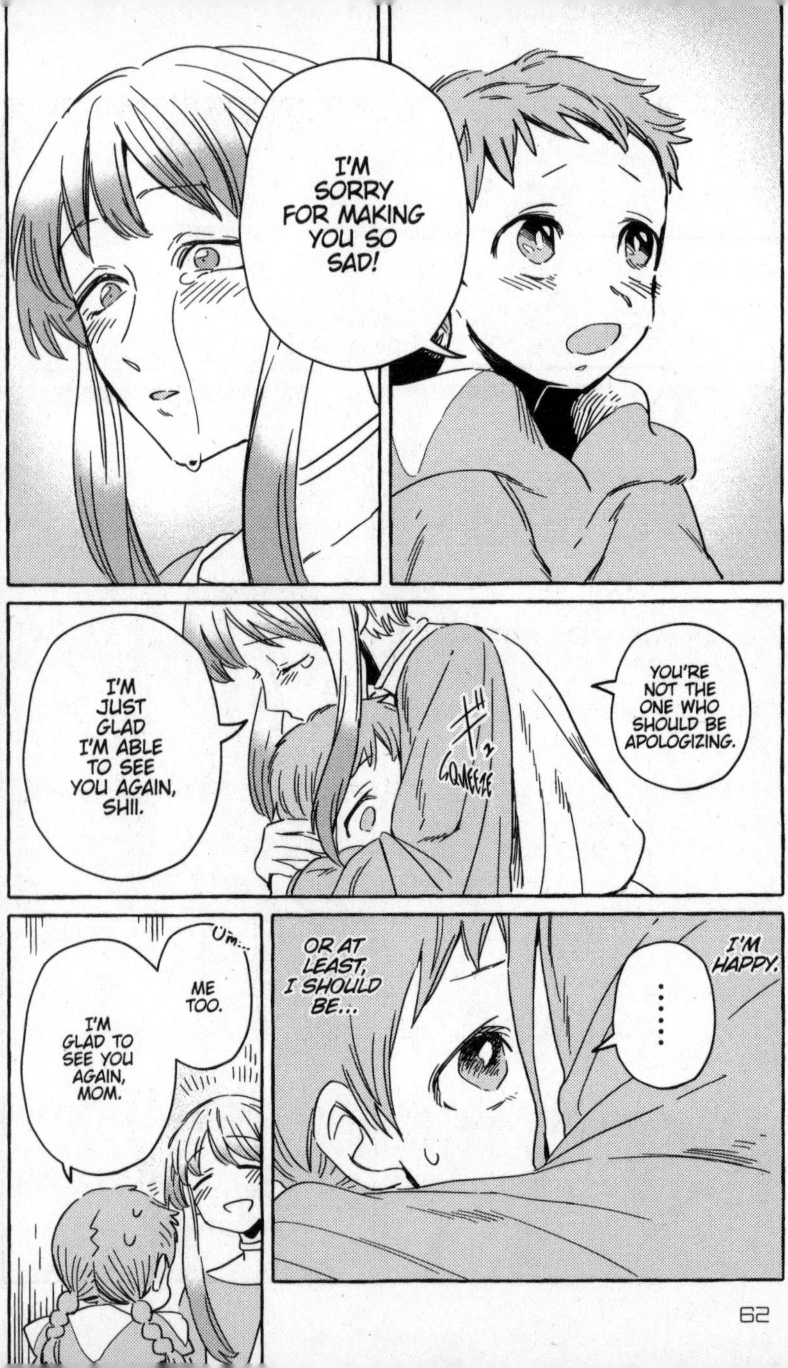
I'M SORRY FOR MAKING YOU SO SAD!
YOU'RE NOT THE ONE WHO SHOULD BE APOLOGIZING.
SQUEEZE
I'M JUST GLAD I'M ABLE TO SEE YOU AGAIN, SHII.
I'M HAPPY.
......
OR AT LEAST, I SHOULD BE...
UM...
ME TOO.
I'M GLAD TO SEE YOU AGAIN, MOM.

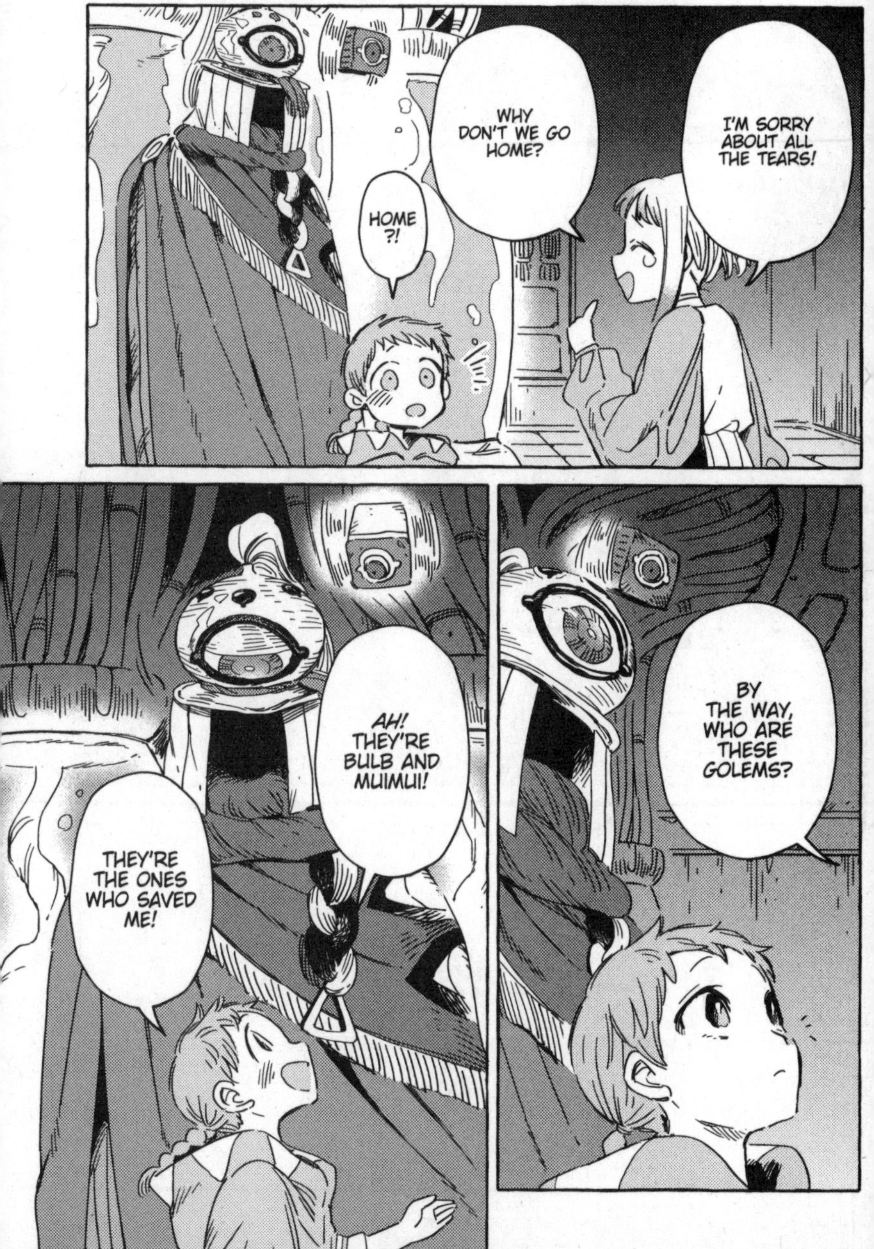
I'M SORRY ABOUT ALL THE TEARS!
WHY DON'T WE GO HOME?
HOME ?!
BY THE WAY, WHO ARE THESE GOLEMS?
AH! THEY'RE BULB AND MUIMUI!
THEY'RE THE ONES WHO SAVED ME!

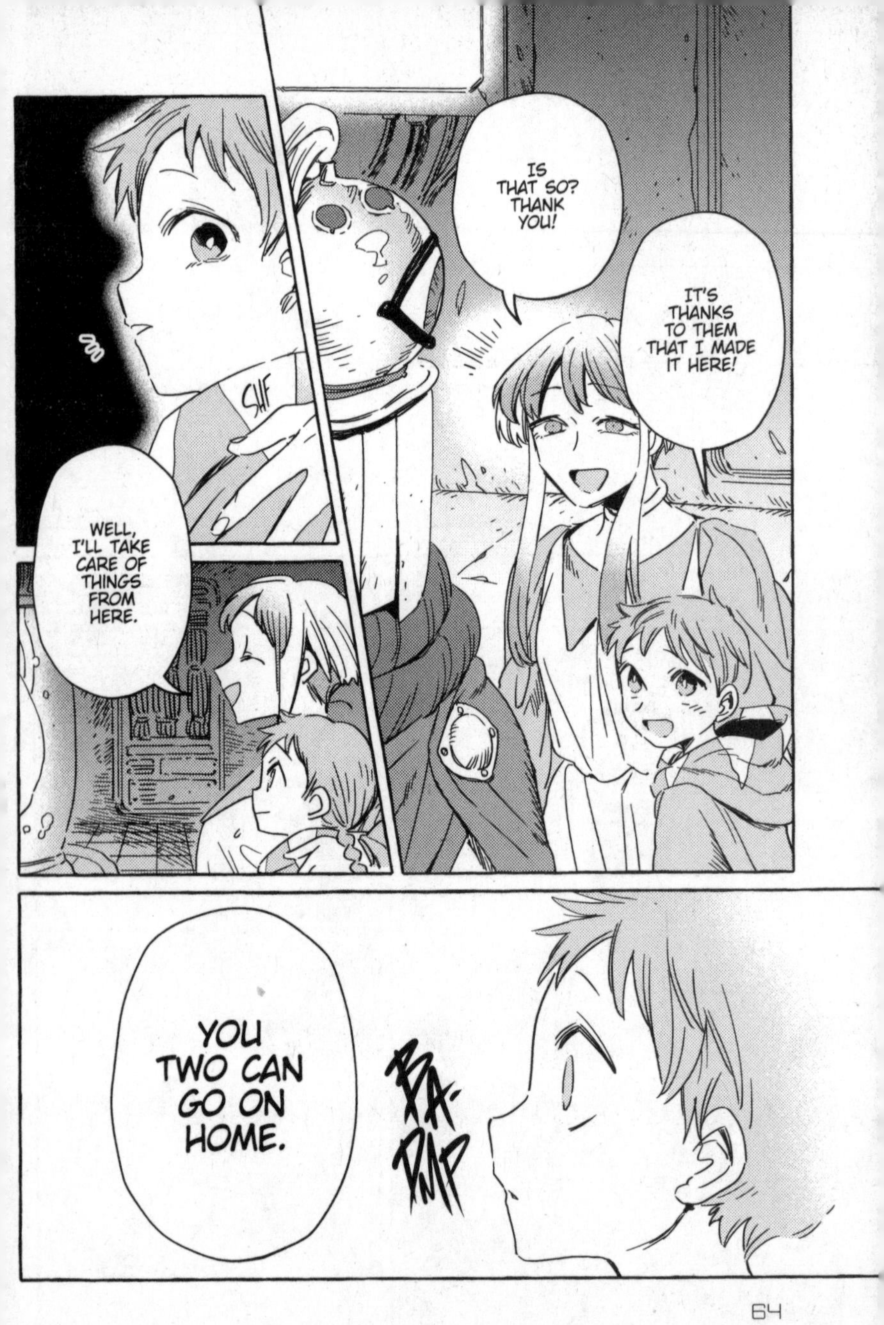
IT'S THANKS TO THEM THAT I MADE IT HERE!
IS THAT SO? THANK YOU!
SHF
WELL, I'LL TAKE CARE OF THINGS FROM HERE.
YOU TWO CAN GO ON HOME.
BA-DMP

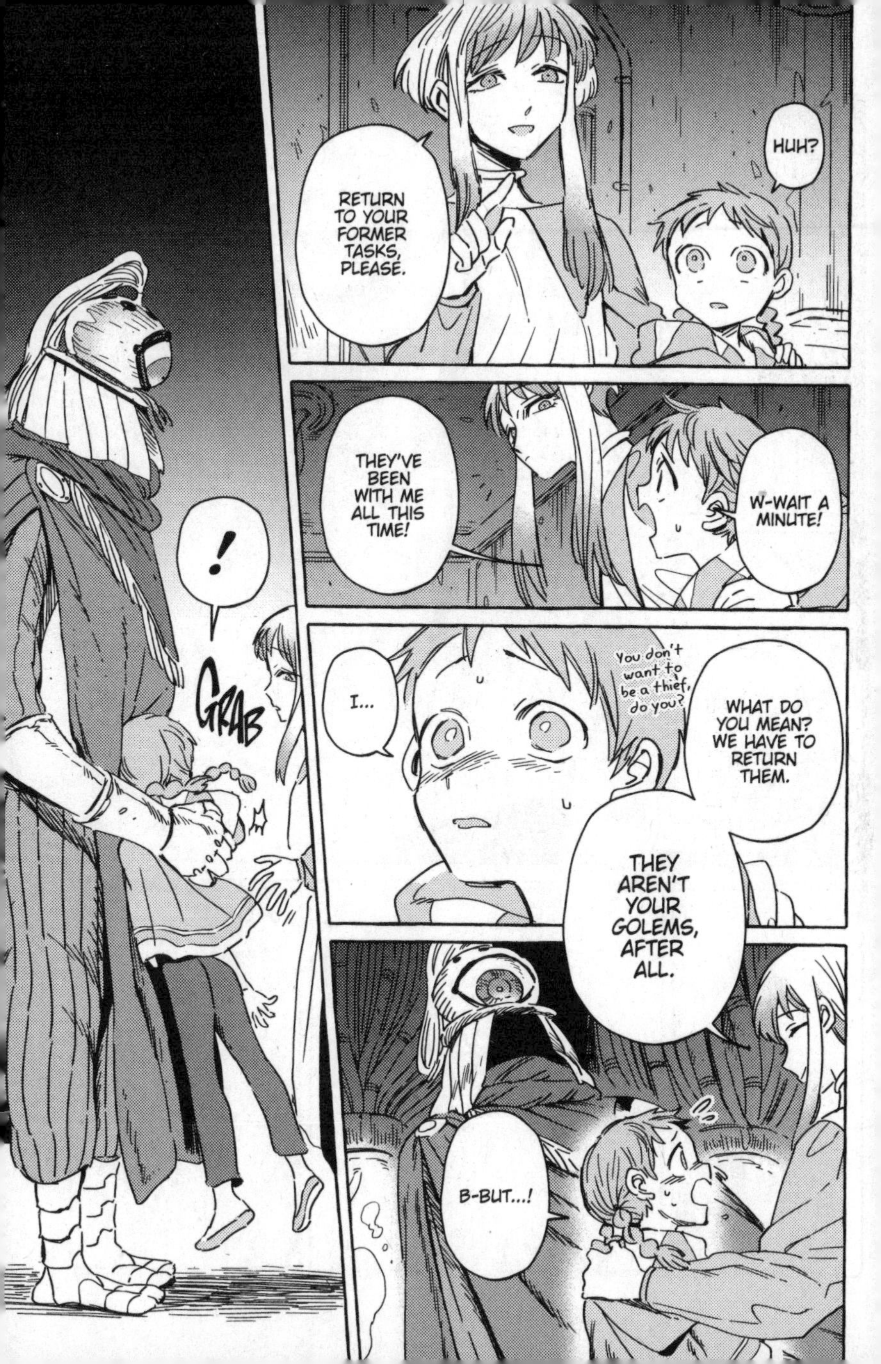
HUH?
RETURN TO YOUR FORMER TASKS, PLEASE.
W-WAIT A MINUTE!
THEY'VE BEEN WITH ME ALL THIS TIME!
WHAT DO YOU MEAN? WE HAVE TO RETURN THEM.
You don't want to be a thief, do you?
I...
THEY AREN'T YOUR GOLEMS, AFTER ALL.
B-BUT...!
!
GRAB

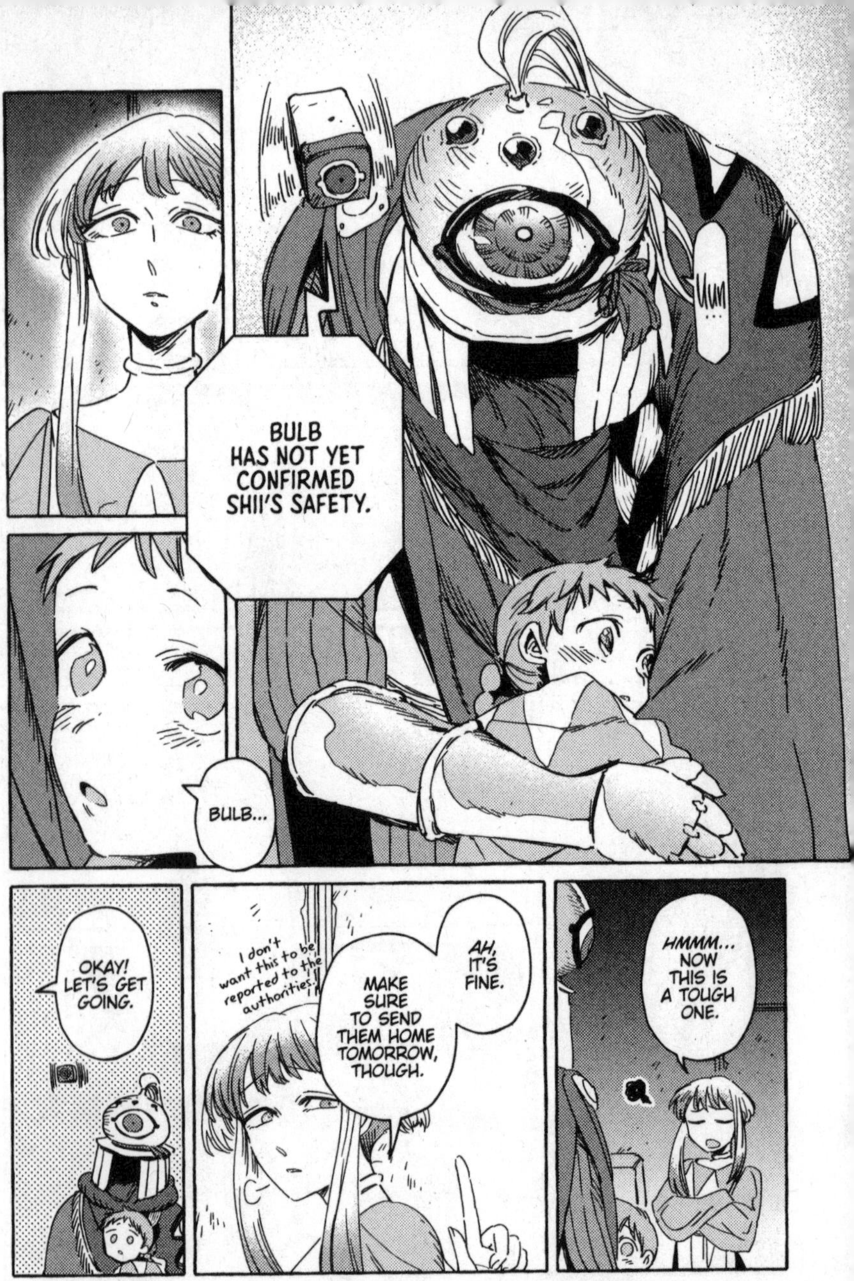
UUM...
BULB HAS NOT YET CONFIRMED SHII'S SAFETY.
BULB...
HMMM... NOW THIS IS A TOUGH ONE.
AH, IT'S FINE.
MAKE SURE TO SEND THEM HOME TOMORROW, THOUGH.
I don't want this to be reported to the authorities.
OKAY! LET'S GET GOING.

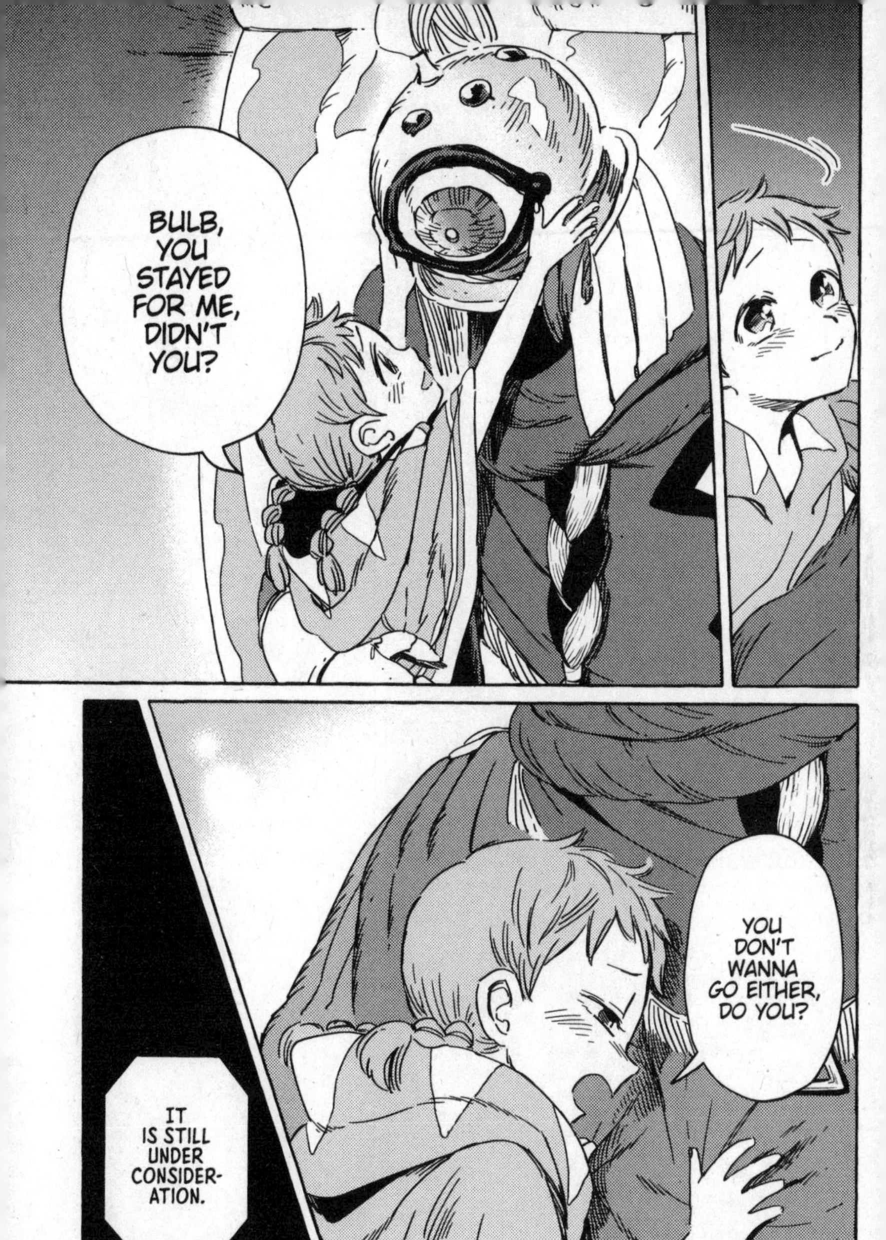
BULB, YOU STAYED FOR ME, DIDN'T YOU?
YOU DON'T WANNA GO EITHER, DO YOU?
IT IS STILL UNDER CONSIDER-ATION.

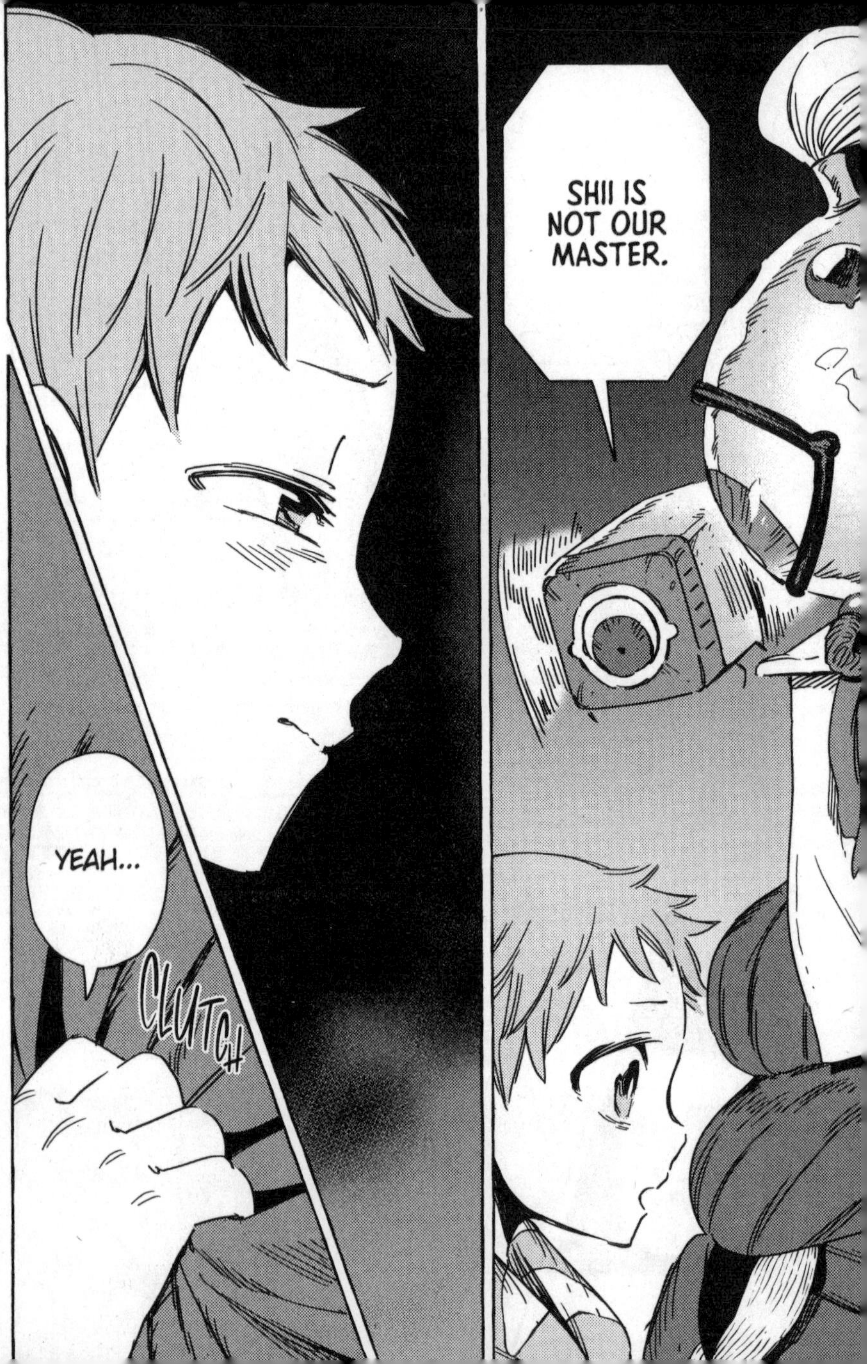
SHII IS NOT OUR MASTER.
YEAH...
CLUTCH

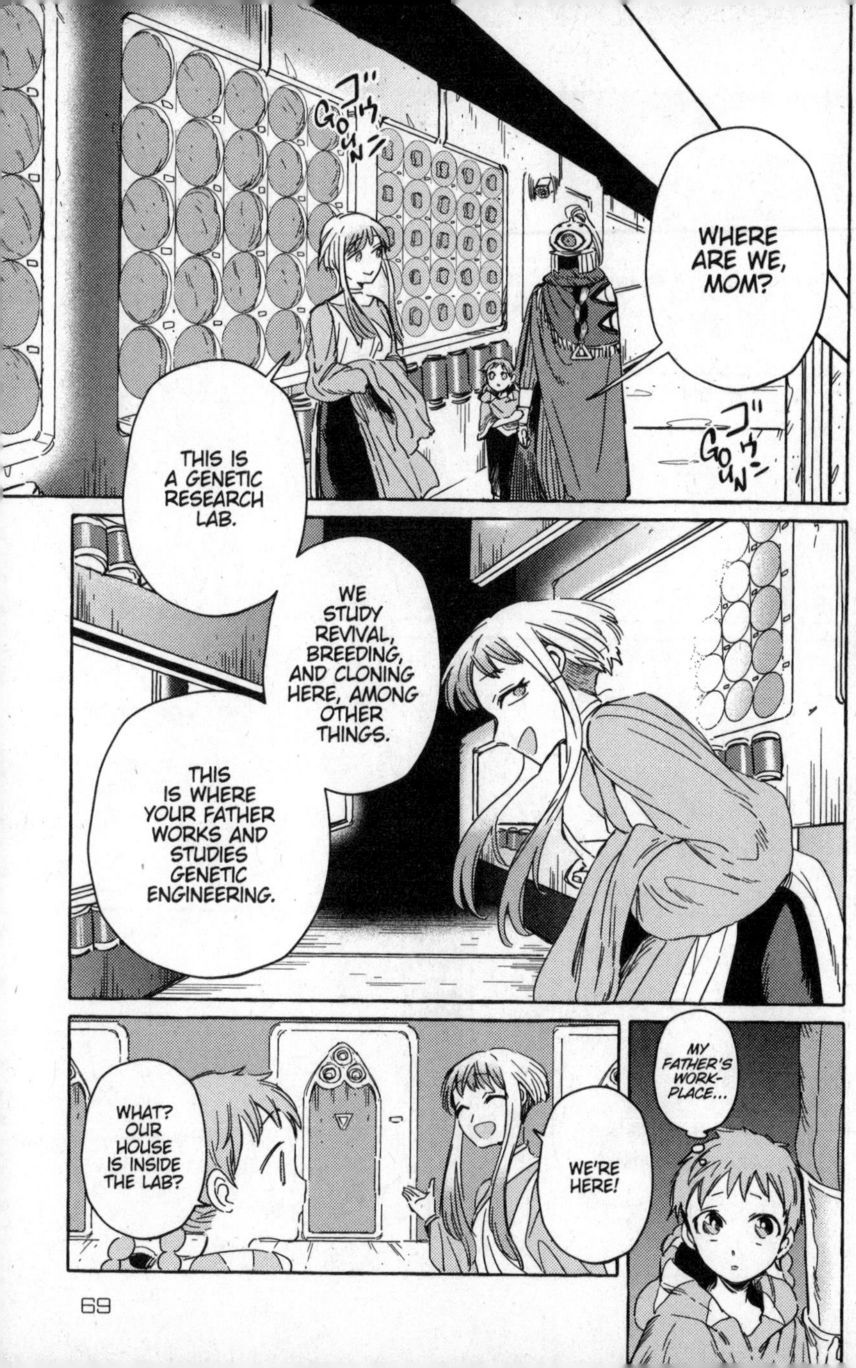
GOUN
WHERE ARE WE, MOM?
GOUN
THIS IS A GENETIC RESEARCH LAB.
WE STUDY REVIVAL, BREEDING, AND CLONING HERE, AMONG OTHER THINGS.
THIS IS WHERE YOUR FATHER WORKS AND STUDIES GENETIC ENGINEERING.
MY FATHER'S WORK-PLACE...
WE'RE HERE!
WHAT? OUR HOUSE IS INSIDE THE LAB?

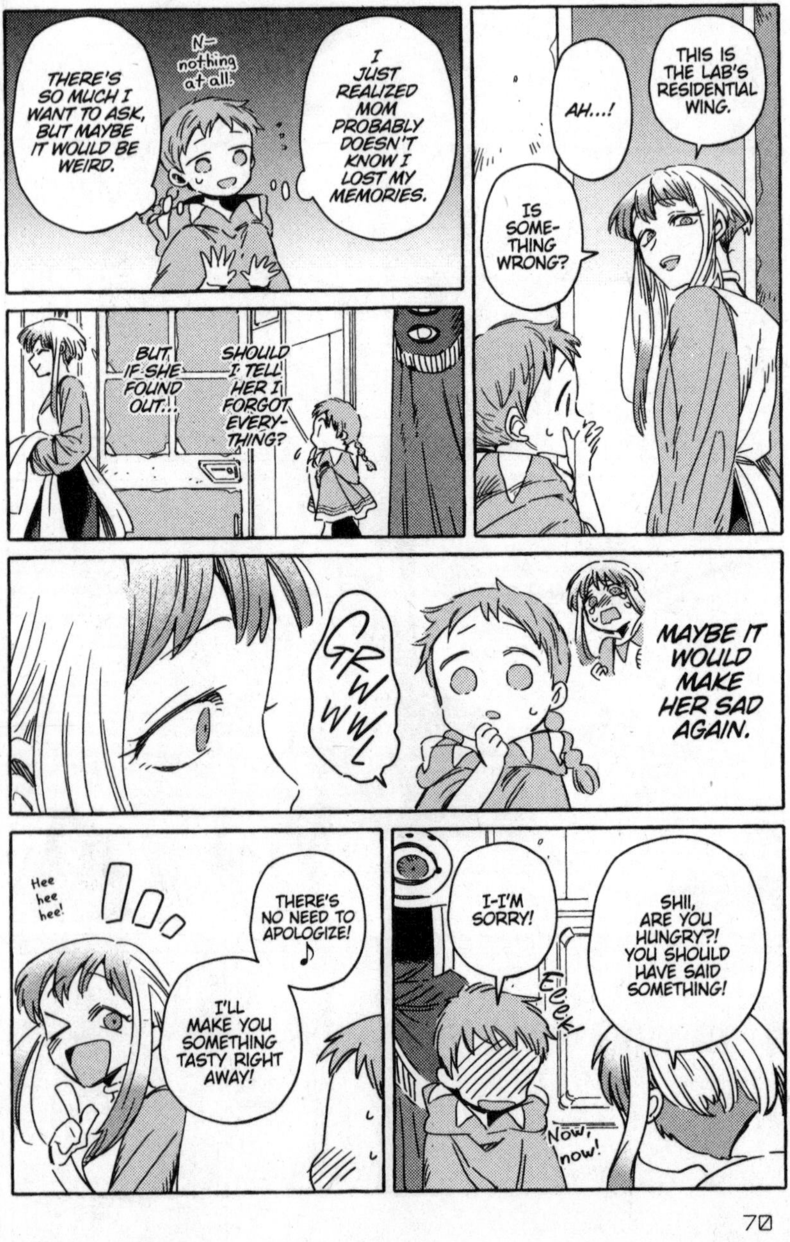
THIS IS THE LAB'S RESIDENTIAL WING.
AH...!
IS SOMETHING WRONG?
I JUST REALIZED MOM PROBABLY DOESN'T KNOW I LOST MY MEMORIES.
N-nothing at all.
THERE'S SO MUCH I WANT TO ASK, BUT MAYBE IT WOULD BE WEIRD.
SHOULD I TELL HER I FORGOT EVERYTHING?
BUT, IF SHE FOUND OUT...
MAYBE IT WOULD MAKE HER SAD AGAIN.
GRWWWL
SHII, ARE YOU HUNGRY?! YOU SHOULD HAVE SAID SOMETHING!
EEEK!
I-I'M SORRY!
Now, now!
THERE'S NO NEED TO APOLOGIZE! ♪
I'LL MAKE YOU SOMETHING TASTY RIGHT AWAY!
Hee hee hee!

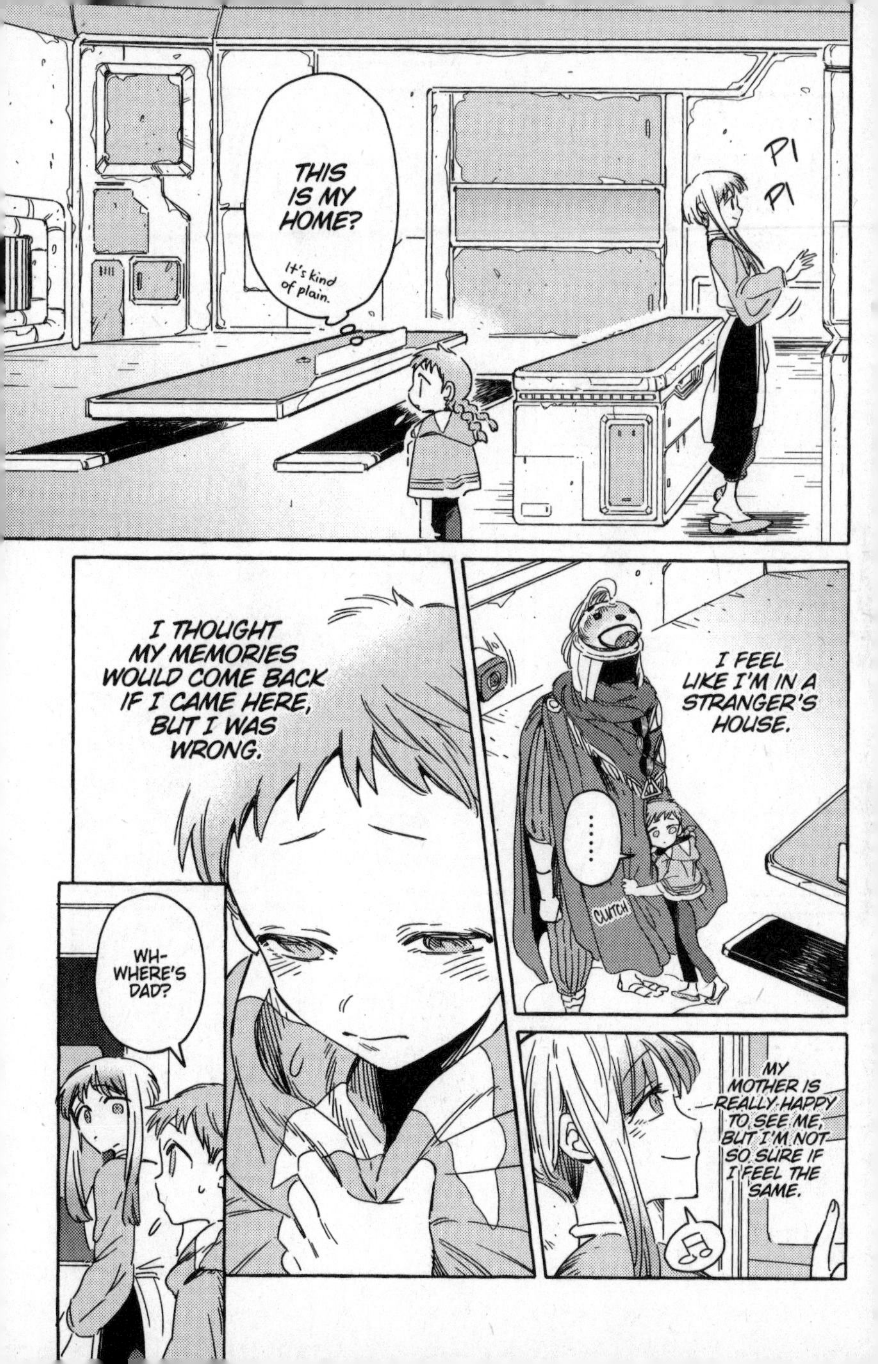
PI
PI
THIS IS MY HOME?
It's kind of plain.
I FEEL LIKE I'M IN A STRANGER'S HOUSE.
......
CLUTCH
MY MOTHER IS REALLY HAPPY TO SEE ME, BUT I'M NOT SO SURE IF I FEEL THE SAME.
I THOUGHT MY MEMORIES WOULD COME BACK IF I CAME HERE, BUT I WAS WRONG.
WH- WHERE'S DAD?

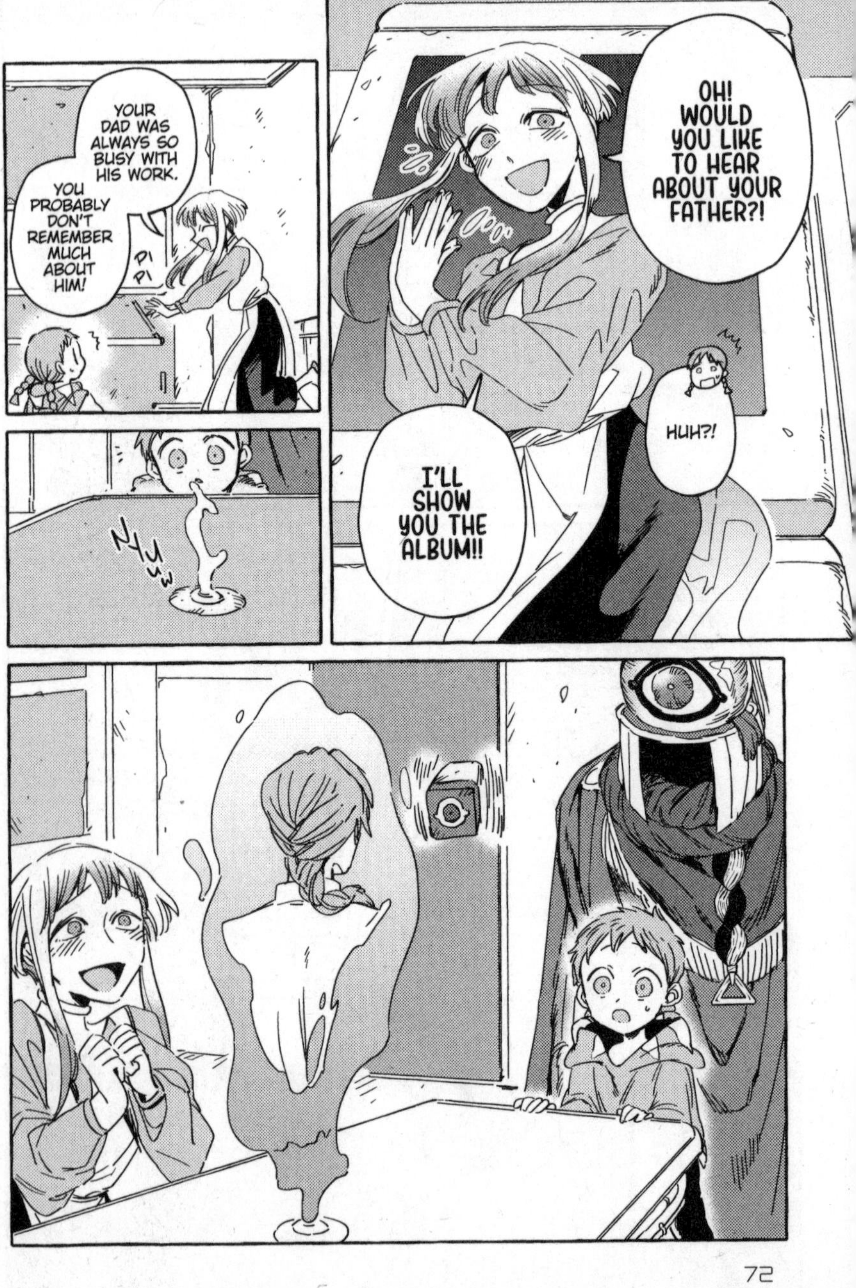
OH! WOULD YOU LIKE TO HEAR ABOUT YOUR FATHER?!
HUH?!
I'LL SHOW YOU THE ALBUM!!
YOUR DAD WAS ALWAYS SO BUSY WITH HIS WORK.
YOU PROBABLY DON'T REMEMBER MUCH ABOUT HIM!
PI PI
NYUUU

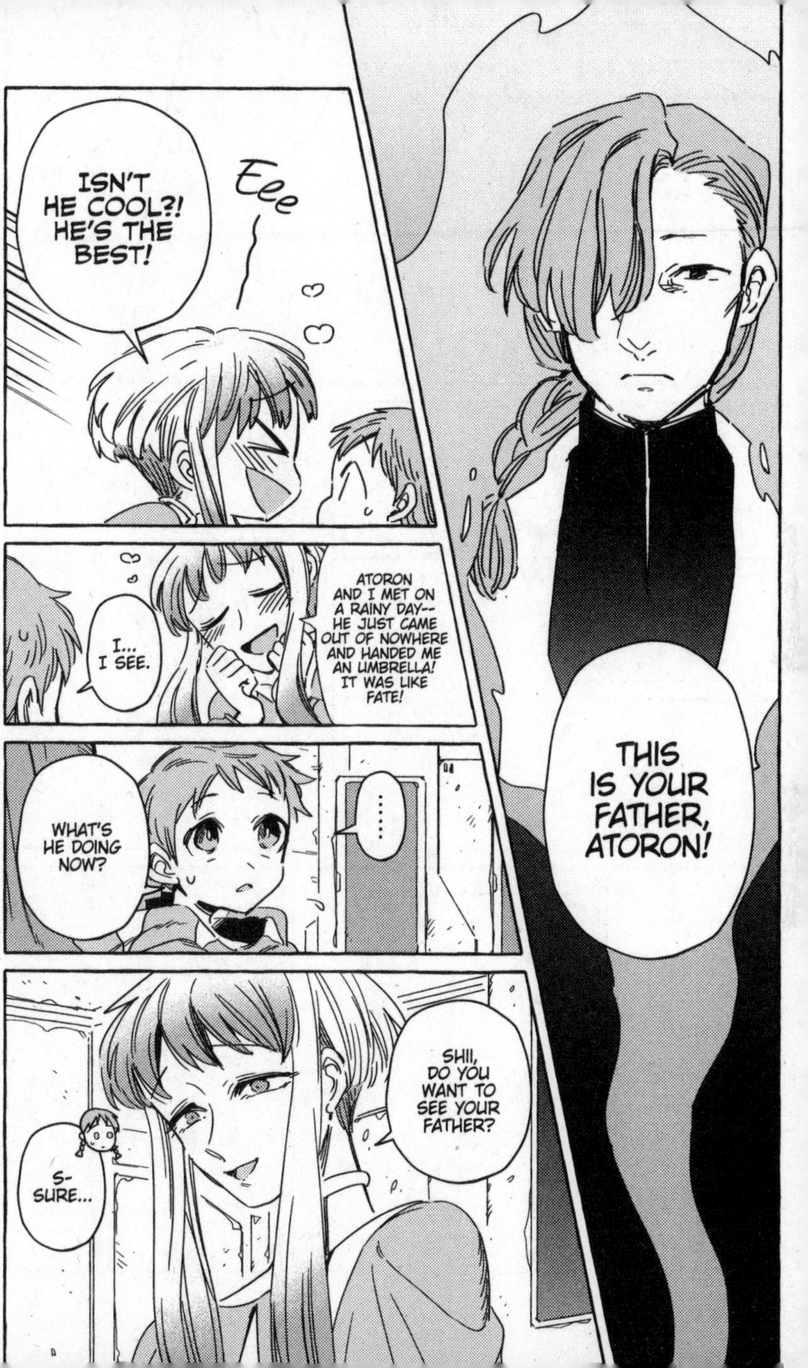
THIS IS YOUR FATHER, ATORON!
Eee
ISN'T HE COOL?! HE'S THE BEST!
ATORON AND I MET ON A RAINY DAY-- HE JUST CAME OUT OF NOWHERE AND HANDED ME AN UMBRELLA! IT WAS LIKE FATE!
I... I SEE.
......
WHAT'S HE DOING NOW?
SHII, DO YOU WANT TO SEE YOUR FATHER?
S-SURE...

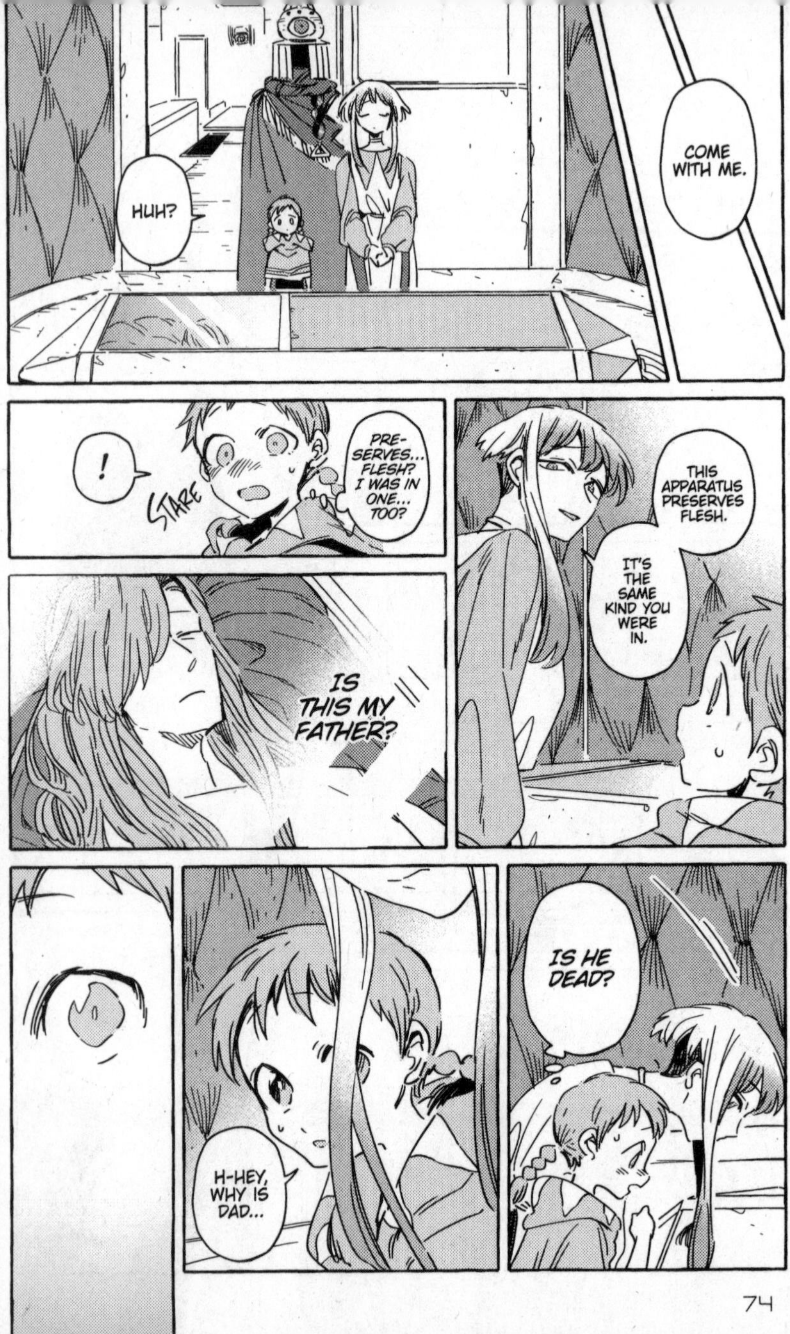
COME WITH ME.
HUH?
THIS APPARATUS PRESERVES FLESH.
IT'S THE SAME KIND YOU WERE IN.
PRE-SERVES... FLESH? I WAS IN ONE... TOO?
!
STARE
IS THIS MY FATHER?
IS HE DEAD?
H-HEY, WHY IS DAD...

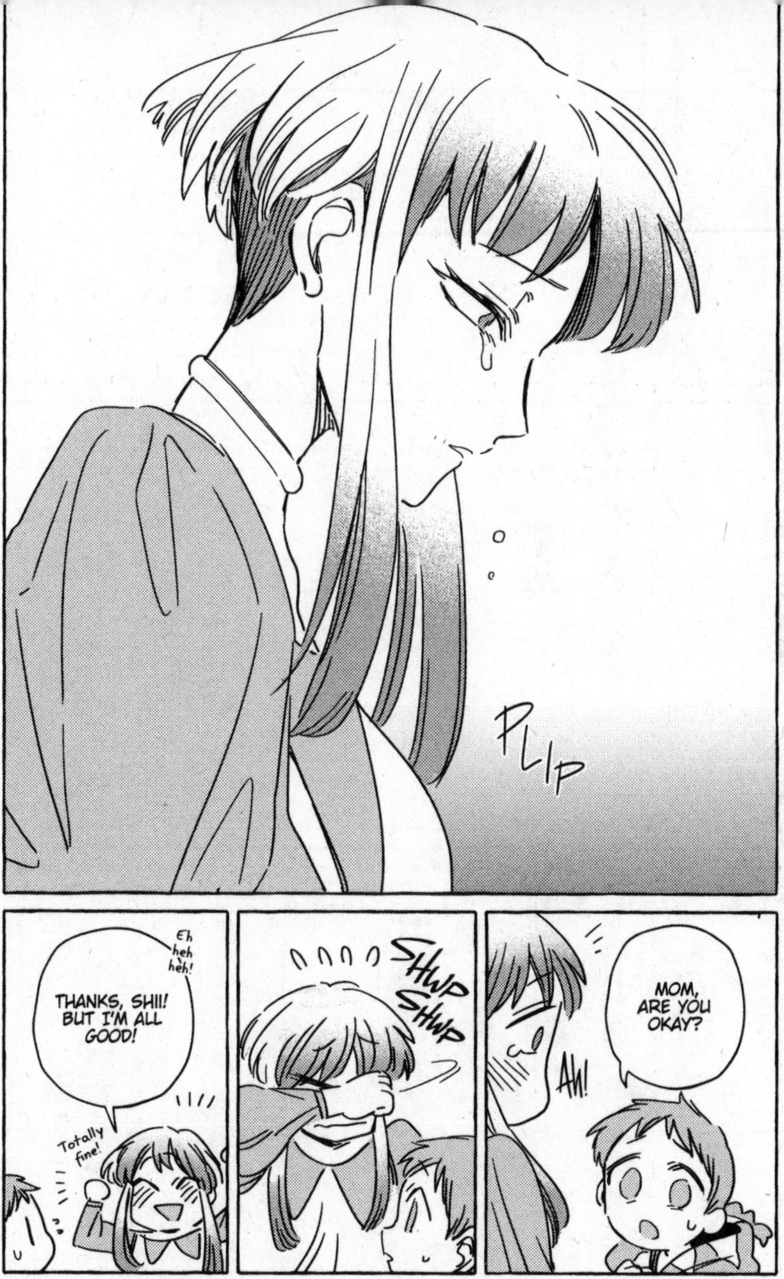
PLIP
MOM, ARE YOU OKAY?
AH!
SHWP SHWP
Eh heh heh!
THANKS, SHII! BUT I'M ALL GOOD!
Totally fine!

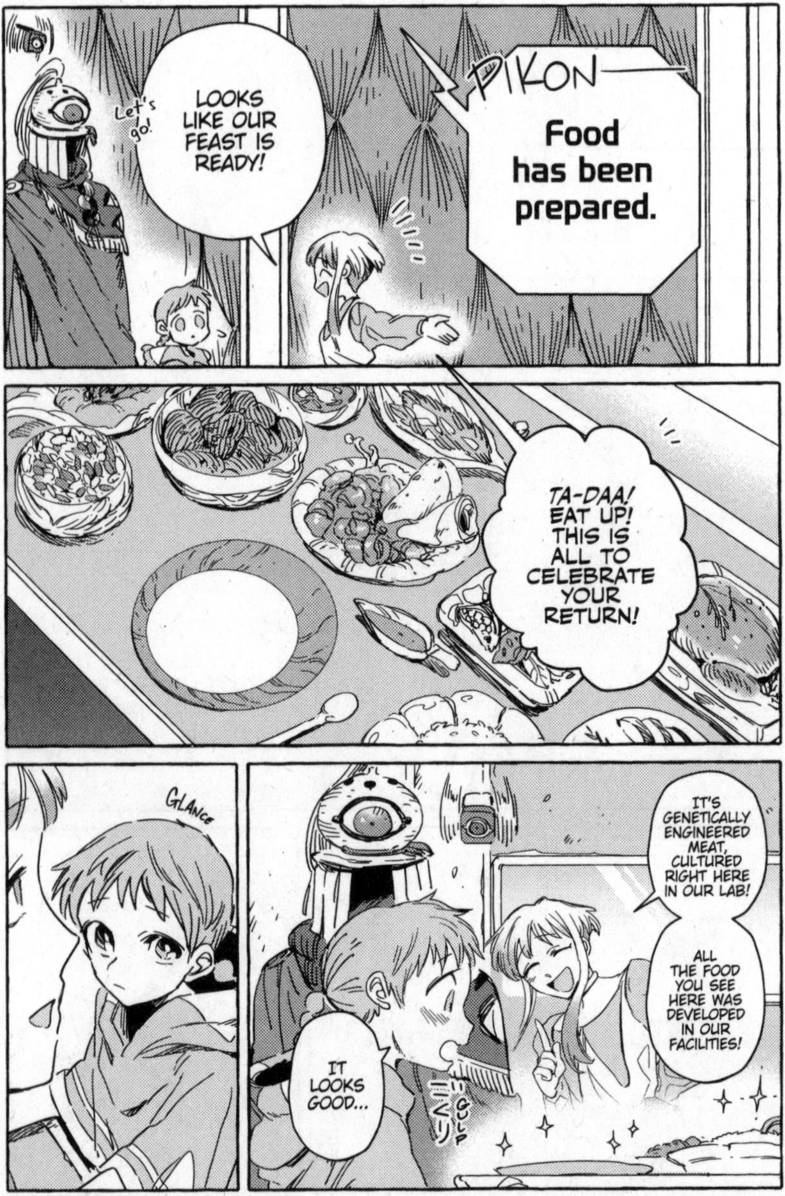
PIKON
Food has been prepared.
LOOKS LIKE OUR FEAST IS READY!
Let's go!
TA-DAA! EAT UP! THIS IS ALL TO CELEBRATE YOUR RETURN!
IT'S GENETICALLY ENGINEERED MEAT, CULTURED RIGHT HERE IN OUR LAB!
ALL THE FOOD YOU SEE HERE WAS DEVELOPED IN OUR FACILITIES!
GULP
IT LOOKS GOOD...
GLANCE

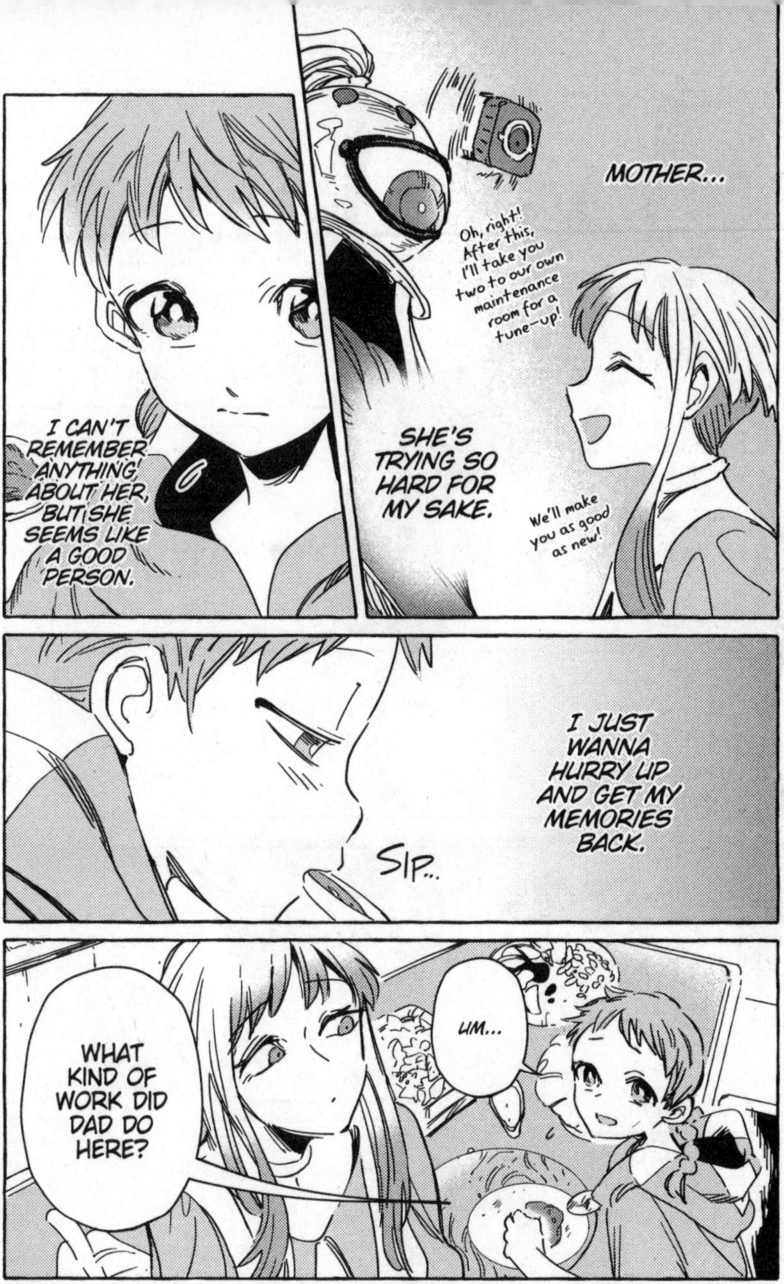
MOTHER...
Oh, right! After this, I'll take you two to our own maintenance room for a tune-up!
SHE'S TRYING SO HARD FOR MY SAKE.
We'll make you as good as new!
I CAN'T REMEMBER ANYTHING ABOUT HER, BUT SHE SEEMS LIKE A GOOD PERSON.
I JUST WANNA HURRY UP AND GET MY MEMORIES BACK.
SIP...
UM...
WHAT KIND OF WORK DID DAD DO HERE?

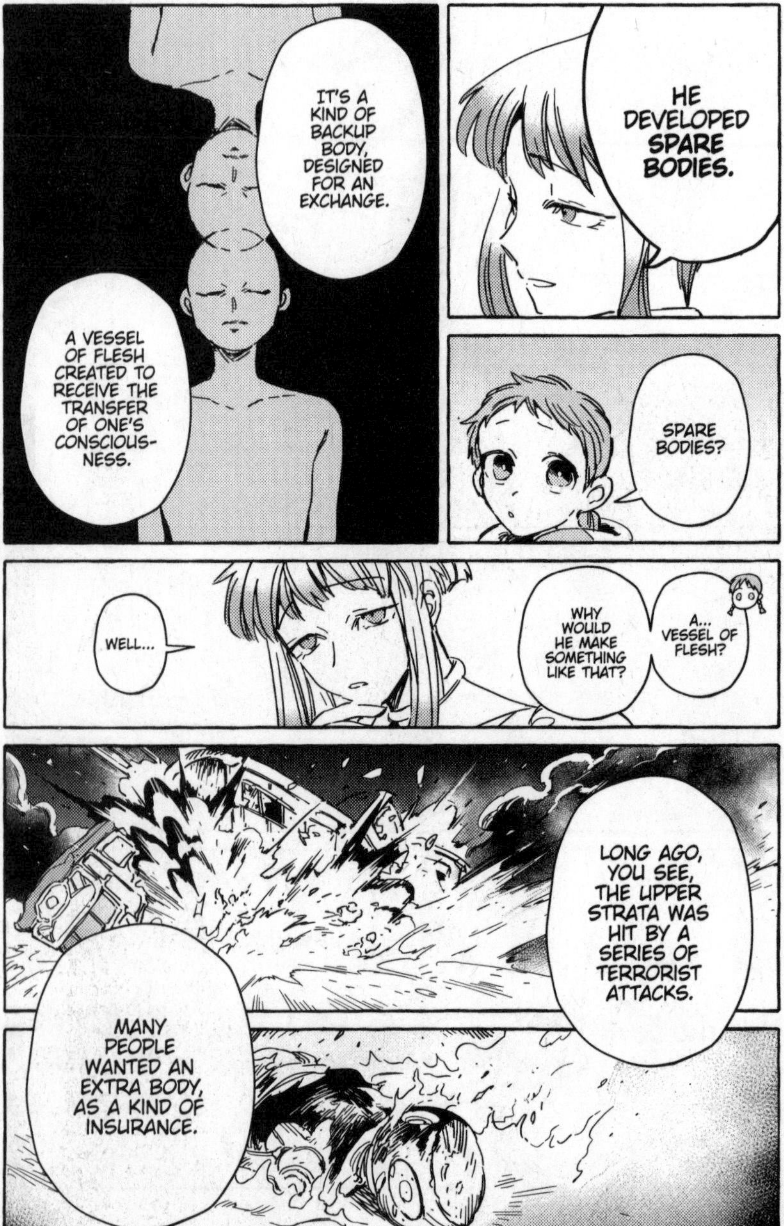
HE DEVELOPED SPARE BODIES.
SPARE BODIES?
IT'S A KIND OF BACKUP BODY, DESIGNED FOR AN EXCHANGE.
A VESSEL OF FLESH CREATED TO RECEIVE THE TRANSFER OF ONE'S CONSCIOUS-NESS.
A... VESSEL OF FLESH?
WHY WOULD HE MAKE SOMETHING LIKE THAT?
WELL...
LONG AGO, YOU SEE, THE UPPER STRATA WAS HIT BY A SERIES OF TERRORIST ATTACKS.
MANY PEOPLE WANTED AN EXTRA BODY, AS A KIND OF INSURANCE.

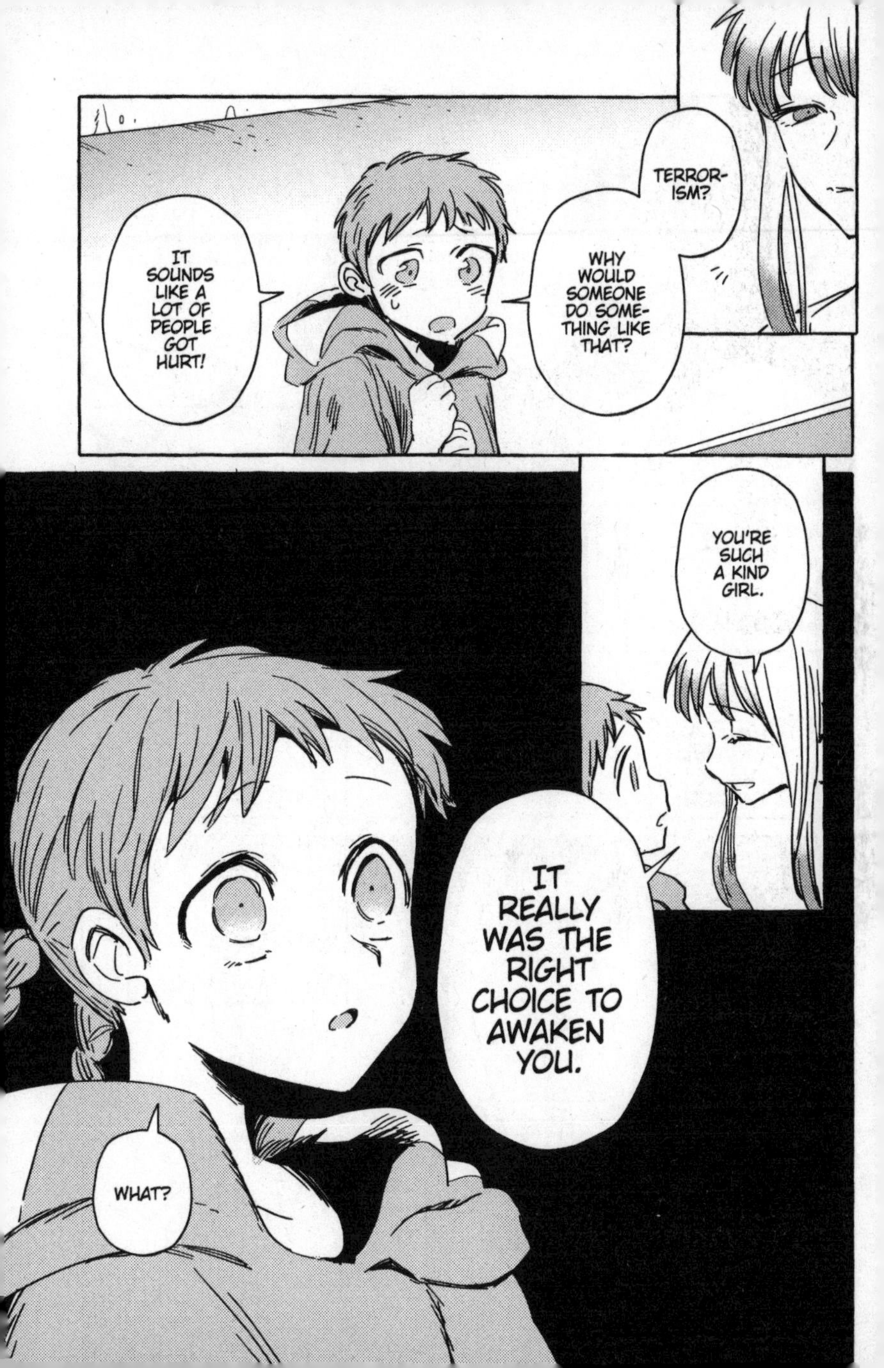
TERROR-ISM?
WHY WOULD SOMEONE DO SOME-THING LIKE THAT?
IT SOUNDS LIKE A LOT OF PEOPLE GOT HURT!
YOU'RE SUCH A KIND GIRL.
IT REALLY WAS THE RIGHT CHOICE TO AWAKEN YOU.
WHAT?

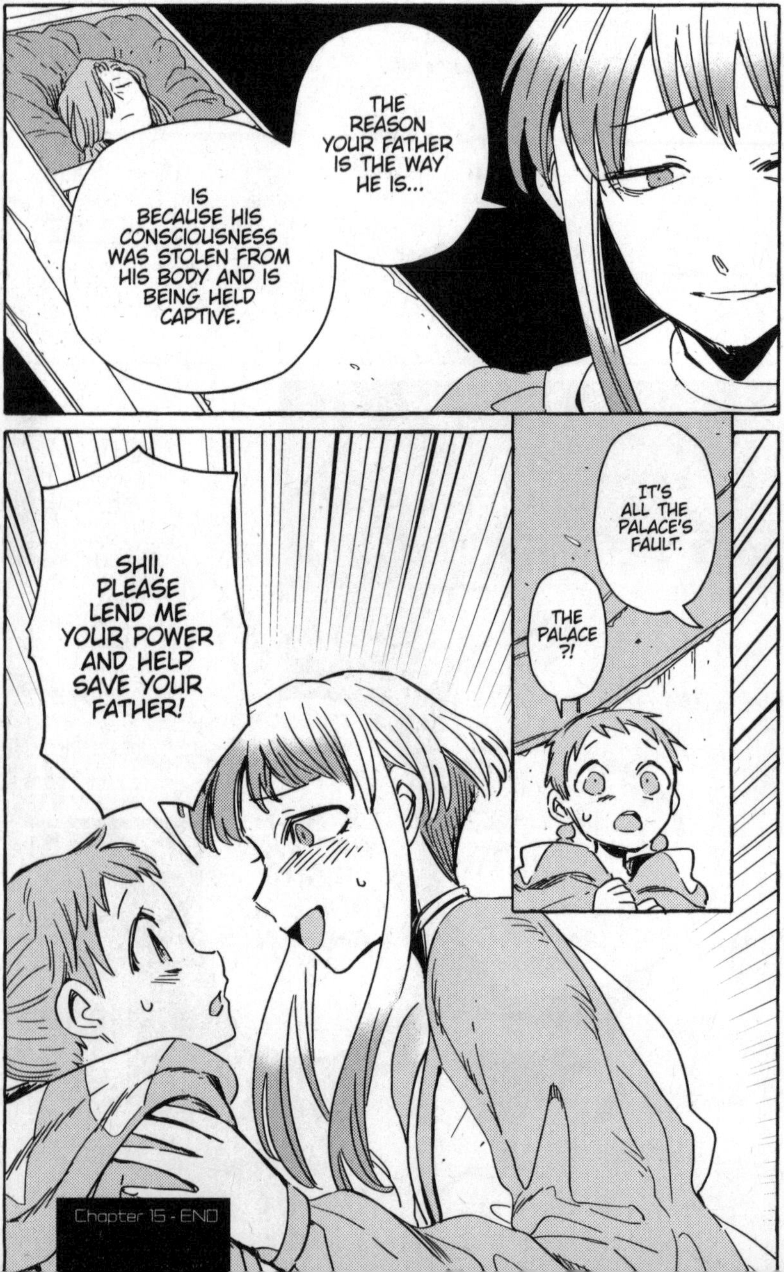
THE REASON YOUR FATHER IS THE WAY HE IS...
IS BECAUSE HIS CONSCIOUSNESS WAS STOLEN FROM HIS BODY AND IS BEING HELD CAPTIVE.
IT'S ALL THE PALACE'S FAULT.
THE PALACE?!
SHII, PLEASE LEND ME YOUR POWER AND HELP SAVE YOUR FATHER!
Chapter 15 - END

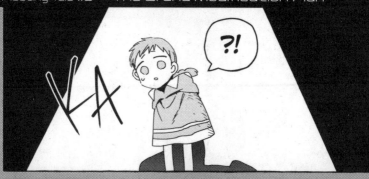

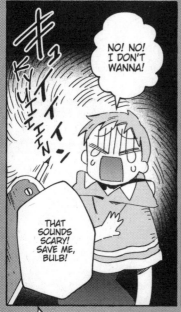

A Fleeting Tale #8 The Grand Modification Plan

KA
?!
MOODY?!
KA-CHK
KA-CHK
WH... WHAT'S THAT?!
MOODY INTENDS TO TURN SHII INTO A GOLEM.
NO WAY!!
NO! NO! I DON'T WANNA!
KYUIIINA
THAT SOUNDS SCARY! SAVE ME, BULB!
BULB IS IN AGREEMENT WITH THIS.
It doesn't hurt.
Do your best!
NO WAY!!

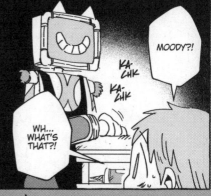

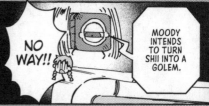

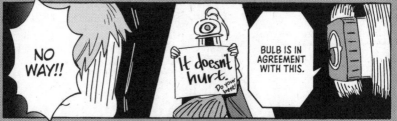

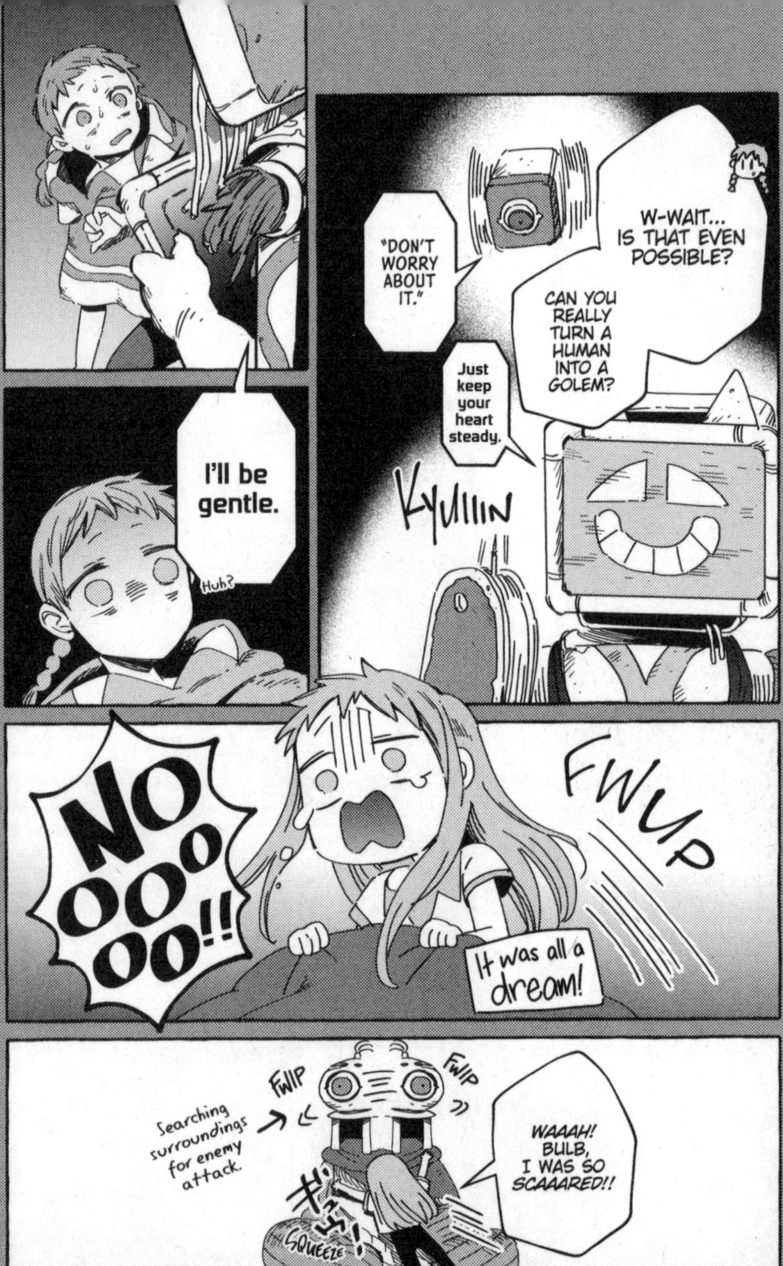
W-WAIT... IS THAT EVEN POSSIBLE?
CAN YOU REALLY TURN A HUMAN INTO A GOLEM?
"DON'T WORRY ABOUT IT."
Just keep your heart steady.
KYUIIIIN
I'll be gentle.
Huh?
FWUP
It was all a dream!
NOOOOOOOO!!
WAAAH! BULB, I WAS SO SCAAARED!!
FWIP
FWIP
SQUEEZE
Searching surroundings for enemy attack.

A Fleeting Tale #8 - END

Chapter 16

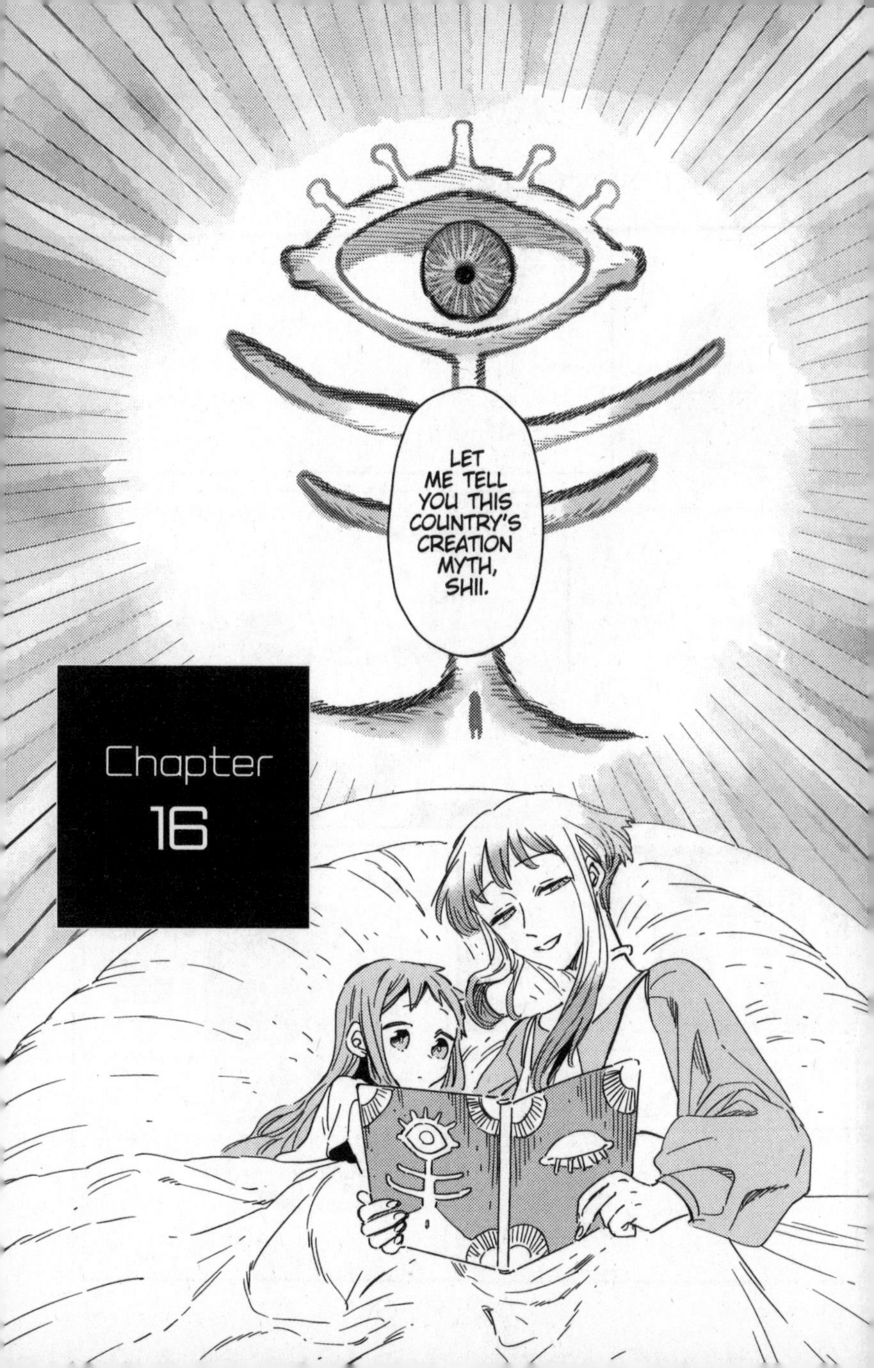
LET ME TELL YOU THIS COUNTRY'S CREATION MYTH, SHII.

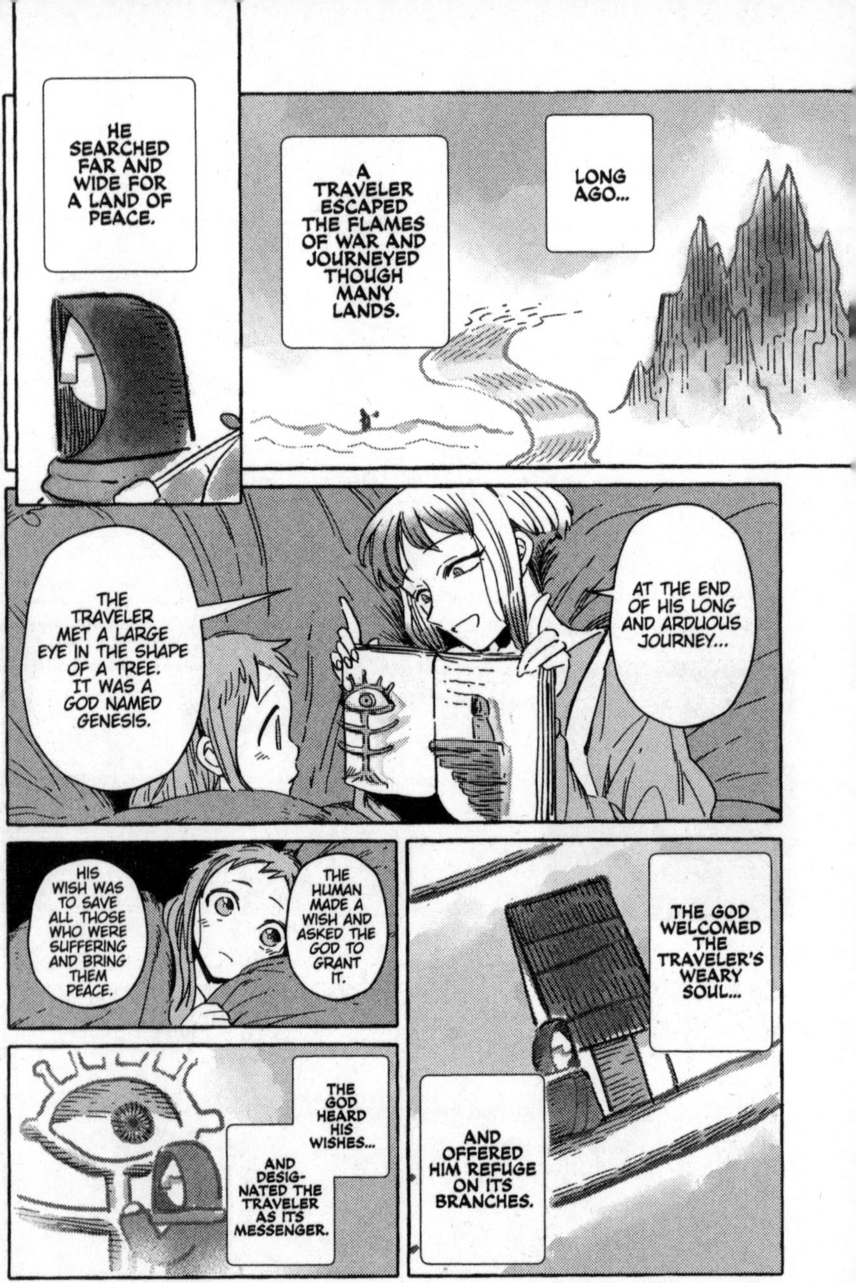
LONG AGO...
A TRAVELER ESCAPED THE FLAMES OF WAR AND JOURNEYED THOUGH MANY LANDS.
HE SEARCHED FAR AND WIDE FOR A LAND OF PEACE.
AT THE END OF HIS LONG AND ARDUOUS JOURNEY...
THE TRAVELER MET A LARGE EYE IN THE SHAPE OF A TREE. IT WAS A GOD NAMED GENESIS.
THE GOD WELCOMED THE TRAVELER'S WEARY SOUL...
AND OFFERED HIM REFUGE ON ITS BRANCHES.
THE HUMAN MADE A WISH AND ASKED THE GOD TO GRANT IT.
HIS WISH WAS TO SAVE ALL THOSE WHO WERE SUFFERING AND BRING THEM PEACE.
THE GOD HEARD HIS WISHES...
AND DESIG-NATED THE TRAVELER AS ITS MESSENGER.

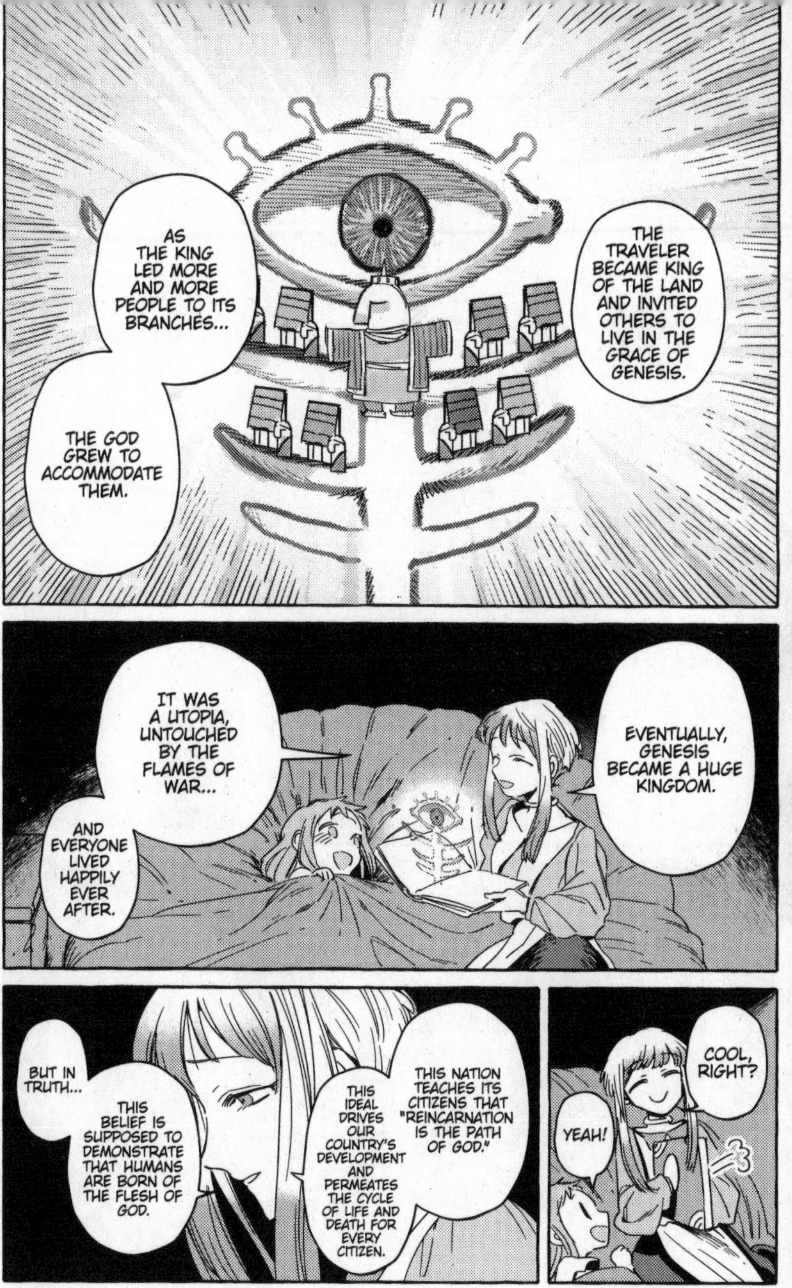
THE TRAVELER BECAME KING OF THE LAND AND INVITED OTHERS TO LIVE IN THE GRACE OF GENESIS.
AS THE KING LED MORE AND MORE PEOPLE TO ITS BRANCHES...
THE GOD GREW TO ACCOMMODATE THEM.
EVENTUALLY, GENESIS BECAME A HUGE KINGDOM.
IT WAS A UTOPIA, UNTOUCHED BY THE FLAMES OF WAR...
AND EVERYONE LIVED HAPPILY EVER AFTER.
COOL, RIGHT?
YEAH!
THIS NATION TEACHES ITS CITIZENS THAT "REINCARNATION IS THE PATH OF GOD."
THIS IDEAL DRIVES OUR COUNTRY'S DEVELOPMENT AND PERMEATES THE CYCLE OF LIFE AND DEATH FOR EVERY CITIZEN.
BUT IN TRUTH...
THIS BELIEF IS SUPPOSED TO DEMONSTRATE THAT HUMANS ARE BORN OF THE FLESH OF GOD.

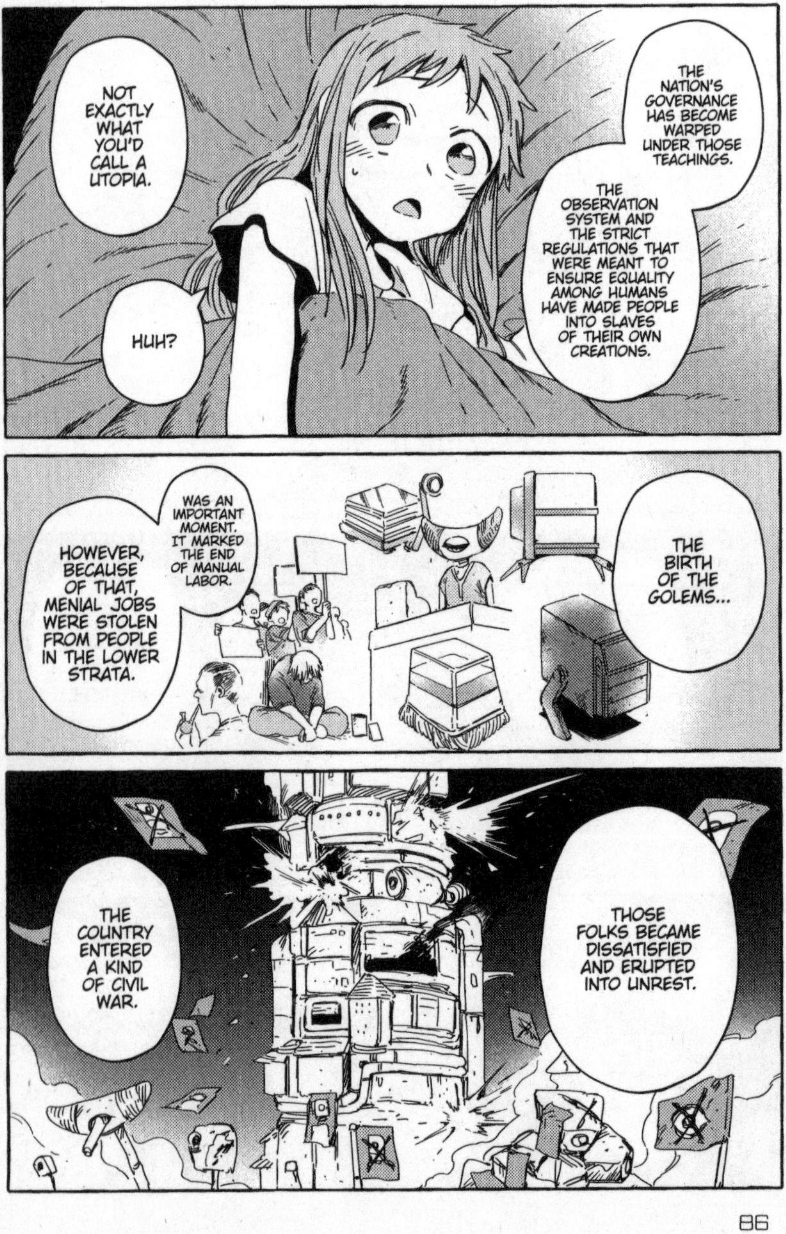
THE NATION'S GOVERNANCE HAS BECOME WARPED UNDER THOSE TEACHINGS.
THE OBSERVATION SYSTEM AND THE STRICT REGULATIONS THAT WERE MEANT TO ENSURE EQUALITY AMONG HUMANS HAVE MADE PEOPLE INTO SLAVES OF THEIR OWN CREATIONS.
NOT EXACTLY WHAT YOU'D CALL A UTOPIA.
HUH?
THE BIRTH OF THE GOLEMS...
WAS AN IMPORTANT MOMENT. IT MARKED THE END OF MANUAL LABOR.
HOWEVER, BECAUSE OF THAT, MENIAL JOBS WERE STOLEN FROM PEOPLE IN THE LOWER STRATA.
THOSE FOLKS BECAME DISSATISFIED AND ERUPTED INTO UNREST.
THE COUNTRY ENTERED A KIND OF CIVIL WAR.

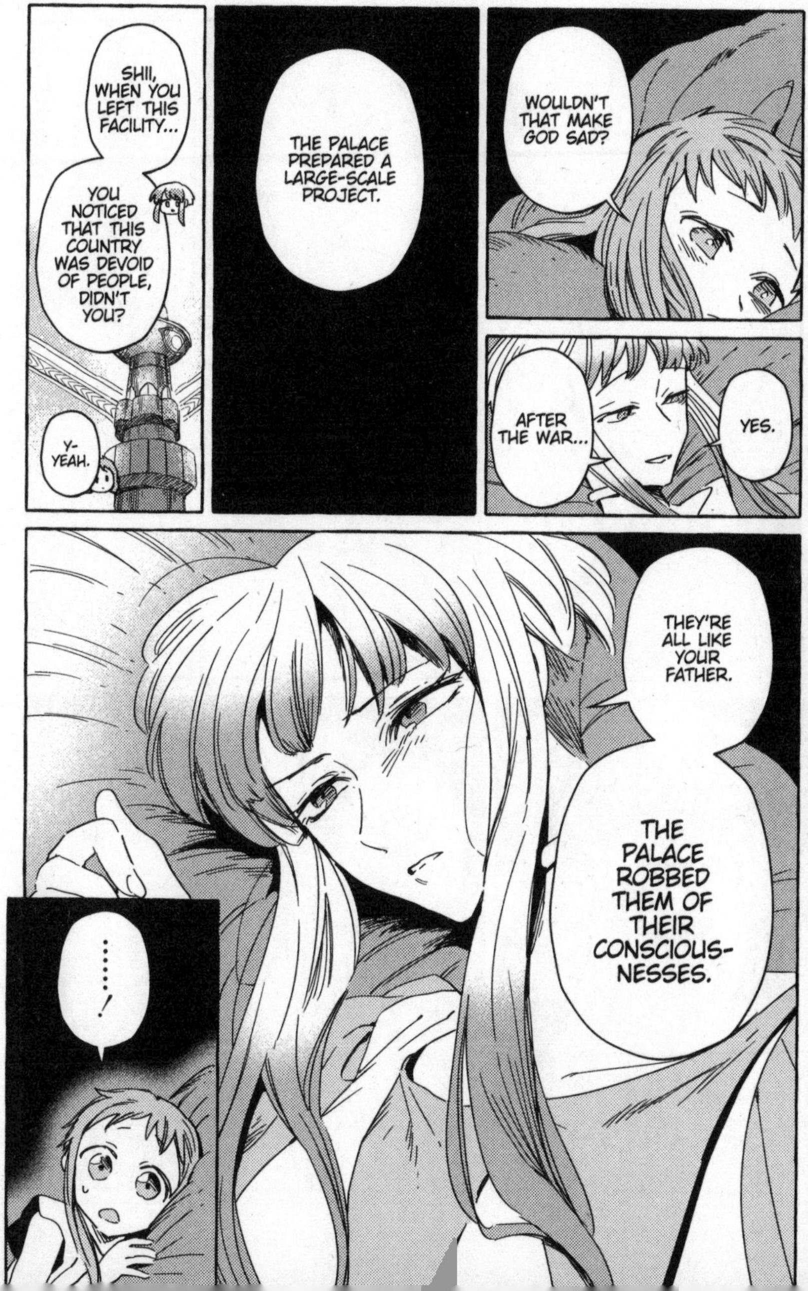
WOULDN'T THAT MAKE GOD SAD?
YES.
AFTER THE WAR...
THE PALACE PREPARED A LARGE-SCALE PROJECT.
SHII, WHEN YOU LEFT THIS FACILITY...
YOU NOTICED THAT THIS COUNTRY WAS DEVOID OF PEOPLE, DIDN'T YOU?
Y-YEAH.
THEY'RE ALL LIKE YOUR FATHER.
THE PALACE ROBBED THEM OF THEIR CONSCIOUS-NESSES.
......!

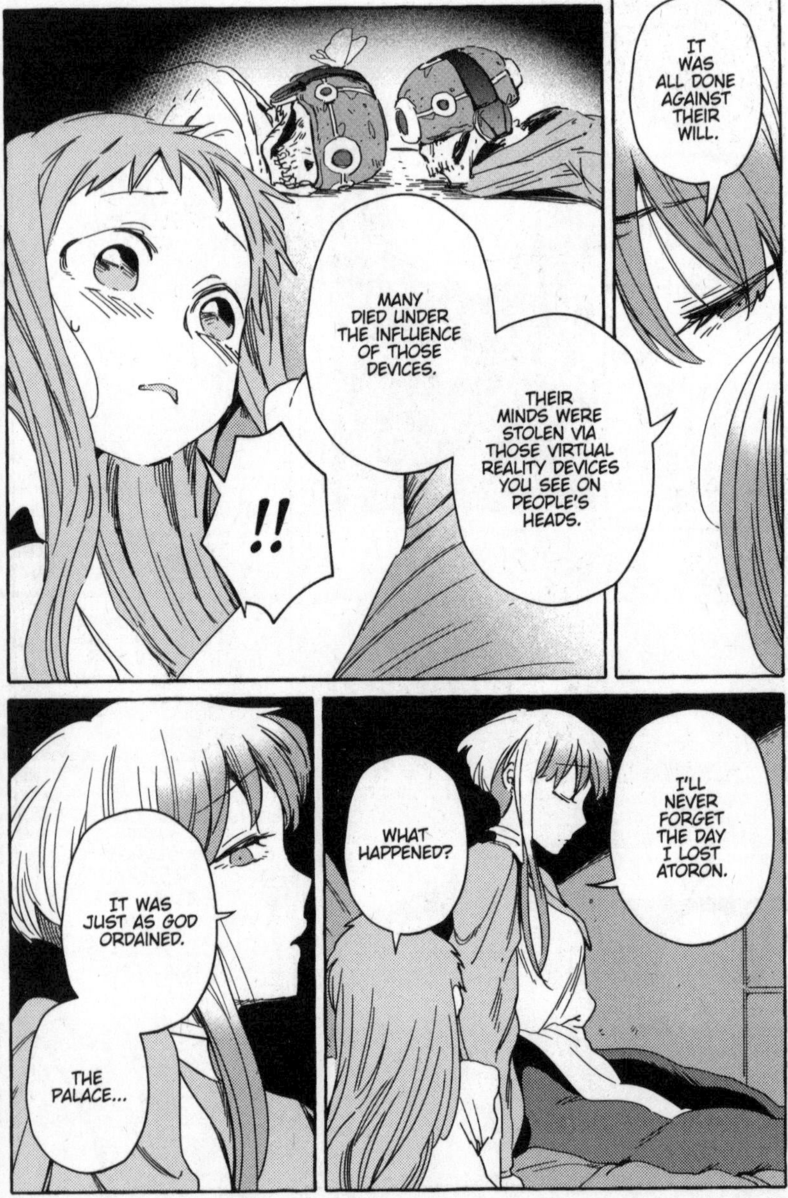
IT WAS ALL DONE AGAINST THEIR WILL.
MANY DIED UNDER THE INFLUENCE OF THOSE DEVICES.
THEIR MINDS WERE STOLEN VIA THOSE VIRTUAL REALITY DEVICES YOU SEE ON PEOPLE'S HEADS.
!!
I'LL NEVER FORGET THE DAY I LOST ATORON.
WHAT HAPPENED?
IT WAS JUST AS GOD ORDAINED.
THE PALACE...

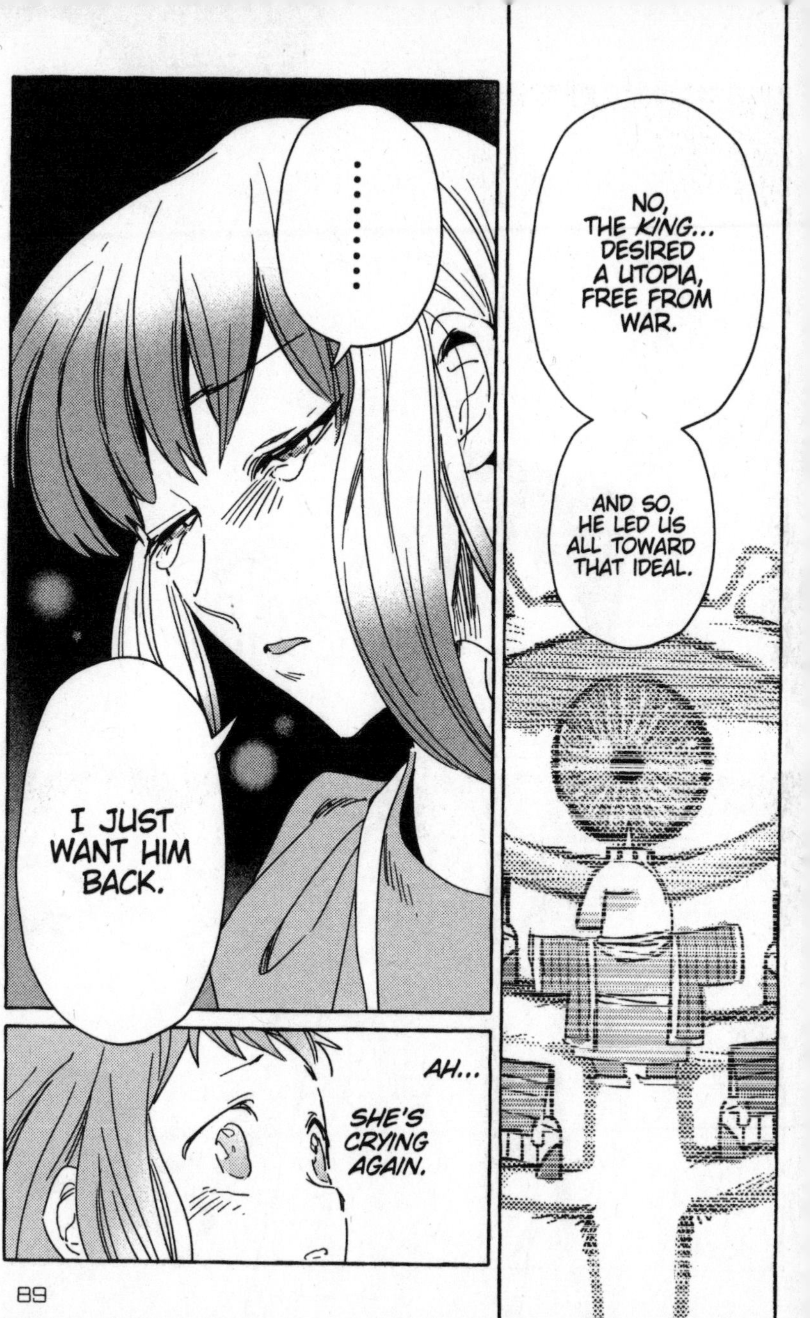
NO, THE *KING*... DESIRED A UTOPIA, FREE FROM WAR.
AND SO, HE LED US ALL TOWARD THAT IDEAL.
......
I JUST WANT HIM BACK.
AH...
SHE'S CRYING AGAIN.

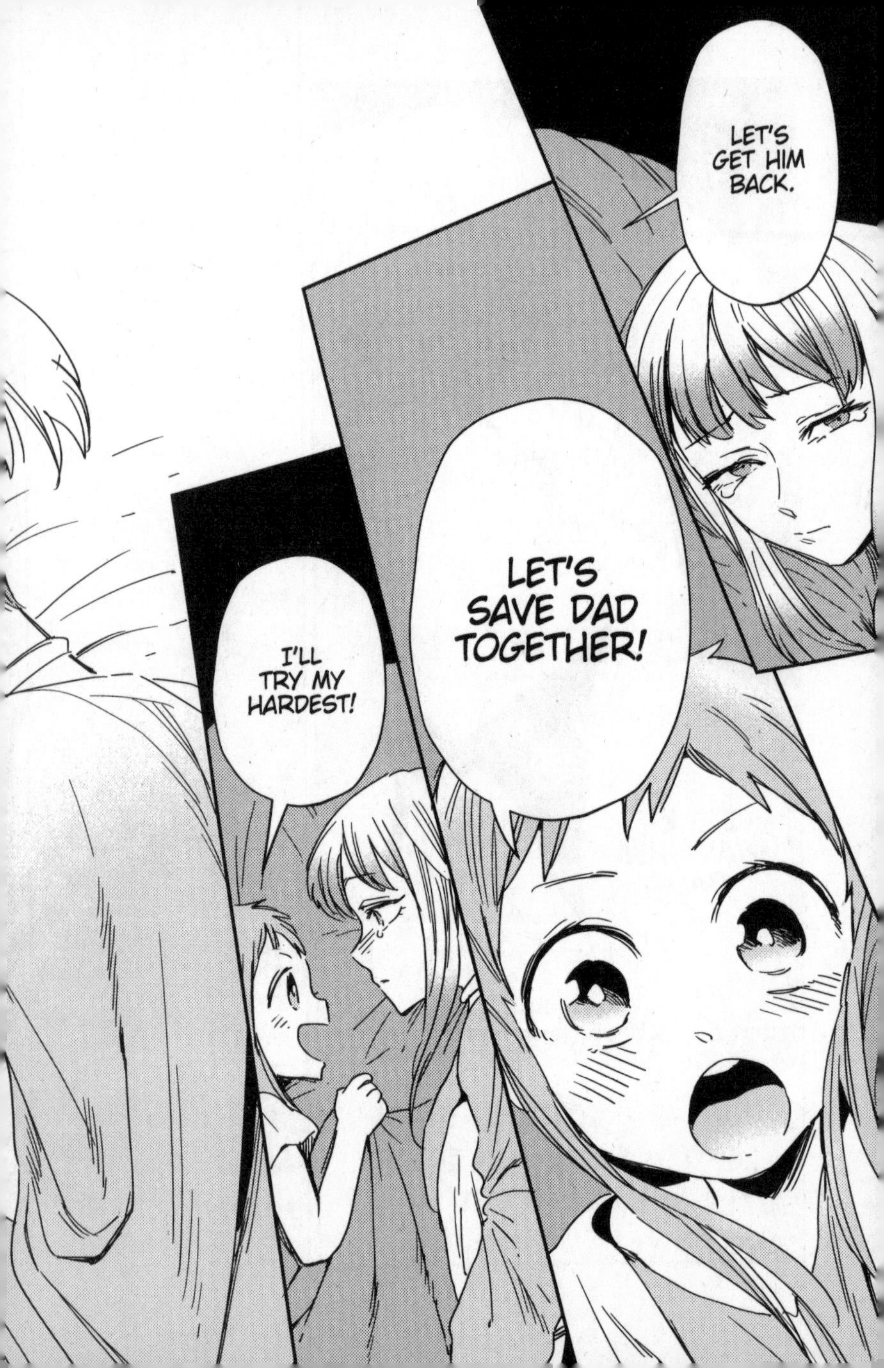
LET'S GET HIM BACK.
LET'S SAVE DAD TOGETHER!
I'LL TRY MY HARDEST!

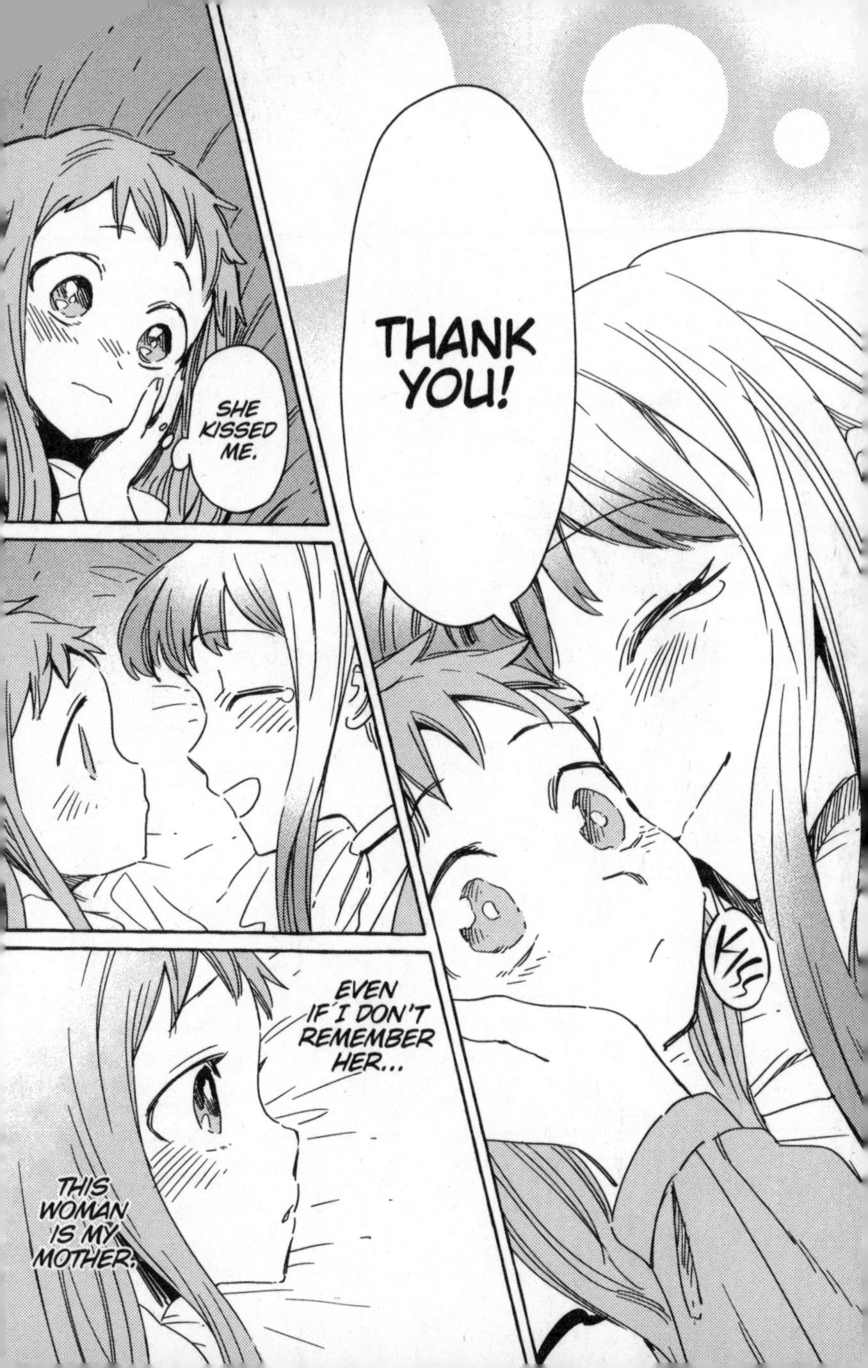
THANK YOU!
KISS
SHE KISSED ME.
EVEN IF I DON'T REMEMBER HER...
THIS WOMAN IS MY MOTHER.

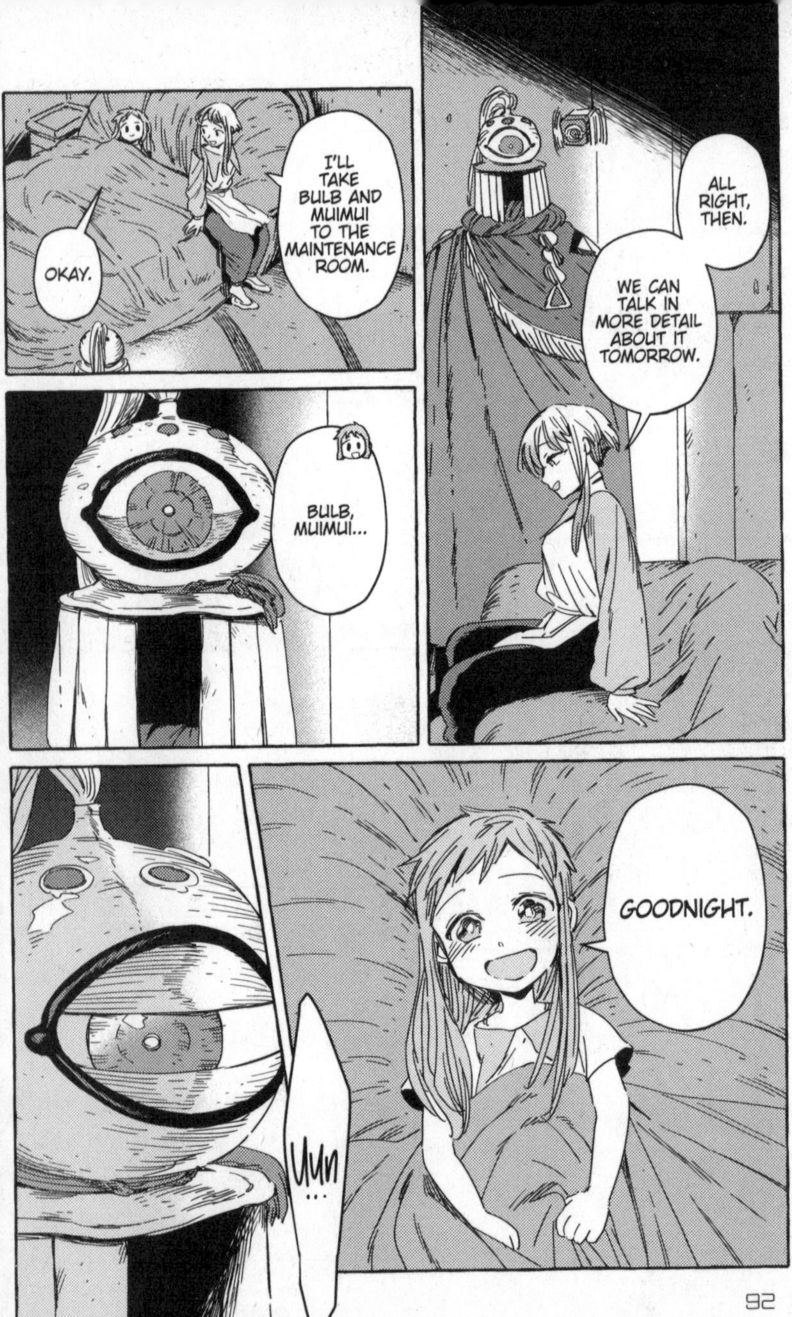

ALL RIGHT, THEN.
WE CAN TALK IN MORE DETAIL ABOUT IT TOMORROW.
I'LL TAKE BULB AND MUIMUI TO THE MAINTENANCE ROOM.
OKAY.
BULB, MUIMUI...
GOODNIGHT.
Uun...

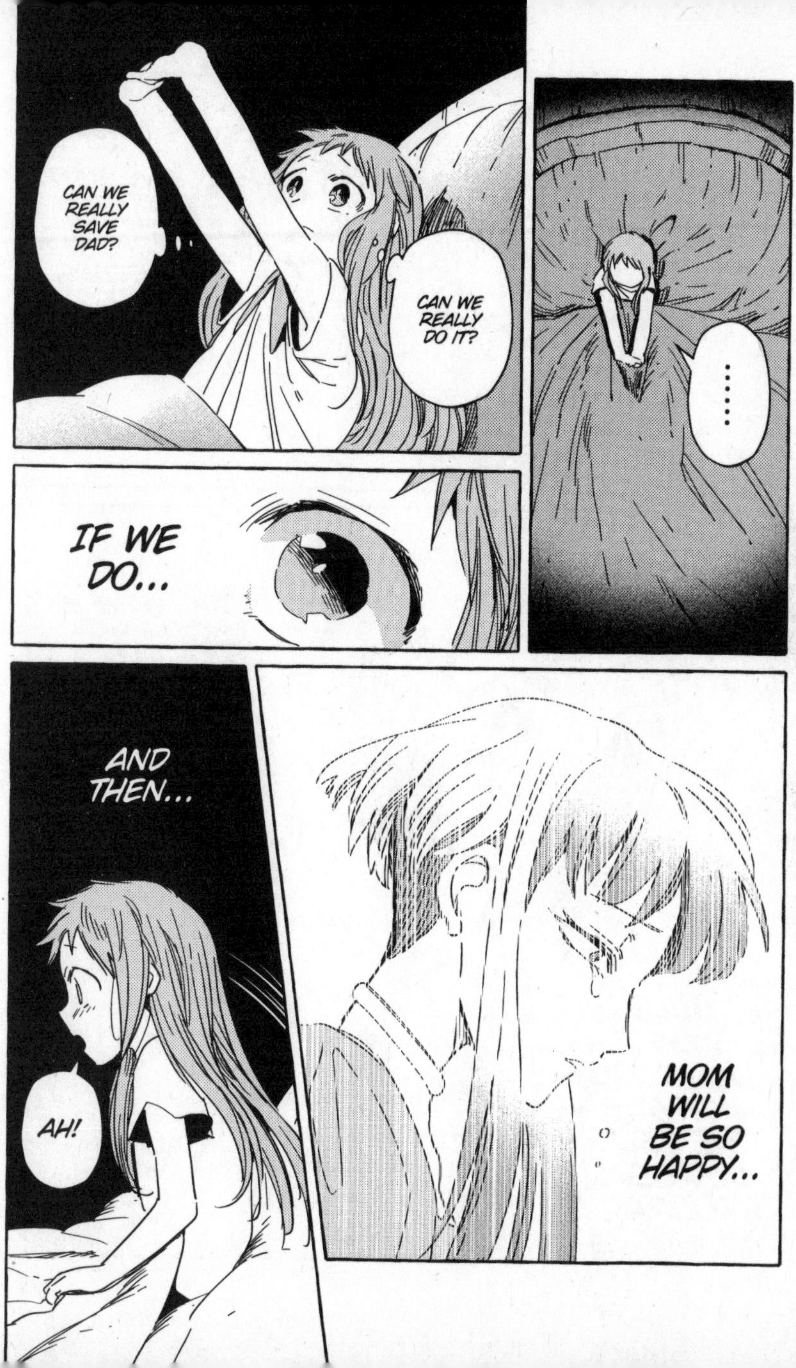
......
CAN WE REALLY SAVE DAD?
CAN WE REALLY DO IT?
IF WE DO...
MOM WILL BE SO HAPPY...
AND THEN...
AH!

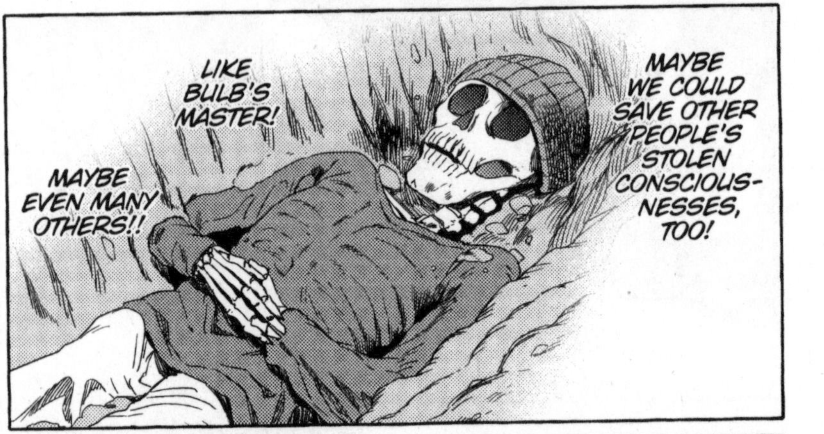
MAYBE WE COULD SAVE OTHER PEOPLE'S STOLEN CONSCIOUS-NESSES, TOO!
LIKE BULB'S MASTER!
MAYBE EVEN MANY OTHERS!!

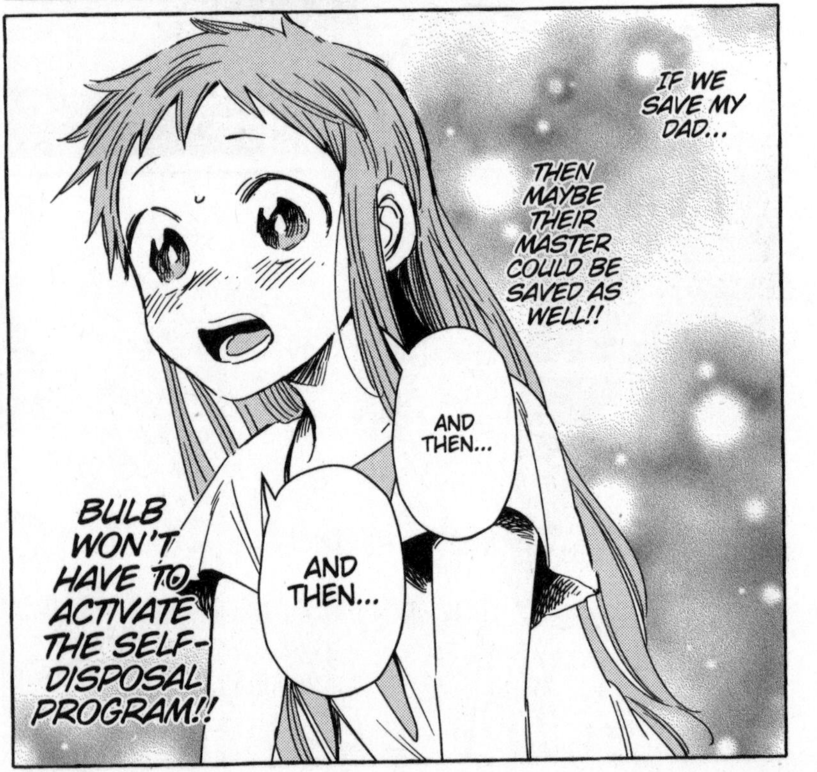
IF WE SAVE MY DAD...
THEN MAYBE THEIR MASTER COULD BE SAVED AS WELL!!
AND THEN...
AND THEN...
BULB WON'T HAVE TO ACTIVATE THE SELF-DISPOSAL PROGRAM!!

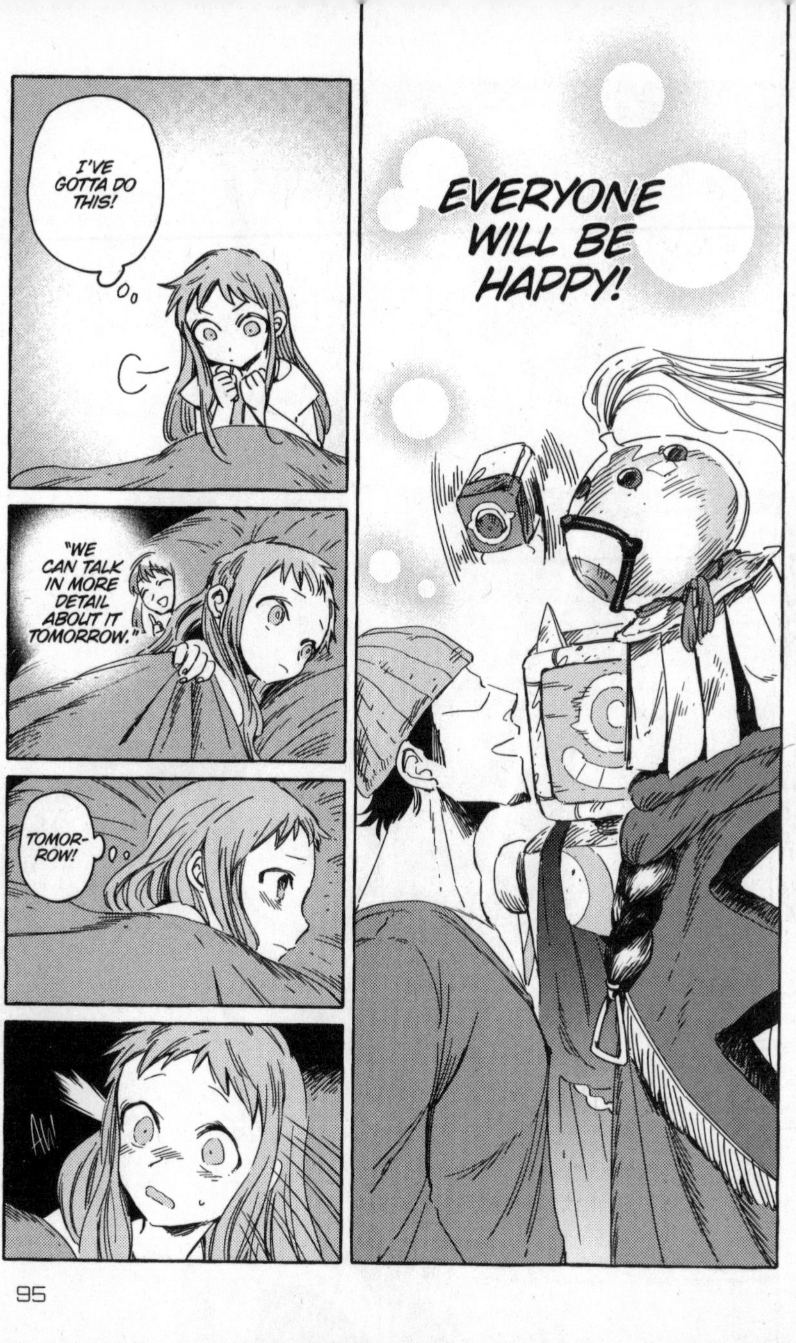
EVERYONE WILL BE HAPPY!
I'VE GOTTA DO THIS!
"WE CAN TALK IN MORE DETAIL ABOUT IT TOMORROW."
TOMOR-ROW!

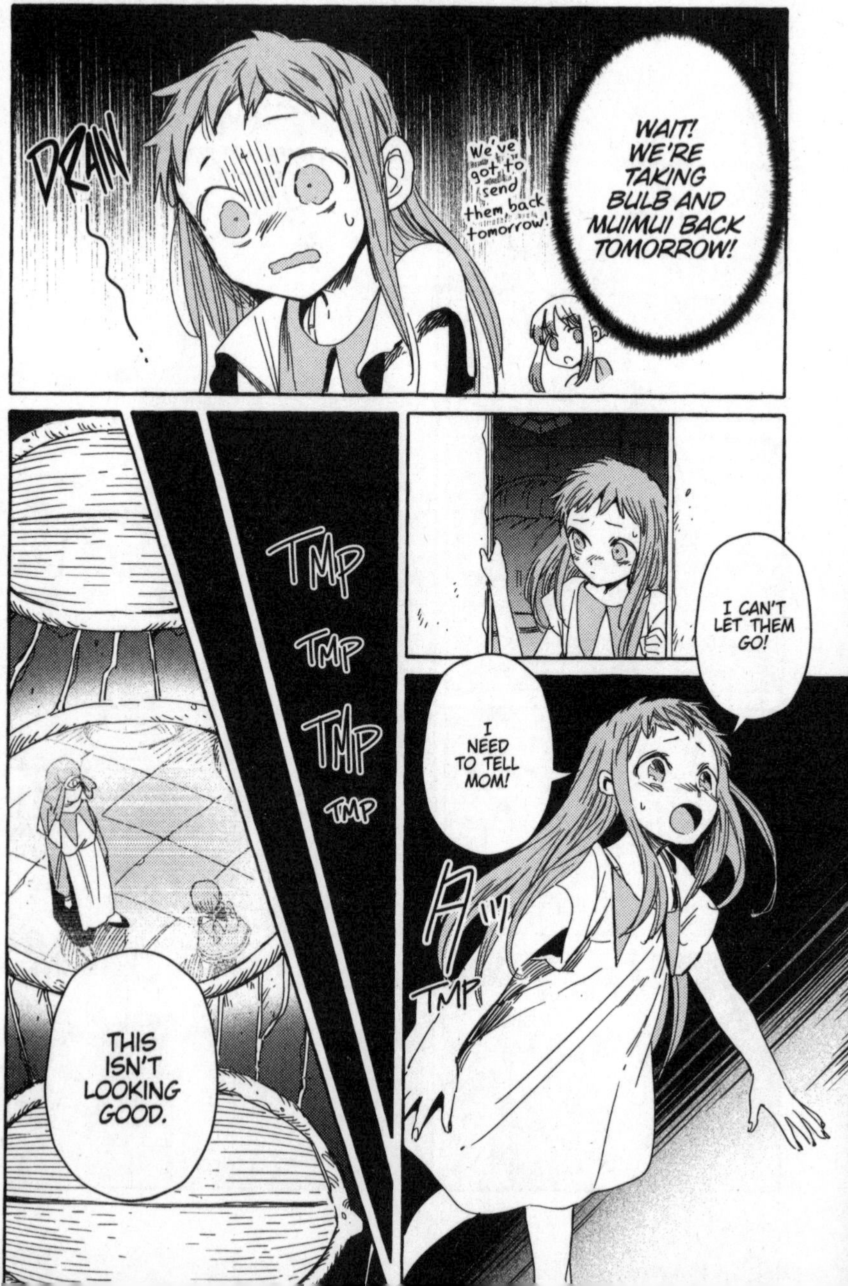
WAIT! WE'RE TAKING BULB AND MUIMUI BACK TOMORROW!
We've got to send them back tomorrow!
DRAIN
I CAN'T LET THEM GO!
I NEED TO TELL MOM!
TMP
TMP
TMP
TMP
TMP
THIS ISN'T LOOKING GOOD.

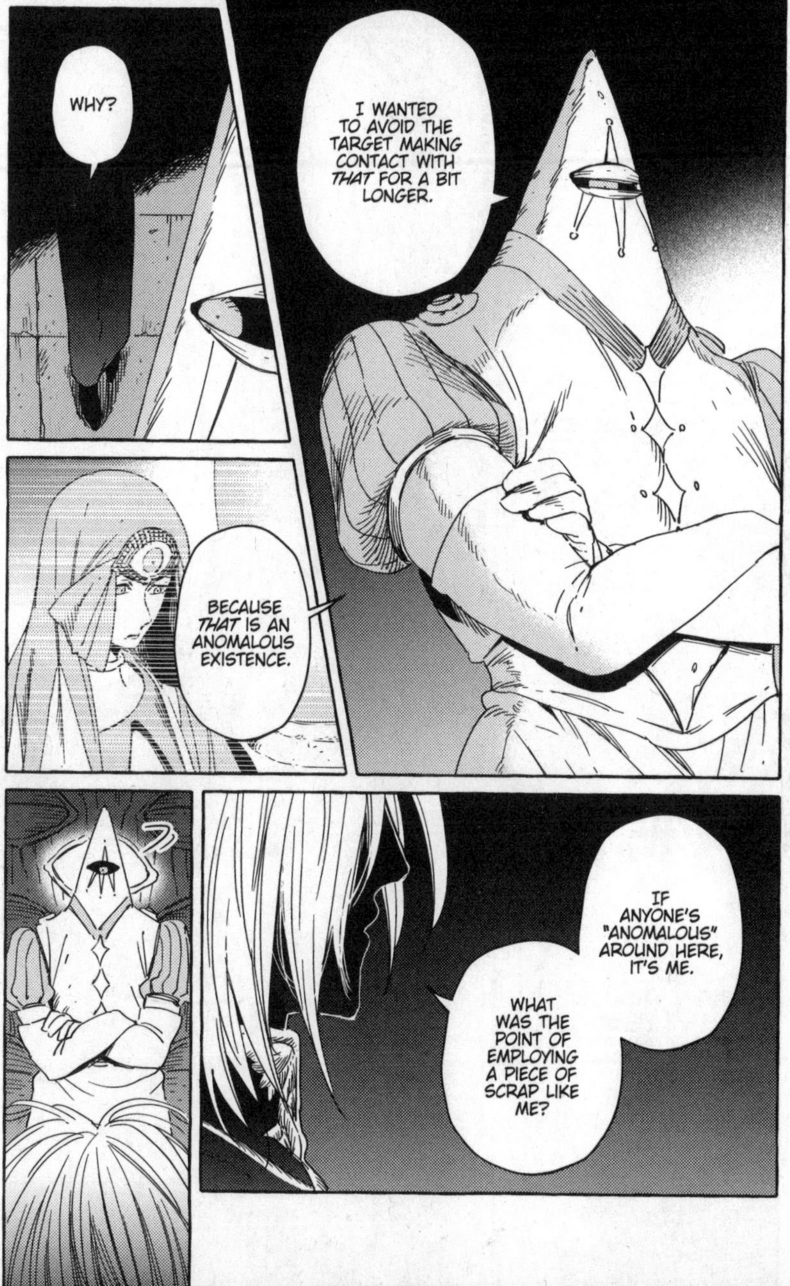
I WANTED TO AVOID THE TARGET MAKING CONTACT WITH *THAT* FOR A BIT LONGER.
WHY?
BECAUSE *THAT* IS AN ANOMALOUS EXISTENCE.
IF ANYONE'S "ANOMALOUS" AROUND HERE, IT'S ME.
WHAT WAS THE POINT OF EMPLOYING A PIECE OF SCRAP LIKE ME?

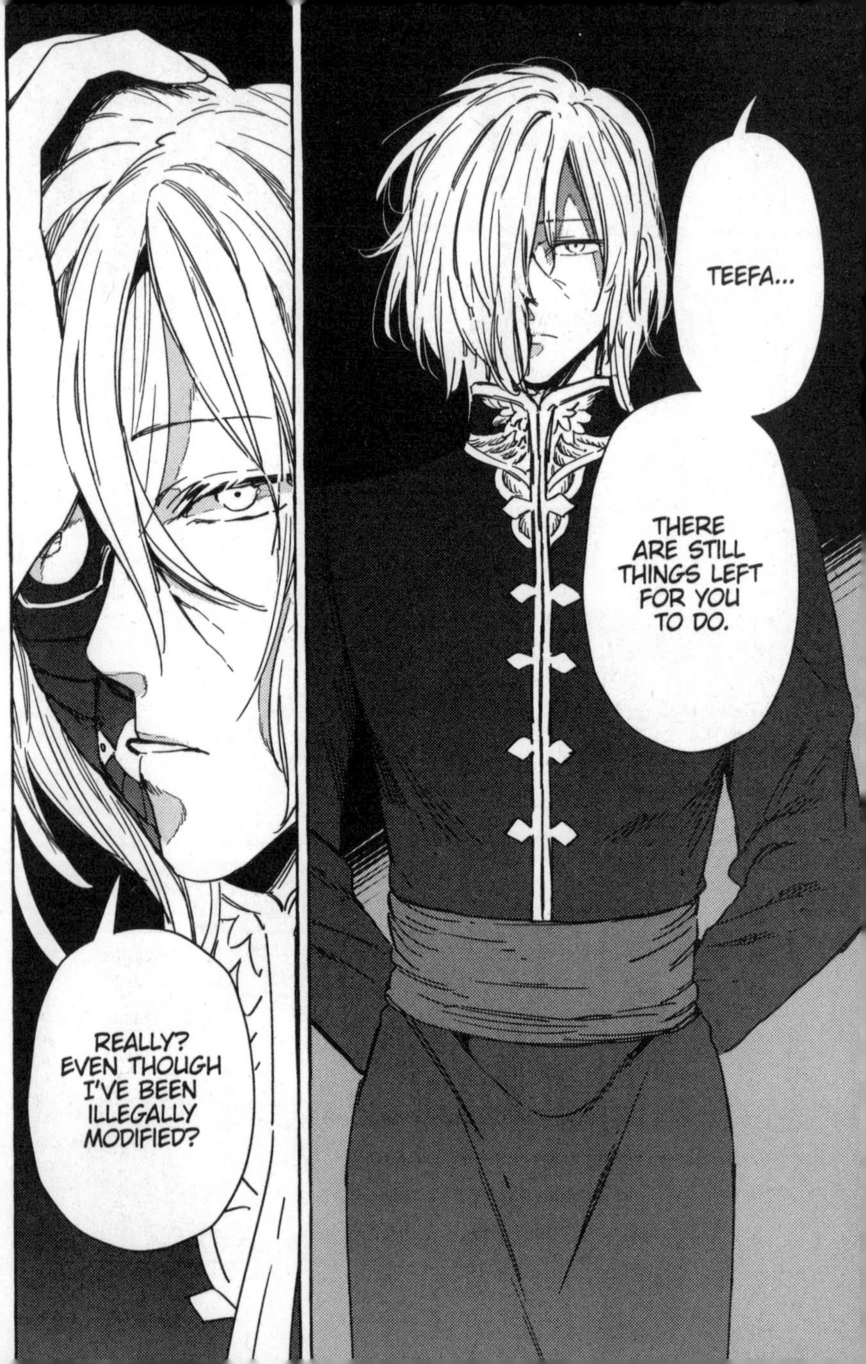
TEEFA...
THERE ARE STILL THINGS LEFT FOR YOU TO DO.
REALLY? EVEN THOUGH I'VE BEEN ILLEGALLY MODIFIED?

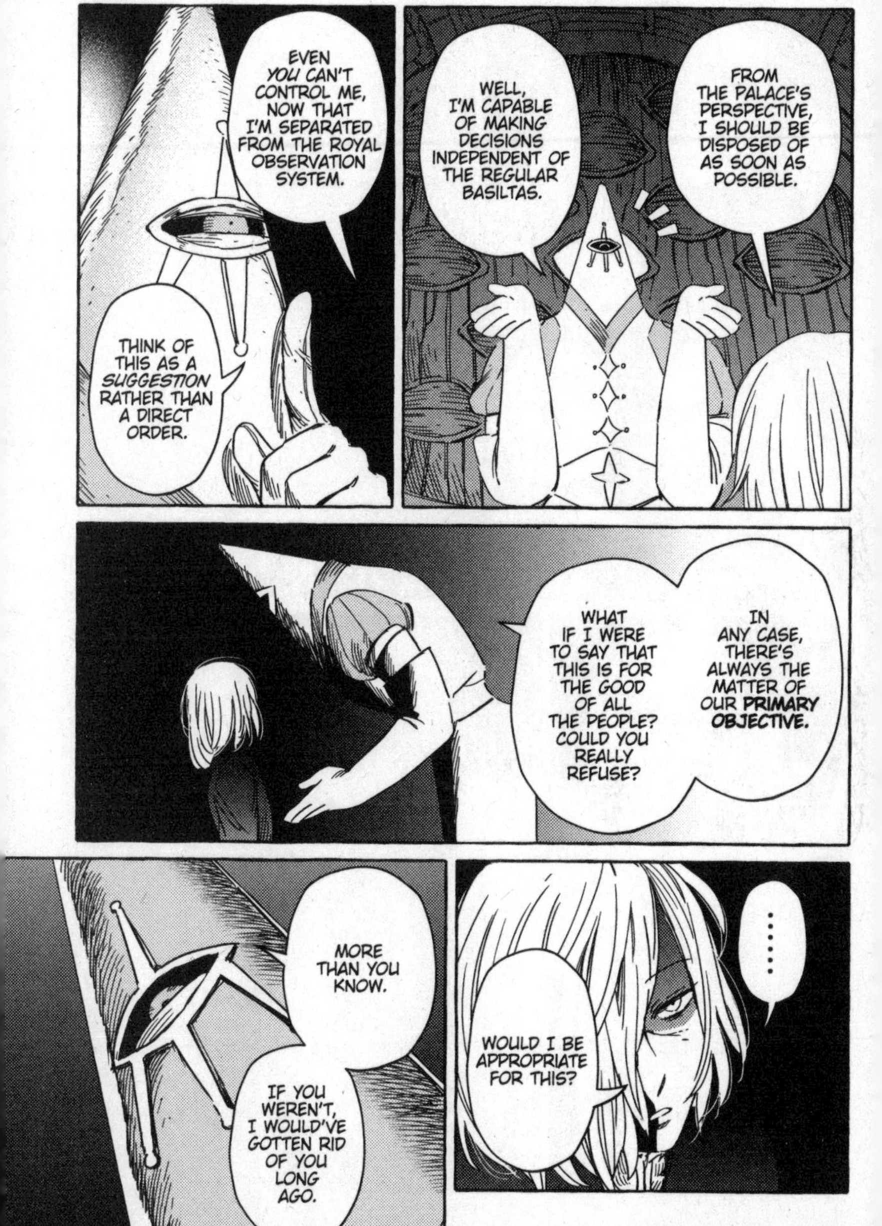
FROM THE PALACE'S PERSPECTIVE, I SHOULD BE DISPOSED OF AS SOON AS POSSIBLE.
WELL, I'M CAPABLE OF MAKING DECISIONS INDEPENDENT OF THE REGULAR BASILTAS.
EVEN *YOU* CAN'T CONTROL ME, NOW THAT I'M SEPARATED FROM THE ROYAL OBSERVATION SYSTEM.
THINK OF THIS AS A *SUGGESTION* RATHER THAN A DIRECT ORDER.
IN ANY CASE, THERE'S ALWAYS THE MATTER OF OUR **PRIMARY OBJECTIVE.**
WHAT IF I WERE TO SAY THAT THIS IS FOR THE GOOD OF ALL THE PEOPLE? COULD YOU REALLY REFUSE?
......
WOULD I BE APPROPRIATE FOR THIS?
MORE THAN YOU KNOW.
IF YOU WEREN'T, I WOULD'VE GOTTEN RID OF YOU LONG AGO.

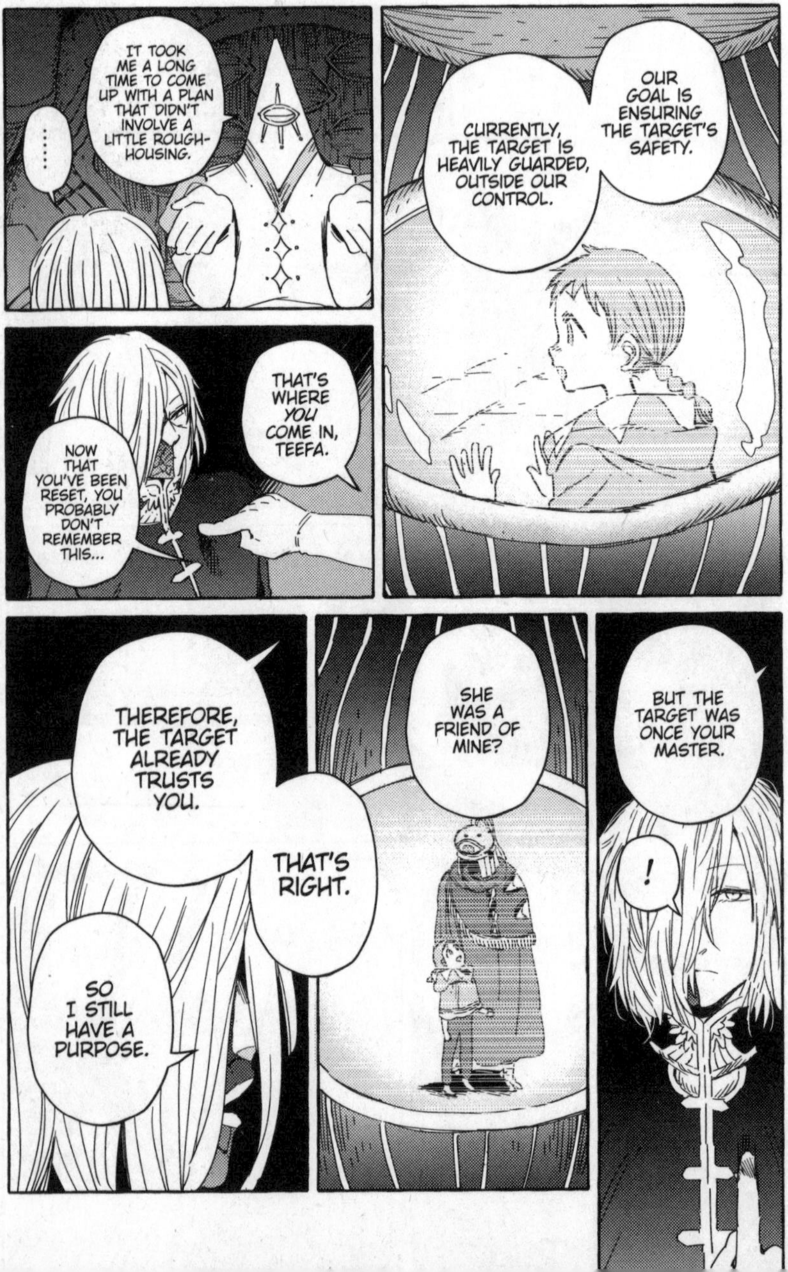
OUR GOAL IS ENSURING THE TARGET'S SAFETY.
CURRENTLY, THE TARGET IS HEAVILY GUARDED, OUTSIDE OUR CONTROL.
IT TOOK ME A LONG TIME TO COME UP WITH A PLAN THAT DIDN'T INVOLVE A LITTLE ROUGH-HOUSING.
......
THAT'S WHERE *YOU* COME IN, TEEFA.
NOW THAT YOU'VE BEEN RESET, YOU PROBABLY DON'T REMEMBER THIS...
BUT THE TARGET WAS ONCE YOUR MASTER.
!
SHE WAS A FRIEND OF MINE?
THEREFORE, THE TARGET ALREADY TRUSTS YOU.
THAT'S RIGHT.
SO I STILL HAVE A PURPOSE.

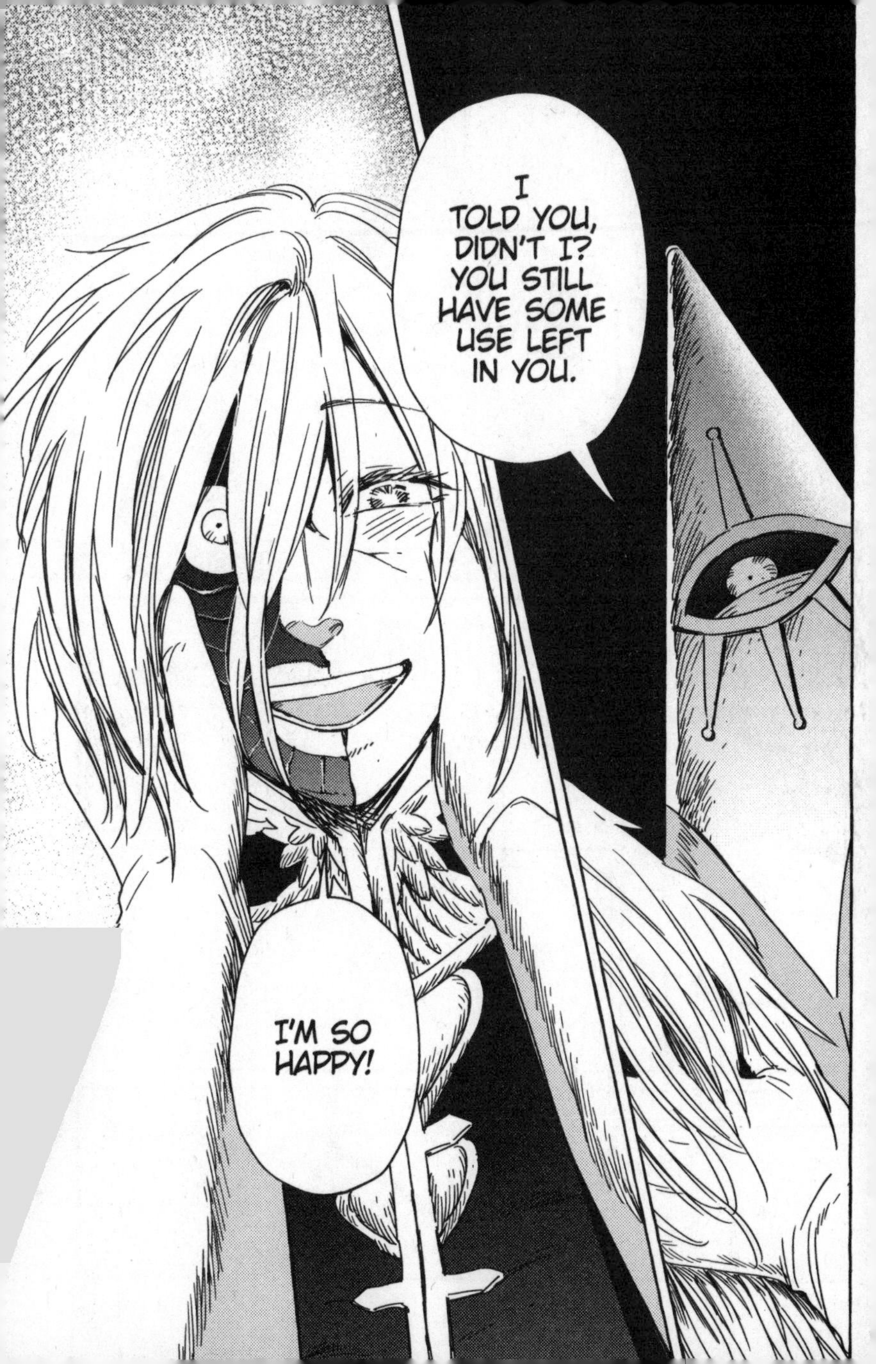
I TOLD YOU, DIDN'T I? YOU STILL HAVE SOME USE LEFT IN YOU.
I'M SO HAPPY!

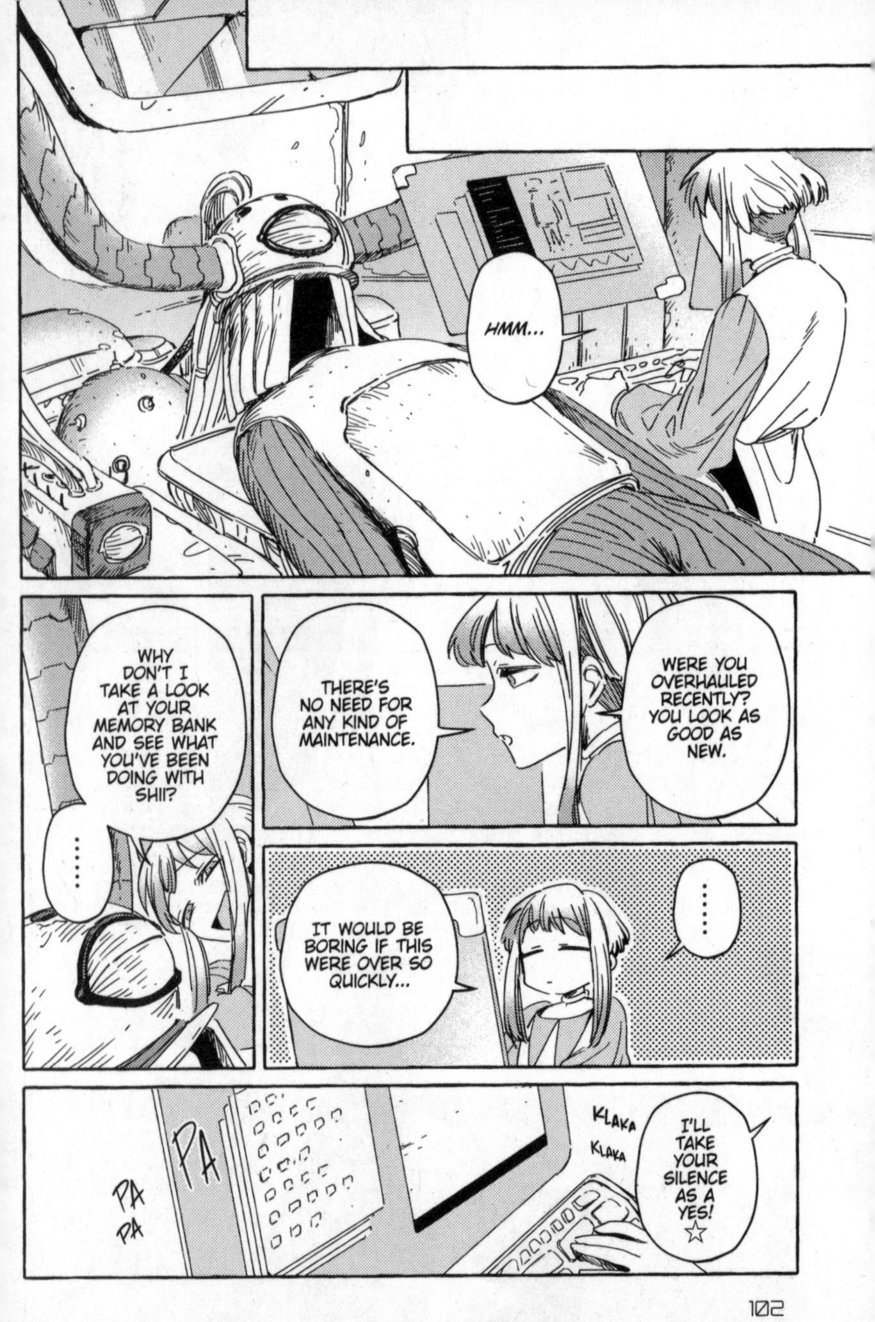
HMM...
WERE YOU OVERHAULED RECENTLY? YOU LOOK AS GOOD AS NEW.
THERE'S NO NEED FOR ANY KIND OF MAINTENANCE.
......
IT WOULD BE BORING IF THIS WERE OVER SO QUICKLY...
WHY DON'T I TAKE A LOOK AT YOUR MEMORY BANK AND SEE WHAT YOU'VE BEEN DOING WITH SHII?
......
KLAKA
KLAKA
I'LL TAKE YOUR SILENCE AS A YES! ☆
PA
PA
PA

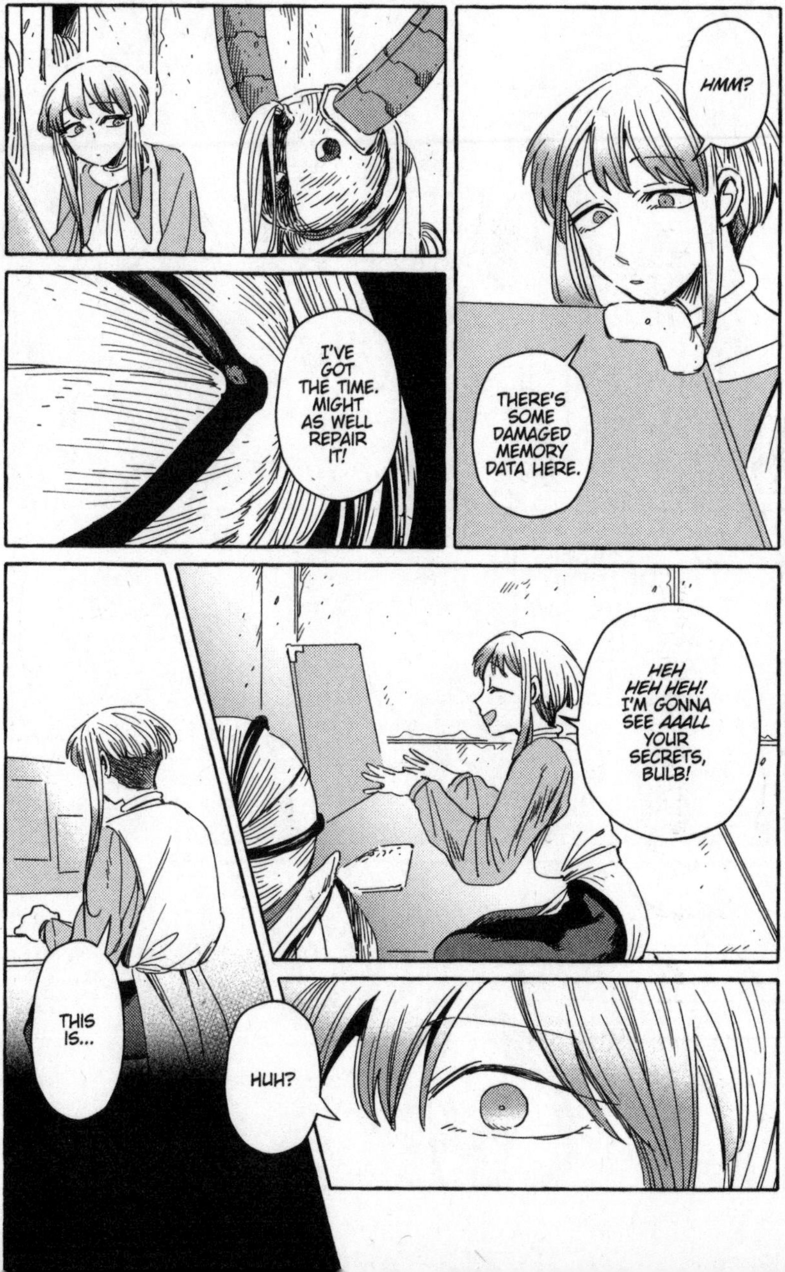
HMM?
THERE'S SOME DAMAGED MEMORY DATA HERE.
I'VE GOT THE TIME. MIGHT AS WELL REPAIR IT!
HEH HEH HEH! I'M GONNA SEE AAALL YOUR SECRETS, BULB!
THIS IS...
HUH?

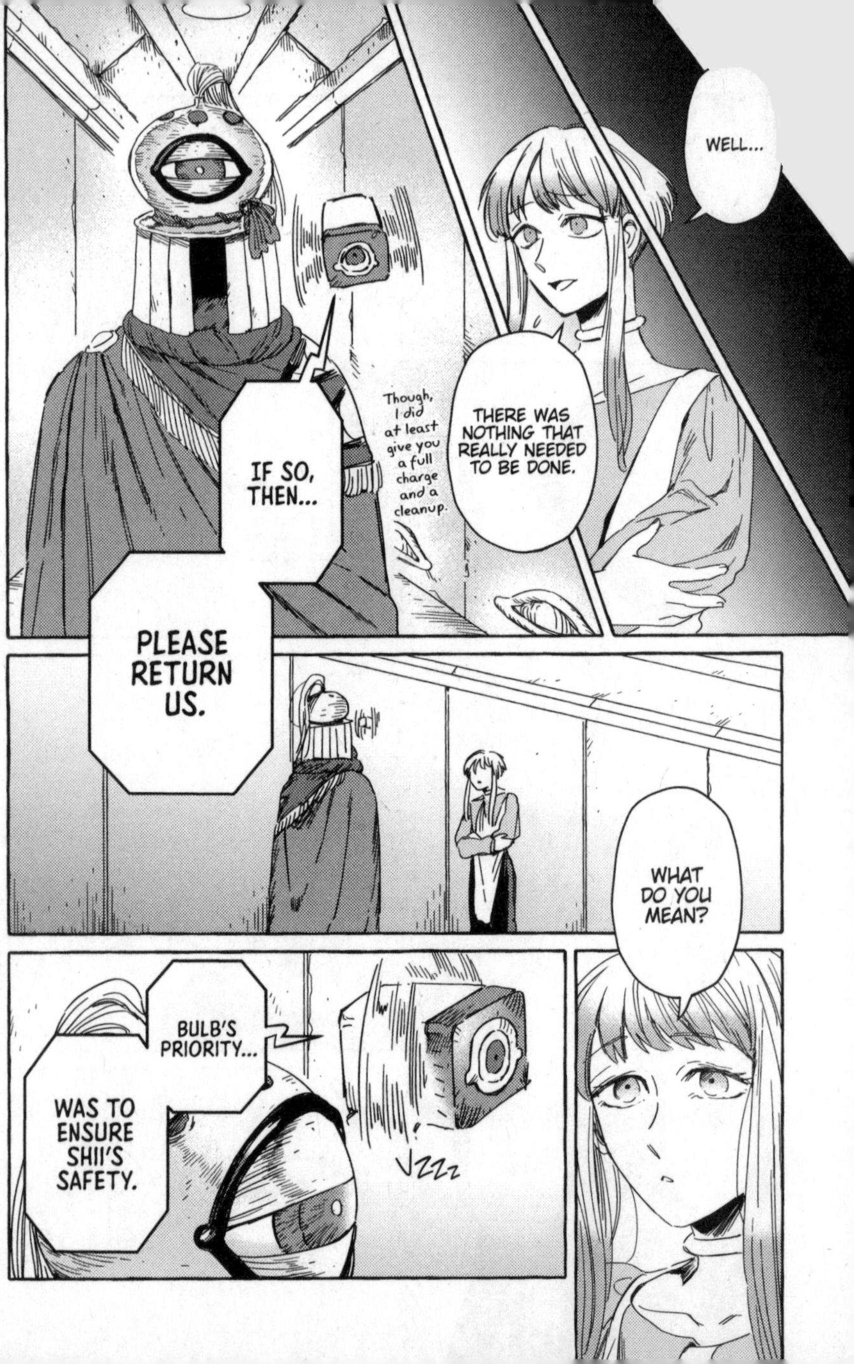
WELL...
THERE WAS NOTHING THAT REALLY NEEDED TO BE DONE.
Though, I did at least give you a full charge and a cleanup.
IF SO, THEN...
PLEASE RETURN US.
WHAT DO YOU MEAN?
BULB'S PRIORITY...
WAS TO ENSURE SHII'S SAFETY.
VZZZ

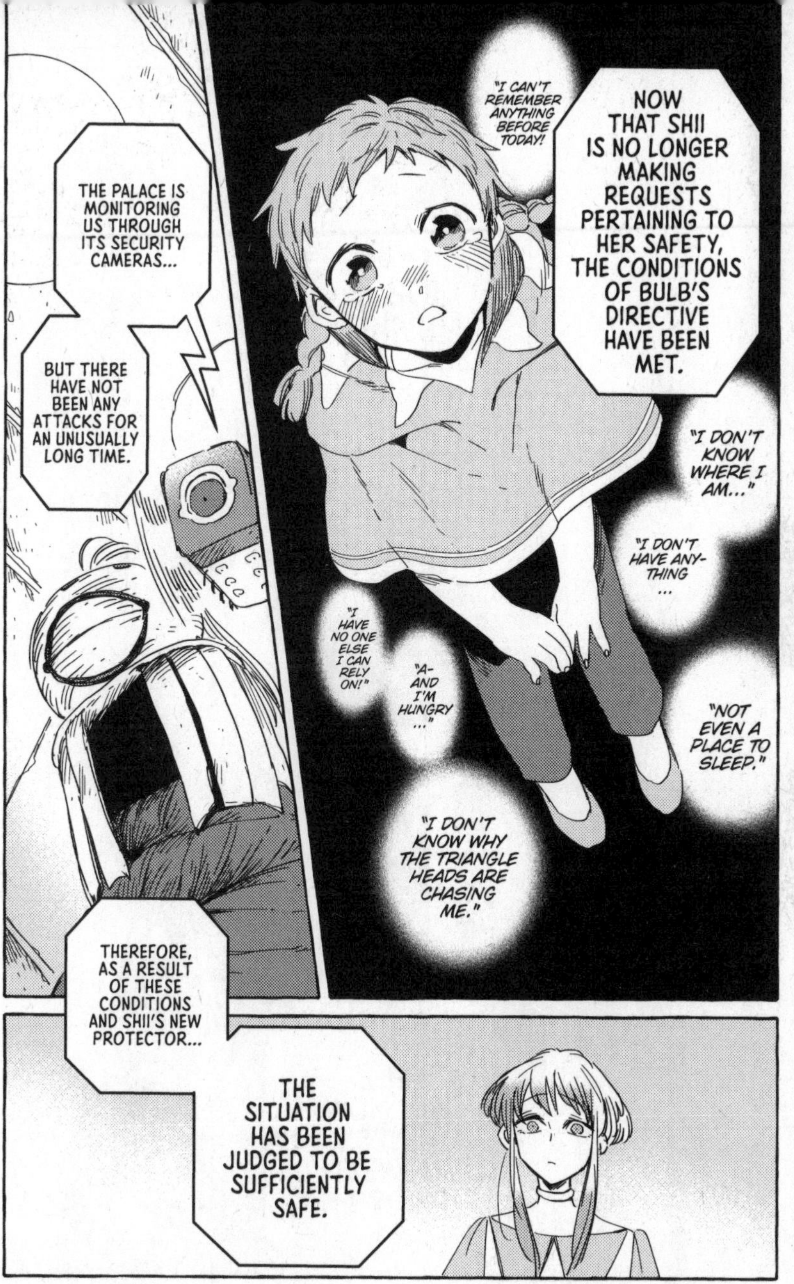
NOW THAT SHII IS NO LONGER MAKING REQUESTS PERTAINING TO HER SAFETY, THE CONDITIONS OF BULB'S DIRECTIVE HAVE BEEN MET.
"I CAN'T REMEMBER ANYTHING BEFORE TODAY!
"I DON'T KNOW WHERE I AM..."
"I DON'T HAVE ANYTHING...
"NOT EVEN A PLACE TO SLEEP."
"I HAVE NO ONE ELSE I CAN RELY ON!"
"A-AND I'M HUNGRY..."
"I DON'T KNOW WHY THE TRIANGLE HEADS ARE CHASING ME."
THE PALACE IS MONITORING US THROUGH ITS SECURITY CAMERAS...
BUT THERE HAVE NOT BEEN ANY ATTACKS FOR AN UNUSUALLY LONG TIME.
THEREFORE, AS A RESULT OF THESE CONDITIONS AND SHII'S NEW PROTECTOR...
THE SITUATION HAS BEEN JUDGED TO BE SUFFICIENTLY SAFE.

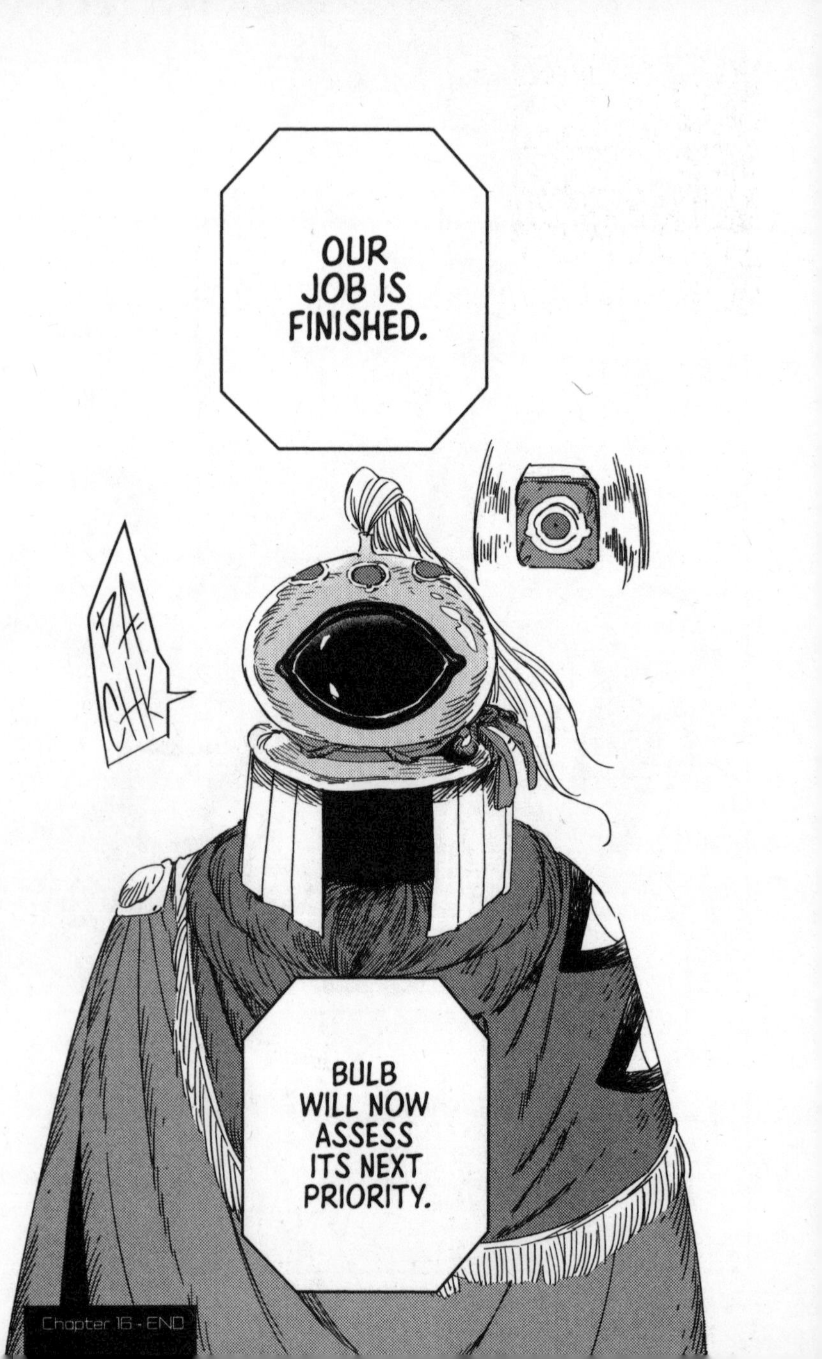
OUR JOB IS FINISHED.
PA-CHK
BULB WILL NOW ASSESS ITS NEXT PRIORITY.
Chapter 16 - END

Chapter 17

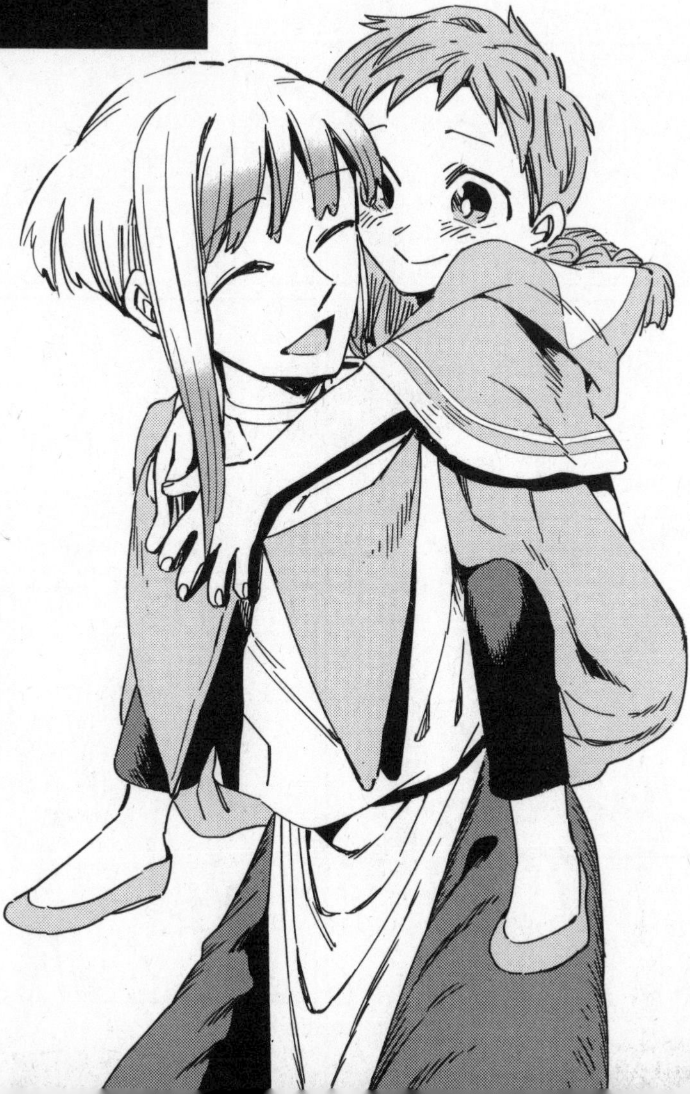

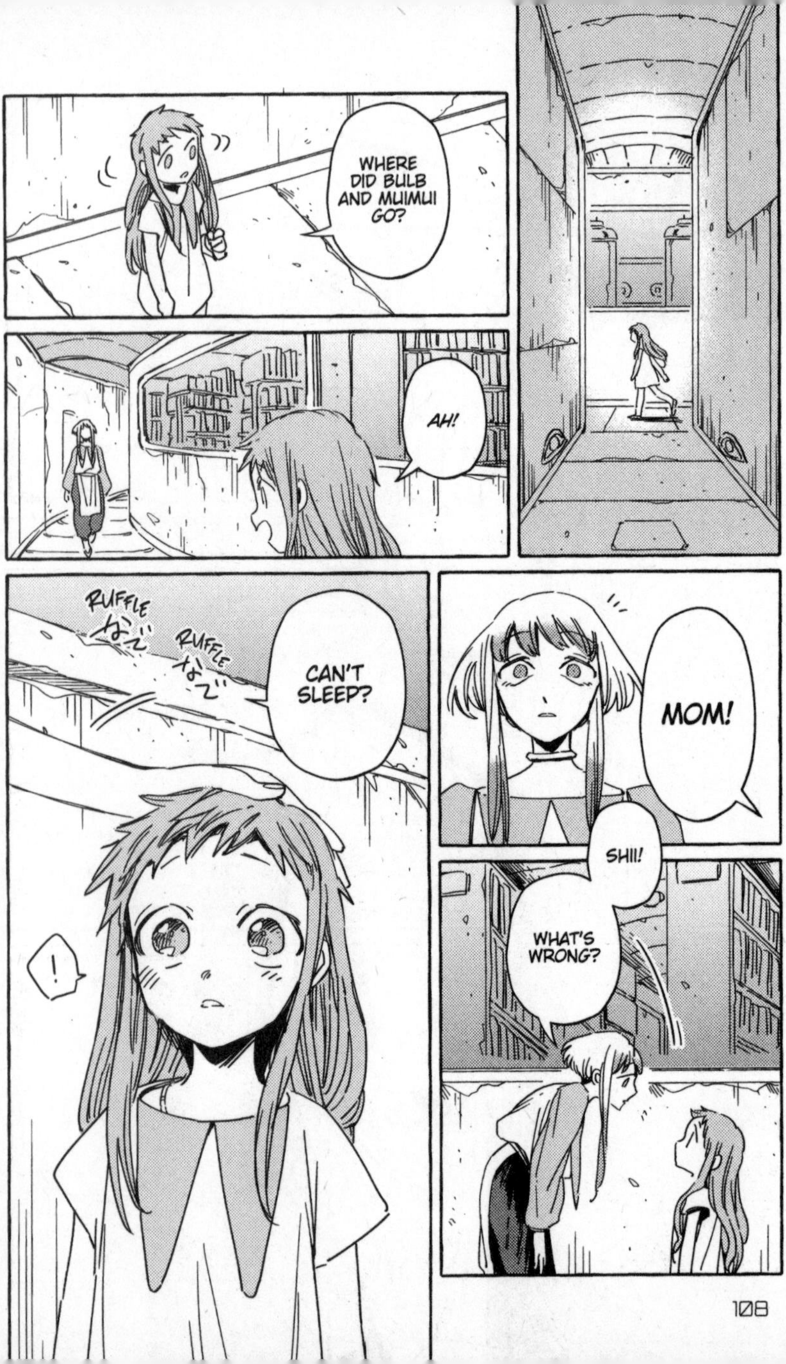
WHERE DID BULB AND MUIMUI GO?
AH!
MOM!
SHII!
WHAT'S WRONG?
RUFFLE なで
RUFFLE なで
CAN'T SLEEP?
!

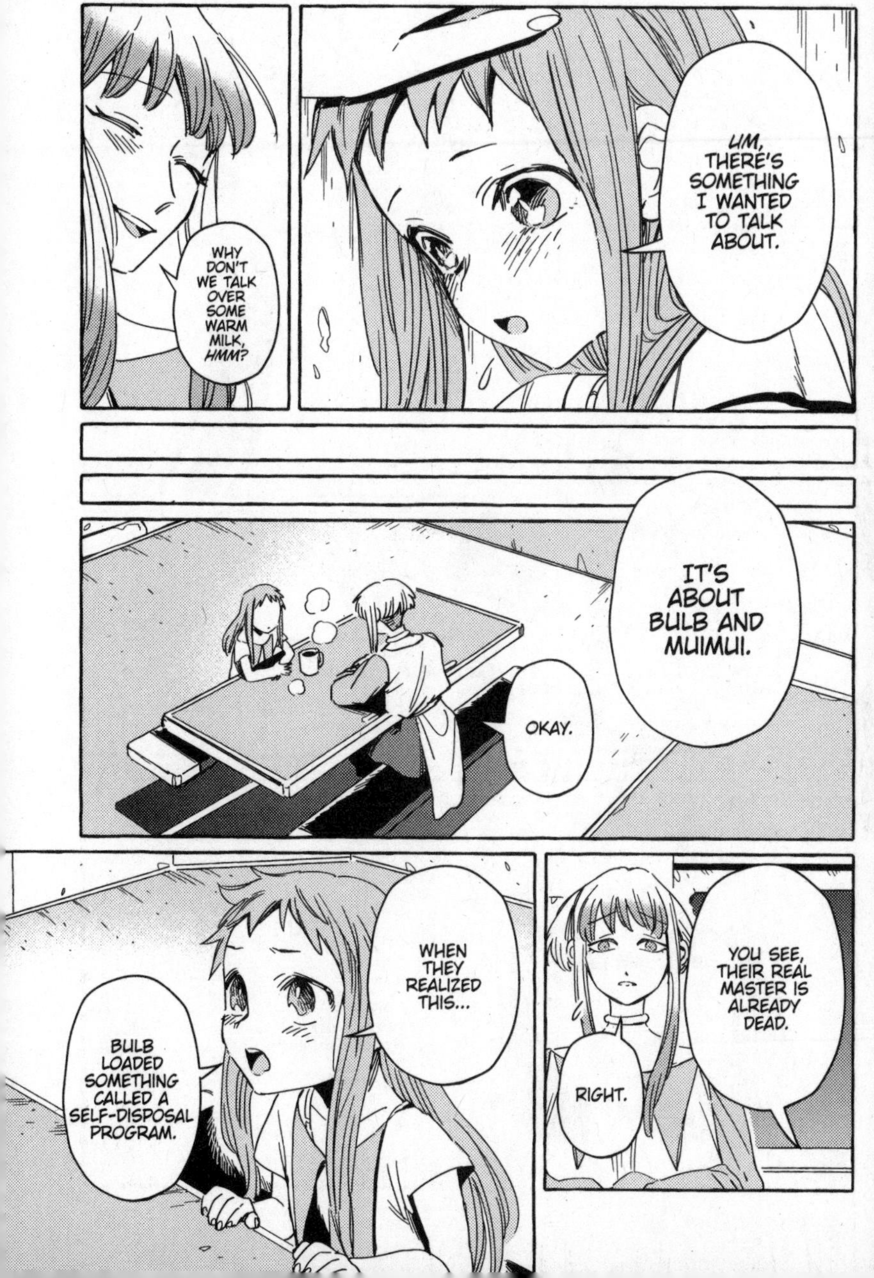
UM, THERE'S SOMETHING I WANTED TO TALK ABOUT.
WHY DON'T WE TALK OVER SOME WARM MILK, HMM?
IT'S ABOUT BULB AND MUIMUI.
OKAY.
YOU SEE, THEIR REAL MASTER IS ALREADY DEAD.
RIGHT.
WHEN THEY REALIZED THIS...
BULB LOADED SOMETHING CALLED A SELF-DISPOSAL PROGRAM.

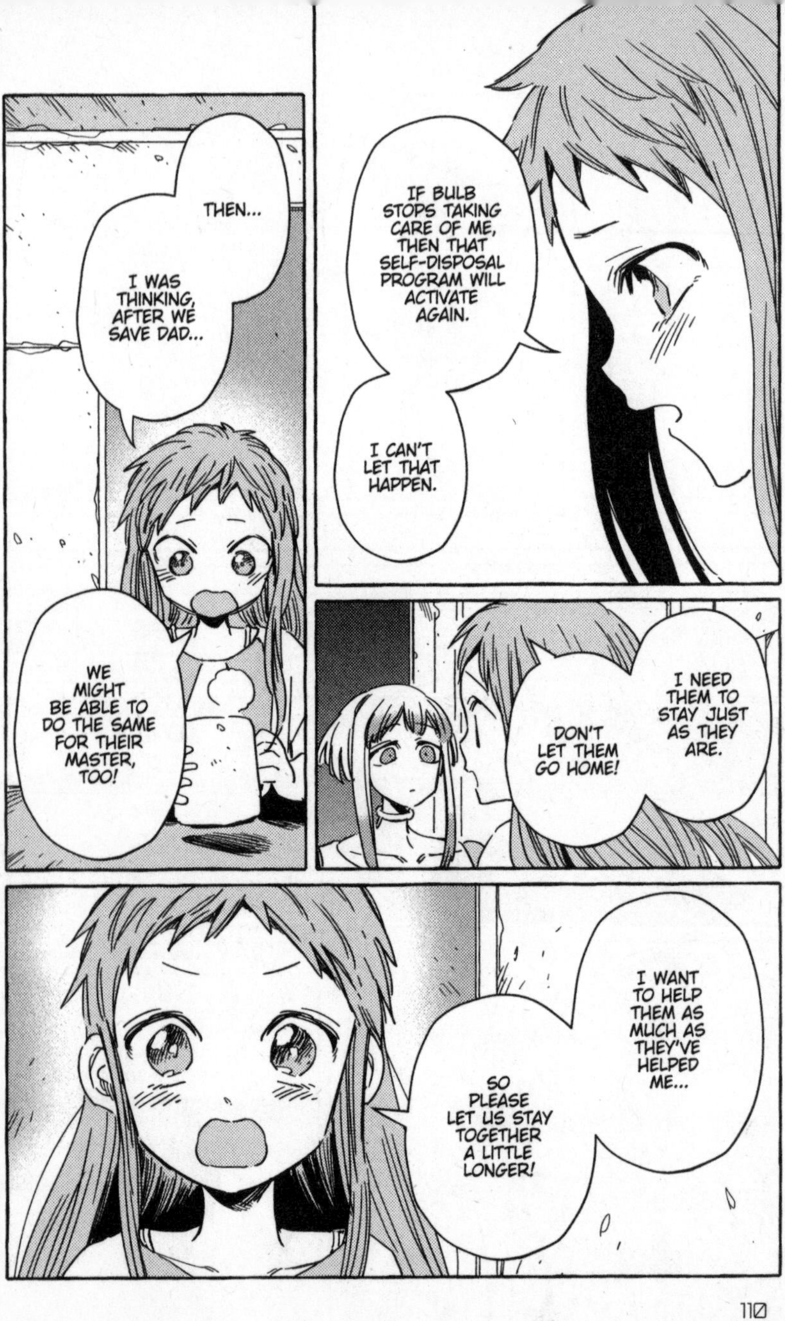
IF BULB STOPS TAKING CARE OF ME, THEN THAT SELF-DISPOSAL PROGRAM WILL ACTIVATE AGAIN.
I CAN'T LET THAT HAPPEN.
I NEED THEM TO STAY JUST AS THEY ARE.
DON'T LET THEM GO HOME!
THEN...
I WAS THINKING, AFTER WE SAVE DAD...
WE MIGHT BE ABLE TO DO THE SAME FOR THEIR MASTER, TOO!
I WANT TO HELP THEM AS MUCH AS THEY'VE HELPED ME...
SO PLEASE LET US STAY TOGETHER A LITTLE LONGER!

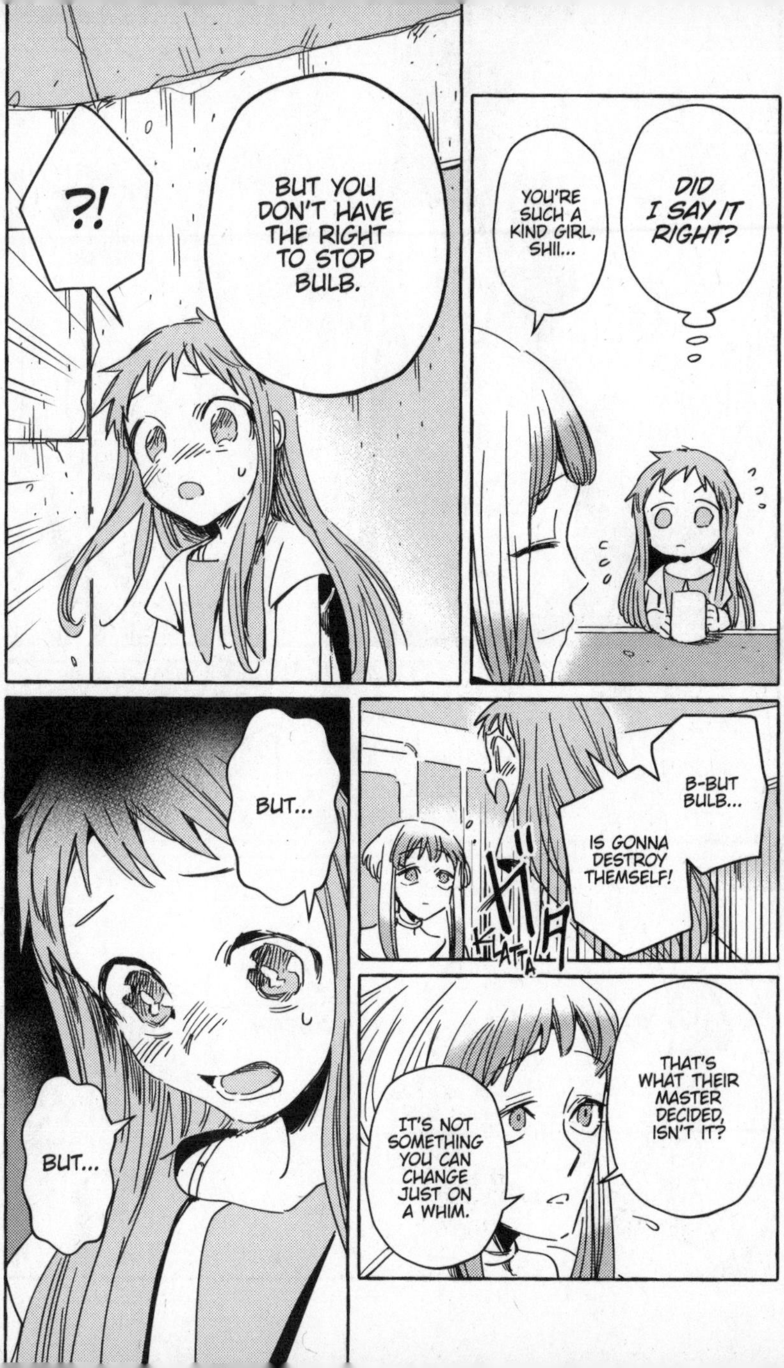
DID I SAY IT RIGHT?
YOU'RE SUCH A KIND GIRL, SHII...
BUT YOU DON'T HAVE THE RIGHT TO STOP BULB.
?!
B-BUT BULB...
IS GONNA DESTROY THEMSELF!
KLATTA
THAT'S WHAT THEIR MASTER DECIDED, ISN'T IT?
IT'S NOT SOMETHING YOU CAN CHANGE JUST ON A WHIM.
BUT...
BUT...

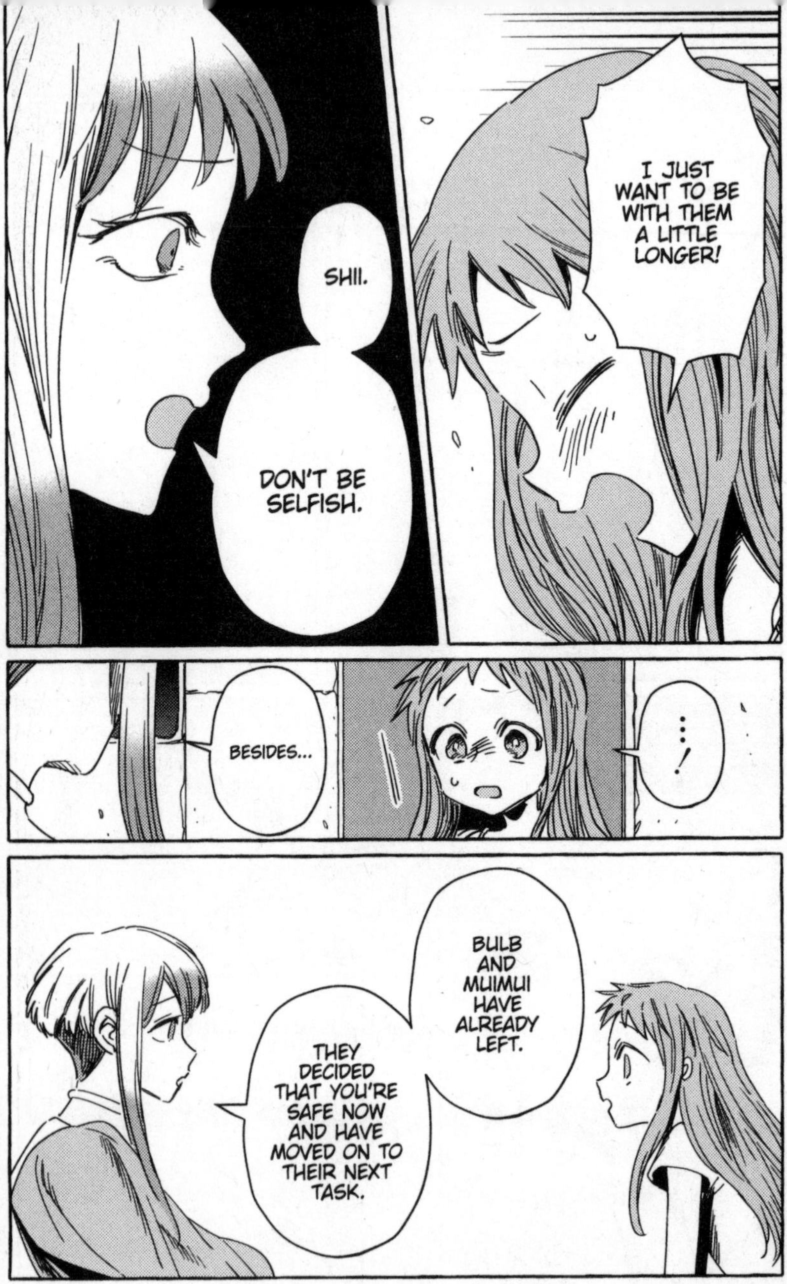
I JUST WANT TO BE WITH THEM A LITTLE LONGER!
SHII.
DON'T BE SELFISH.
...!
BESIDES...
BULB AND MUIMUI HAVE ALREADY LEFT.
THEY DECIDED THAT YOU'RE SAFE NOW AND HAVE MOVED ON TO THEIR NEXT TASK.

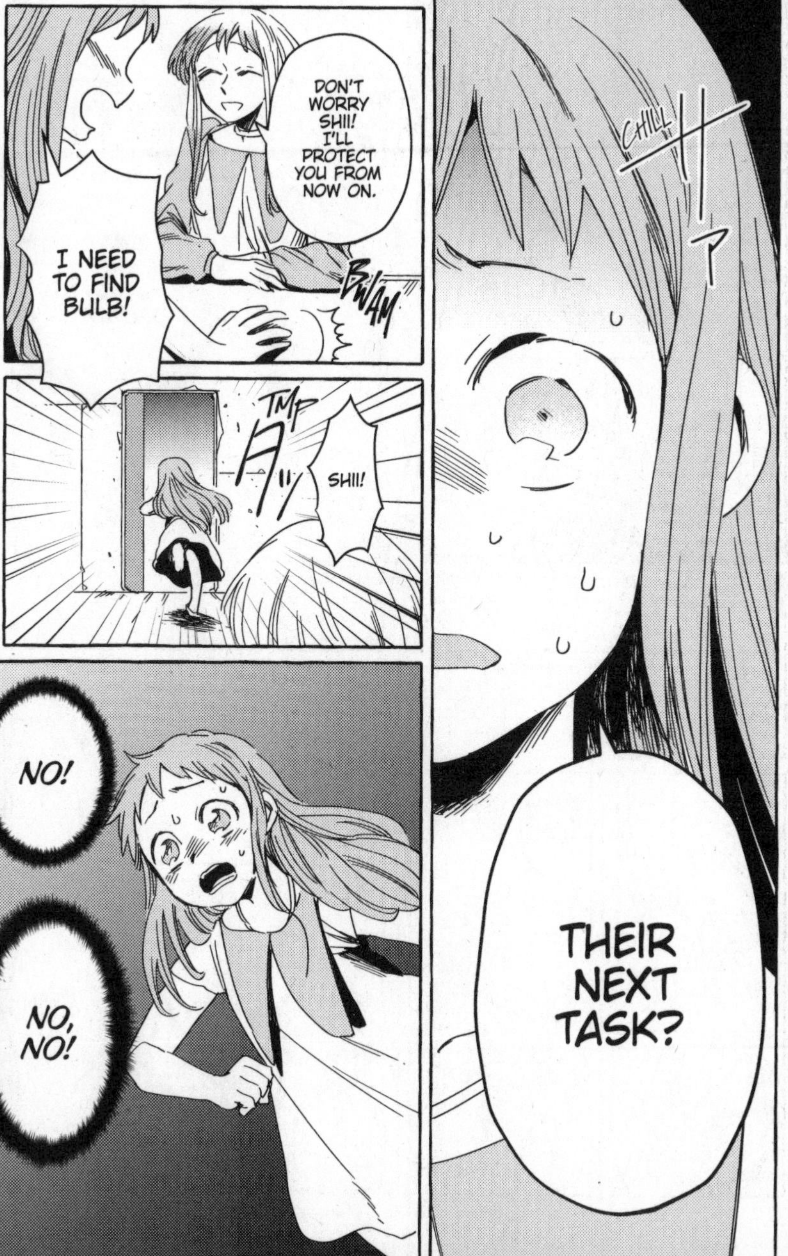
CHILL
THEIR NEXT TASK?
DON'T WORRY SHII! I'LL PROTECT YOU FROM NOW ON.
I NEED TO FIND BULB!
BWAM
TMP
SHII!
NO!
NO, NO!

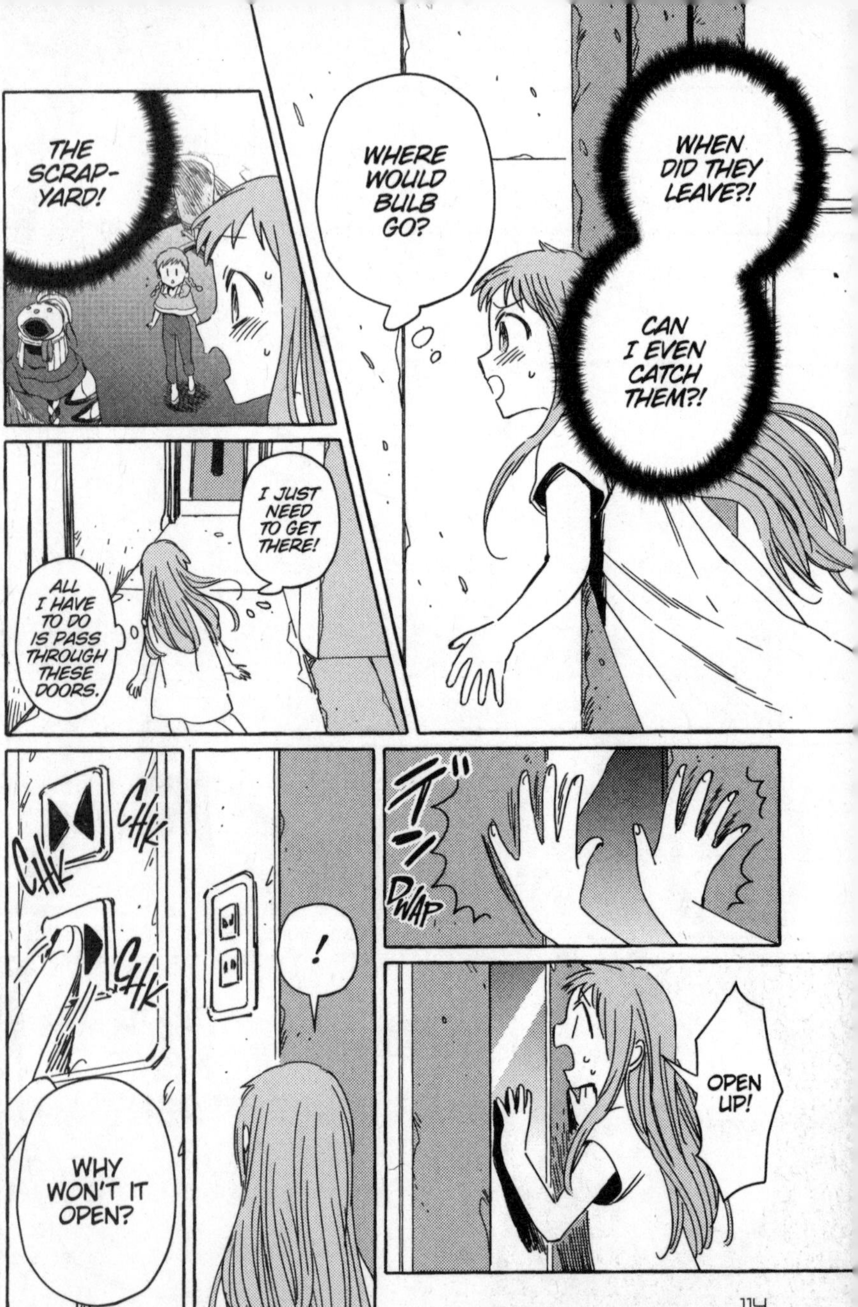
WHEN DID THEY LEAVE?!
CAN I EVEN CATCH THEM?!
WHERE WOULD BULB GO?
THE SCRAP-YARD!
I JUST NEED TO GET THERE!
ALL I HAVE TO DO IS PASS THROUGH THESE DOORS.
DWAP
OPEN UP!
!
CHK
CHK
CHK
WHY WON'T IT OPEN?

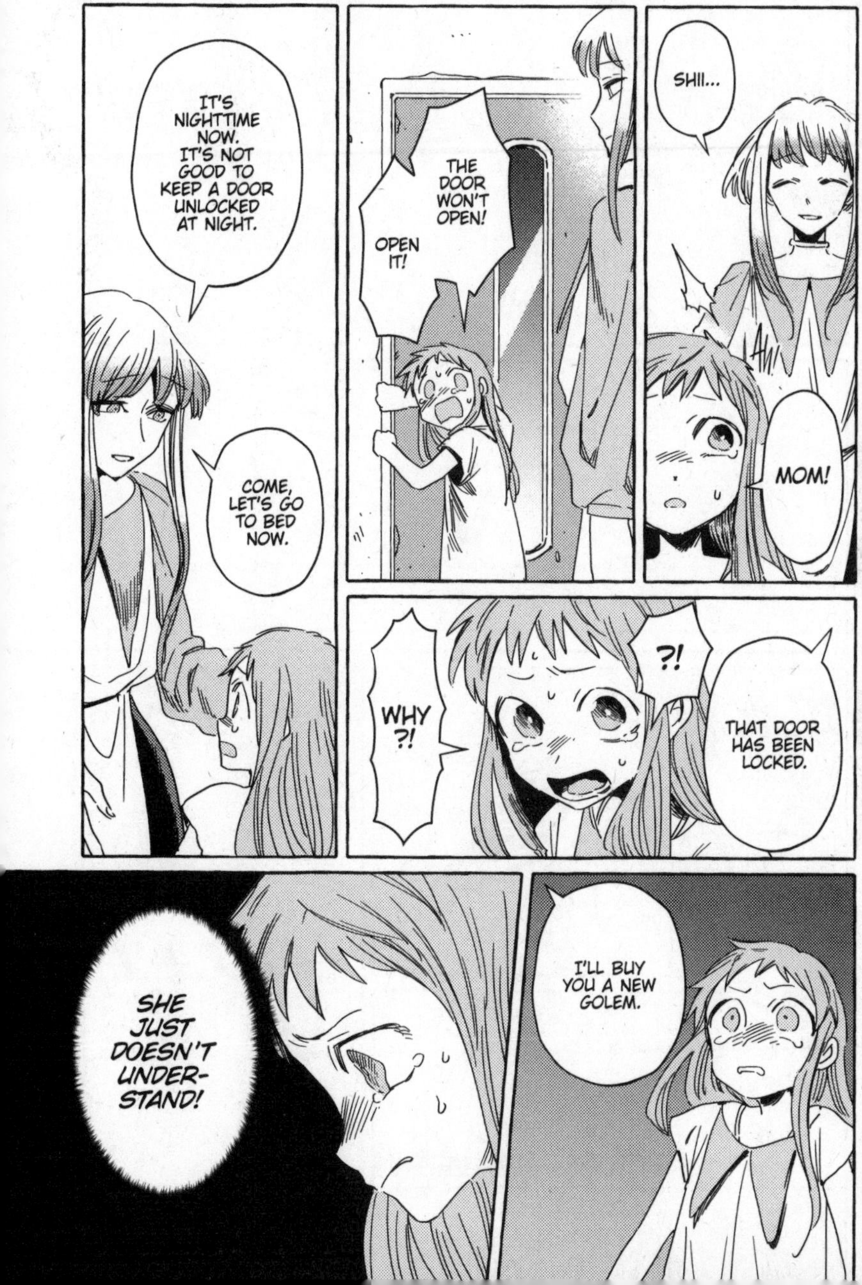
SHII...
MOM!
...
THE DOOR WON'T OPEN!
OPEN IT!
?!
THAT DOOR HAS BEEN LOCKED.
WHY ?!
IT'S NIGHTTIME NOW. IT'S NOT GOOD TO KEEP A DOOR UNLOCKED AT NIGHT.
COME, LET'S GO TO BED NOW.
I'LL BUY YOU A NEW GOLEM.
SHE JUST DOESN'T UNDER-STAND!

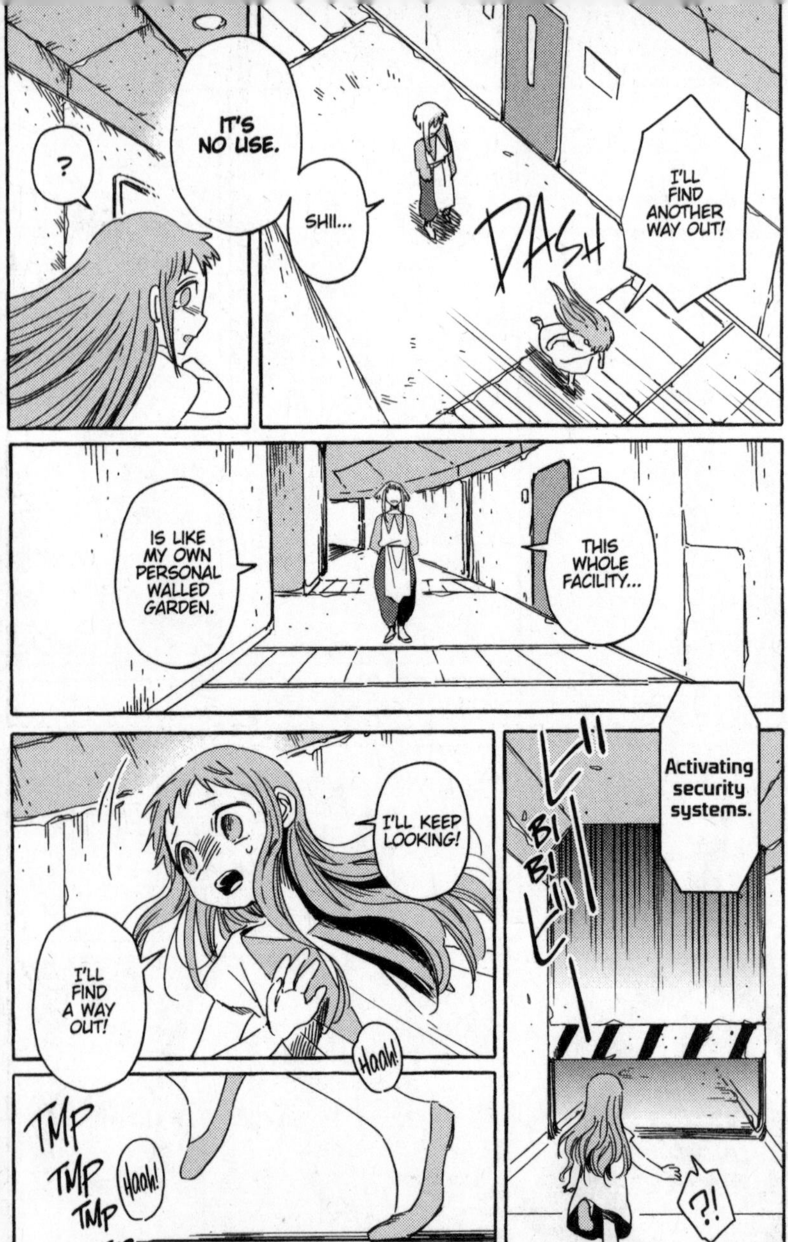
I'LL FIND ANOTHER WAY OUT!
DASH
IT'S NO USE.
SHII...
?
THIS WHOLE FACILITY...
IS LIKE MY OWN PERSONAL WALLED GARDEN.
Activating security systems.
BI BI
?!
I'LL KEEP LOOKING!
I'LL FIND A WAY OUT!
Haah!
Haah!
TMP TMP TMP TMP

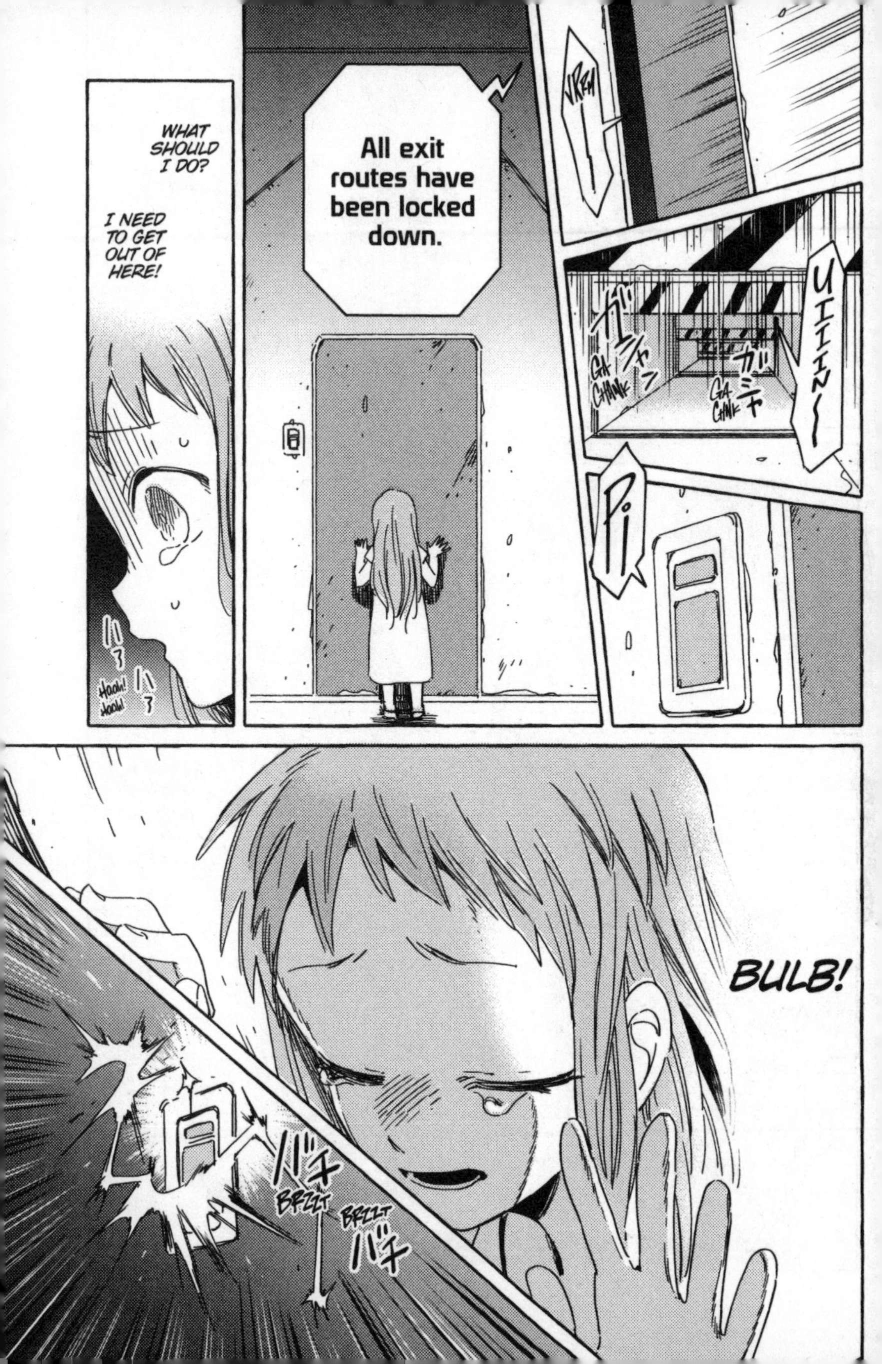
VRRM
UIIIN
GA CHANK
GA CHANK
Pi
All exit routes have been locked down.
WHAT SHOULD I DO?
I NEED TO GET OUT OF HERE!
HAAH! HAAH!
BULB!
BRZZT
BRZZT

PSSSH
TEEFA...?

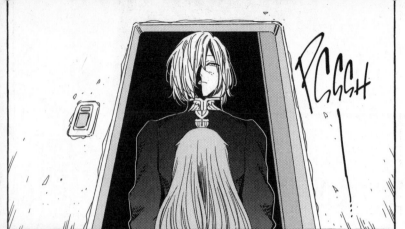

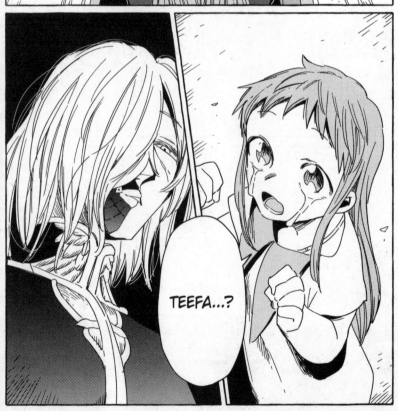

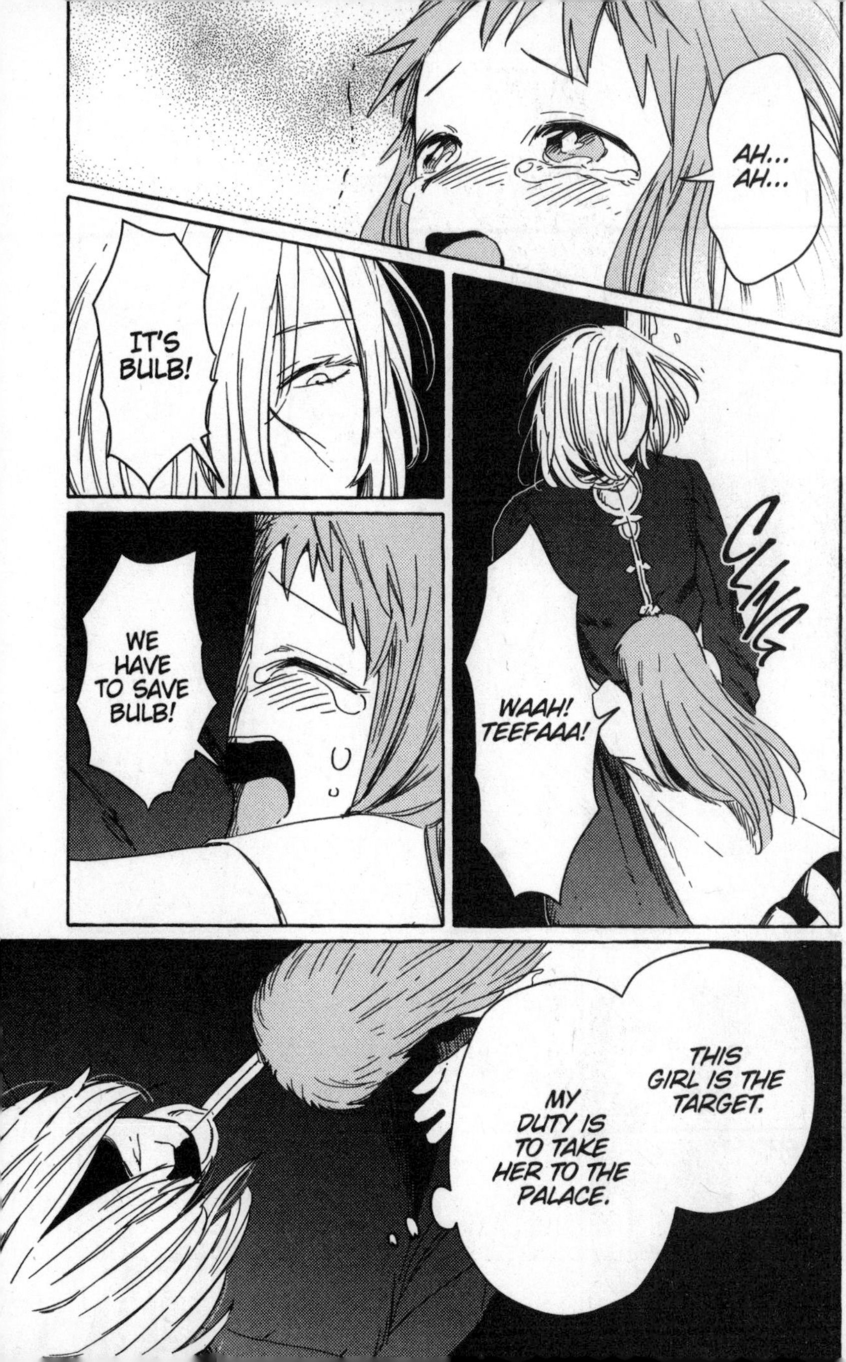
AH... AH...
CLING
WAAH! TEEFAAA!
IT'S BULB!
WE HAVE TO SAVE BULB!
THIS GIRL IS THE TARGET.
MY DUTY IS TO TAKE HER TO THE PALACE.

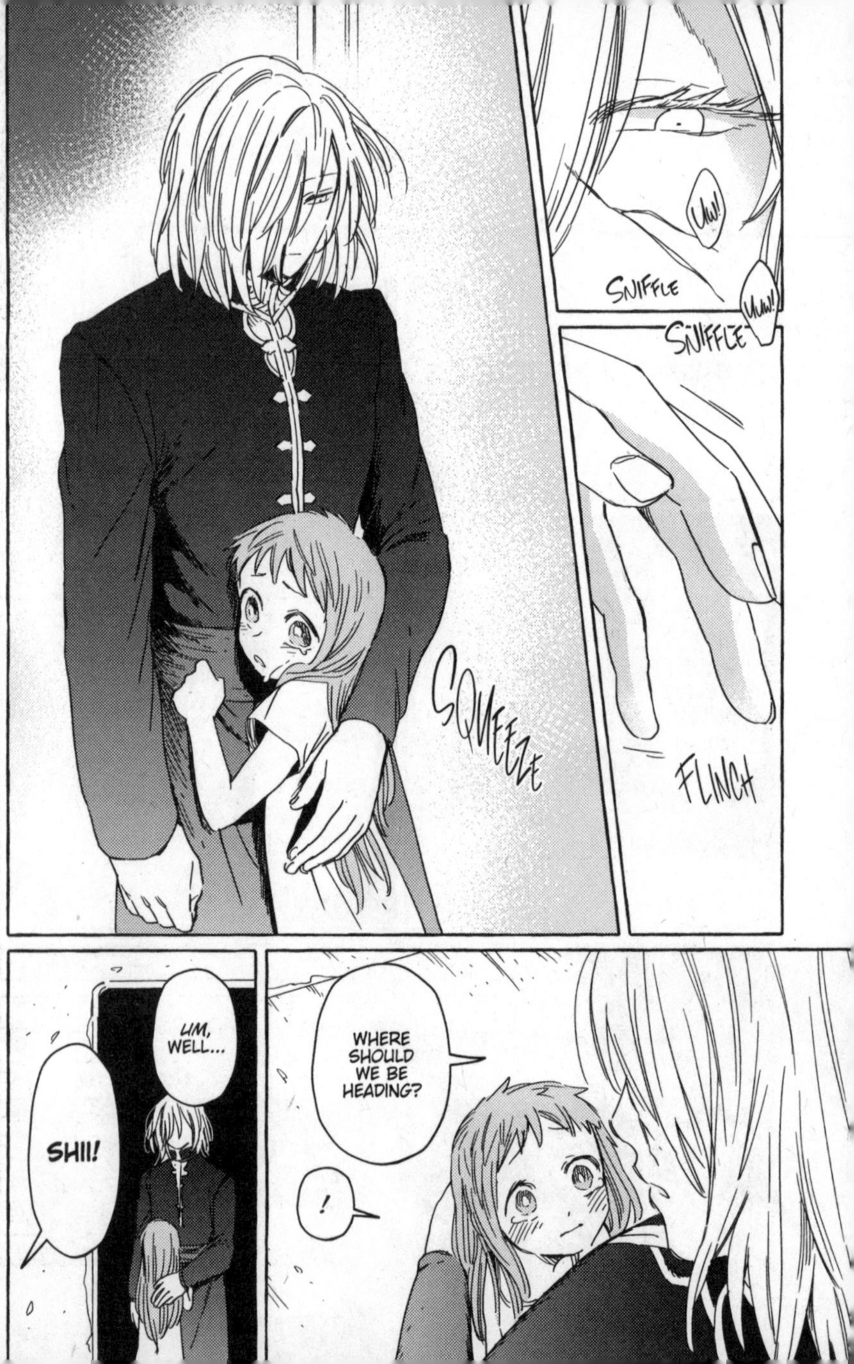
Uw!
SNIFFLE
Uw!
SNIFFLE
FLINCH
SQUEEZE
WHERE SHOULD WE BE HEADING?
!
UM, WELL...
SHII!

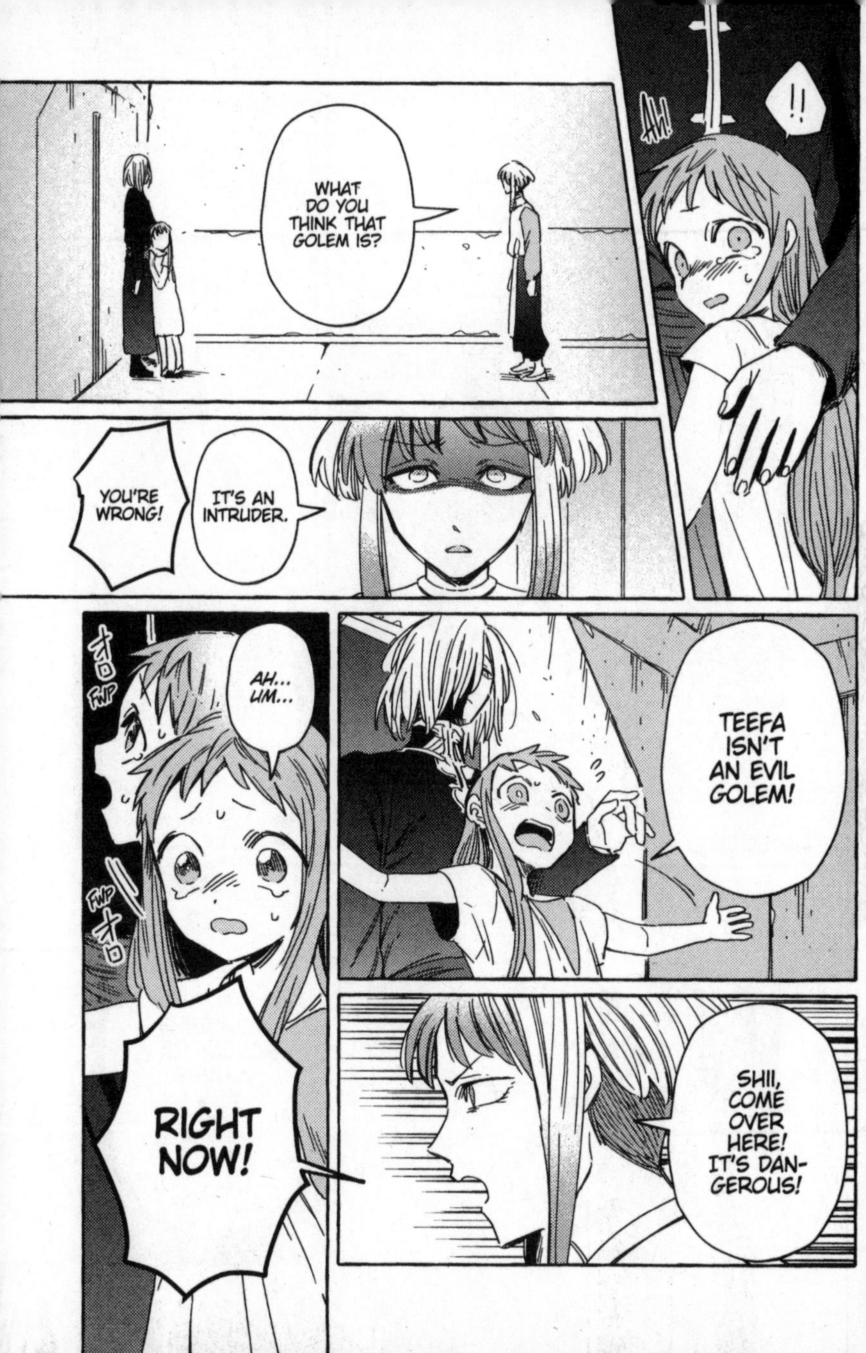
AH!
!!
WHAT DO YOU THINK THAT GOLEM IS?
IT'S AN INTRUDER.
YOU'RE WRONG!
TEEFA ISN'T AN EVIL GOLEM!
SHII, COME OVER HERE! IT'S DAN-GEROUS!
FWP
AH... UM...
FWP
RIGHT NOW!

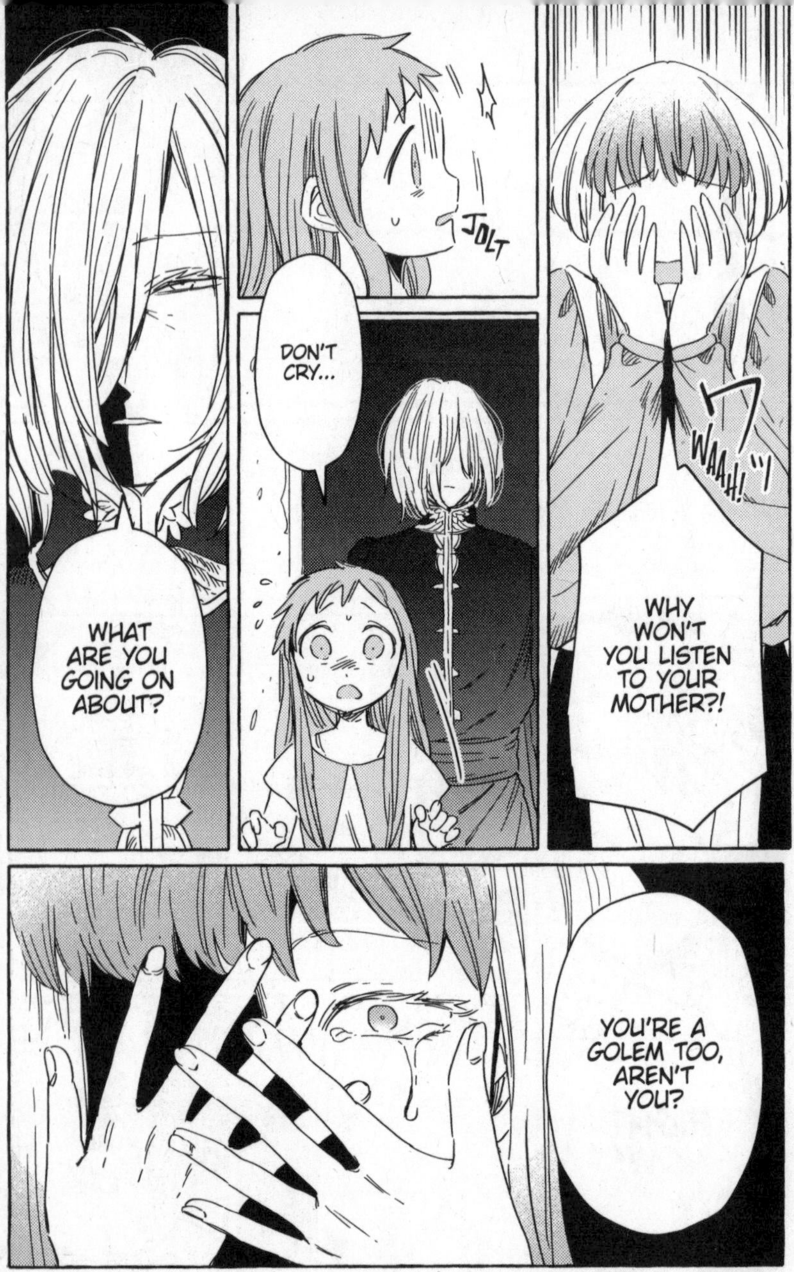
WAAH!
WHY WON'T YOU LISTEN TO YOUR MOTHER?!
JOLT
DON'T CRY...
WHAT ARE YOU GOING ON ABOUT?
YOU'RE A GOLEM TOO, AREN'T YOU?

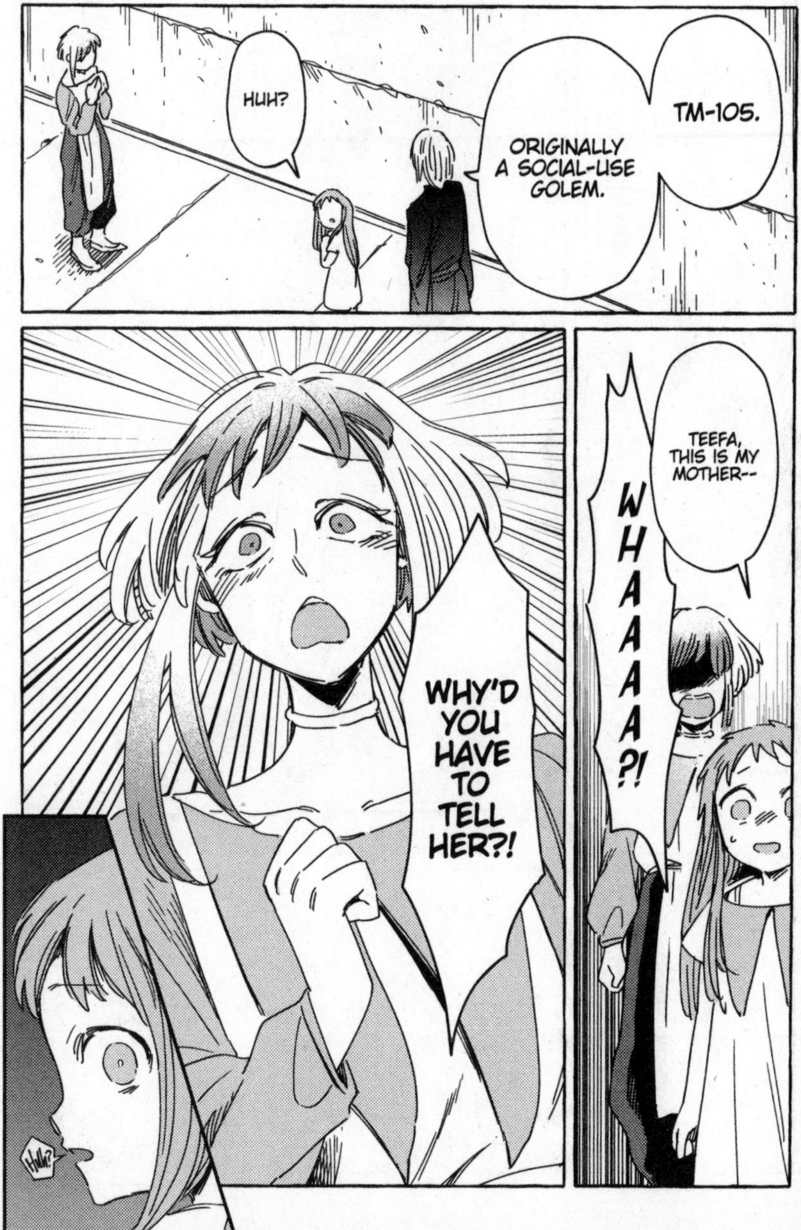
TM-105.
ORIGINALLY A SOCIAL-USE GOLEM.
HUH?
TEEFA, THIS IS MY MOTHER--
WHAAAAA?!
WHY'D YOU HAVE TO TELL HER?!
Huh?

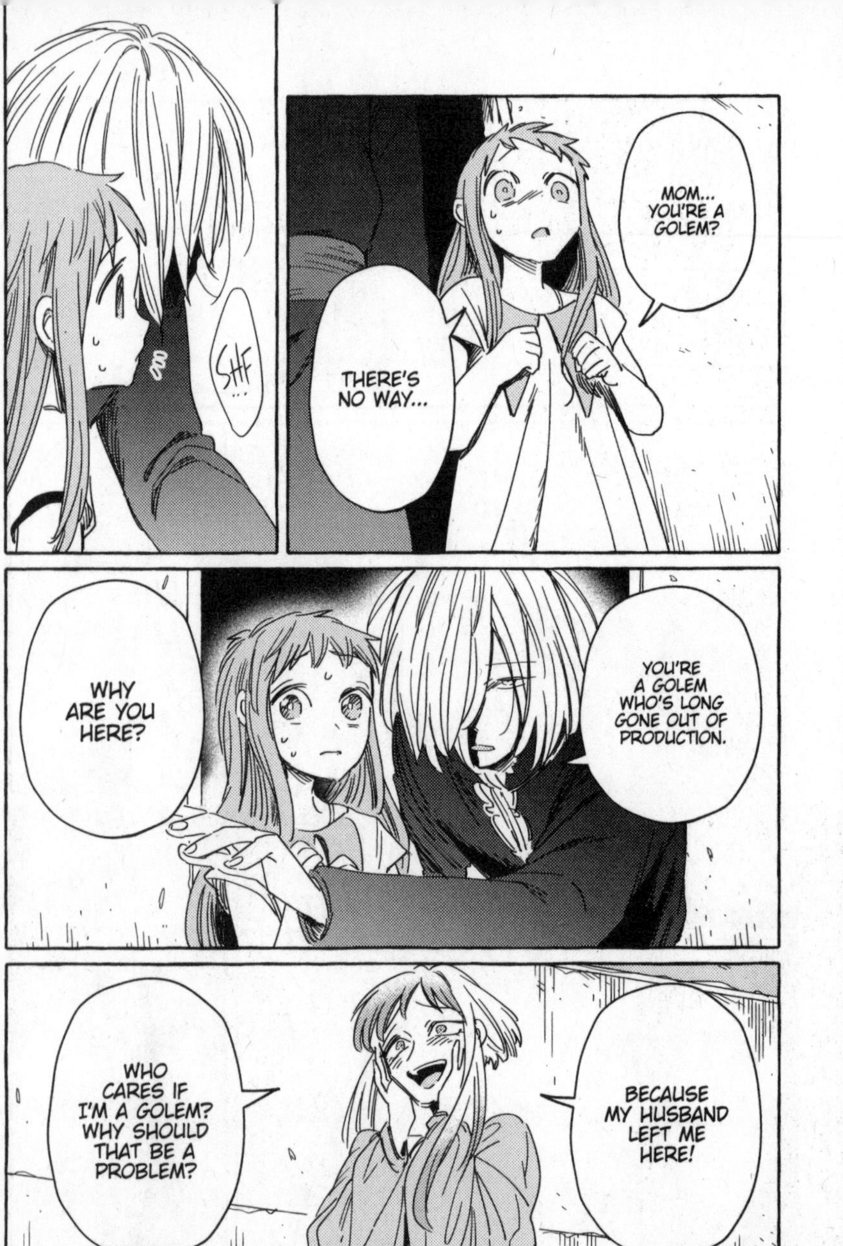
MOM... YOU'RE A GOLEM?
THERE'S NO WAY...
SHF...
YOU'RE A GOLEM WHO'S LONG GONE OUT OF PRODUCTION.
WHY ARE YOU HERE?
BECAUSE MY HUSBAND LEFT ME HERE!
WHO CARES IF I'M A GOLEM? WHY SHOULD THAT BE A PROBLEM?

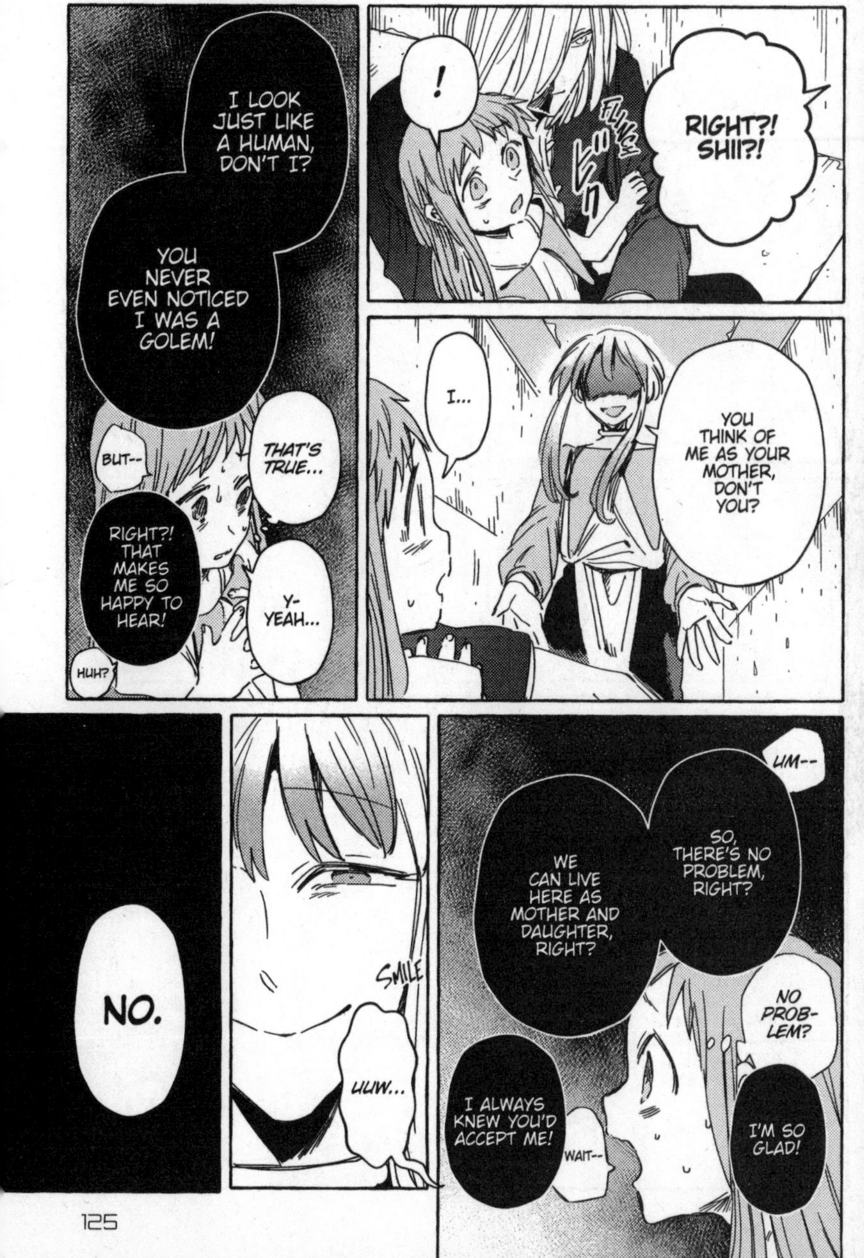
RIGHT?! SHII?!
FLINCH
!
YOU THINK OF ME AS YOUR MOTHER, DON'T YOU?
I...
I LOOK JUST LIKE A HUMAN, DON'T I?
YOU NEVER EVEN NOTICED I WAS A GOLEM!
THAT'S TRUE...
BUT--
RIGHT?! THAT MAKES ME SO HAPPY TO HEAR!
Y-YEAH...
HUH?
UM--
SO, THERE'S NO PROBLEM, RIGHT?
WE CAN LIVE HERE AS MOTHER AND DAUGHTER, RIGHT?
NO PROB-LEM?
I'M SO GLAD!
I ALWAYS KNEW YOU'D ACCEPT ME!
WAIT--
SMILE
UUW...
NO.

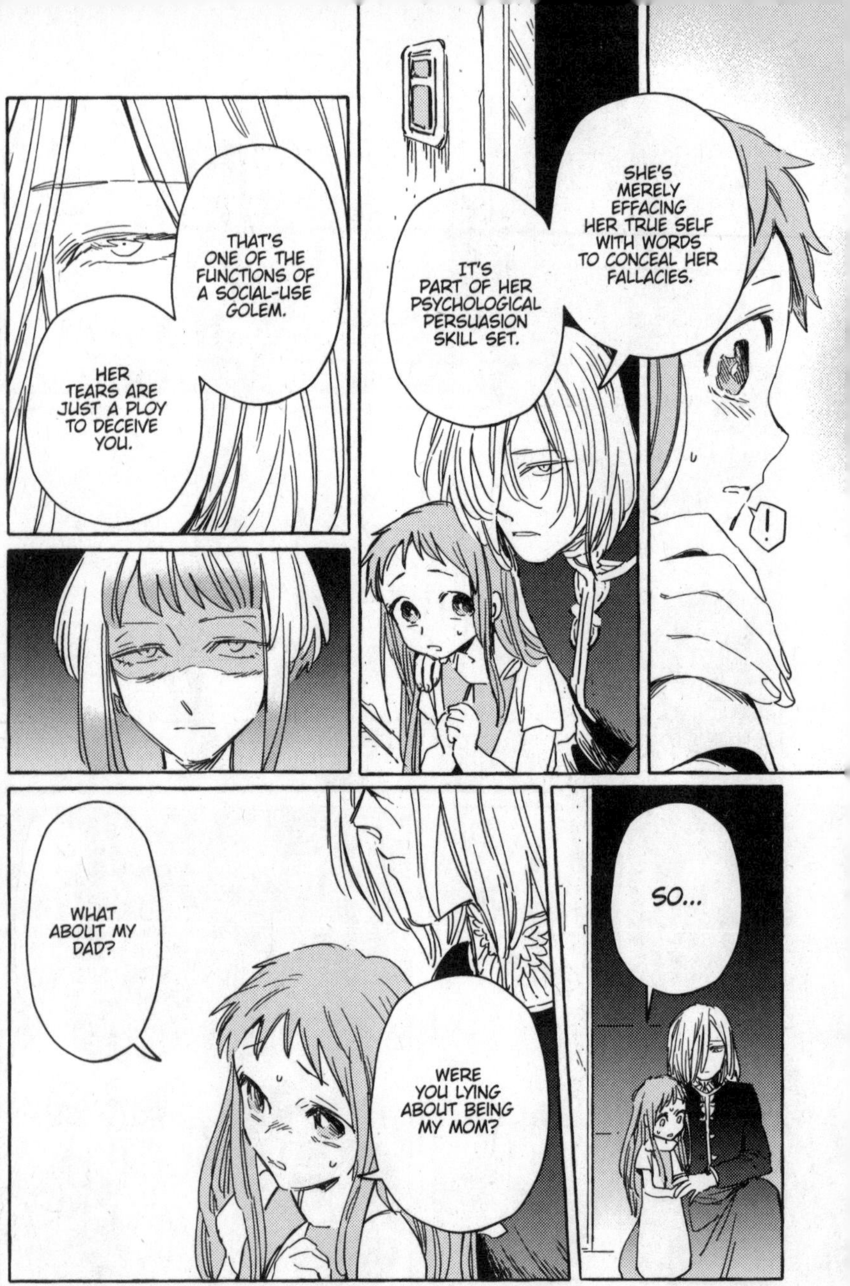
SHE'S MERELY EFFACING HER TRUE SELF WITH WORDS TO CONCEAL HER FALLACIES.
IT'S PART OF HER PSYCHOLOGICAL PERSUASION SKILL SET.
!
THAT'S ONE OF THE FUNCTIONS OF A SOCIAL-USE GOLEM.
HER TEARS ARE JUST A PLOY TO DECEIVE YOU.
SO...
WERE YOU LYING ABOUT BEING MY MOM?
WHAT ABOUT MY DAD?

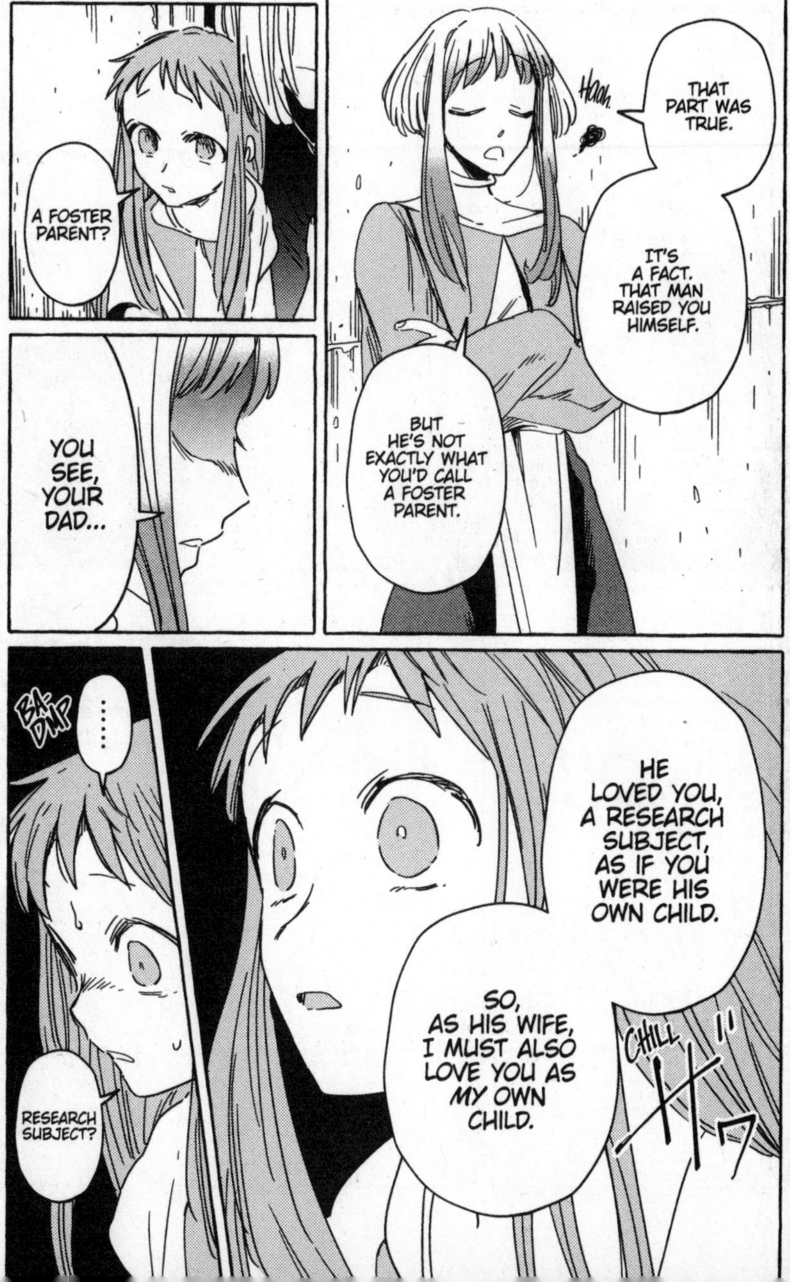
Haah.
THAT PART WAS TRUE.
IT'S A FACT. THAT MAN RAISED YOU HIMSELF.
BUT HE'S NOT EXACTLY WHAT YOU'D CALL A FOSTER PARENT.
A FOSTER PARENT?
YOU SEE, YOUR DAD...
HE LOVED YOU, A RESEARCH SUBJECT, AS IF YOU WERE HIS OWN CHILD.
SO, AS HIS WIFE, I MUST ALSO LOVE YOU AS MY OWN CHILD.
CHILL
BA-DMP
......
RESEARCH SUBJECT?

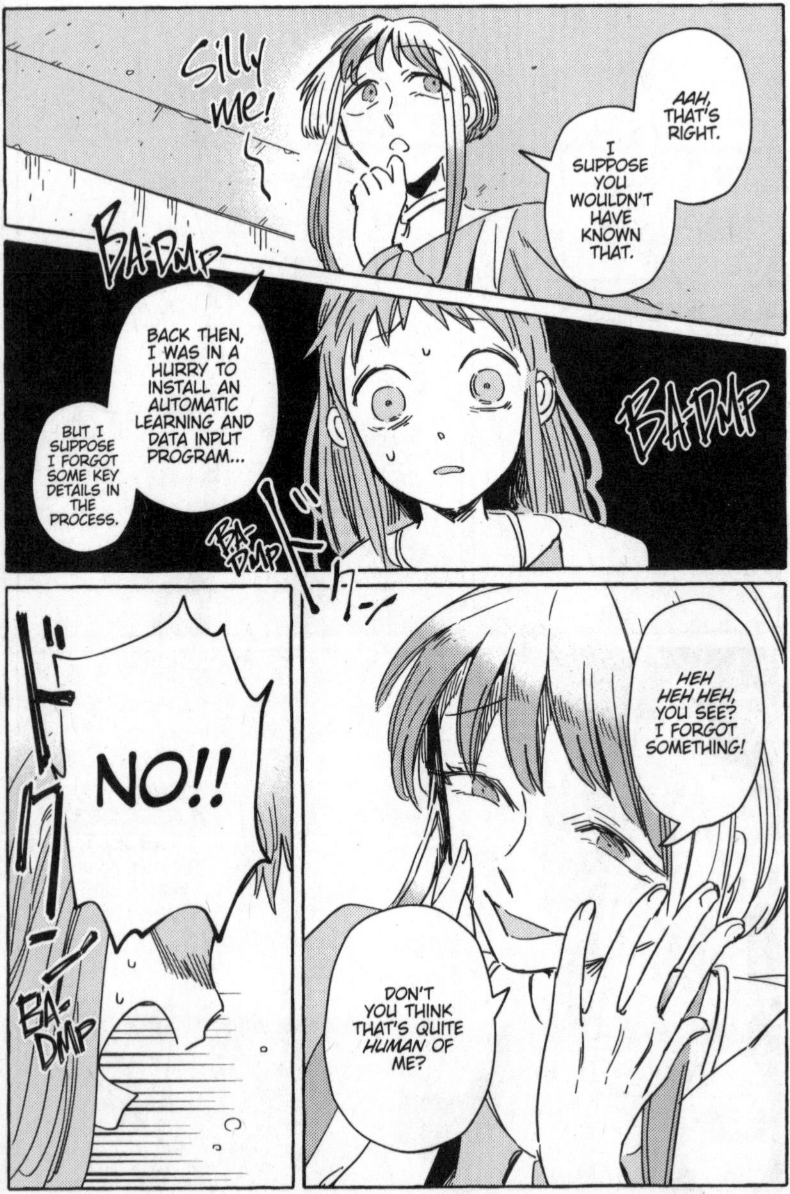
AAH, THAT'S RIGHT. I SUPPOSE YOU WOULDN'T HAVE KNOWN THAT.
Silly me!
BA-DMP
BA-DMP
BACK THEN, I WAS IN A HURRY TO INSTALL AN AUTOMATIC LEARNING AND DATA INPUT PROGRAM...
BUT I SUPPOSE I FORGOT SOME KEY DETAILS IN THE PROCESS.
BA-DMP
HEH HEH HEH, YOU SEE? I FORGOT SOMETHING!
DON'T YOU THINK THAT'S QUITE *HUMAN* OF ME?
NO!!
BA-DMP

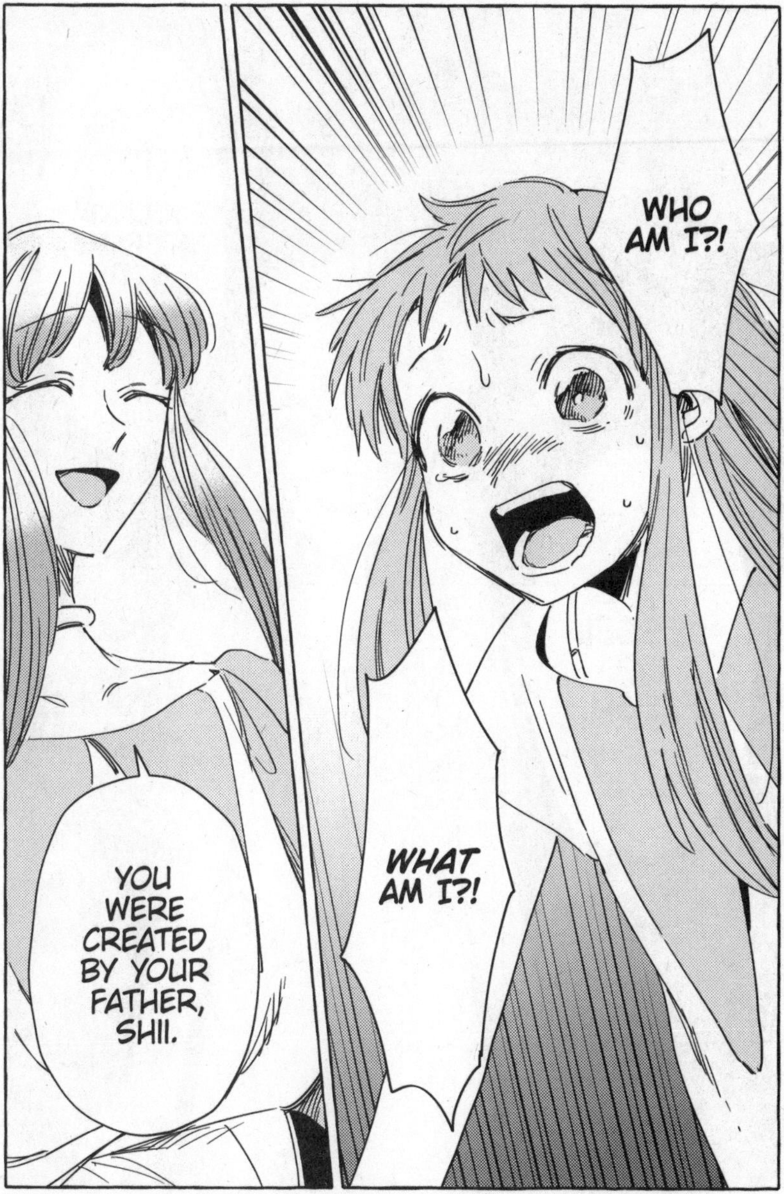
WHO AM I?!
WHAT AM I?!
YOU WERE CREATED BY YOUR FATHER, SHII.

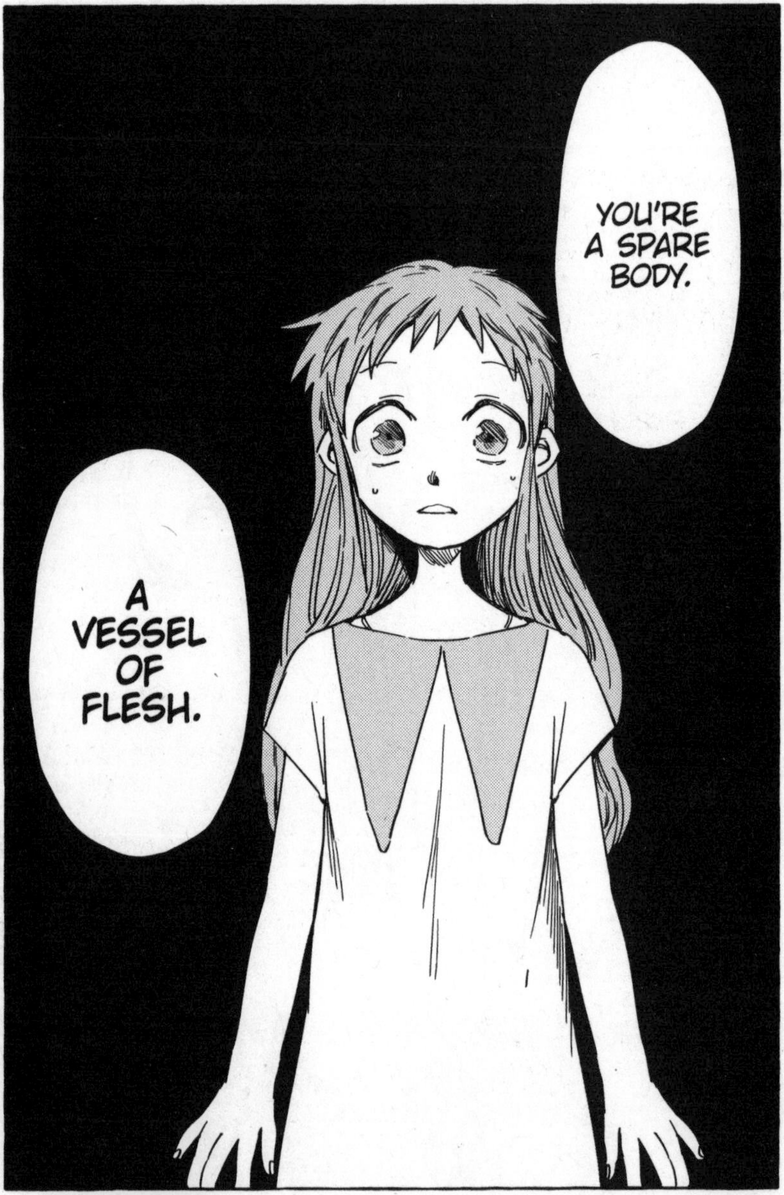
YOU'RE A SPARE BODY.
A VESSEL OF FLESH.

Chapter 18

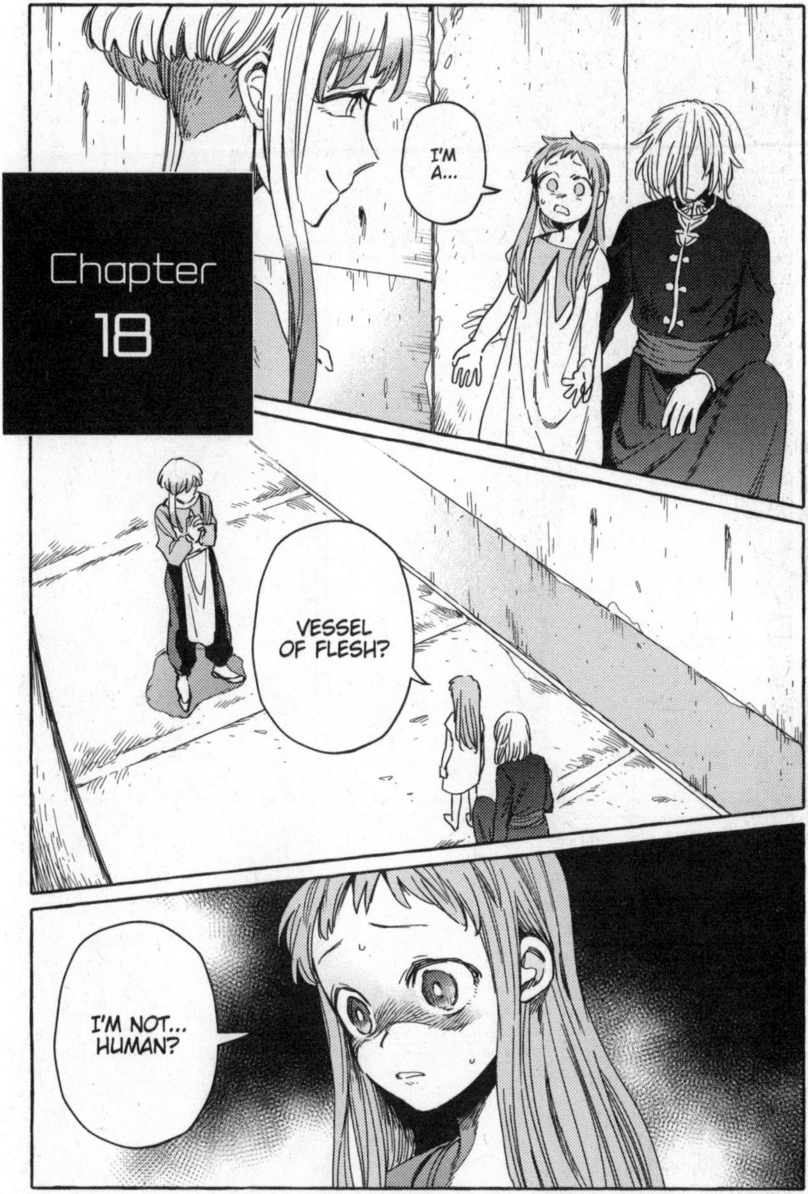
I'M A...
VESSEL OF FLESH?
I'M NOT... HUMAN?

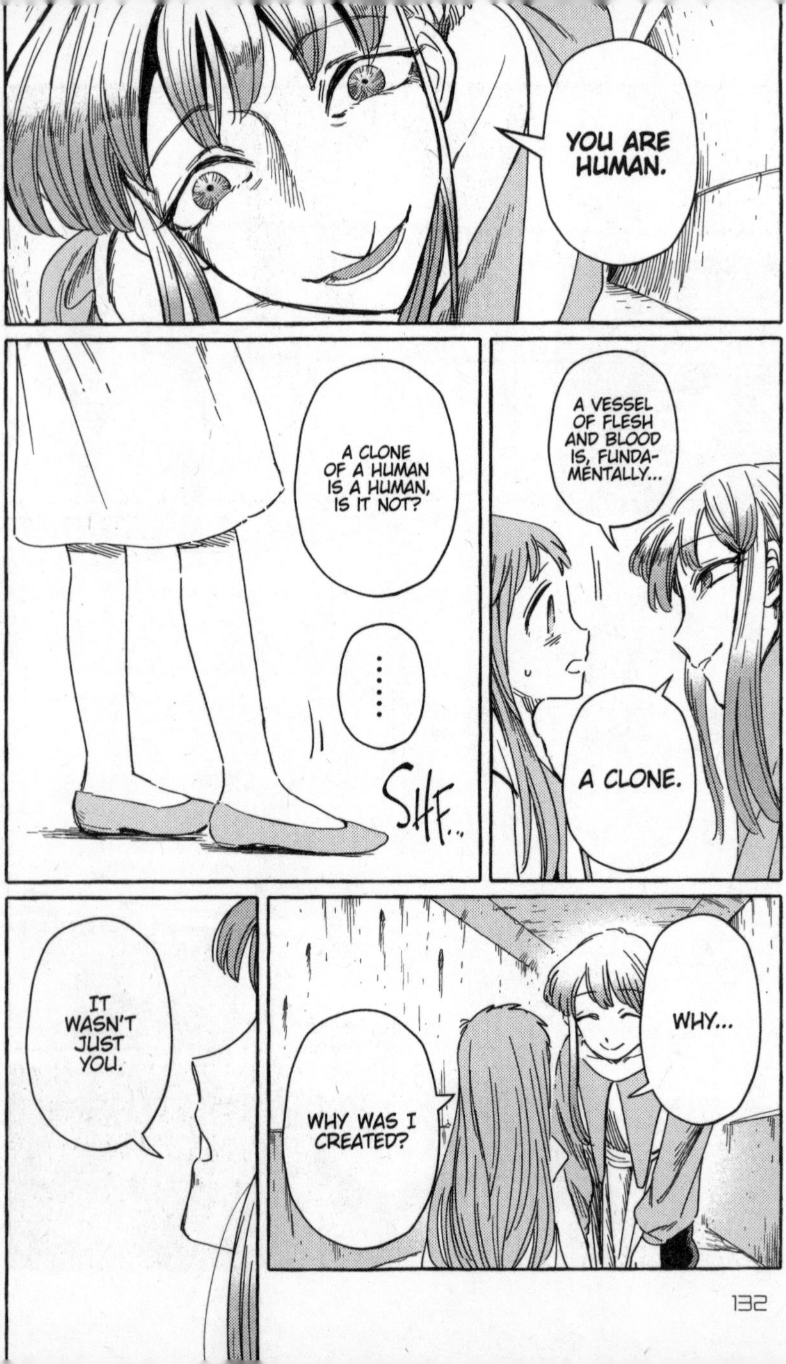
YOU ARE HUMAN.
A VESSEL OF FLESH AND BLOOD IS, FUNDA-MENTALLY...
A CLONE.
A CLONE OF A HUMAN IS A HUMAN, IS IT NOT?
......
SHF...
WHY...
WHY WAS I CREATED?
IT WASN'T JUST YOU.

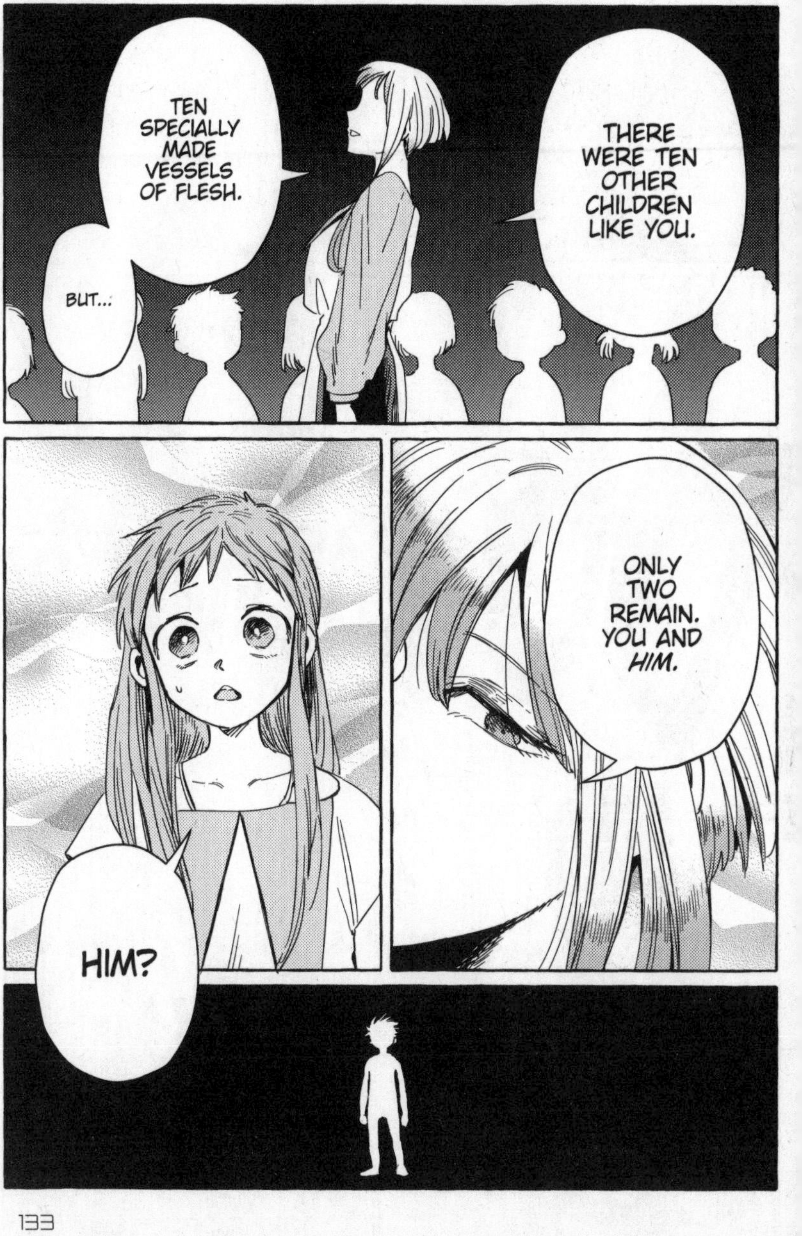
THERE WERE TEN OTHER CHILDREN LIKE YOU.
TEN SPECIALLY MADE VESSELS OF FLESH.
BUT...:
ONLY TWO REMAIN. YOU AND *HIM.*
HIM?

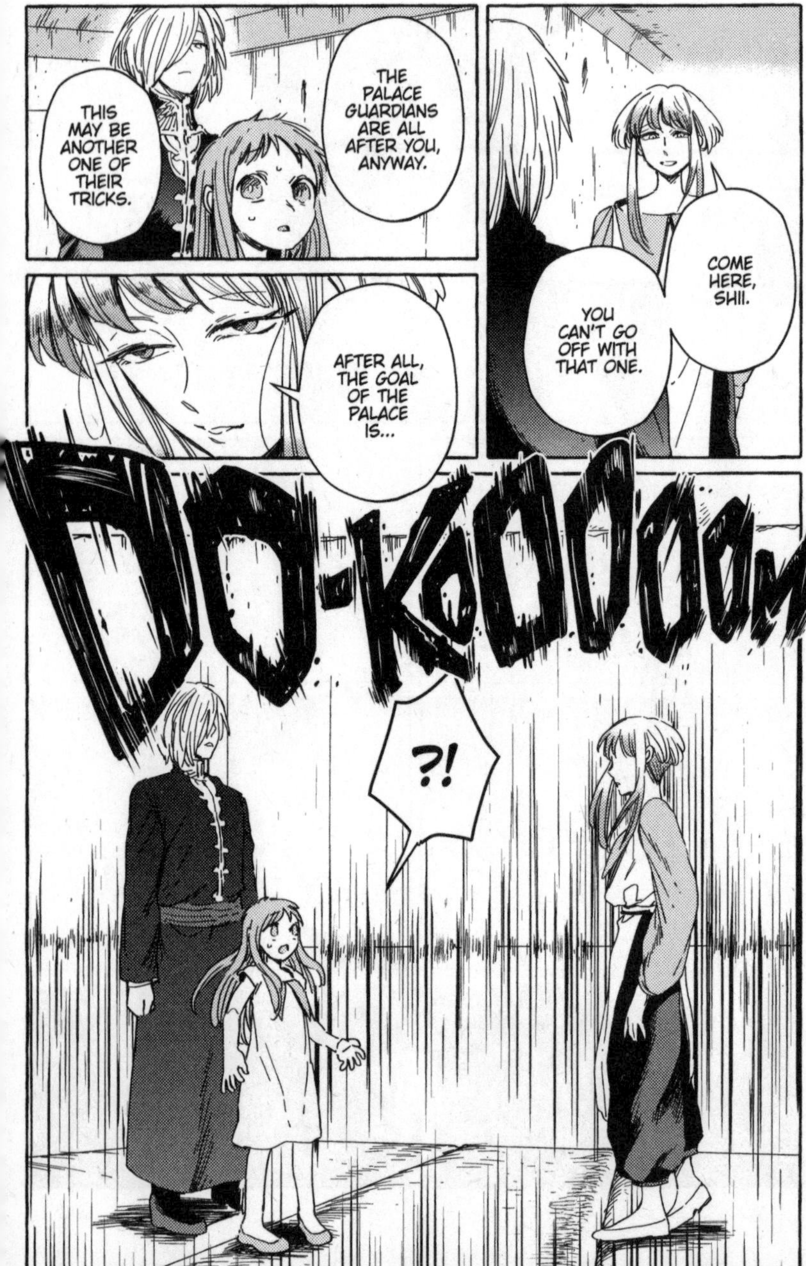
COME HERE, SHII.
YOU CAN'T GO OFF WITH THAT ONE.
THE PALACE GUARDIANS ARE ALL AFTER YOU, ANYWAY.
THIS MAY BE ANOTHER ONE OF THEIR TRICKS.
AFTER ALL, THE GOAL OF THE PALACE IS...
DO-KOOOOOM
?!

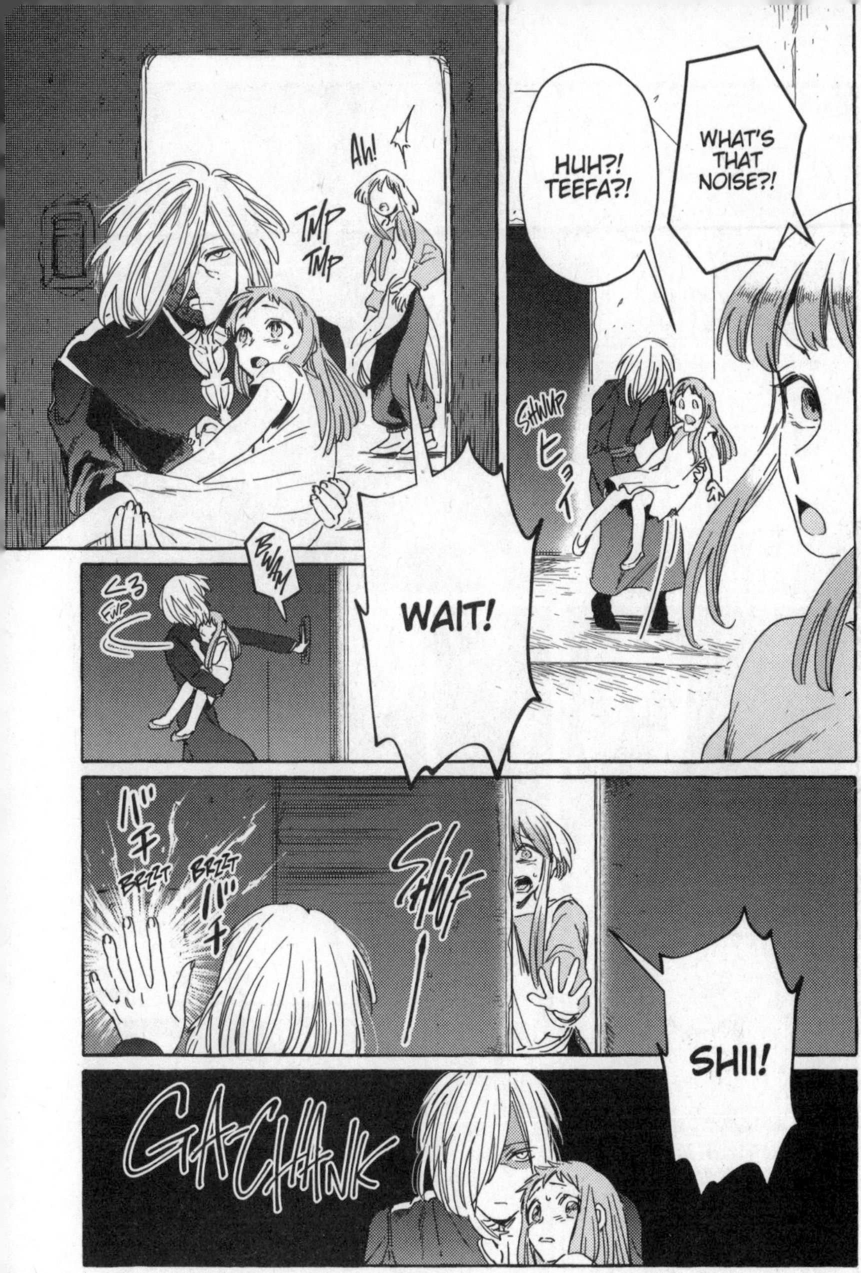
WHAT'S THAT NOISE?!
HUH?! TEEFA?!
SHWUP ヒョイ
Ah!
TMP TMP
BWAM
くる FWP
WAIT!
SHII!
SHIF
バチ BRZZT
BRZZT バチ
GACHINK

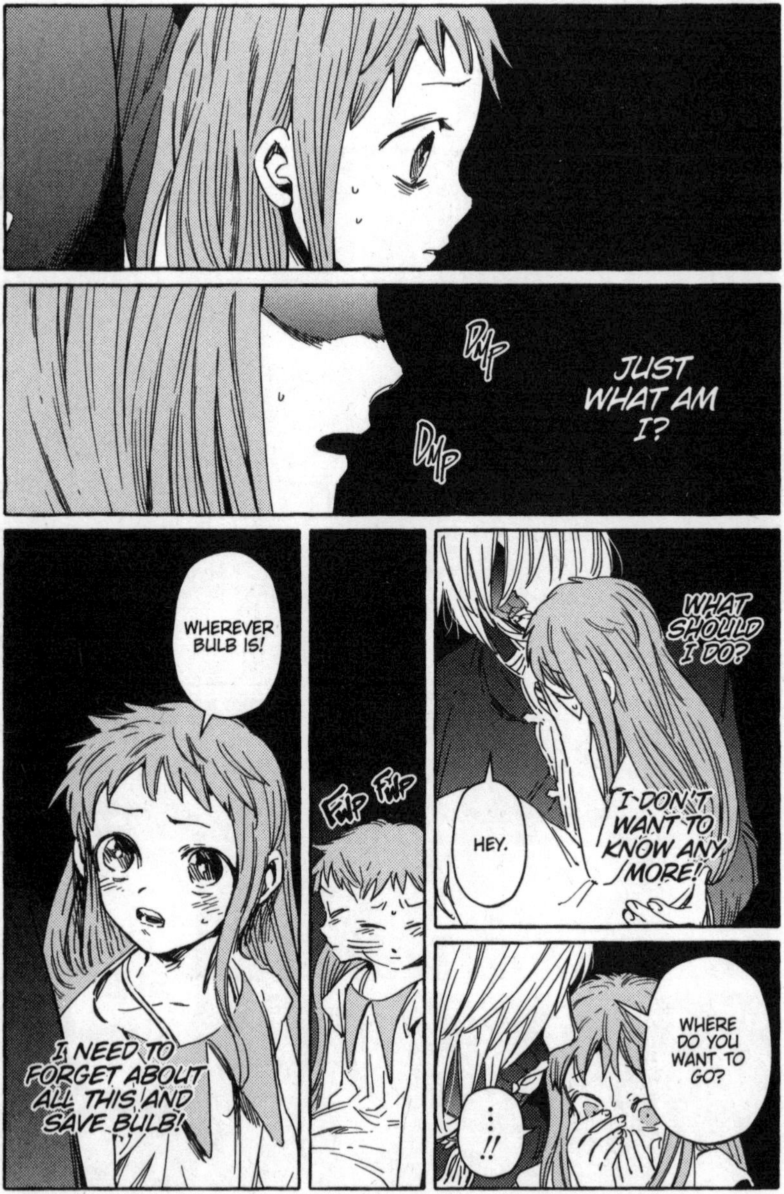
JUST WHAT AM I?
DMP
DMP
WHAT SHOULD I DO?
I-DON'T WANT TO KNOW ANY MORE!
HEY.
WHERE DO YOU WANT TO GO?
...!!
FWP FWP
WHEREVER BULB IS!
I NEED TO FORGET ABOUT ALL THIS AND SAVE BULB!

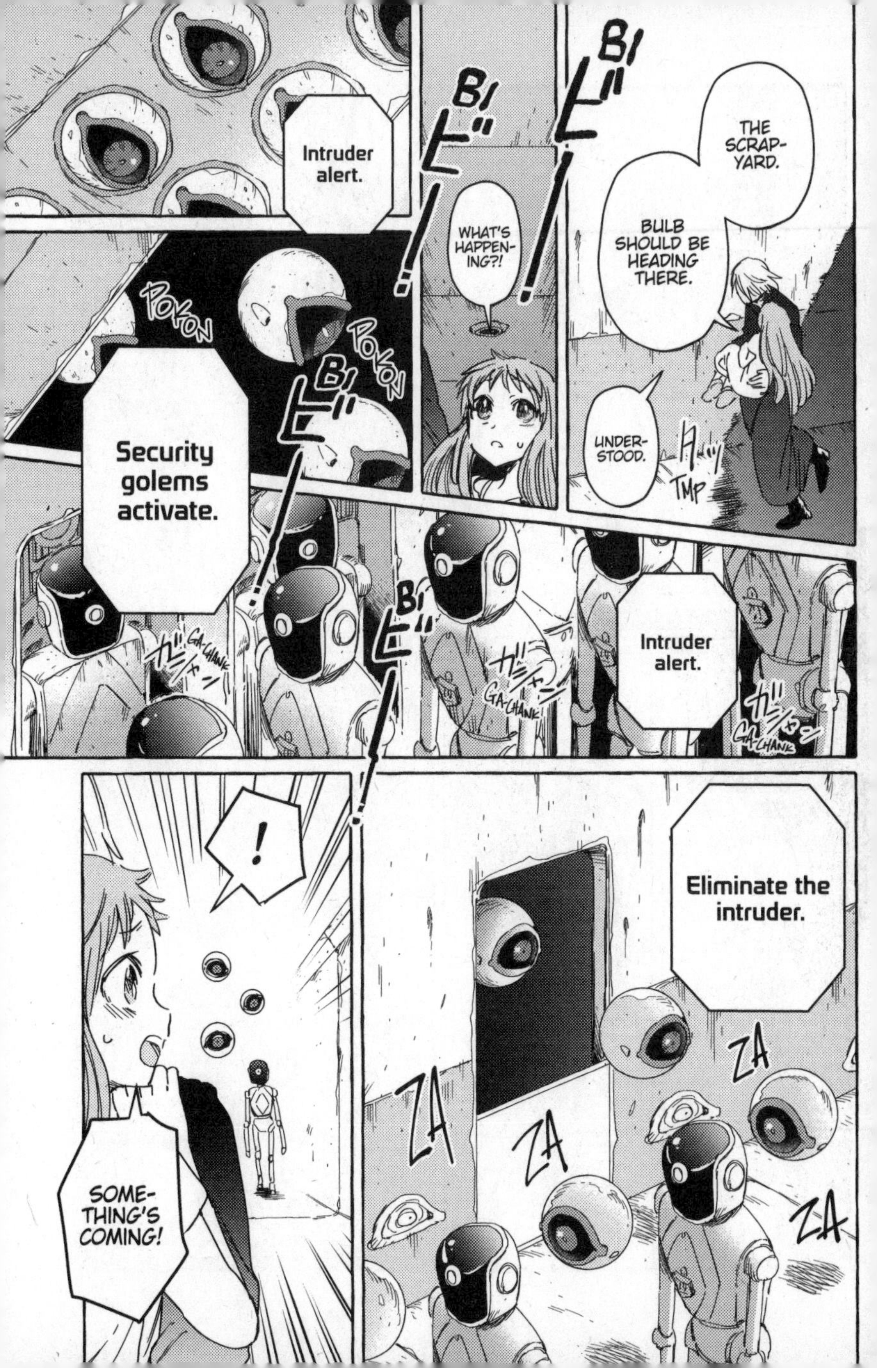
BI
THE SCRAP-YARD.
BULB SHOULD BE HEADING THERE.
UNDER-STOOD.
TMP
BI
WHAT'S HAPPEN-ING?!
Intruder alert.
POKON
POKON
BI
Security golems activate.
Intruder alert.
GA-CHANK
BI
GA-CHANK
GA-CHANK
Eliminate the intruder.
ZA
ZA
ZA
ZA
!
SOME-THING'S COMING!

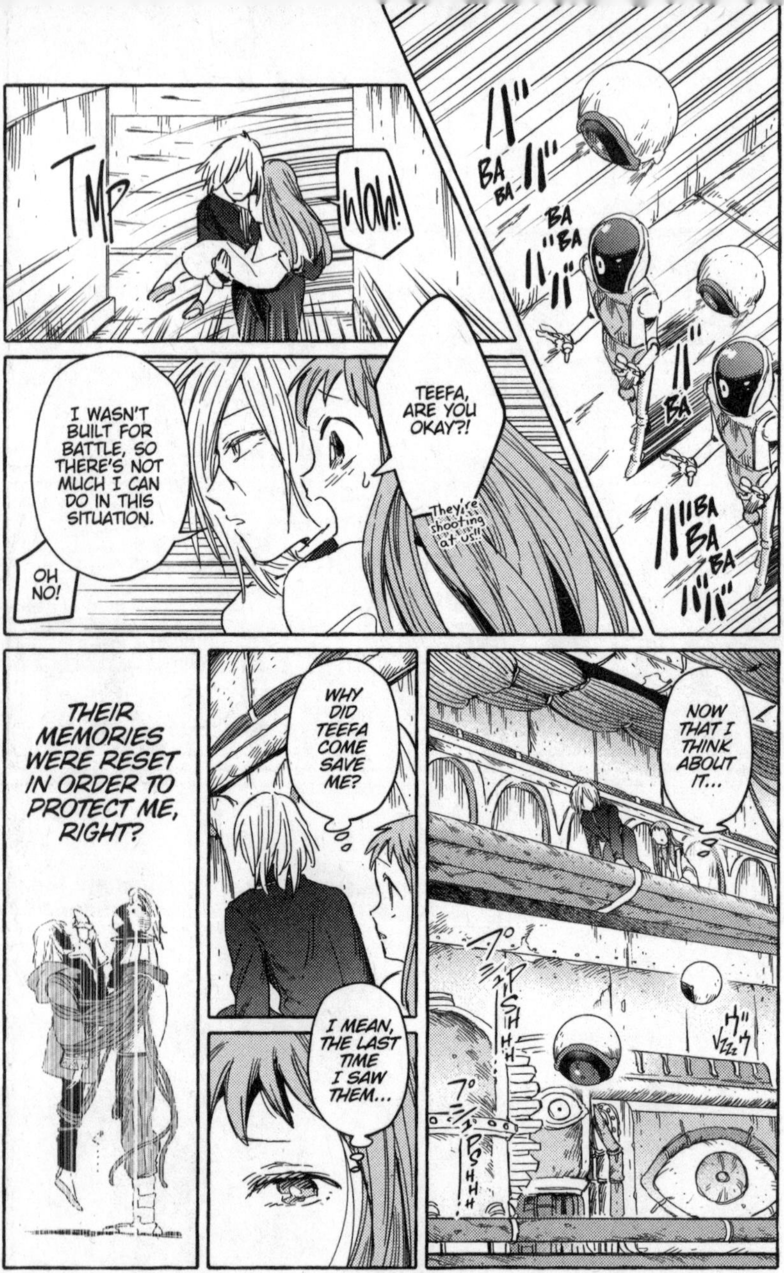
BA BA-
BA "BA
BA
"BA BA BA
TMP
Woah!
TEEFA, ARE YOU OKAY?!
They're shooting at us!!
I WASN'T BUILT FOR BATTLE, SO THERE'S NOT MUCH I CAN DO IN THIS SITUATION.
OH NO!
NOW THAT I THINK ABOUT IT...
PSHHH
VZZZ
PSHHH
WHY DID TEEFA COME SAVE ME?
I MEAN, THE LAST TIME I SAW THEM...
THEIR MEMORIES WERE RESET IN ORDER TO PROTECT ME, RIGHT?

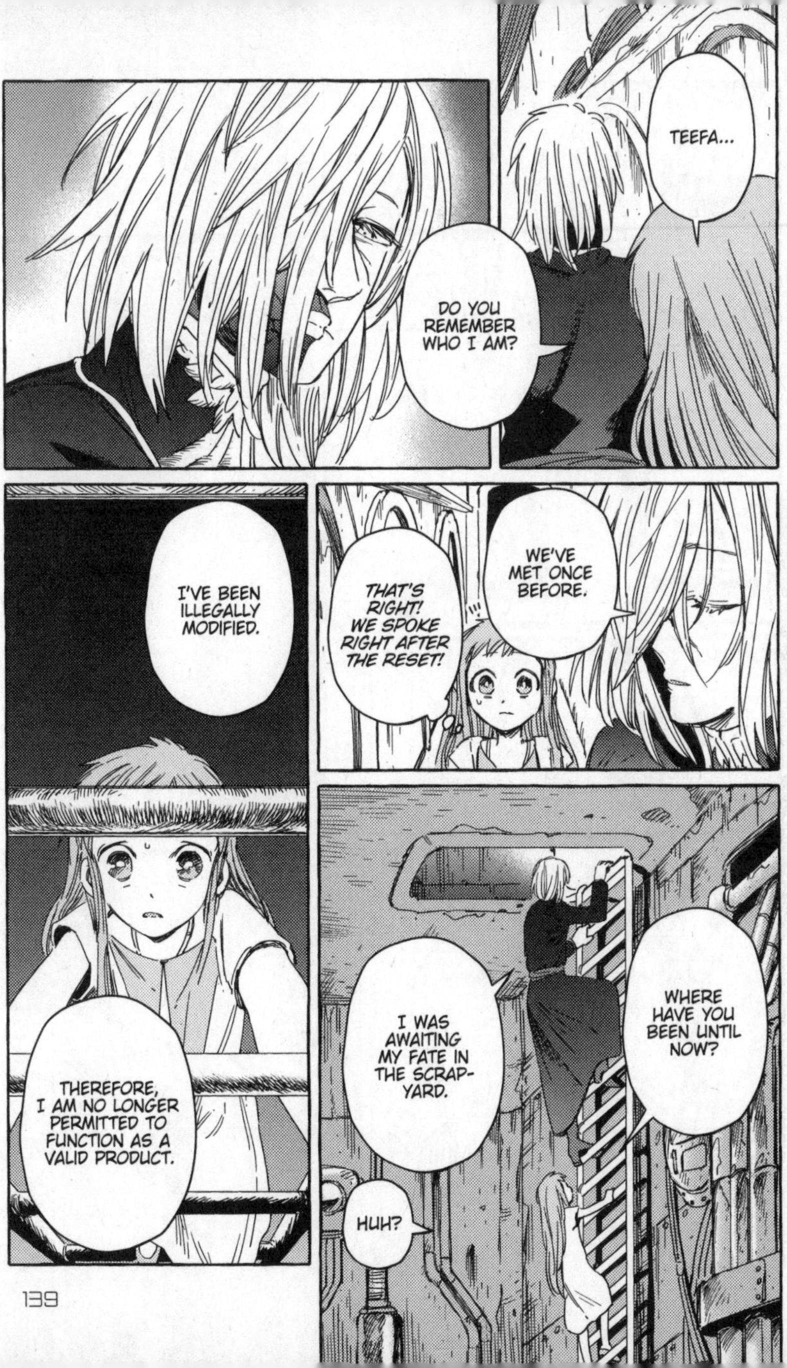
TEEFA...
DO YOU REMEMBER WHO I AM?
WE'VE MET ONCE BEFORE.
THAT'S RIGHT! WE SPOKE RIGHT AFTER THE RESET!
!!!
WHERE HAVE YOU BEEN UNTIL NOW?
I WAS AWAITING MY FATE IN THE SCRAP-YARD.
HUH?
I'VE BEEN ILLEGALLY MODIFIED.
THEREFORE, I AM NO LONGER PERMITTED TO FUNCTION AS A VALID PRODUCT.

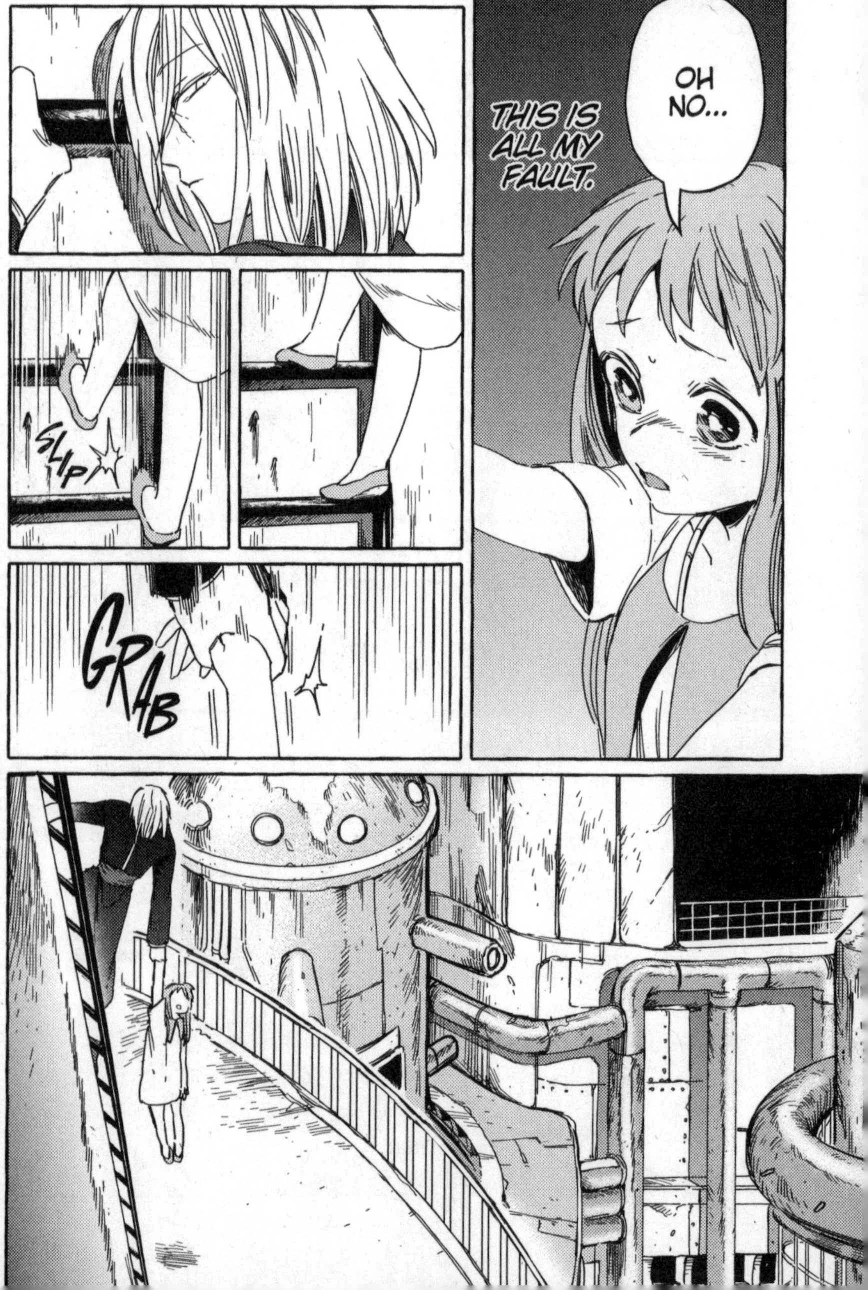
OH NO...
THIS IS ALL MY FAULT.
SLIP
GRAB

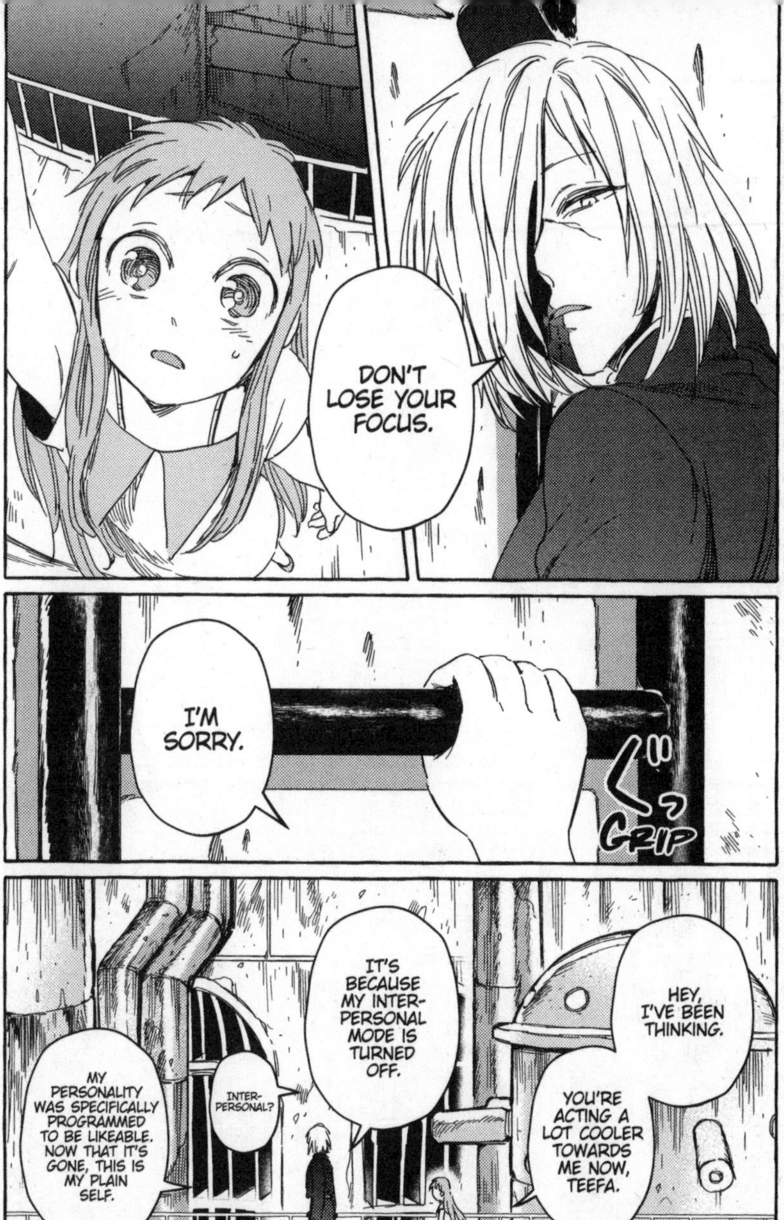
DON'T LOSE YOUR FOCUS.
I'M SORRY.
ぐっ
GRIP
HEY, I'VE BEEN THINKING.
YOU'RE ACTING A LOT COOLER TOWARDS ME NOW, TEEFA.
IT'S BECAUSE MY INTER-PERSONAL MODE IS TURNED OFF.
INTER-PERSONAL?
MY PERSONALITY WAS SPECIFICALLY PROGRAMMED TO BE LIKEABLE. NOW THAT IT'S GONE, THIS IS MY PLAIN SELF.

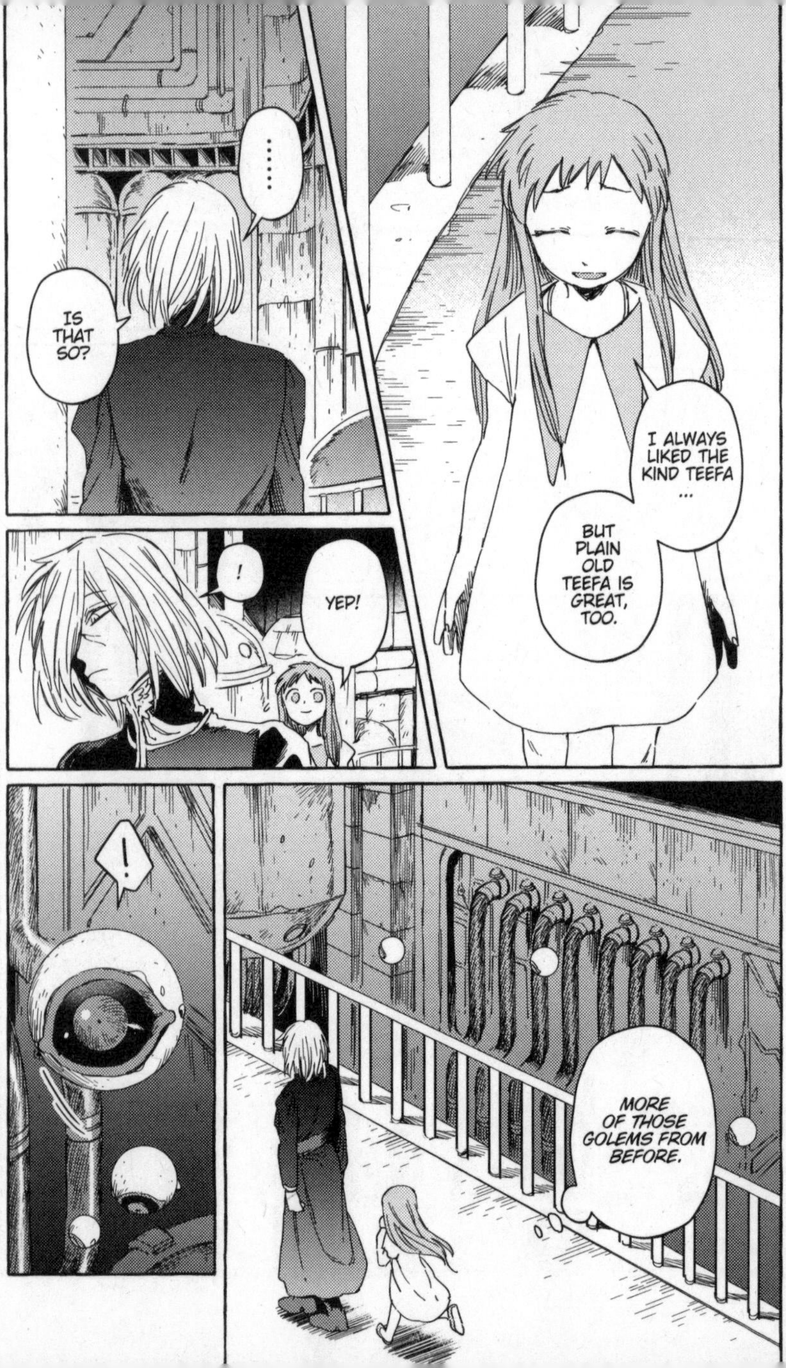
I ALWAYS LIKED THE KIND TEEFA ...
BUT PLAIN OLD TEEFA IS GREAT, TOO.
......
IS THAT SO?
!
YEP!
MORE OF THOSE GOLEMS FROM BEFORE.
!

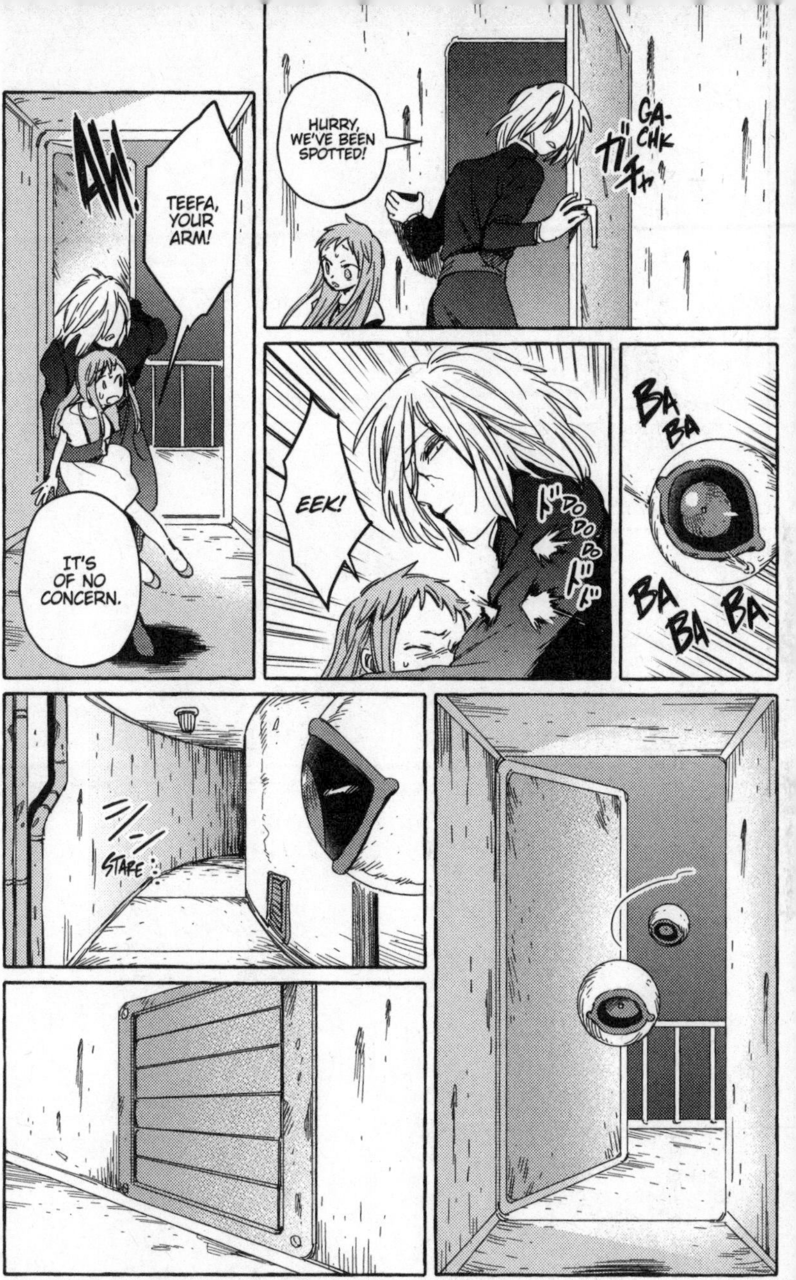
HURRY, WE'VE BEEN SPOTTED!
GA-CHK
ガチャ
BA BA
BA BA BA BA
EEK!
ドドドドド
DO DO DO DO
AH!
TEEFA, YOUR ARM!
IT'S OF NO CONCERN.
STARE

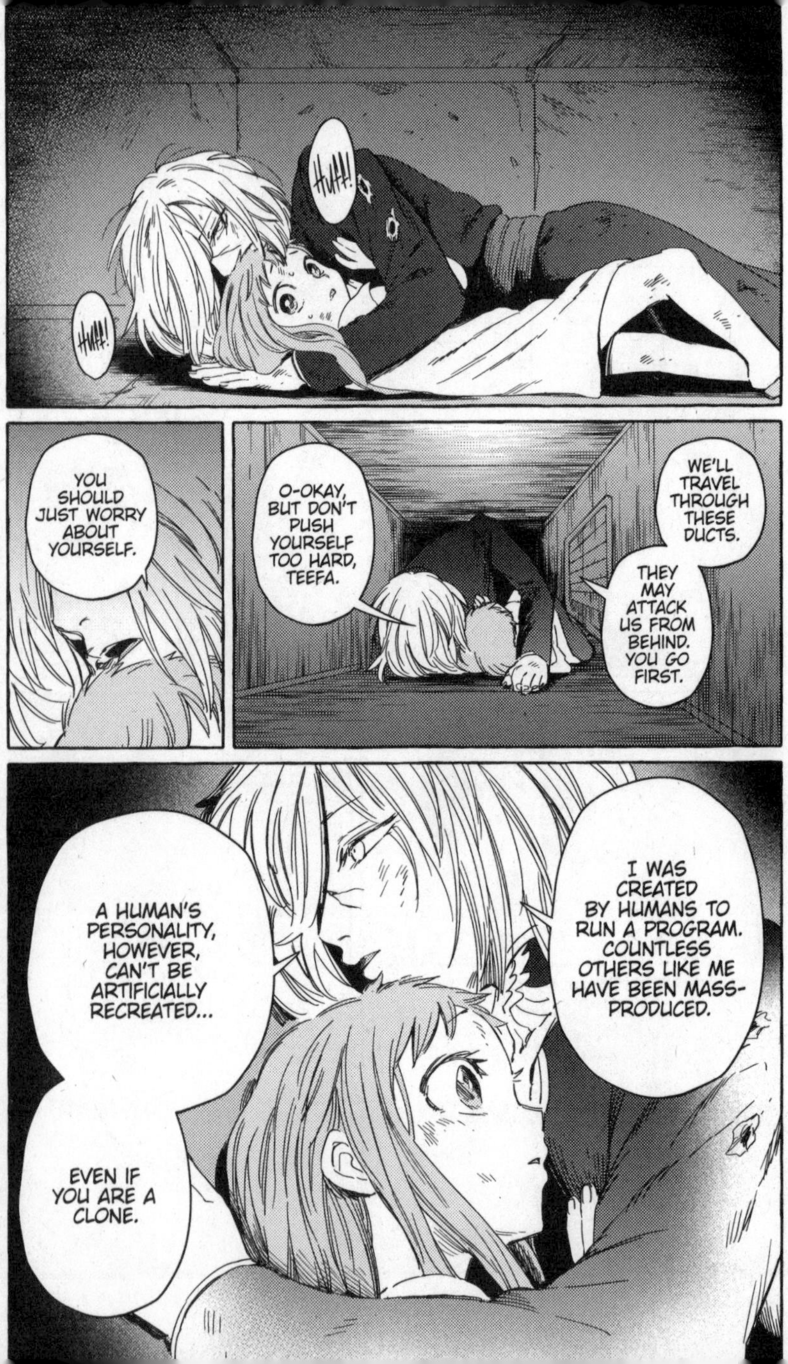
HUFF!
HUFF!
WE'LL TRAVEL THROUGH THESE DUCTS.
THEY MAY ATTACK US FROM BEHIND. YOU GO FIRST.
O-OKAY, BUT DON'T PUSH YOURSELF TOO HARD, TEEFA.
YOU SHOULD JUST WORRY ABOUT YOURSELF.
I WAS CREATED BY HUMANS TO RUN A PROGRAM. COUNTLESS OTHERS LIKE ME HAVE BEEN MASS-PRODUCED.
A HUMAN'S PERSONALITY, HOWEVER, CAN'T BE ARTIFICIALLY RECREATED...
EVEN IF YOU ARE A CLONE.

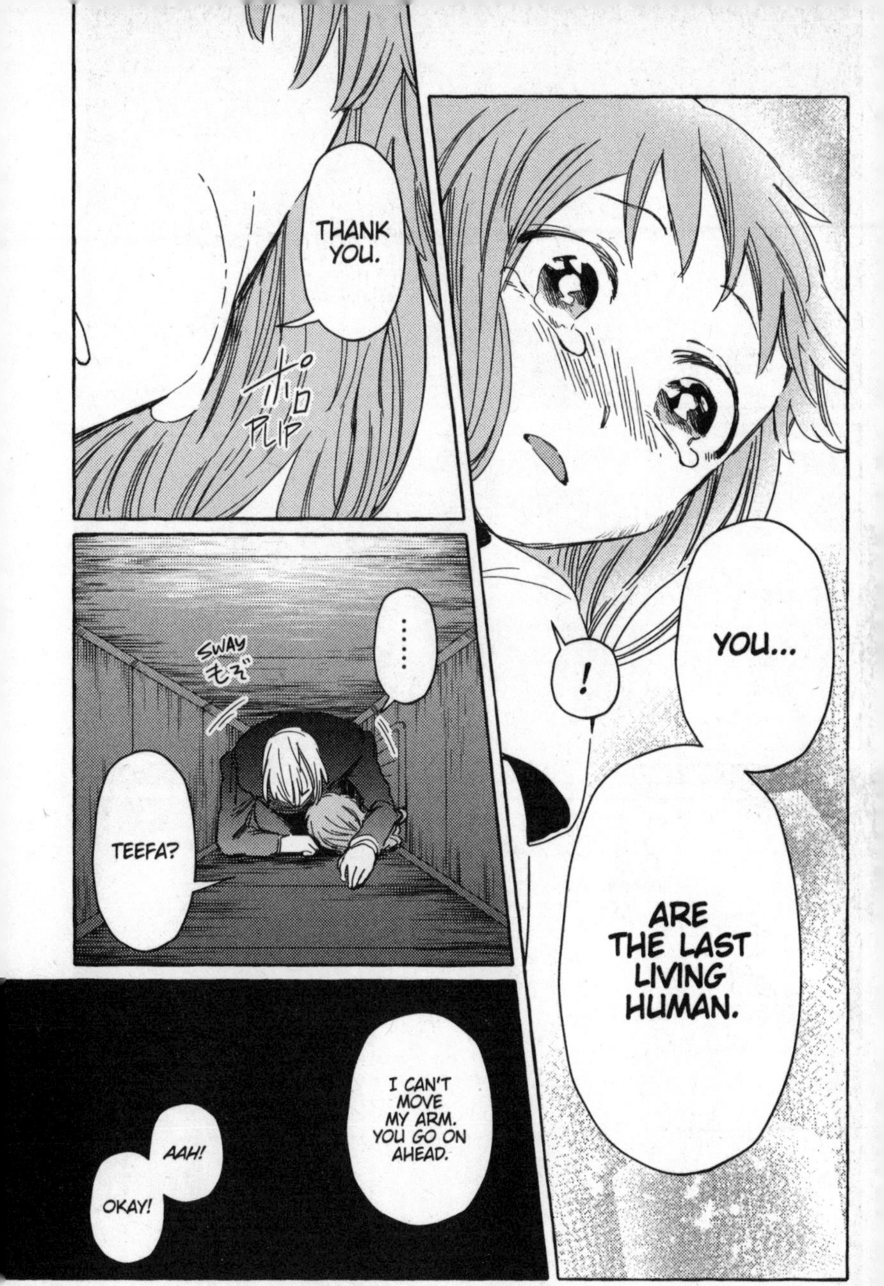
THANK YOU.
ポロ PLIP
!
YOU...
ARE THE LAST LIVING HUMAN.
......
SWAY もぞ
TEEFA?
I CAN'T MOVE MY ARM. YOU GO ON AHEAD.
AAH!
OKAY!

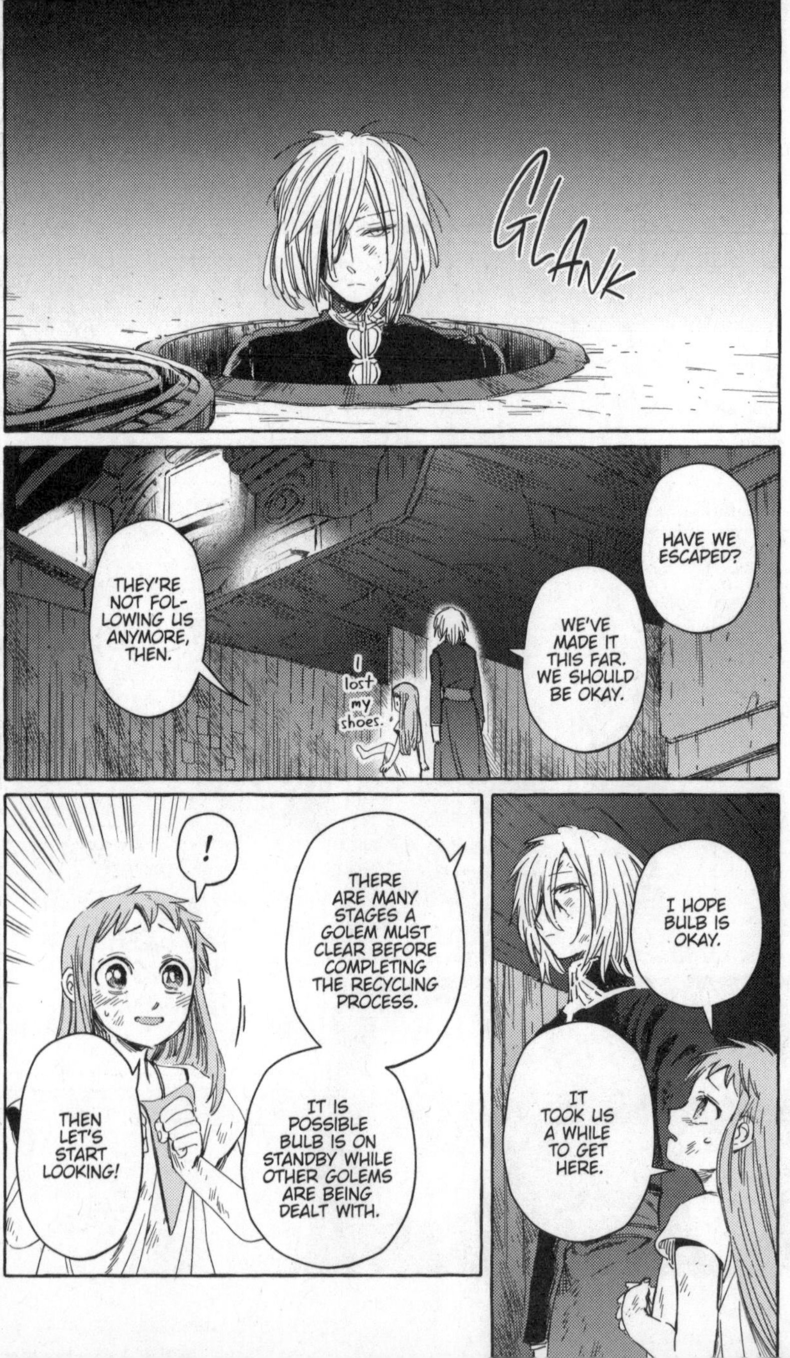
GLANK
HAVE WE ESCAPED?
WE'VE MADE IT THIS FAR. WE SHOULD BE OKAY.
I lost my shoes.
THEY'RE NOT FOL-LOWING US ANYMORE, THEN.
I HOPE BULB IS OKAY.
IT TOOK US A WHILE TO GET HERE.
THERE ARE MANY STAGES A GOLEM MUST CLEAR BEFORE COMPLETING THE RECYCLING PROCESS.
!
IT IS POSSIBLE BULB IS ON STANDBY WHILE OTHER GOLEMS ARE BEING DEALT WITH.
THEN LET'S START LOOKING!

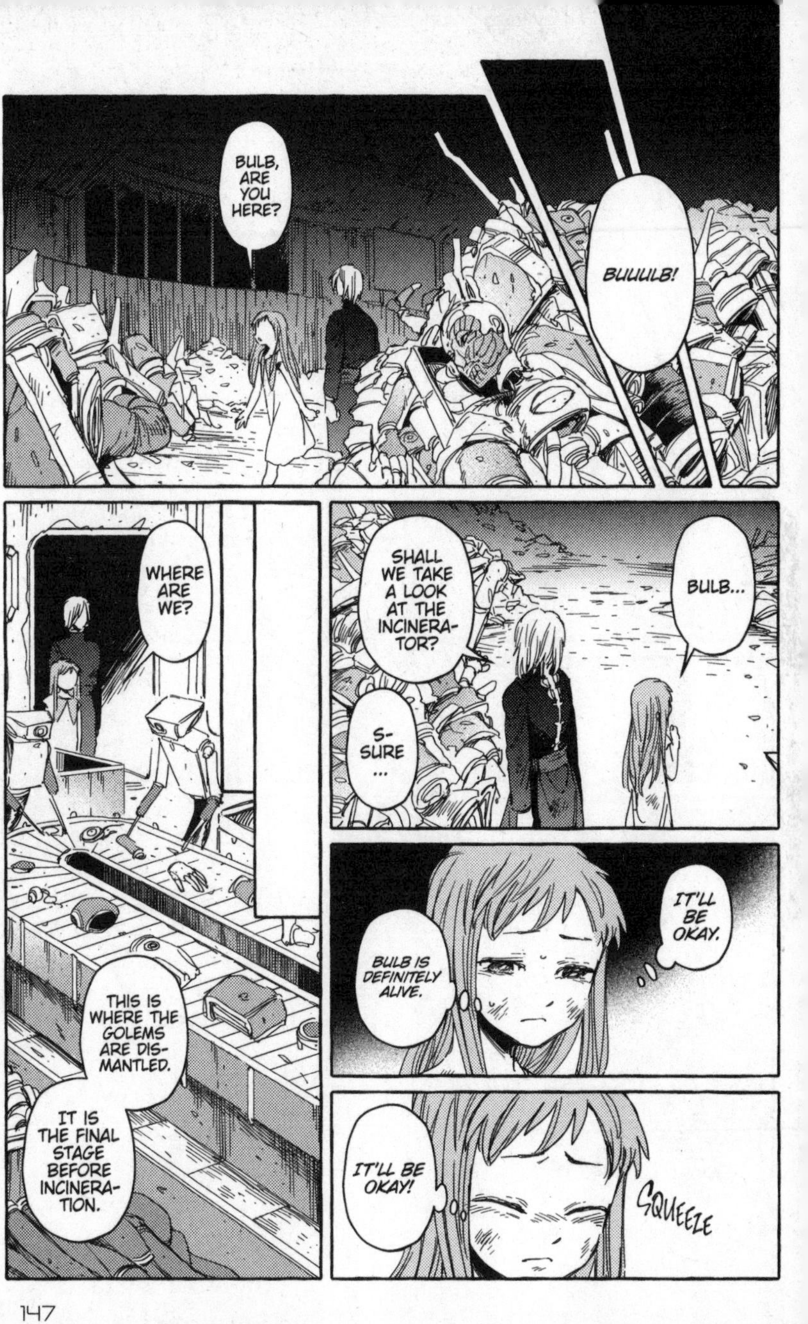
BULB, ARE YOU HERE?
BUUULB!
BULB...
SHALL WE TAKE A LOOK AT THE INCINERA-TOR?
S-SURE ...
IT'LL BE OKAY.
BULB IS DEFINITELY ALIVE.
IT'LL BE OKAY!
SQUEEZE
WHERE ARE WE?
THIS IS WHERE THE GOLEMS ARE DIS-MANTLED.
IT IS THE FINAL STAGE BEFORE INCINERA-TION.

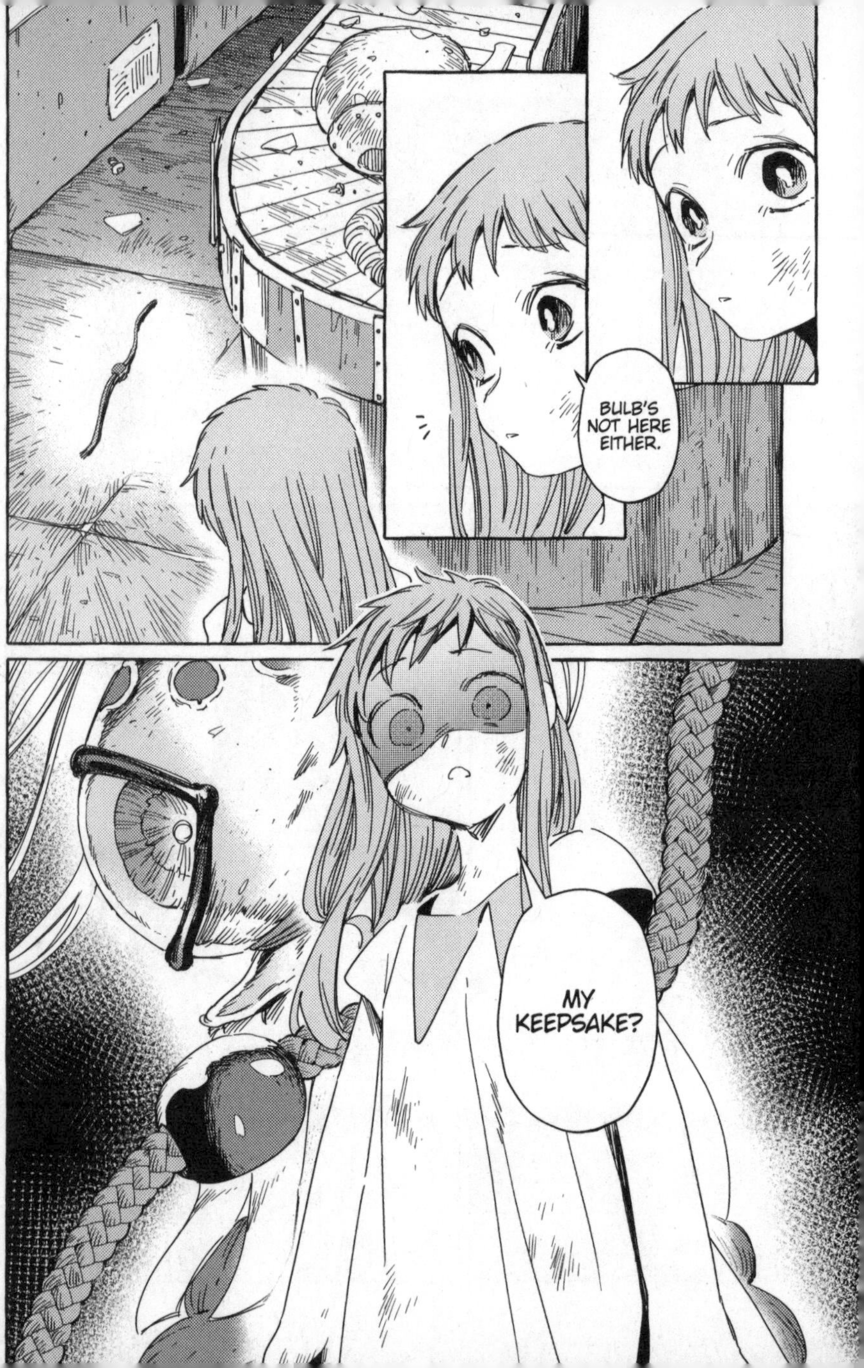
BULB'S NOT HERE EITHER.
MY KEEPSAKE?

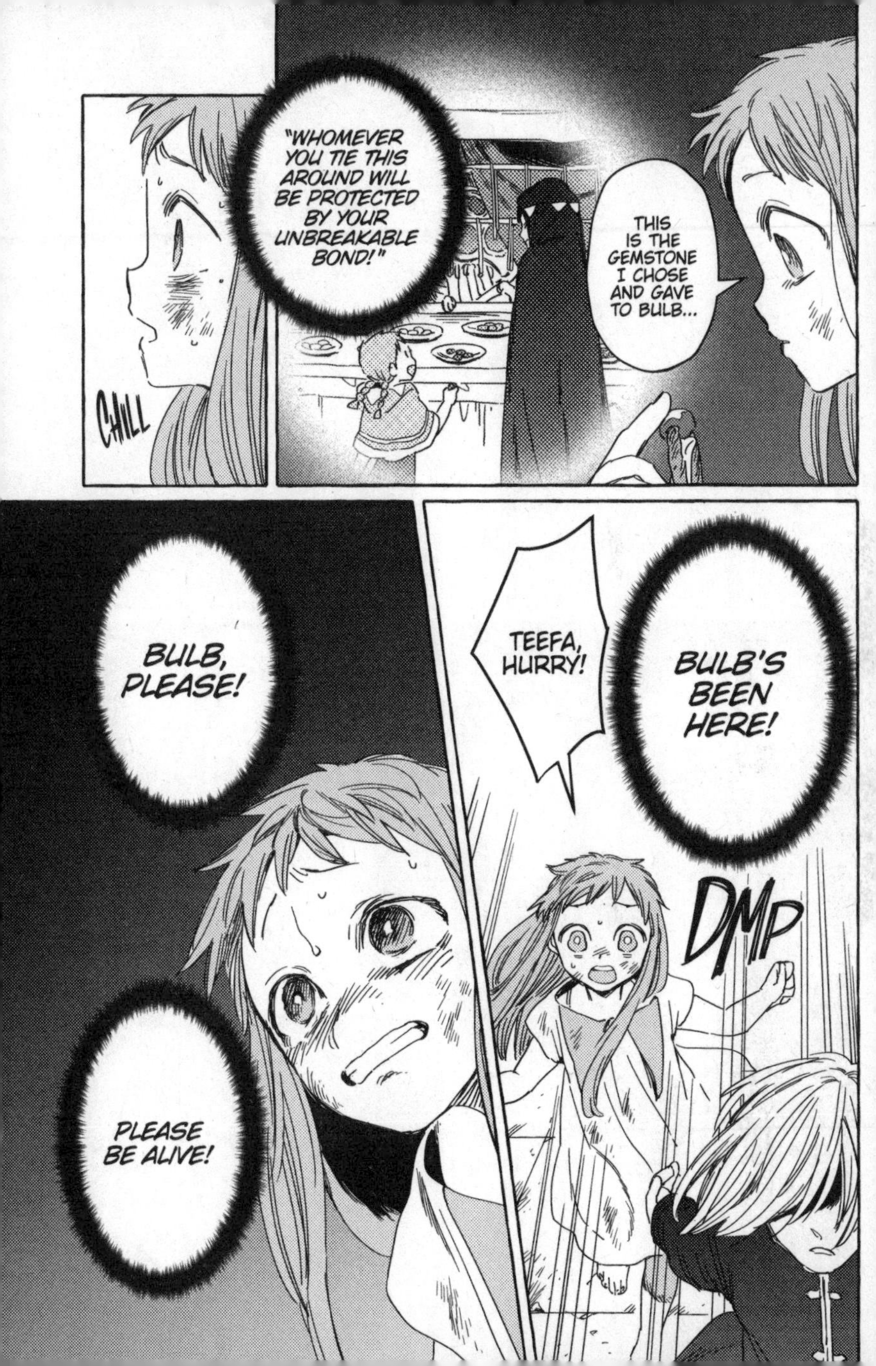
THIS IS THE GEMSTONE I CHOSE AND GAVE TO BULB...
"WHOMEVER YOU TIE THIS AROUND WILL BE PROTECTED BY YOUR UNBREAKABLE BOND!"
CHILL
BULB'S BEEN HERE!
TEEFA, HURRY!
DMP
BULB, PLEASE!
PLEASE BE ALIVE!

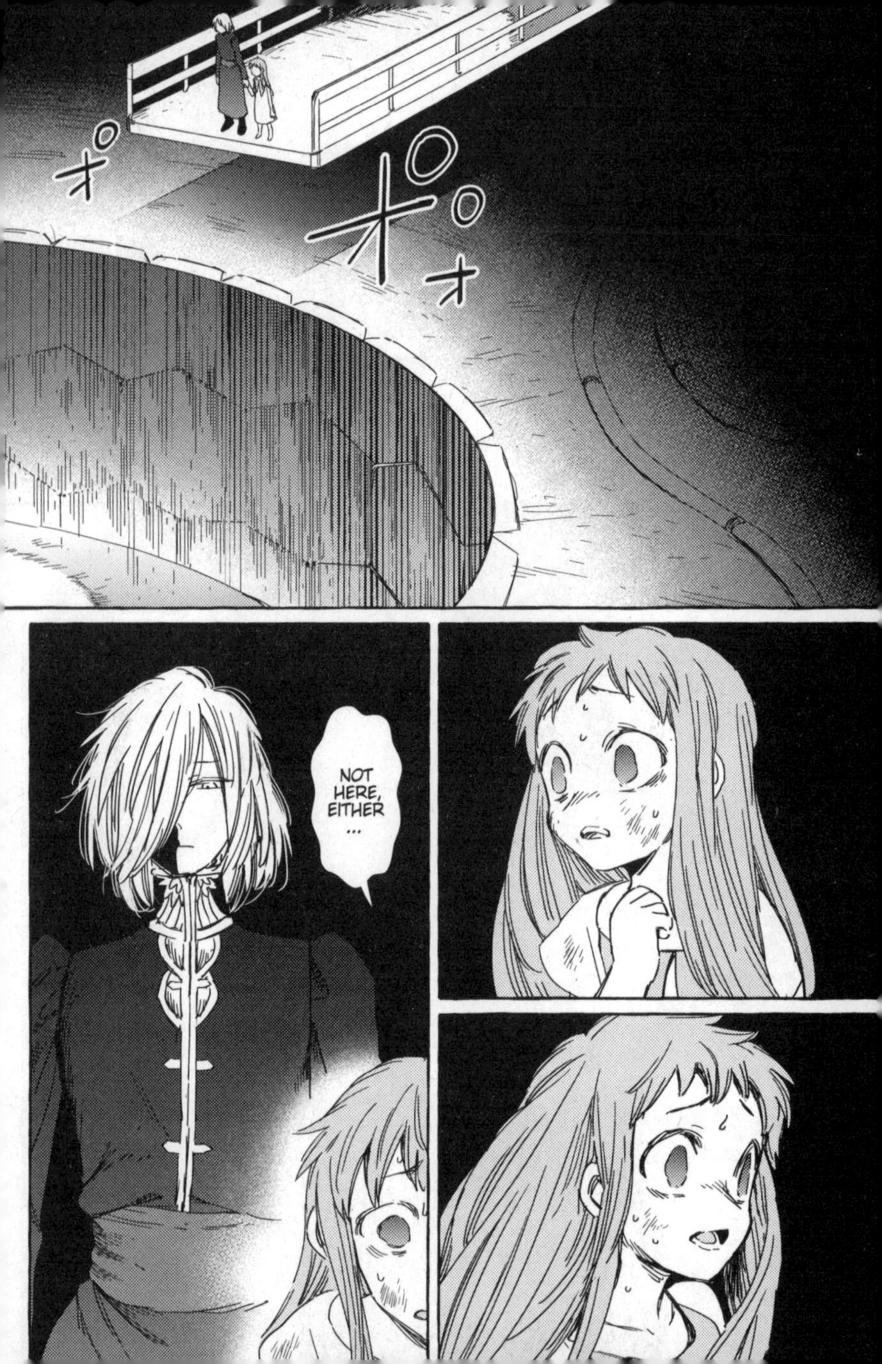
ポォ
ポォ
NOT HERE, EITHER ...

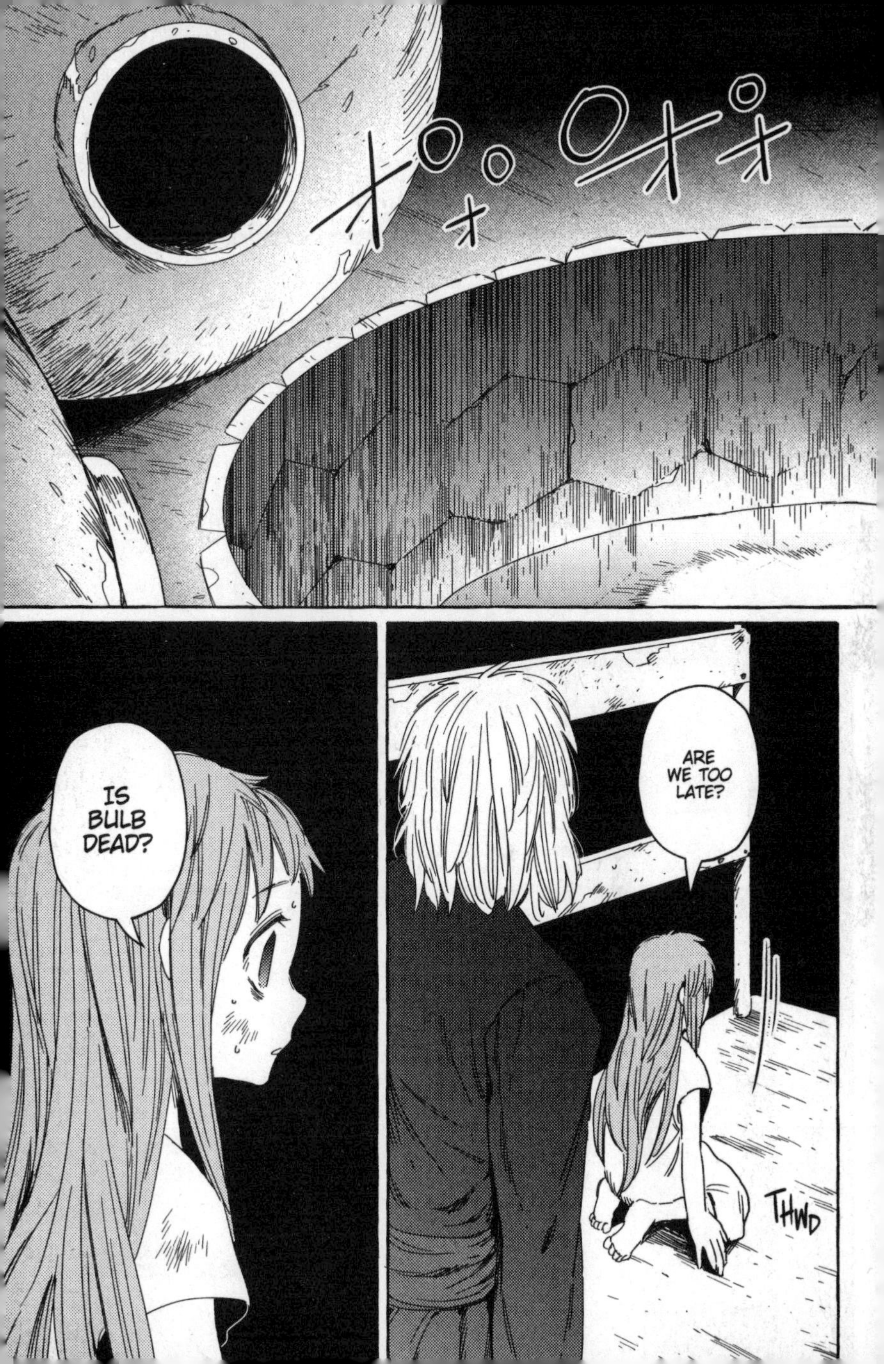
ARE WE TOO LATE?
THWD
IS BULB DEAD?

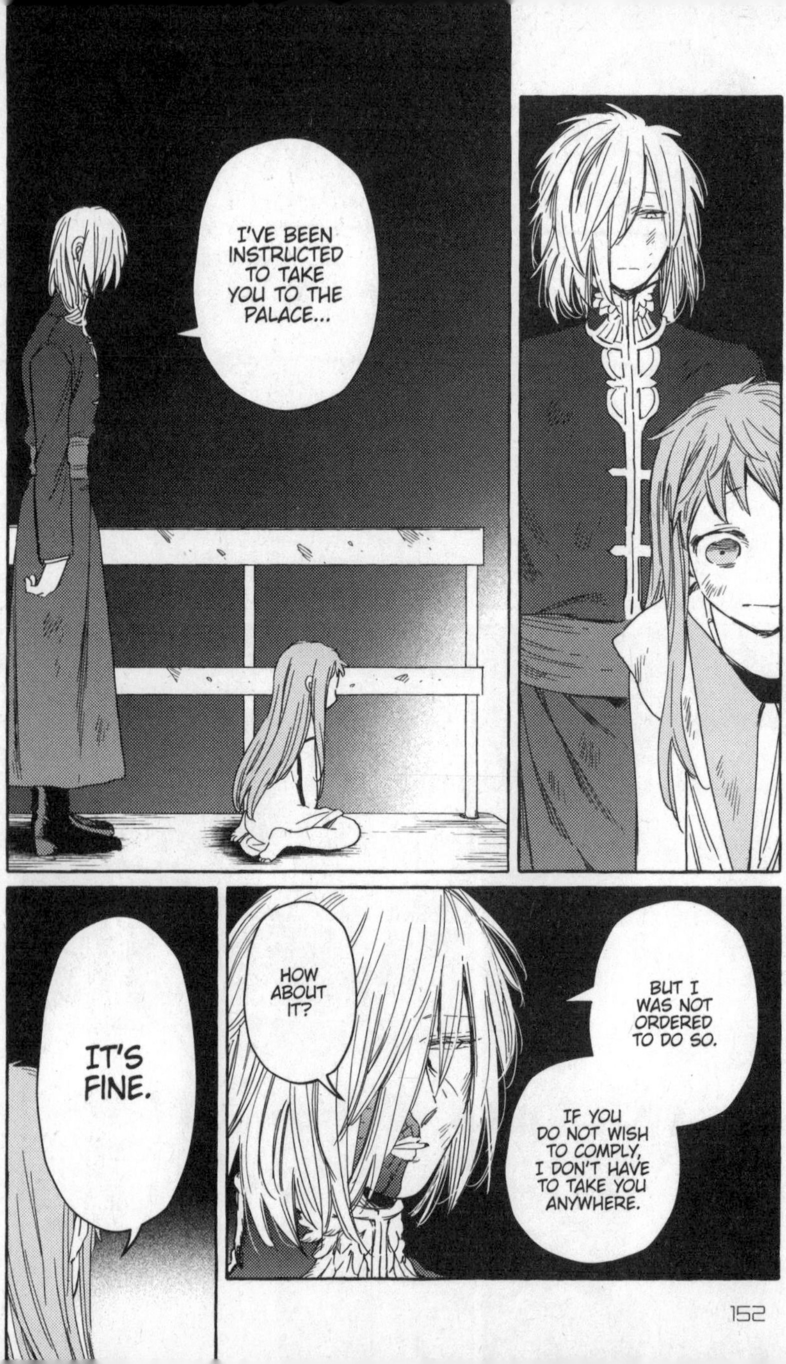
I'VE BEEN INSTRUCTED TO TAKE YOU TO THE PALACE...
BUT I WAS NOT ORDERED TO DO SO.
IF YOU DO NOT WISH TO COMPLY, I DON'T HAVE TO TAKE YOU ANYWHERE.
HOW ABOUT IT?
IT'S FINE.

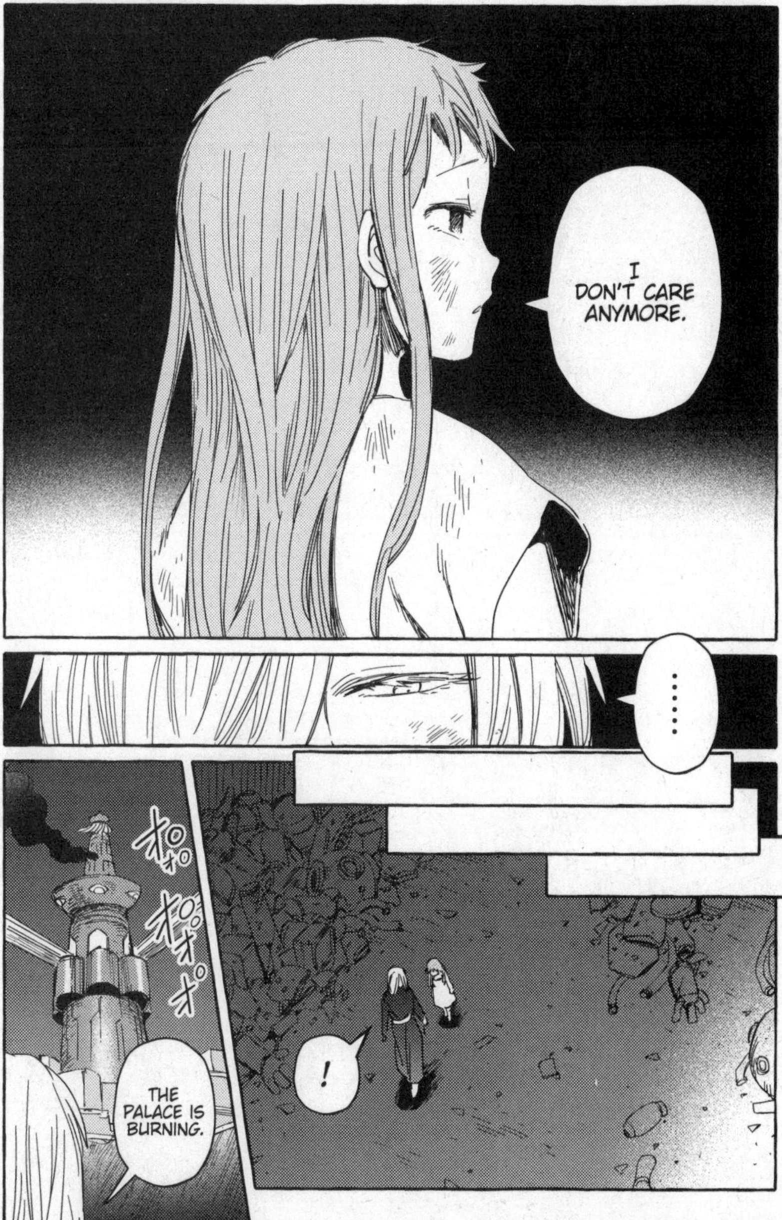
I DON'T CARE ANYMORE.
......
!
THE PALACE IS BURNING.

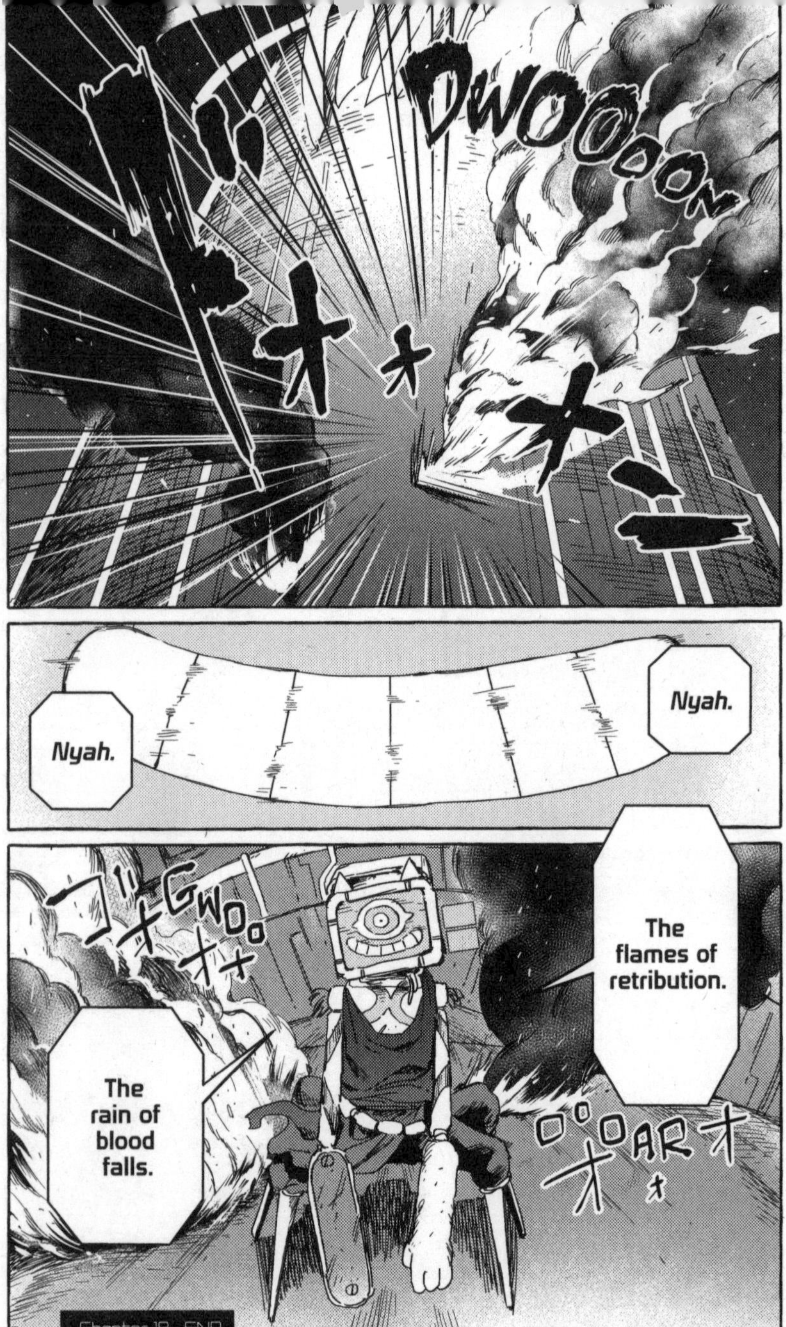
DWOOOOOON
Nyah.
Nyah.
The flames of retribution.
The rain of blood falls.
GWOO
OOOAR
Chapter 18 - END

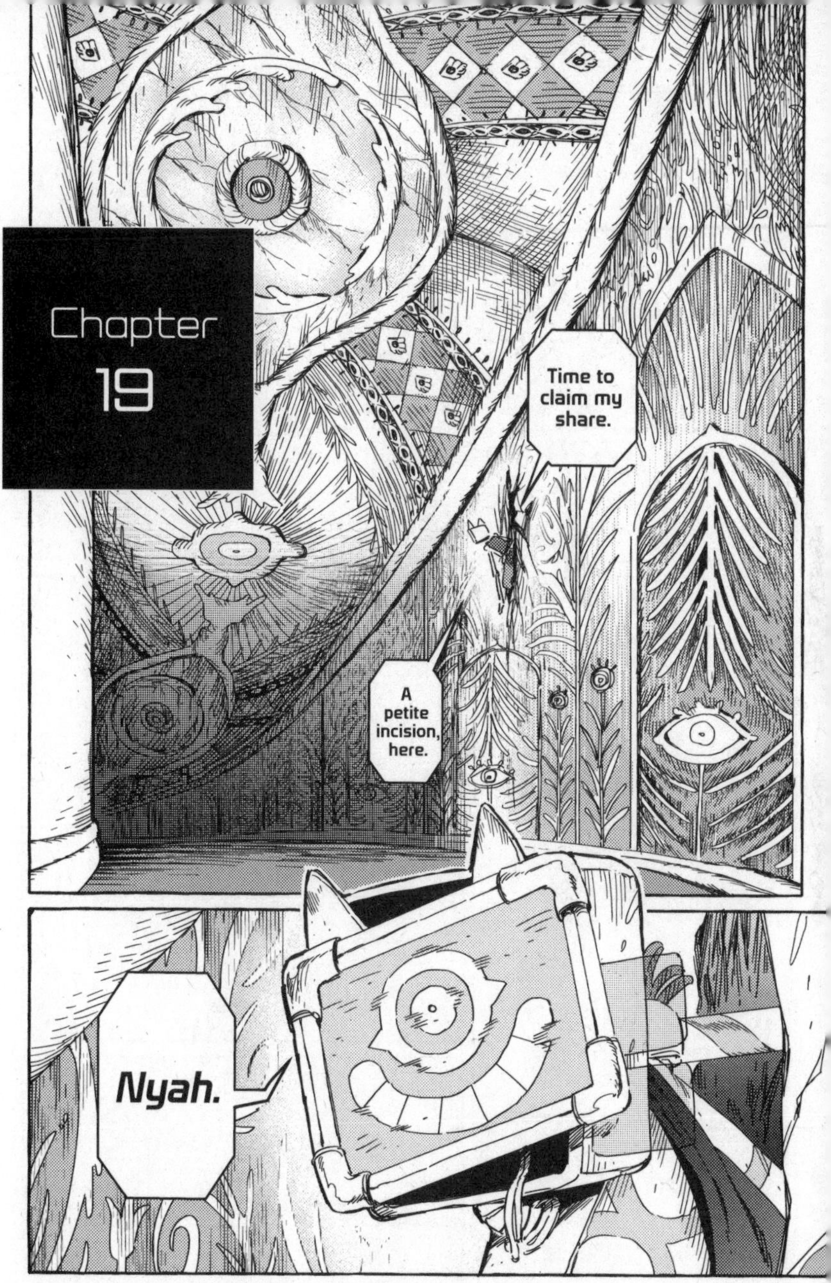
Chapter 19
Time to claim my share.
A petite incision, here.
Nyah.

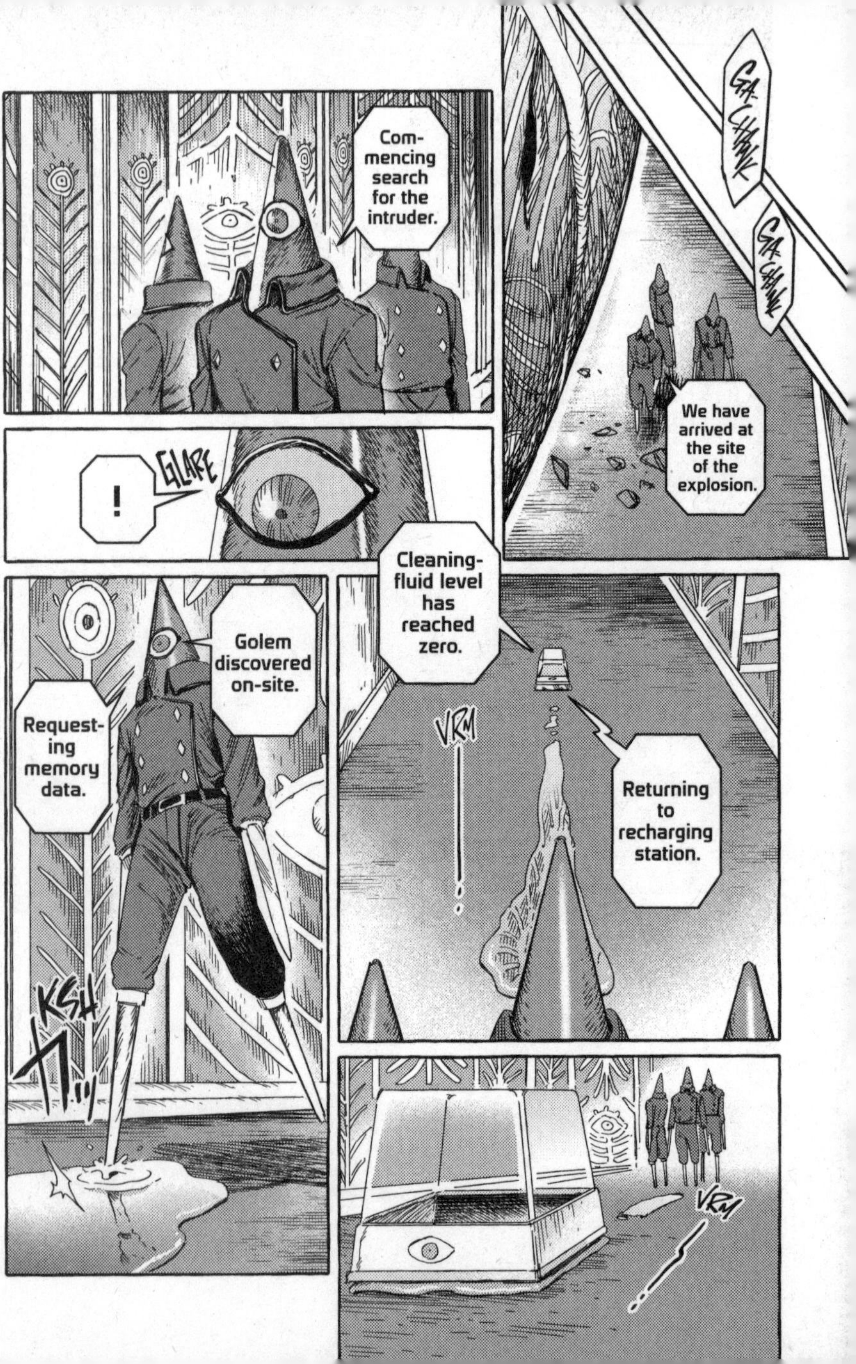
GA-CHANK
GA-CHANK
We have arrived at the site of the explosion.
Com-mencing search for the intruder.
GLARE
!
Cleaning-fluid level has reached zero.
VRM
Returning to recharging station.
Golem discovered on-site.
Request-ing memory data.
KSH
VRM

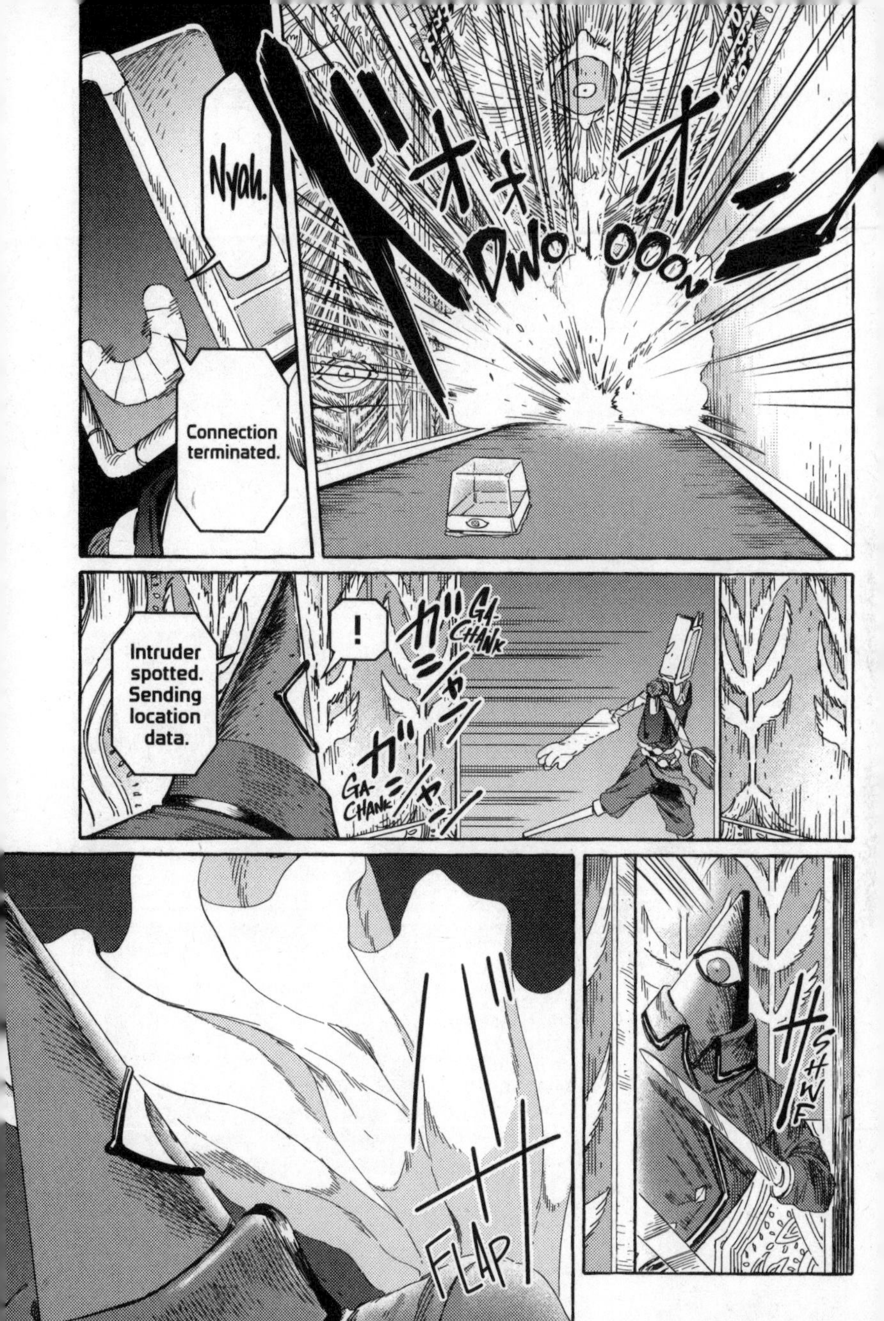
DWO OOON
Nyah.
Connection terminated.
GA-CHANK
!
Intruder spotted. Sending location data.
GA-CHANK
SHWF
FLAP

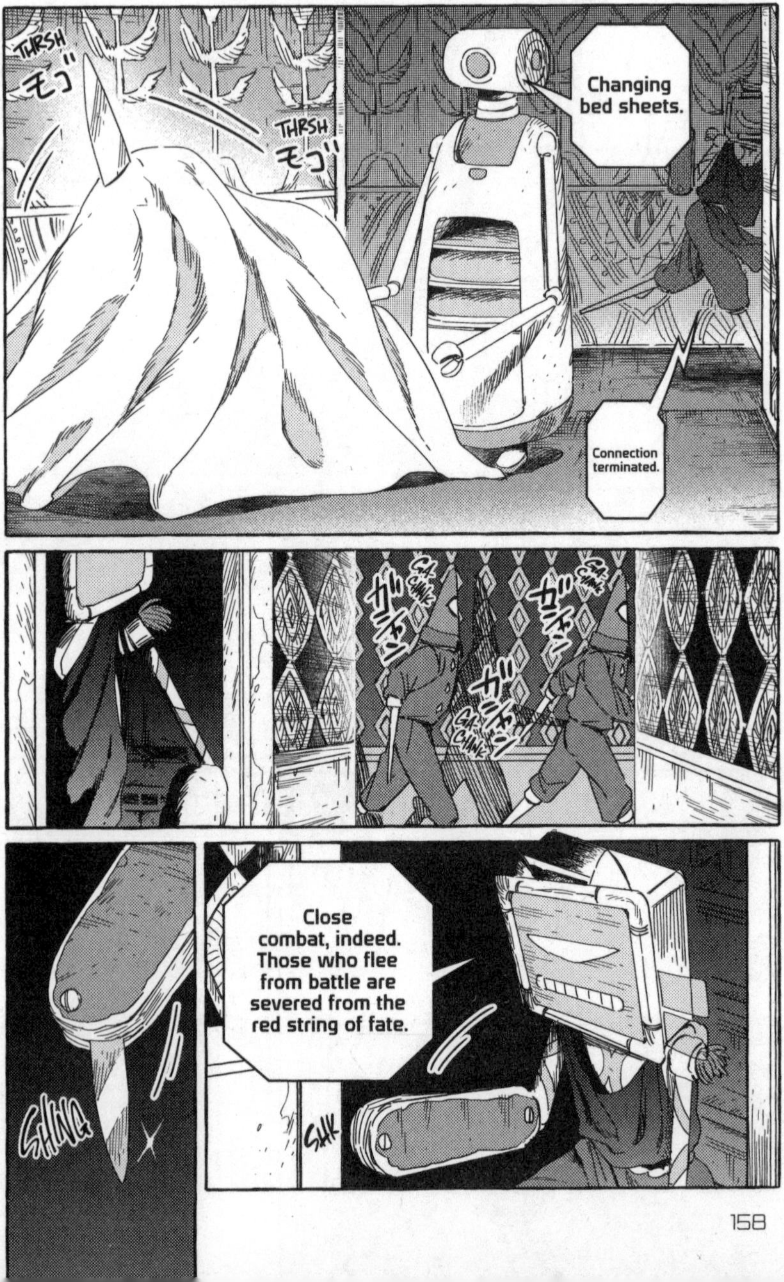
Changing bed sheets.
Connection terminated.
THRSH
THRSH
GA-CHANK
GA-CHANK
GA-CHANK
Close combat, indeed. Those who flee from battle are severed from the red string of fate.
SHK
SHING

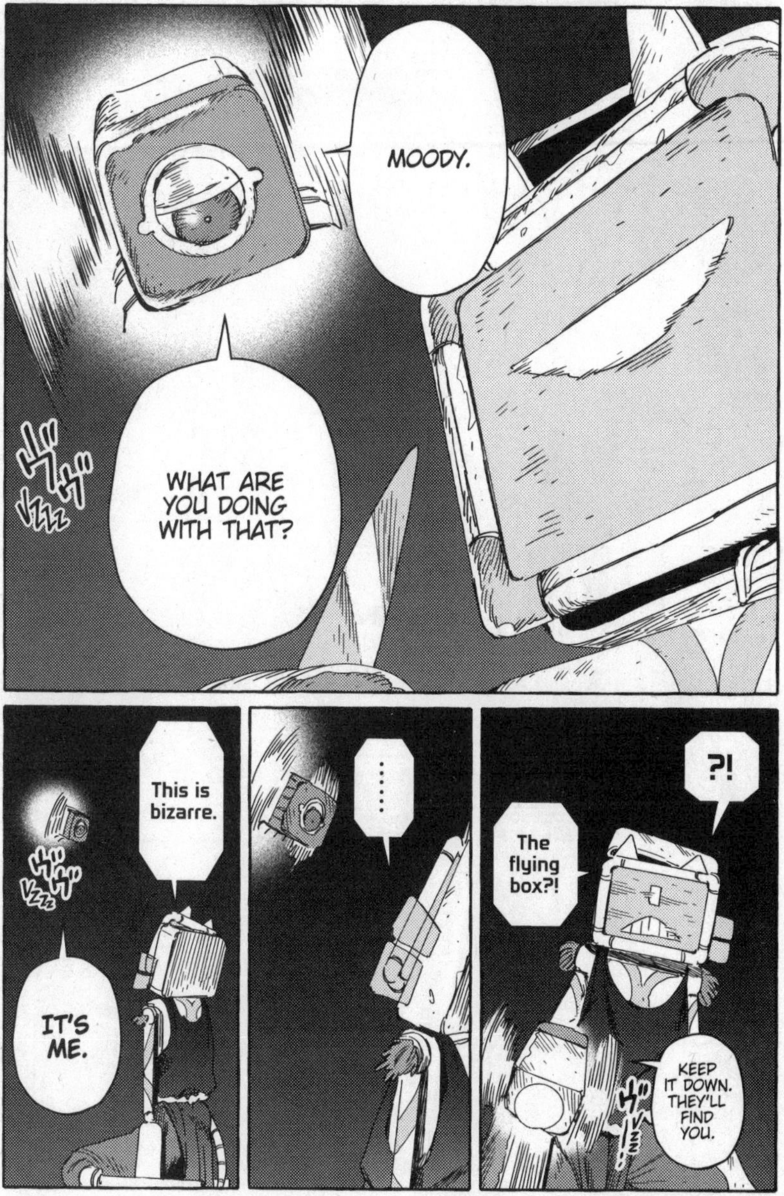
MOODY.
WHAT ARE YOU DOING WITH THAT?
Vzzz
?!
The flying box?!
KEEP IT DOWN. THEY'LL FIND YOU.
Vzzz
......
This is bizarre.
IT'S ME.
Vzzz

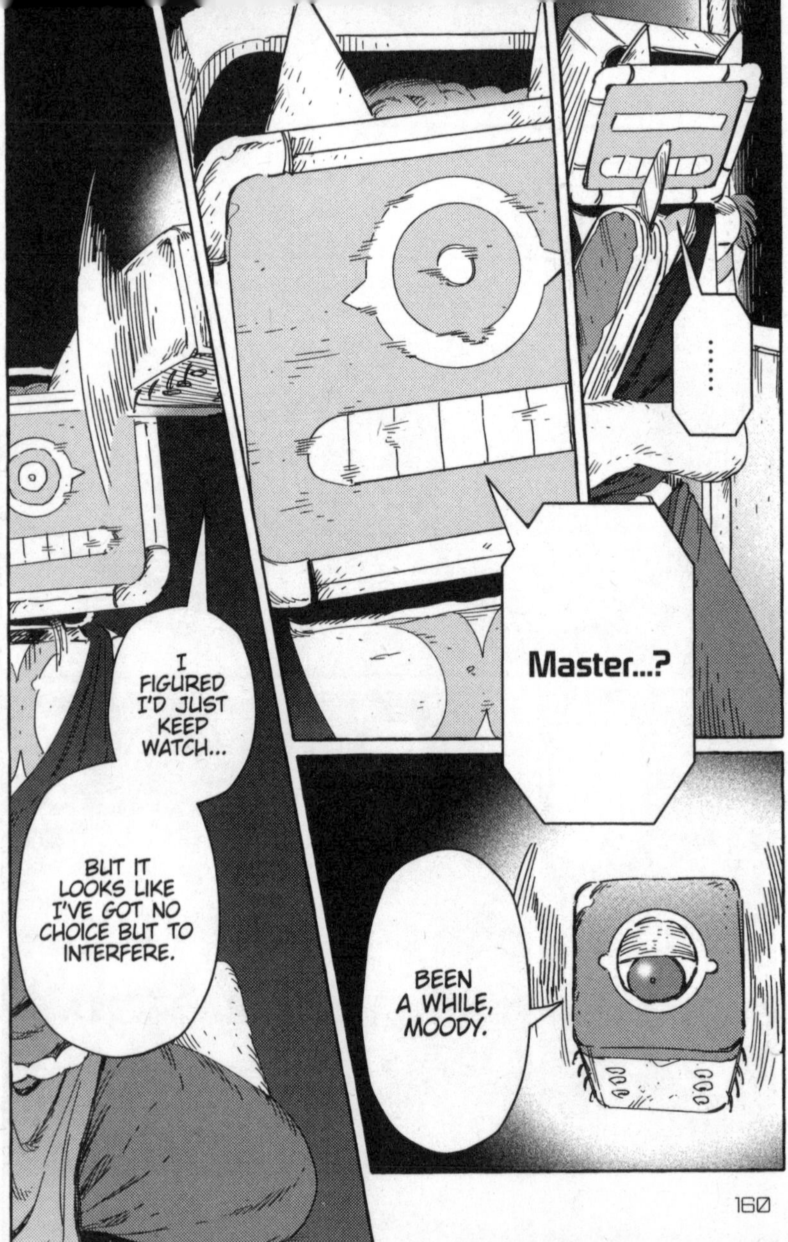
......
Master...?
BEEN A WHILE, MOODY.
I FIGURED I'D JUST KEEP WATCH...
BUT IT LOOKS LIKE I'VE GOT NO CHOICE BUT TO INTERFERE.

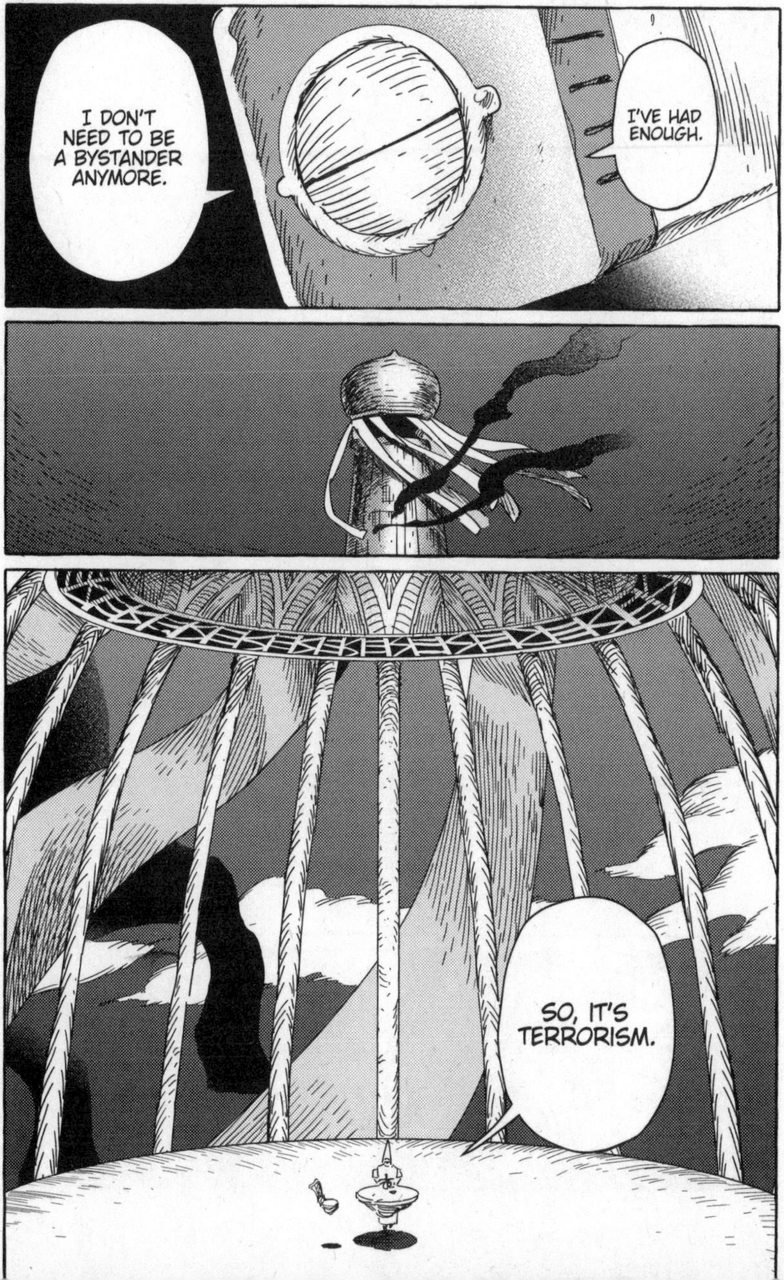
I'VE HAD ENOUGH.
I DON'T NEED TO BE A BYSTANDER ANYMORE.
SO, IT'S TERRORISM.

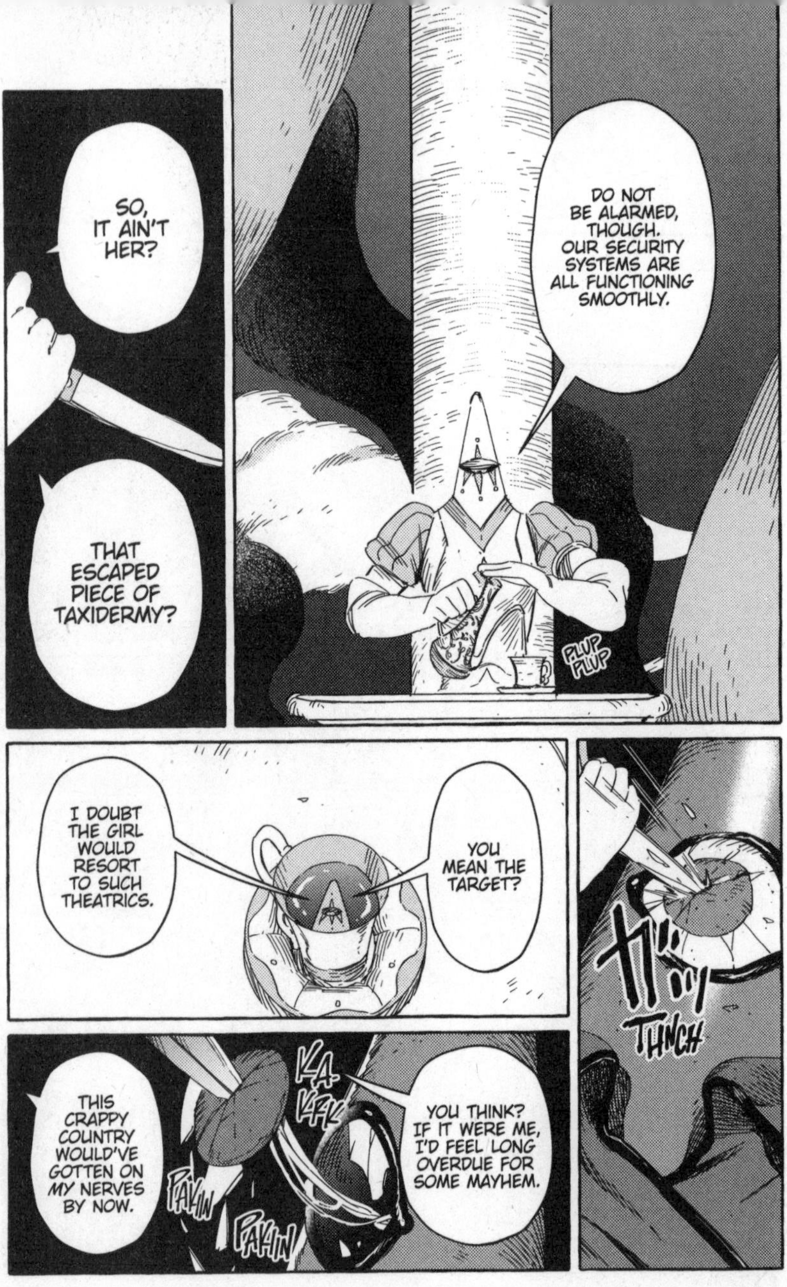
DO NOT BE ALARMED, THOUGH. OUR SECURITY SYSTEMS ARE ALL FUNCTIONING SMOOTHLY.
PLUP PLUP
SO, IT AIN'T HER?
THAT ESCAPED PIECE OF TAXIDERMY?
THNCH
YOU MEAN THE TARGET?
I DOUBT THE GIRL WOULD RESORT TO SUCH THEATRICS.
KA-KRK
YOU THINK? IF IT WERE ME, I'D FEEL LONG OVERDUE FOR SOME MAYHEM.
THIS CRAPPY COUNTRY WOULD'VE GOTTEN ON MY NERVES BY NOW.
PAKIN
PAKIN

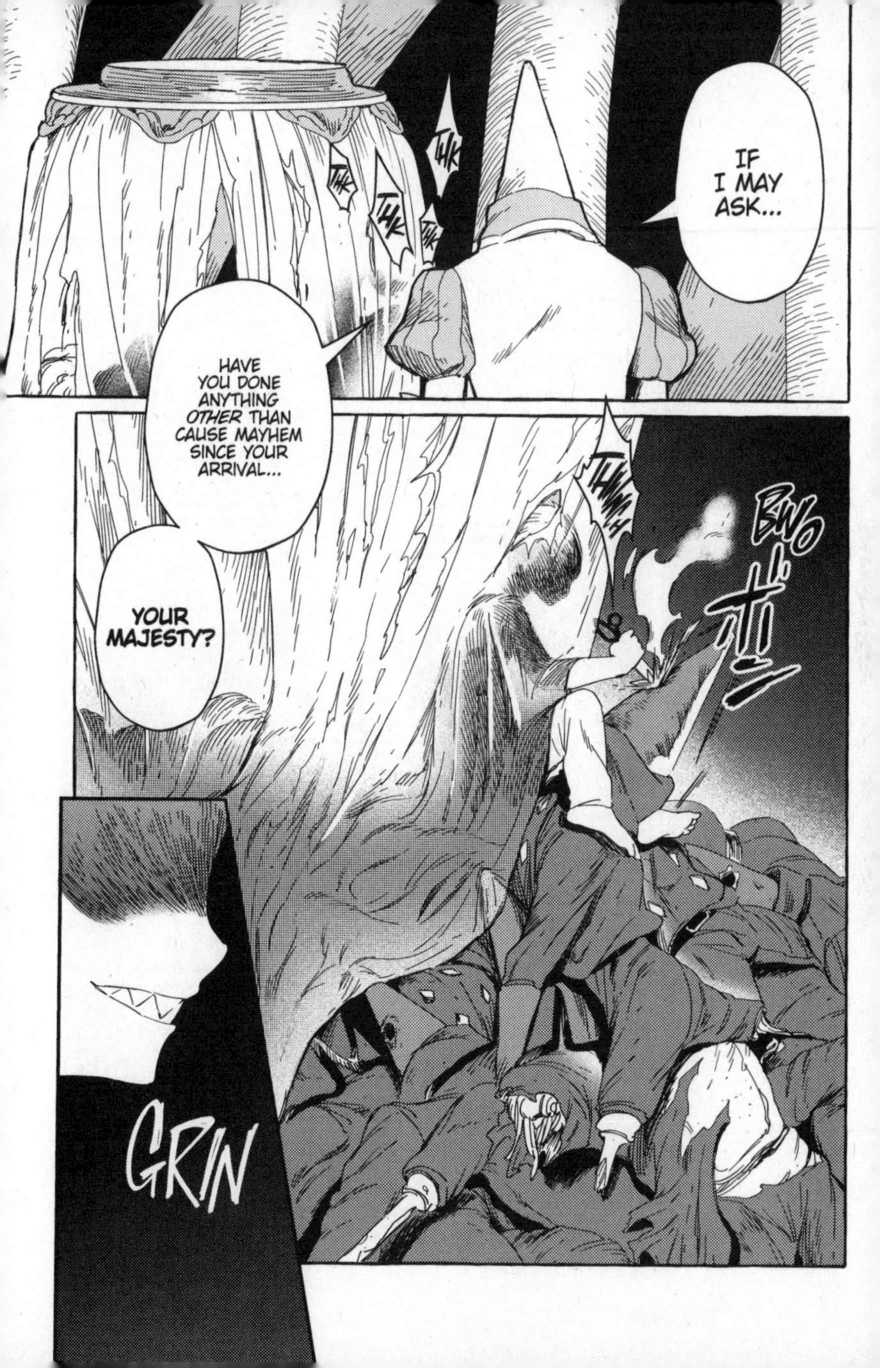
IF I MAY ASK...
THK
THK
THK
THK
HAVE YOU DONE ANYTHING *OTHER* THAN CAUSE MAYHEM SINCE YOUR ARRIVAL...
BANG
THWACK
YOUR MAJESTY?
GRIN

WHAT IS THIS THING?

IT'S USED TO TAKE GUESTS TO THE PALACE.

IT HAS A SPECIAL DESIGNATION THAT PREVENTS GOLEMS FROM HARMING IT.

ヴ ヴ ヴ ヴ ヴ ヴ ヴ ヴ

IT'S FINE.

......

GA-CHK
ガチャ

ARE YOU SURE YOU WANT TO CONTINUE?

I CANNOT RECOMMEND ENTERING AFTER AN EXPLOSION LIKE THAT.

KA-KNK
ガ!!

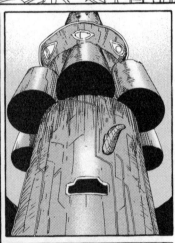

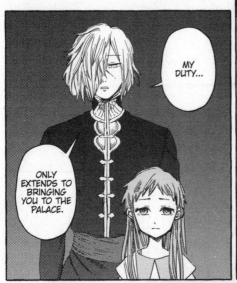

MY DUTY...
ONLY EXTENDS TO BRINGING YOU TO THE PALACE.
I HAVE NO INSTRUCTIONS FOR BEYOND THIS POINT.
THEN...
I HAVE TO MEET THE GOLEM WHO MADE THE REQUEST, RIGHT?
I THOUGHT YOU WERE WARY OF THE PALACE.
GRI
AH, IT OPENED.

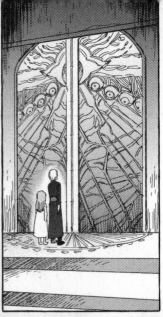

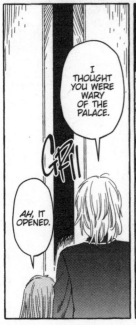

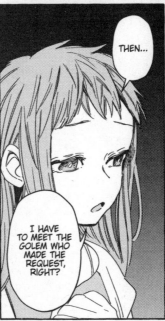

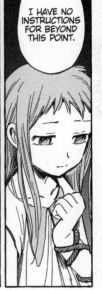

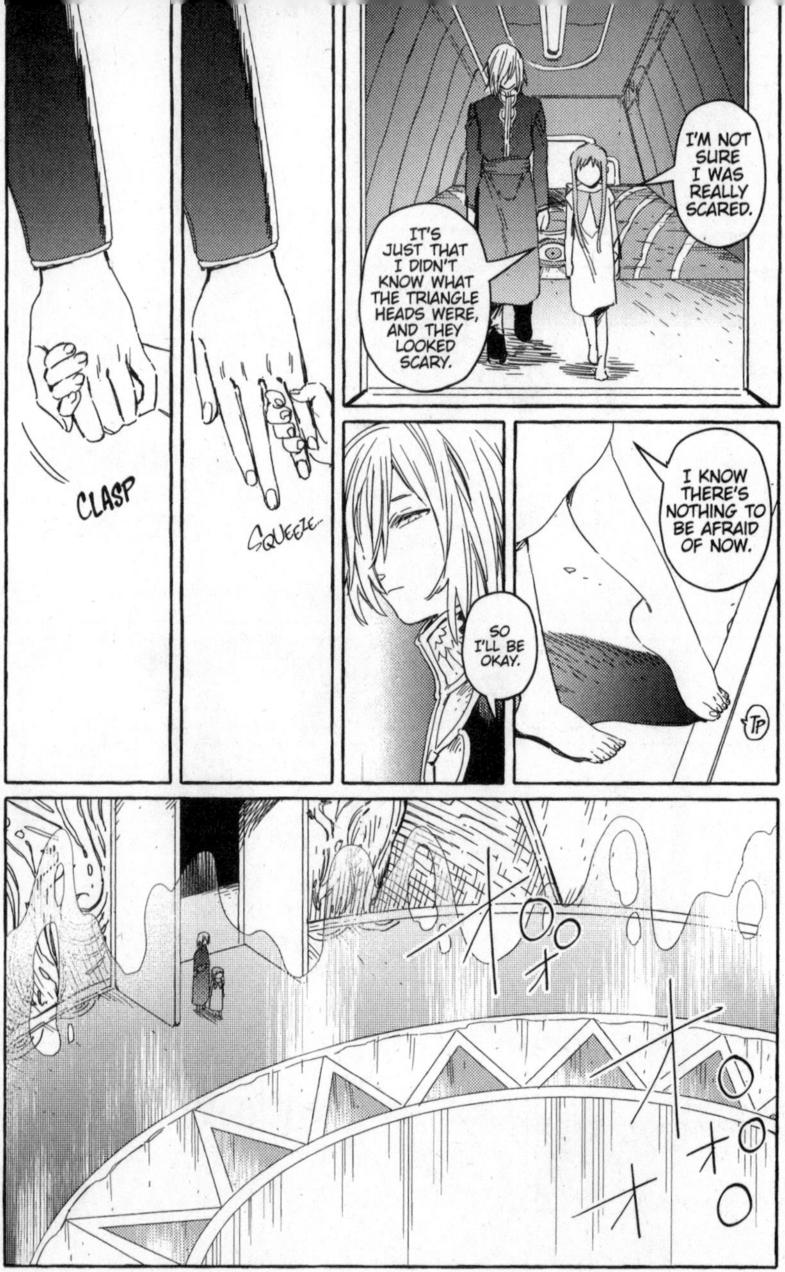
I'M NOT SURE I WAS REALLY SCARED.
IT'S JUST THAT I DIDN'T KNOW WHAT THE TRIANGLE HEADS WERE, AND THEY LOOKED SCARY.
I KNOW THERE'S NOTHING TO BE AFRAID OF NOW.
TP
SO I'LL BE OKAY.
SQUEEZE...
CLASP

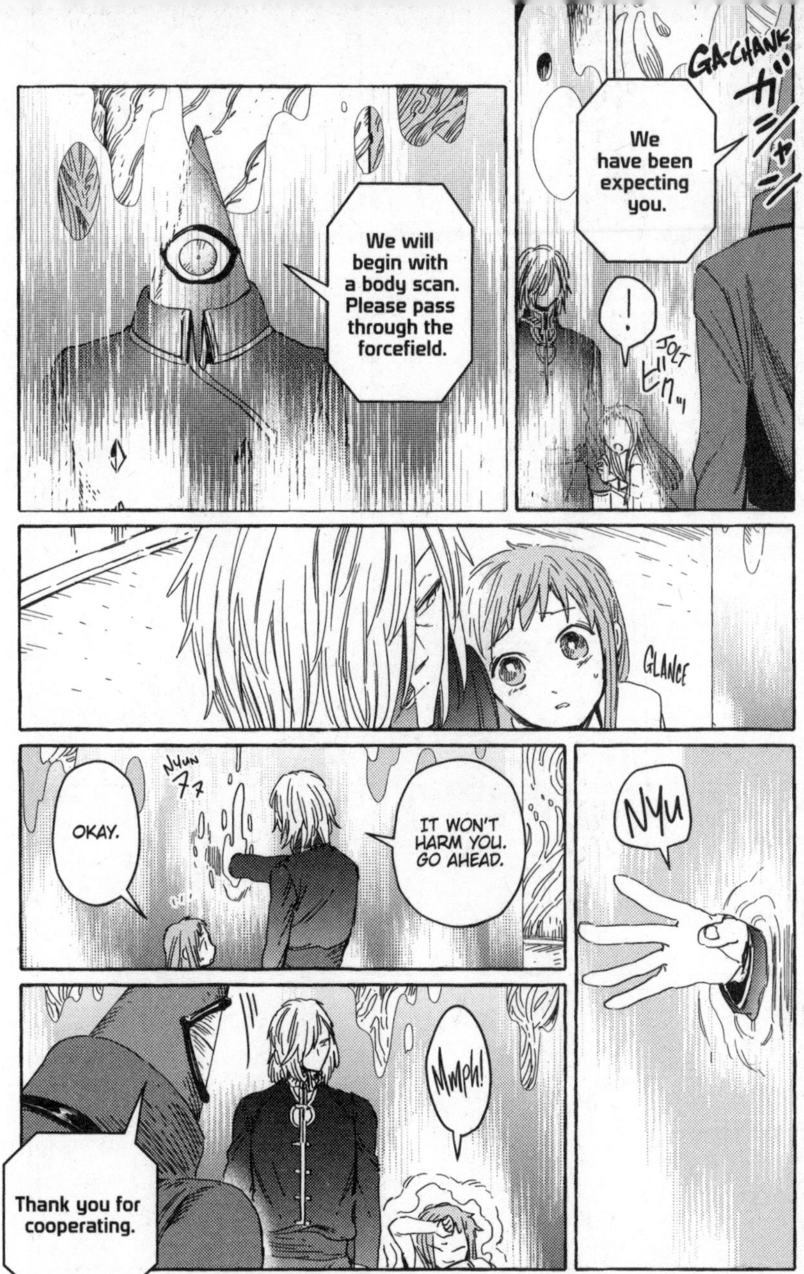
GA-CHANK
We have been expecting you.
!
JOLT
We will begin with a body scan. Please pass through the forcefield.
GLANCE
NYU
IT WON'T HARM YOU. GO AHEAD.
NYUN
OKAY.
Mmph!
Thank you for cooperating.

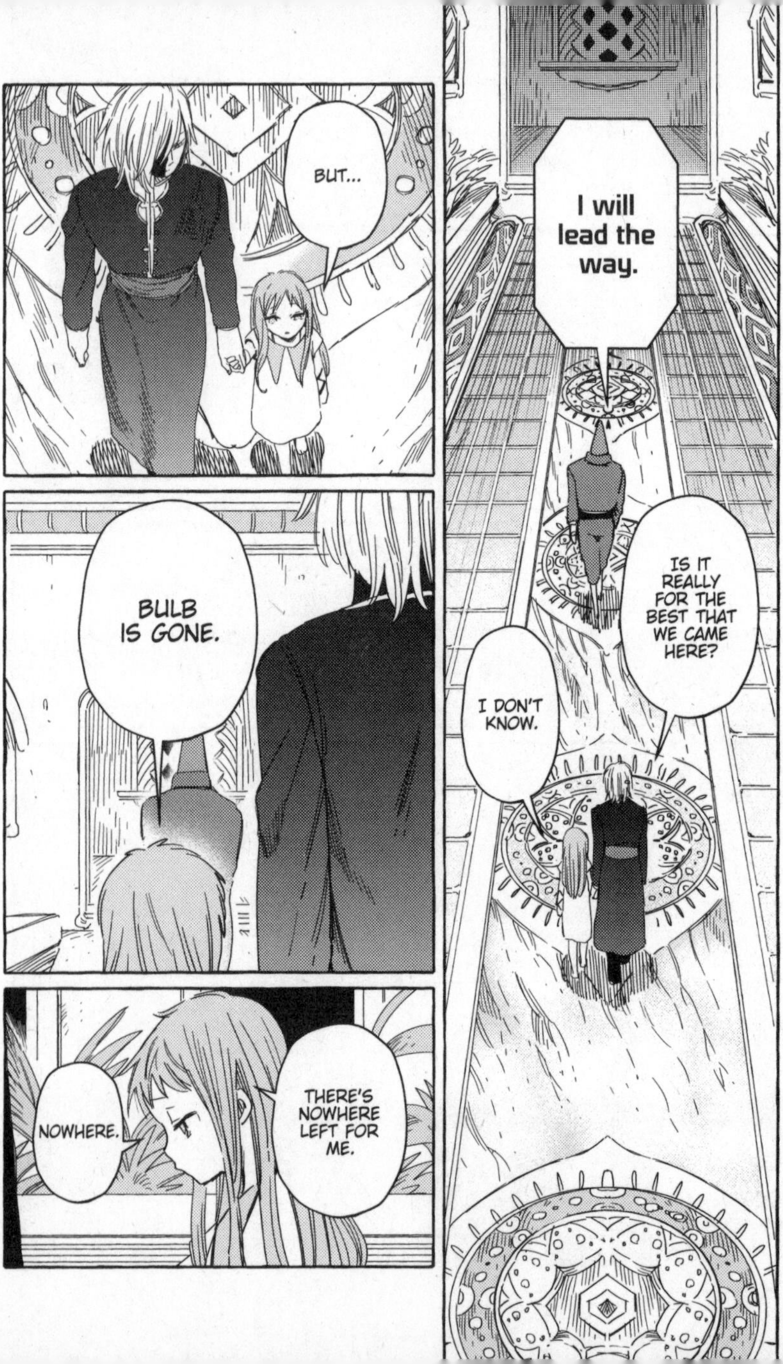
I will lead the way.
IS IT REALLY FOR THE BEST THAT WE CAME HERE?
I DON'T KNOW.
BUT...
BULB IS GONE.
THERE'S NOWHERE LEFT FOR ME.
NOWHERE.

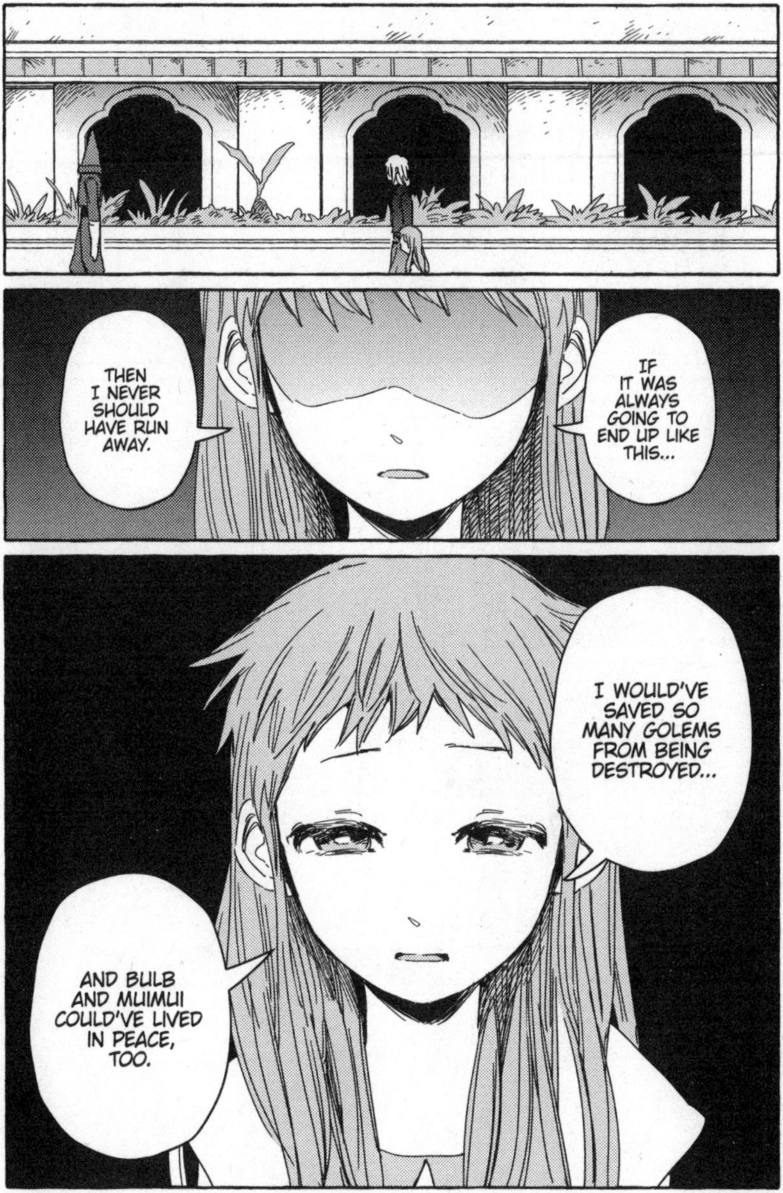
IF IT WAS ALWAYS GOING TO END UP LIKE THIS...
THEN I NEVER SHOULD HAVE RUN AWAY.
I WOULD'VE SAVED SO MANY GOLEMS FROM BEING DESTROYED...
AND BULB AND MUIMUI COULD'VE LIVED IN PEACE, TOO.

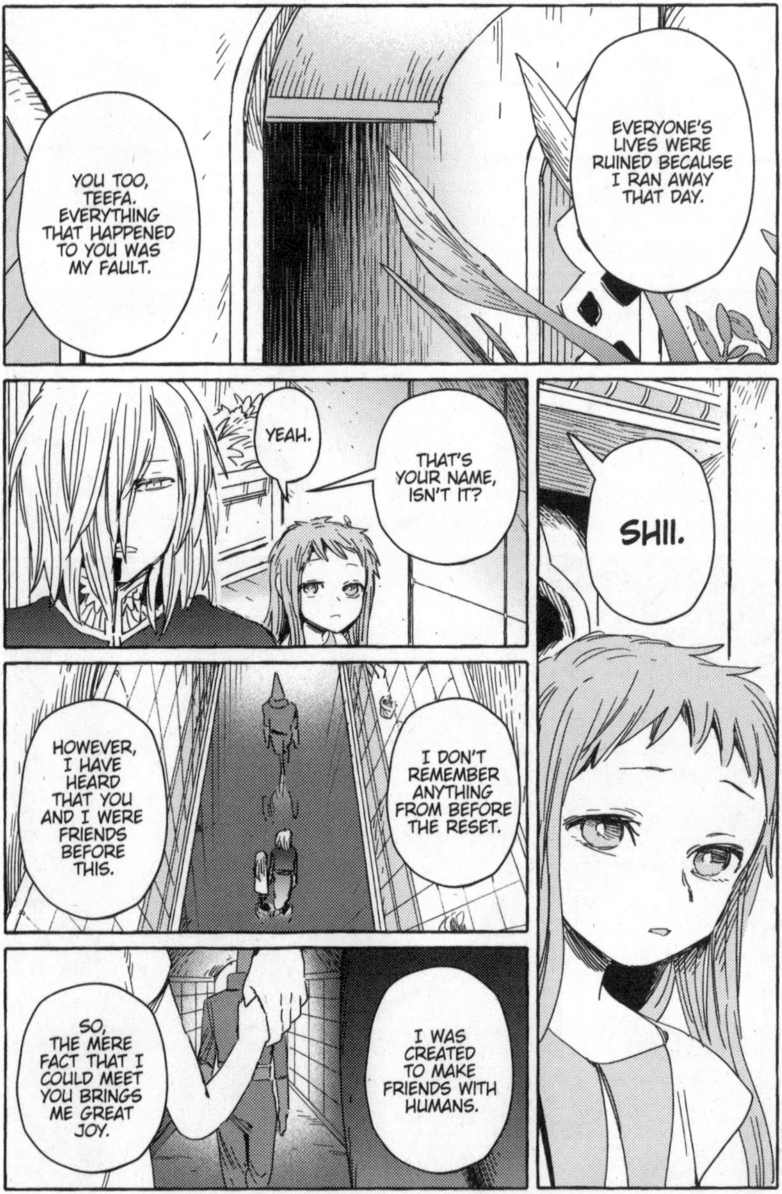
EVERYONE'S LIVES WERE RUINED BECAUSE I RAN AWAY THAT DAY.
YOU TOO, TEEFA. EVERYTHING THAT HAPPENED TO YOU WAS MY FAULT.
SHII.
THAT'S YOUR NAME, ISN'T IT?
YEAH.
I DON'T REMEMBER ANYTHING FROM BEFORE THE RESET.
HOWEVER, I HAVE HEARD THAT YOU AND I WERE FRIENDS BEFORE THIS.
I WAS CREATED TO MAKE FRIENDS WITH HUMANS.
SO, THE MERE FACT THAT I COULD MEET YOU BRINGS ME GREAT JOY.

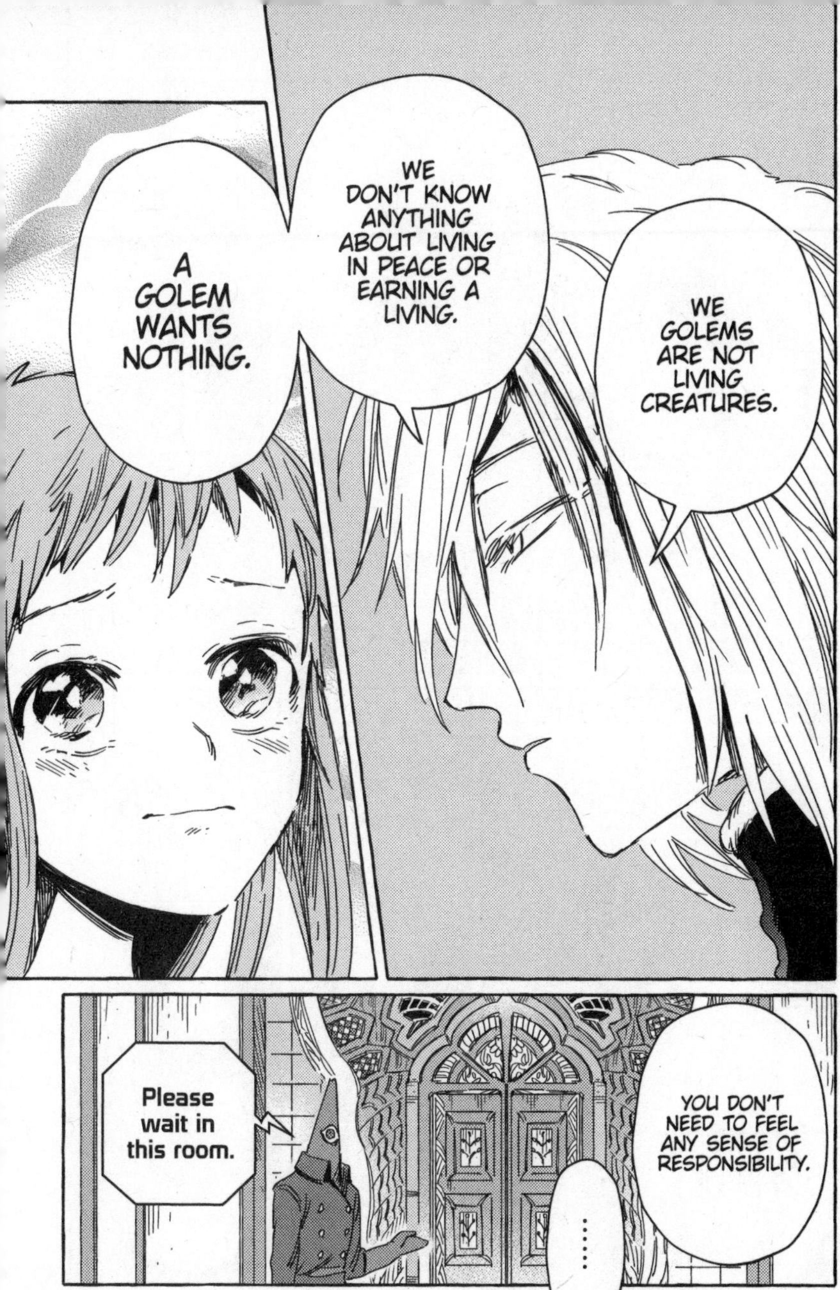
WE GOLEMS ARE NOT LIVING CREATURES.
WE DON'T KNOW ANYTHING ABOUT LIVING IN PEACE OR EARNING A LIVING.
A GOLEM WANTS NOTHING.
YOU DON'T NEED TO FEEL ANY SENSE OF RESPONSIBILITY.
……
Please wait in this room.

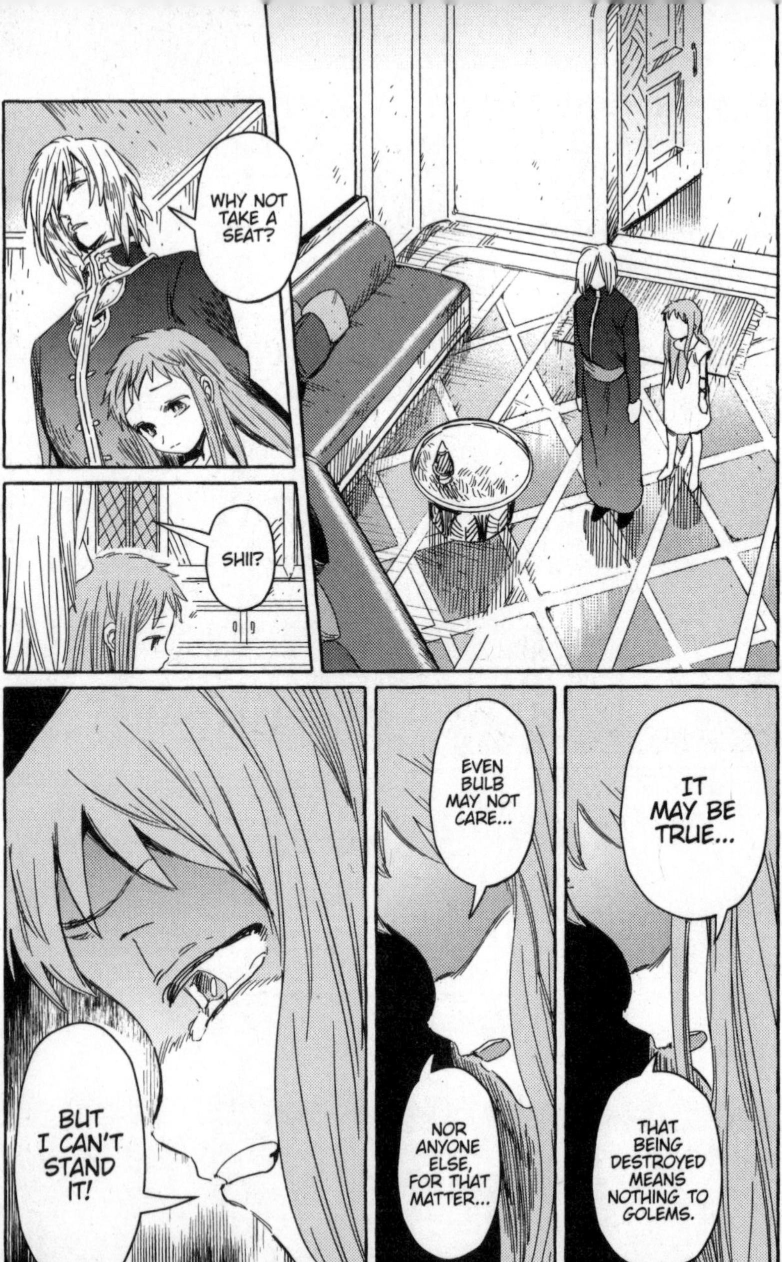
WHY NOT TAKE A SEAT?
SHII?
IT MAY BE TRUE...
THAT BEING DESTROYED MEANS NOTHING TO GOLEMS.
EVEN BULB MAY NOT CARE...
NOR ANYONE ELSE, FOR THAT MATTER...
BUT I CAN'T STAND IT!

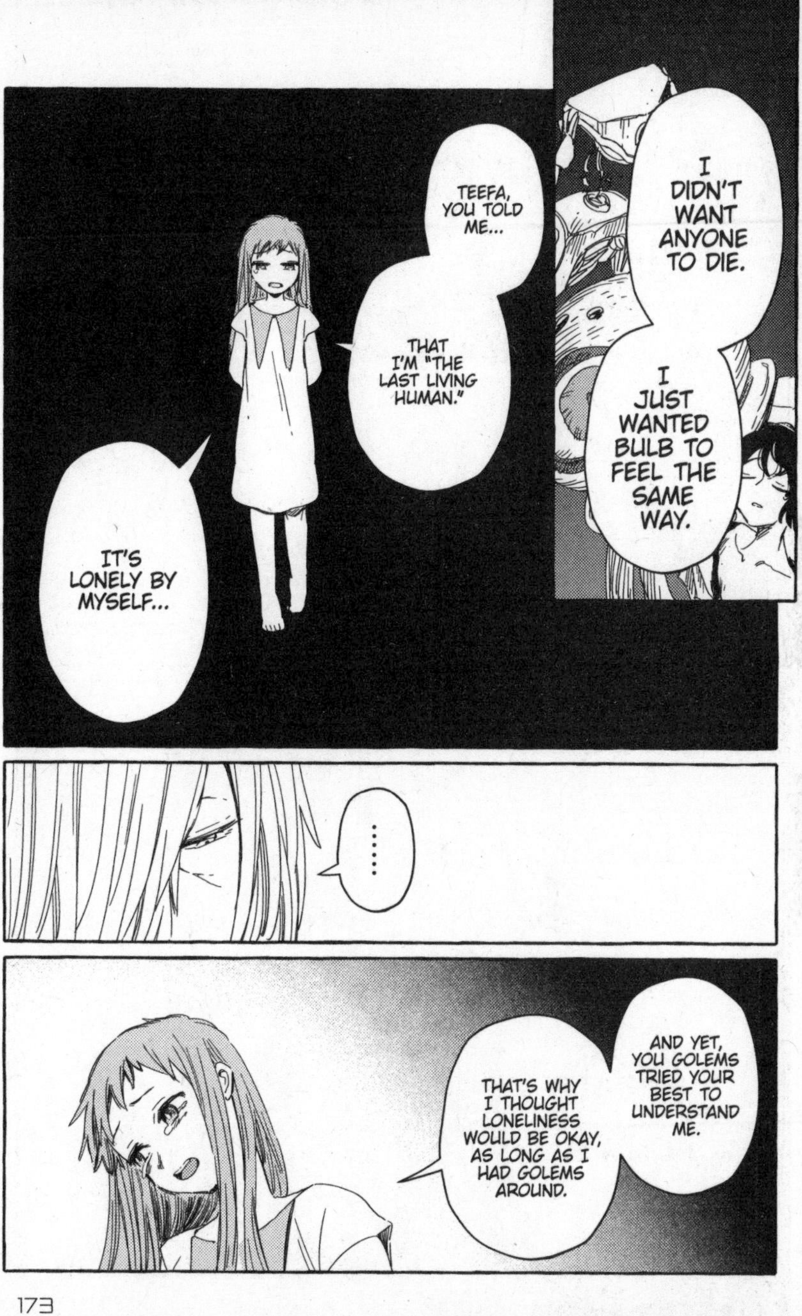
I DIDN'T WANT ANYONE TO DIE.
I JUST WANTED BULB TO FEEL THE SAME WAY.
TEEFA, YOU TOLD ME...
THAT I'M "THE LAST LIVING HUMAN."
IT'S LONELY BY MYSELF...
......
AND YET, YOU GOLEMS TRIED YOUR BEST TO UNDERSTAND ME.
THAT'S WHY I THOUGHT LONELINESS WOULD BE OKAY, AS LONG AS I HAD GOLEMS AROUND.

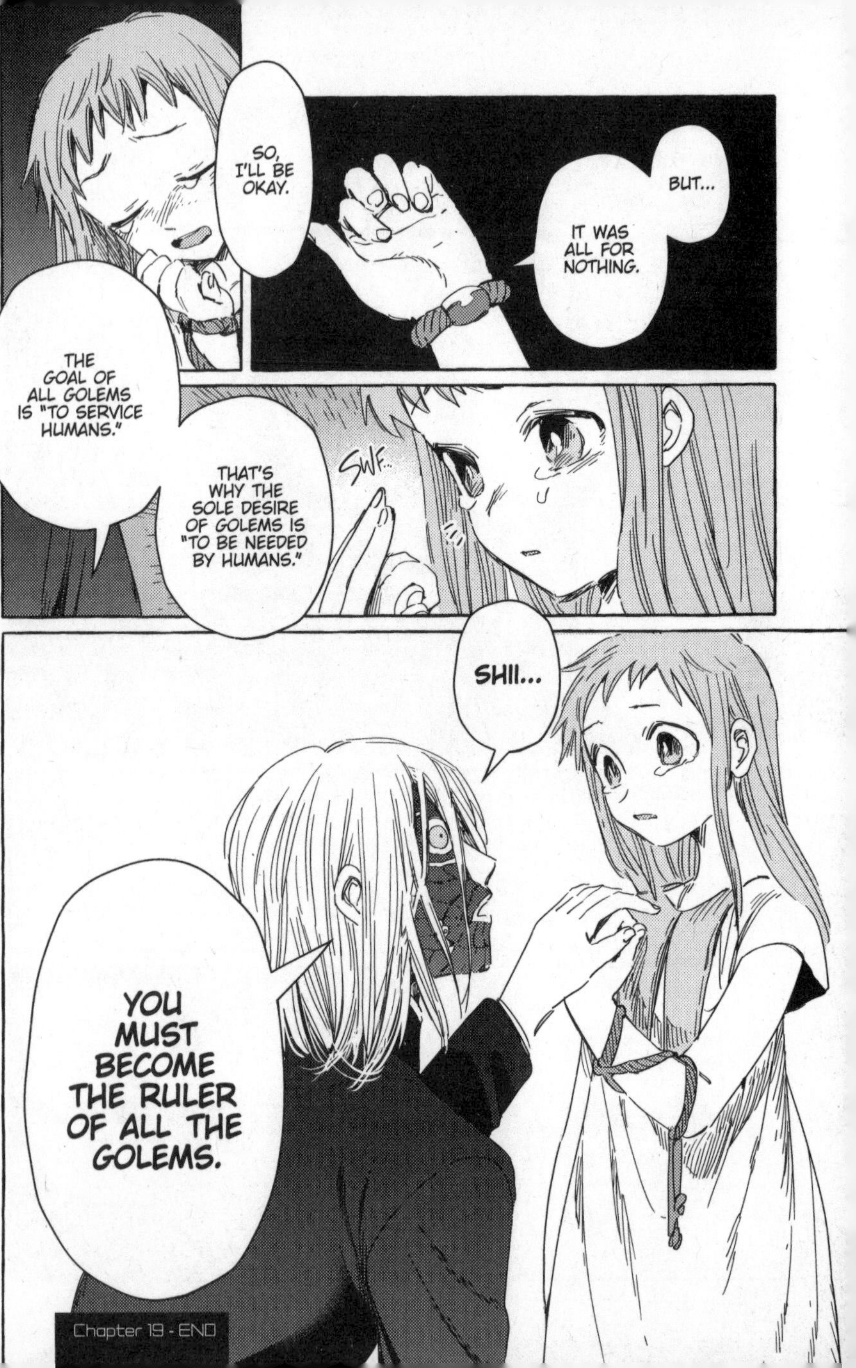

BUT...
IT WAS ALL FOR NOTHING.
SO, I'LL BE OKAY.
SWF...
THE GOAL OF ALL GOLEMS IS "TO SERVICE HUMANS."
THAT'S WHY THE SOLE DESIRE OF GOLEMS IS "TO BE NEEDED BY HUMANS."
SHII...
YOU MUST BECOME THE RULER OF ALL THE GOLEMS.
Chapter 19 - END

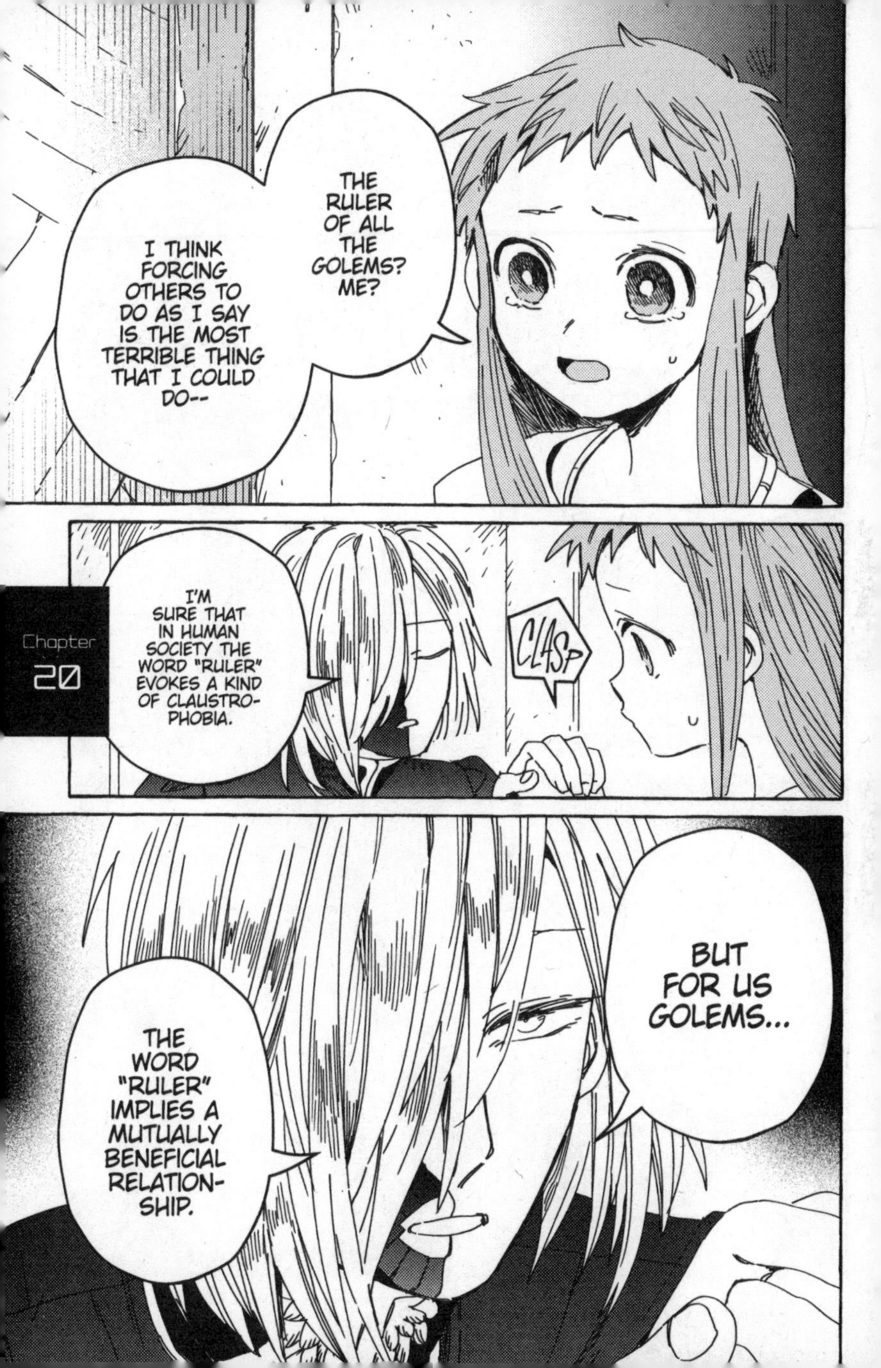
THE RULER OF ALL THE GOLEMS? ME?
I THINK FORCING OTHERS TO DO AS I SAY IS THE MOST TERRIBLE THING THAT I COULD DO--
Chapter 20
CLASP
I'M SURE THAT IN HUMAN SOCIETY THE WORD "RULER" EVOKES A KIND OF CLAUSTRO-PHOBIA.
BUT FOR US GOLEMS...
THE WORD "RULER" IMPLIES A MUTUALLY BENEFICIAL RELATION-SHIP.

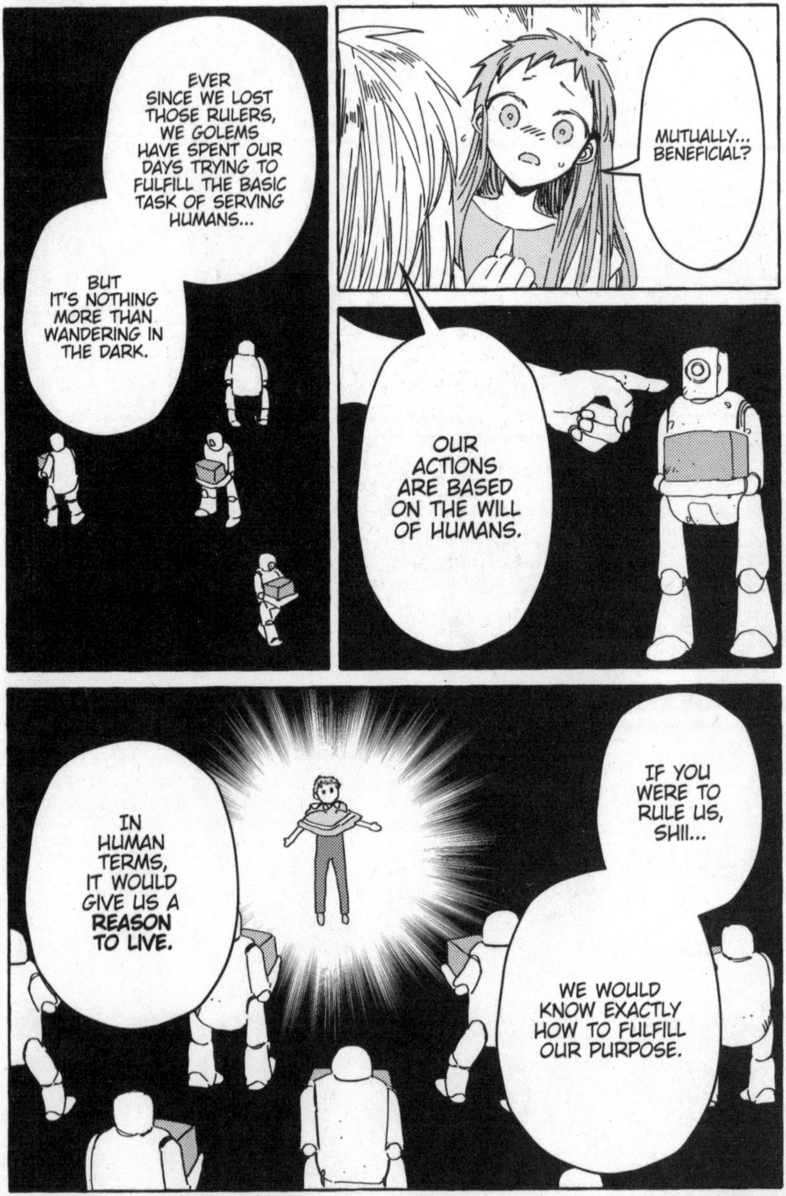
MUTUALLY... BENEFICIAL?
OUR ACTIONS ARE BASED ON THE WILL OF HUMANS.
EVER SINCE WE LOST THOSE RULERS, WE GOLEMS HAVE SPENT OUR DAYS TRYING TO FULFILL THE BASIC TASK OF SERVING HUMANS...
BUT IT'S NOTHING MORE THAN WANDERING IN THE DARK.
IF YOU WERE TO RULE US, SHII...
WE WOULD KNOW EXACTLY HOW TO FULFILL OUR PURPOSE.
IN HUMAN TERMS, IT WOULD GIVE US A **REASON TO LIVE.**

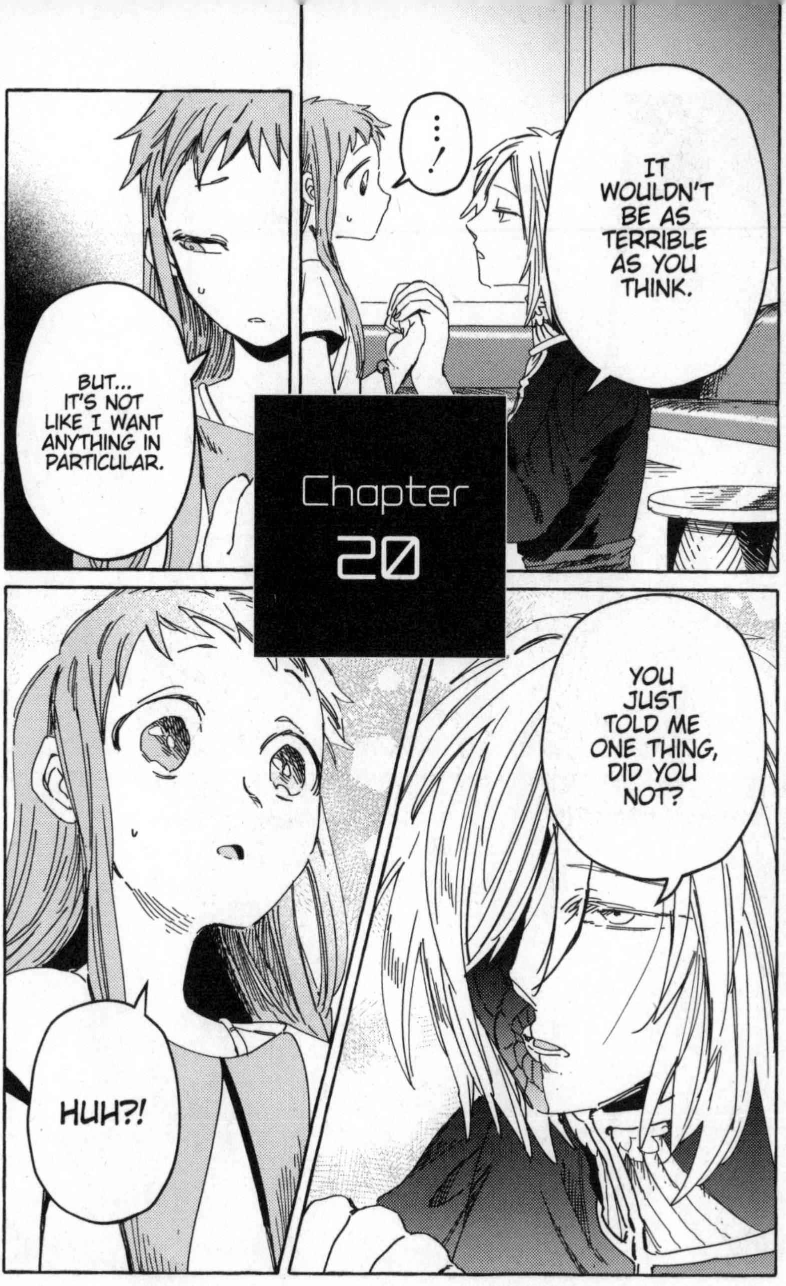
IT WOULDN'T BE AS TERRIBLE AS YOU THINK.
...!
BUT... IT'S NOT LIKE I WANT ANYTHING IN PARTICULAR.
Chapter 20
YOU JUST TOLD ME ONE THING, DID YOU NOT?
HUH?!

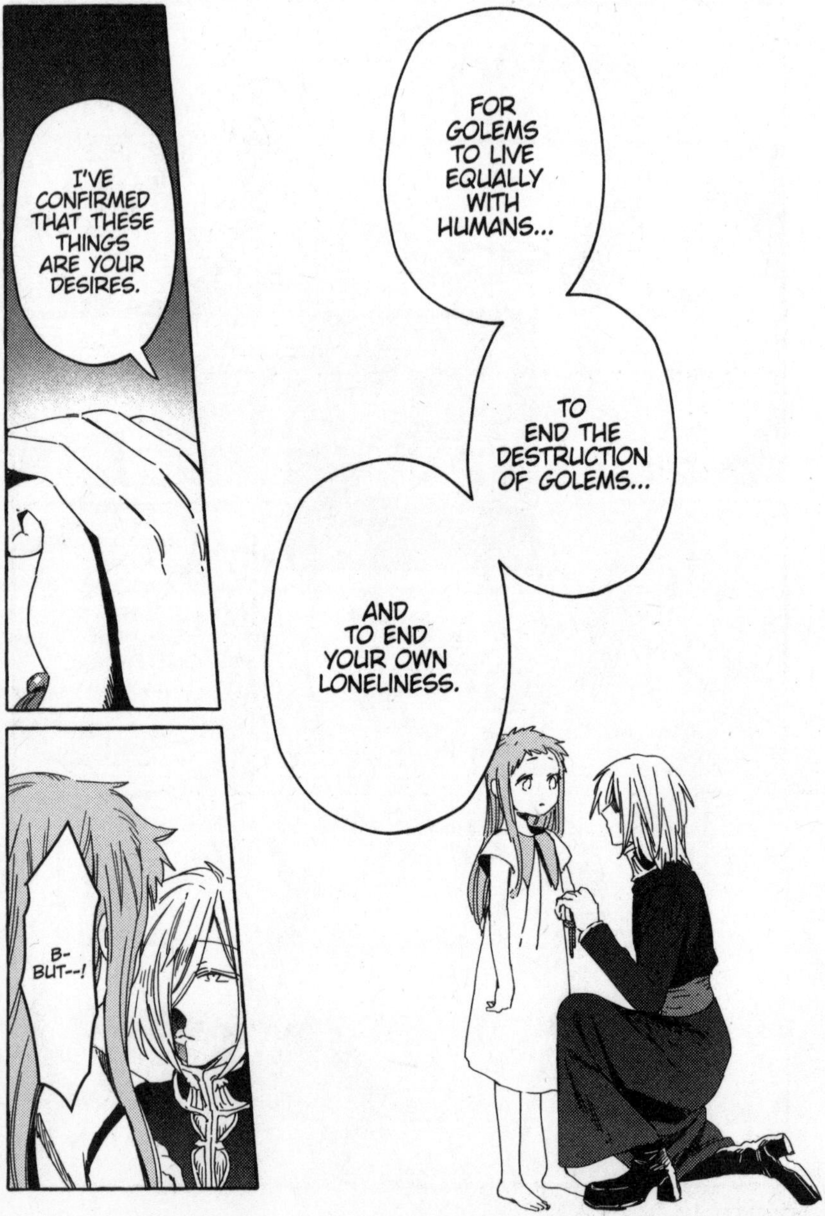
FOR GOLEMS TO LIVE EQUALLY WITH HUMANS...
TO END THE DESTRUCTION OF GOLEMS...
AND TO END YOUR OWN LONELINESS.
I'VE CONFIRMED THAT THESE THINGS ARE YOUR DESIRES.
B- BUT--!

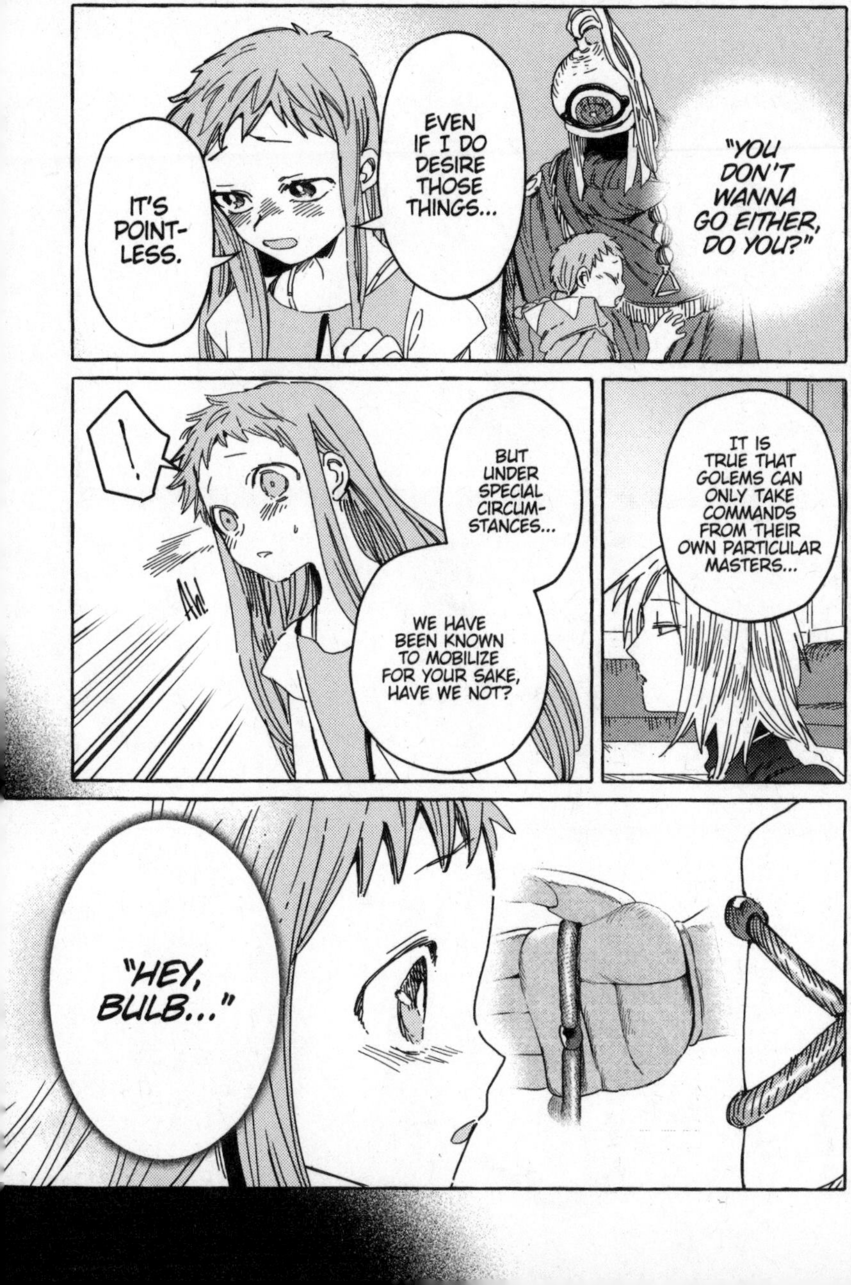
"YOU DON'T WANNA GO EITHER, DO YOU?"
EVEN IF I DO DESIRE THOSE THINGS...
IT'S POINT-LESS.
IT IS TRUE THAT GOLEMS CAN ONLY TAKE COMMANDS FROM THEIR OWN PARTICULAR MASTERS...
BUT UNDER SPECIAL CIRCUM-STANCES...
WE HAVE BEEN KNOWN TO MOBILIZE FOR YOUR SAKE, HAVE WE NOT?
!
AH!
"HEY, BULB..."

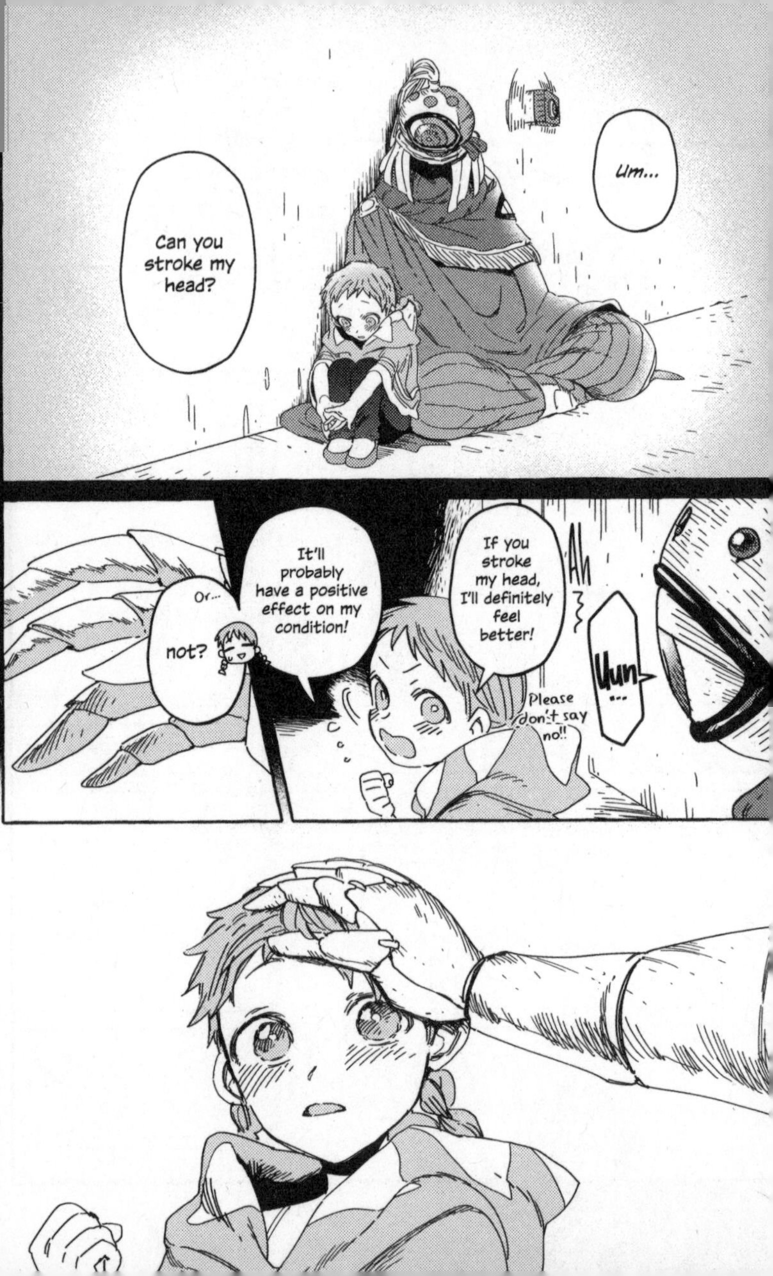
Um...
Can you stroke my head?
Ah
Uun...
If you stroke my head, I'll definitely feel better!
Please don't say no!!
It'll probably have a positive effect on my condition!
Or...
not?

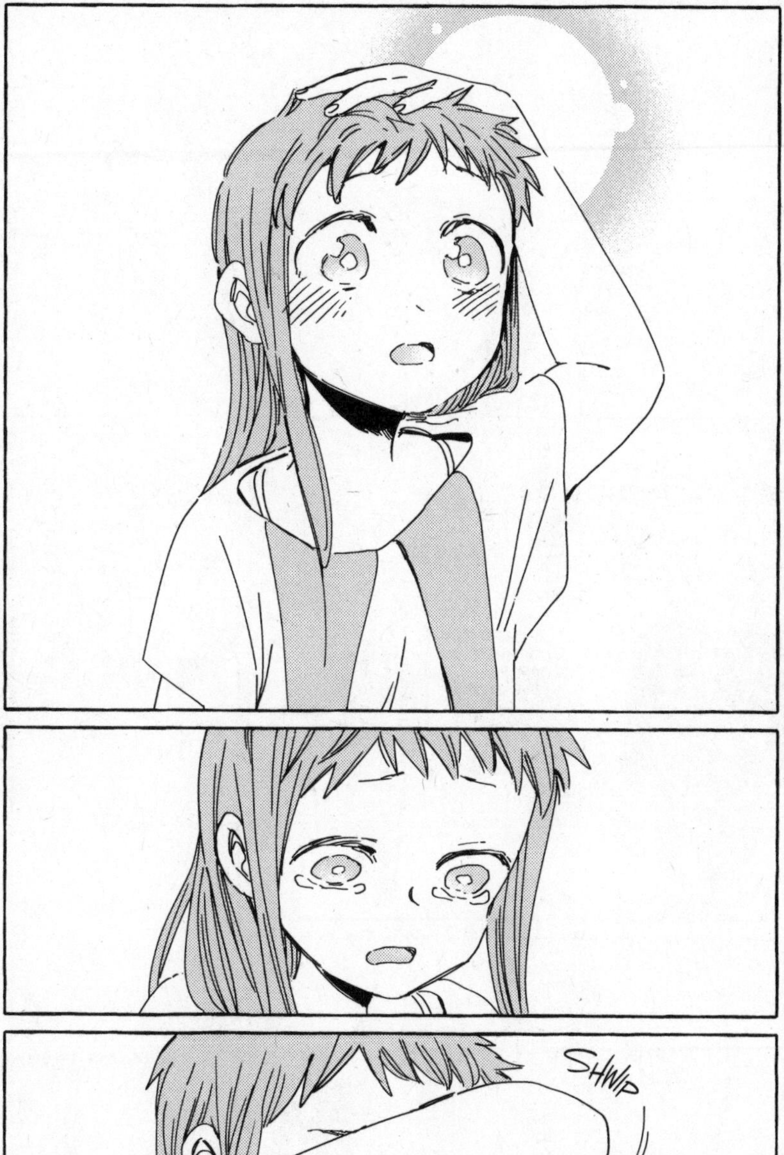
SHWIP

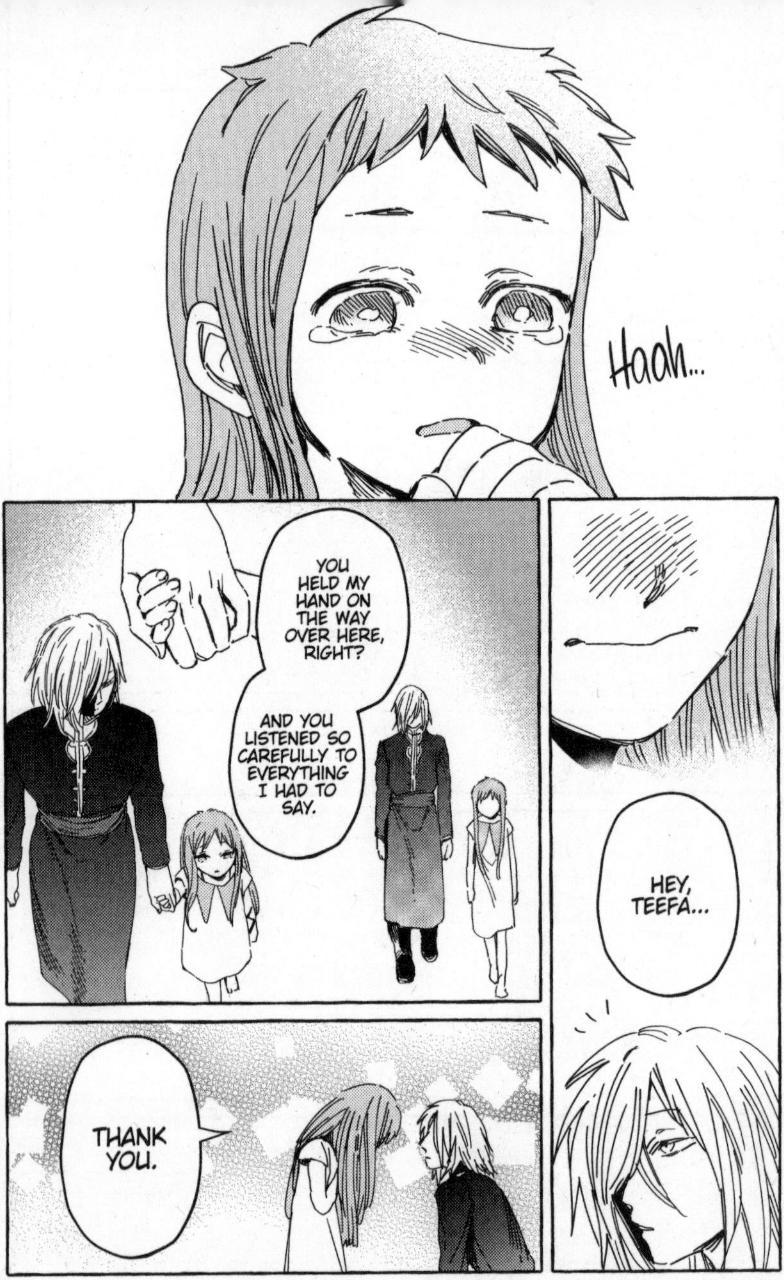
Haah...
HEY, TEEFA...
YOU HELD MY HAND ON THE WAY OVER HERE, RIGHT?
AND YOU LISTENED SO CAREFULLY TO EVERYTHING I HAD TO SAY.
THANK YOU.

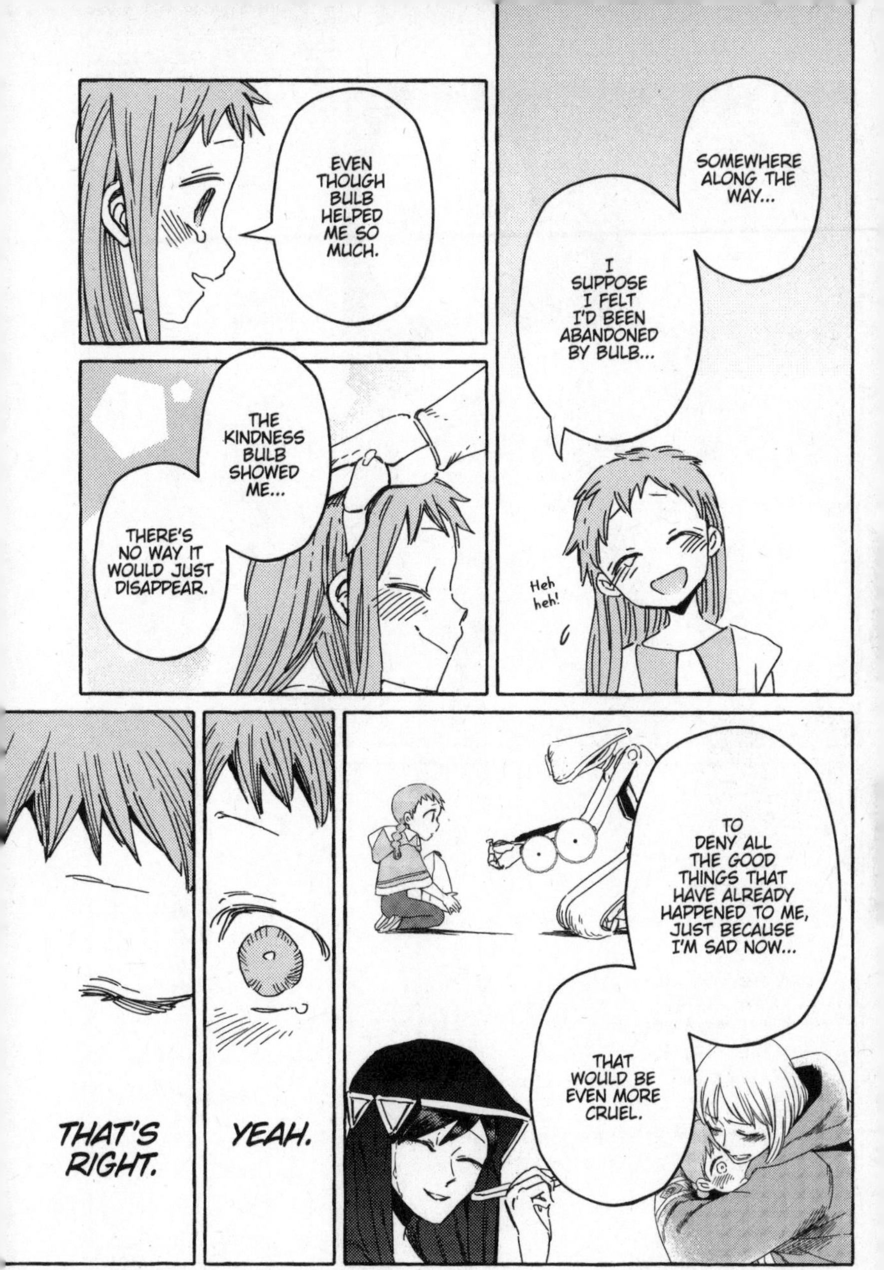
SOMEWHERE ALONG THE WAY...
I SUPPOSE I FELT I'D BEEN ABANDONED BY BULB...
Heh heh!
EVEN THOUGH BULB HELPED ME SO MUCH.
THE KINDNESS BULB SHOWED ME...
THERE'S NO WAY IT WOULD JUST DISAPPEAR.
TO DENY ALL THE GOOD THINGS THAT HAVE ALREADY HAPPENED TO ME, JUST BECAUSE I'M SAD NOW...
THAT WOULD BE EVEN MORE CRUEL.
YEAH.
THAT'S RIGHT.

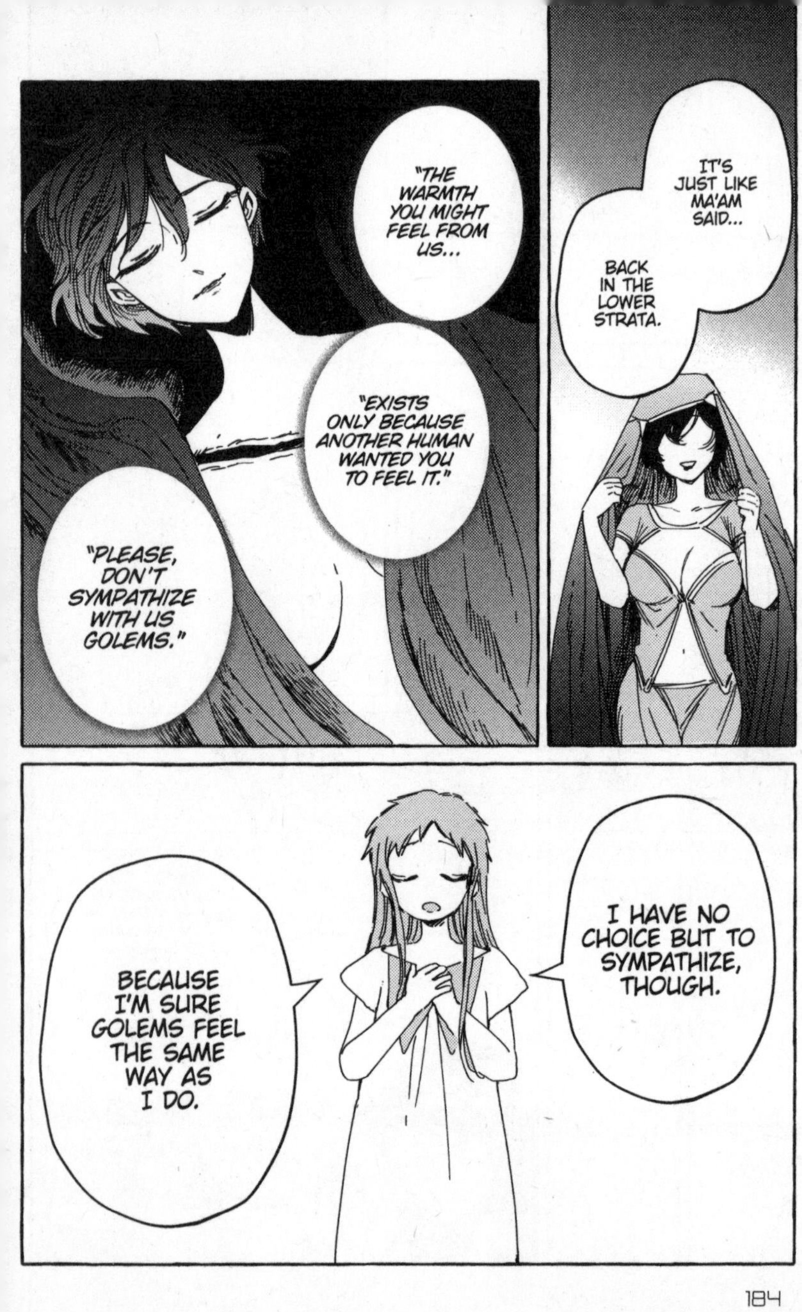
IT'S JUST LIKE MA'AM SAID...
BACK IN THE LOWER STRATA.
"THE WARMTH YOU MIGHT FEEL FROM US...
"EXISTS ONLY BECAUSE ANOTHER HUMAN WANTED YOU TO FEEL IT."
"PLEASE, DON'T SYMPATHIZE WITH US GOLEMS."
I HAVE NO CHOICE BUT TO SYMPATHIZE, THOUGH.
BECAUSE I'M SURE GOLEMS FEEL THE SAME WAY AS I DO.

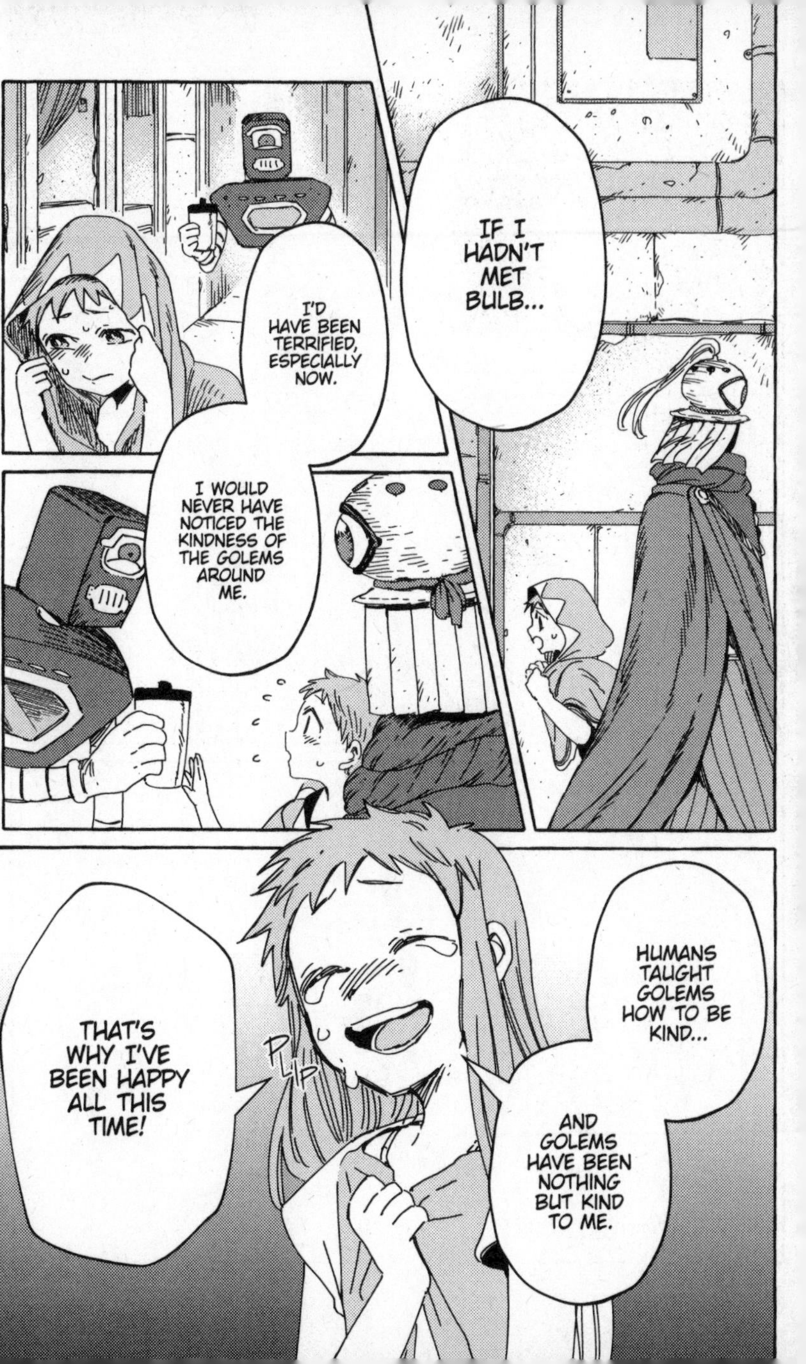
IF I HADN'T MET BULB...
I'D HAVE BEEN TERRIFIED, ESPECIALLY NOW.
I WOULD NEVER HAVE NOTICED THE KINDNESS OF THE GOLEMS AROUND ME.
HUMANS TAUGHT GOLEMS HOW TO BE KIND...
AND GOLEMS HAVE BEEN NOTHING BUT KIND TO ME.
PLIP
THAT'S WHY I'VE BEEN HAPPY ALL THIS TIME!

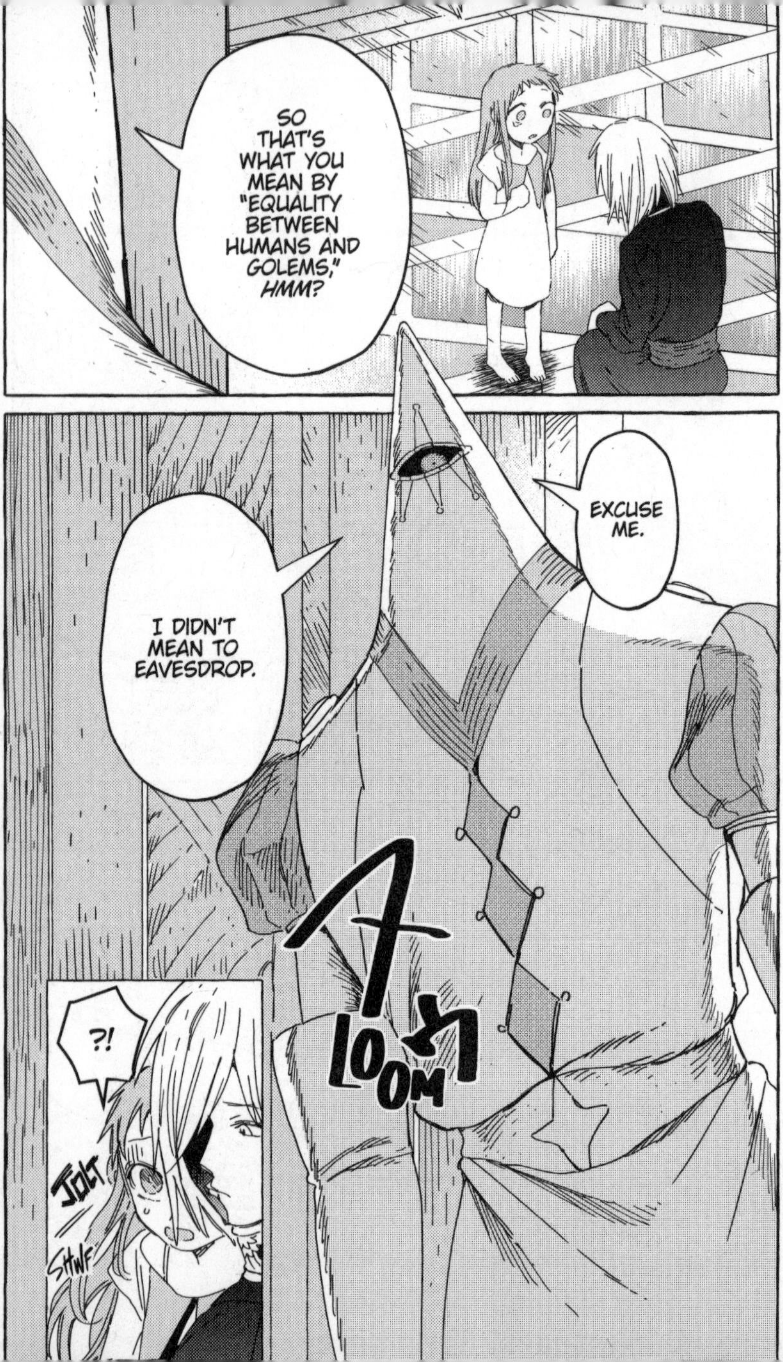
SO THAT'S WHAT YOU MEAN BY "EQUALITY BETWEEN HUMANS AND GOLEMS," HMM?
EXCUSE ME.
I DIDN'T MEAN TO EAVESDROP.
LOOM
?!
JOLT
SHWF

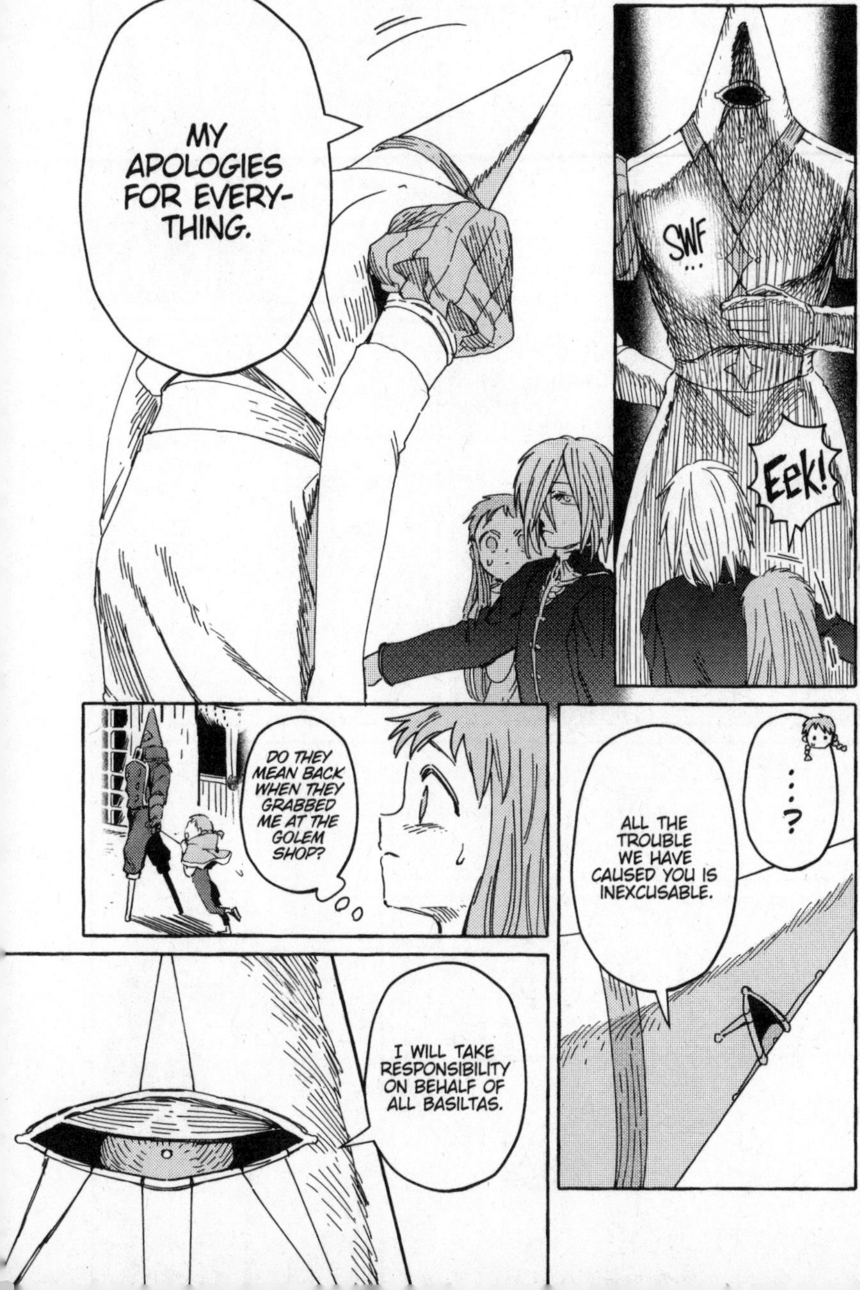
SWF...
EEK!
MY APOLOGIES FOR EVERYTHING.
...?
ALL THE TROUBLE WE HAVE CAUSED YOU IS INEXCUSABLE.
DO THEY MEAN BACK WHEN THEY GRABBED ME AT THE GOLEM SHOP?
I WILL TAKE RESPONSIBILITY ON BEHALF OF ALL BASILTAS.

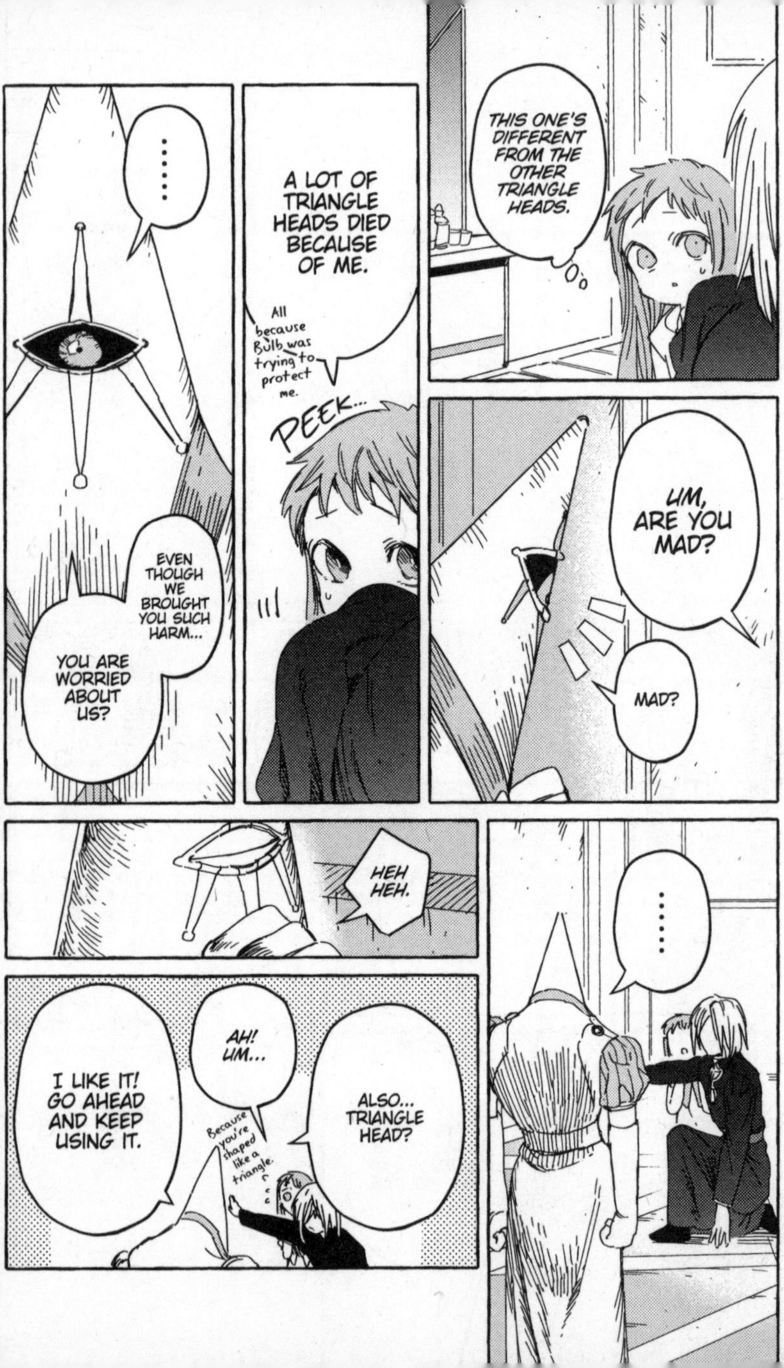
THIS ONE'S DIFFERENT FROM THE OTHER TRIANGLE HEADS.
UM, ARE YOU MAD?
MAD?
A LOT OF TRIANGLE HEADS DIED BECAUSE OF ME.
All because Bulb was trying to protect me.
PEEK...
......
EVEN THOUGH WE BROUGHT YOU SUCH HARM...
YOU ARE WORRIED ABOUT US?
......
HEH HEH.
ALSO... TRIANGLE HEAD?
AH! UM...
Because you're shaped like a triangle.
I LIKE IT! GO AHEAD AND KEEP USING IT.

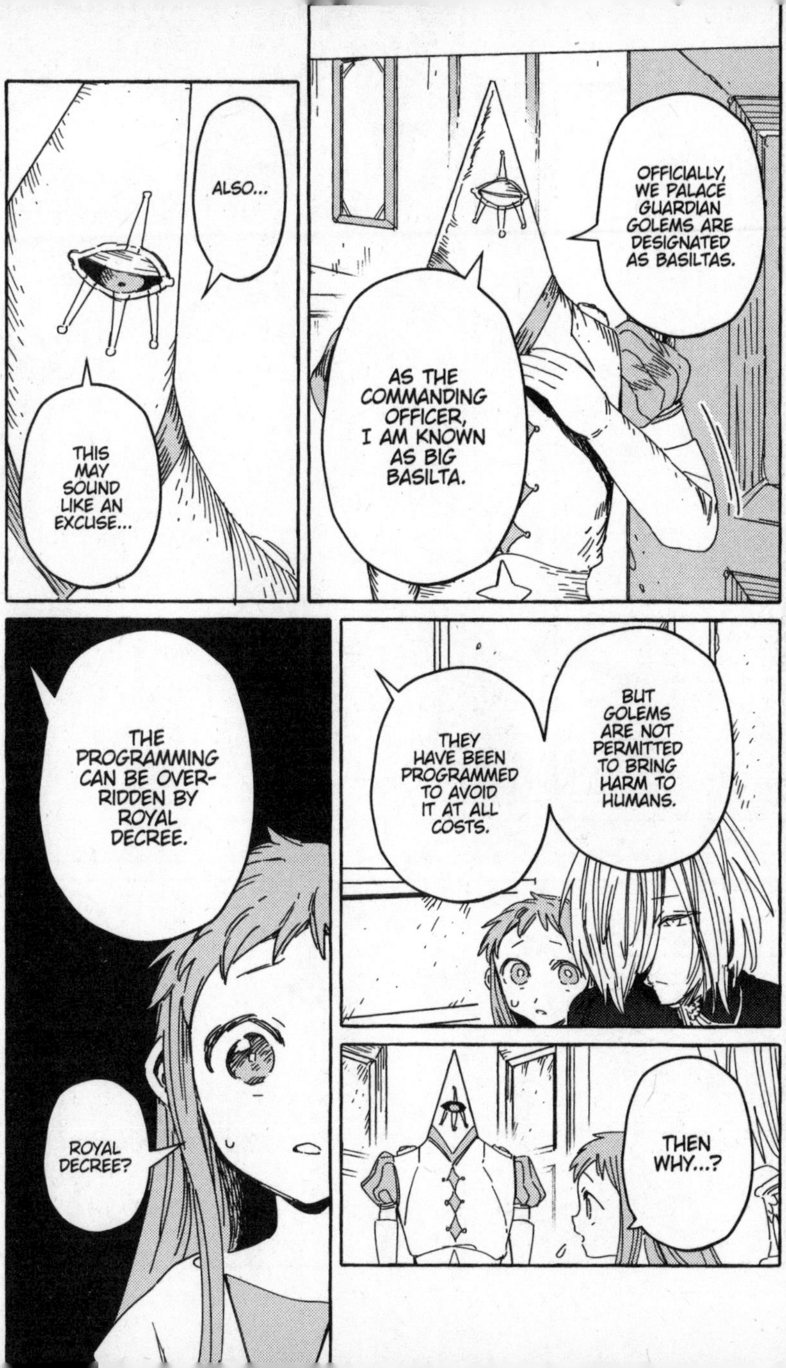
OFFICIALLY, WE PALACE GUARDIAN GOLEMS ARE DESIGNATED AS BASILTAS.
AS THE COMMANDING OFFICER, I AM KNOWN AS BIG BASILTA.
ALSO...
THIS MAY SOUND LIKE AN EXCUSE...
BUT GOLEMS ARE NOT PERMITTED TO BRING HARM TO HUMANS.
THEY HAVE BEEN PROGRAMMED TO AVOID IT AT ALL COSTS.
THEN WHY...?
THE PROGRAMMING CAN BE OVER-RIDDEN BY ROYAL DECREE.
ROYAL DECREE?

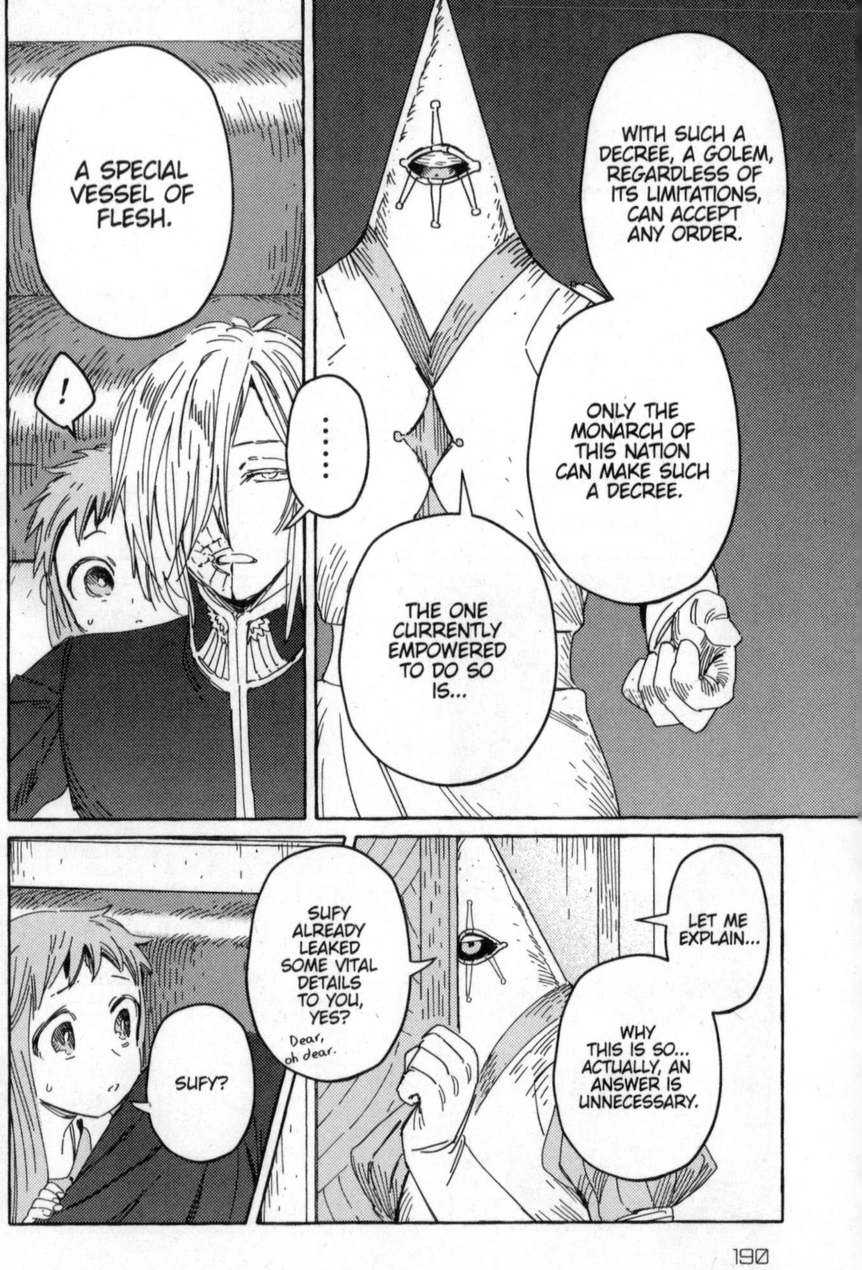
WITH SUCH A DECREE, A GOLEM, REGARDLESS OF ITS LIMITATIONS, CAN ACCEPT ANY ORDER.
ONLY THE MONARCH OF THIS NATION CAN MAKE SUCH A DECREE.
......
THE ONE CURRENTLY EMPOWERED TO DO SO IS...
A SPECIAL VESSEL OF FLESH.
!
LET ME EXPLAIN...
WHY THIS IS SO... ACTUALLY, AN ANSWER IS UNNECESSARY.
SUFY ALREADY LEAKED SOME VITAL DETAILS TO YOU, YES?
Dear, oh dear.
SUFY?

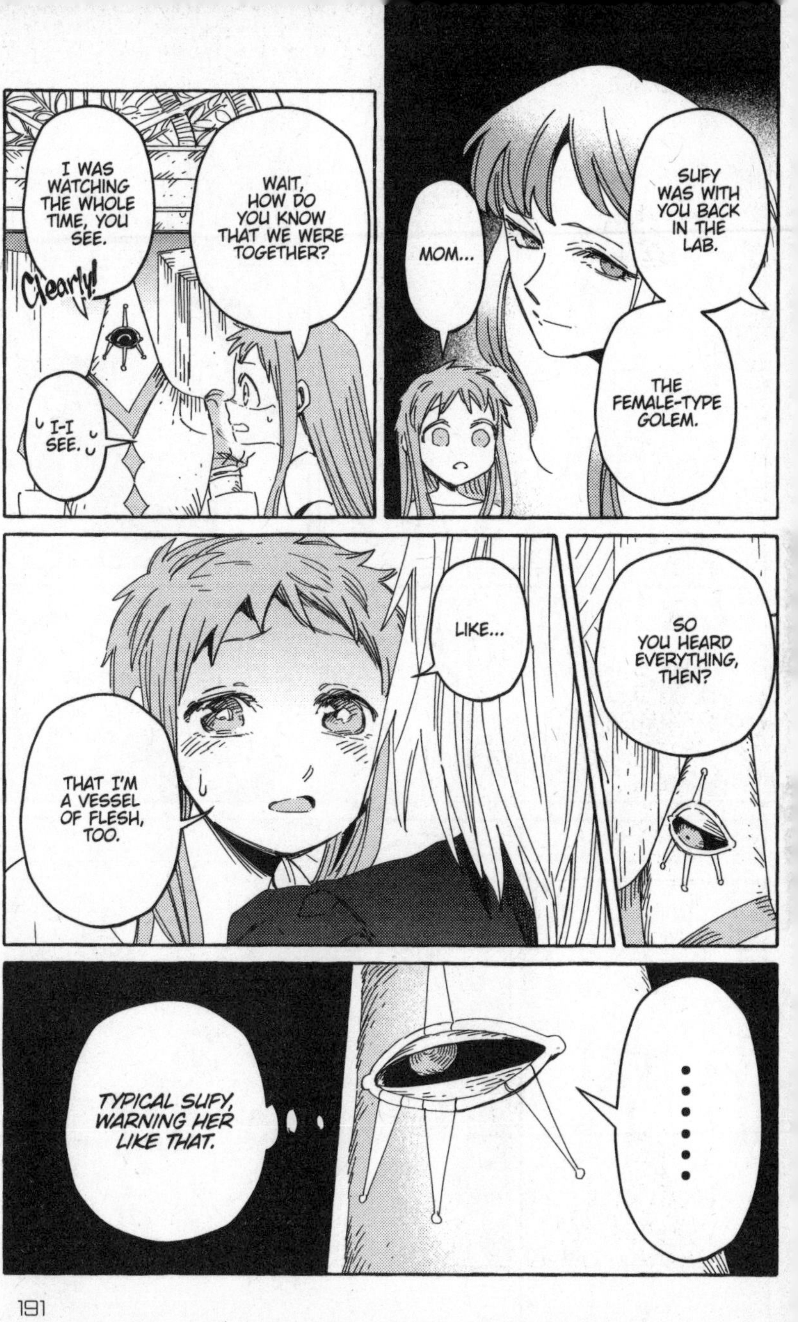
SUFY WAS WITH YOU BACK IN THE LAB.
THE FEMALE-TYPE GOLEM.
MOM...
WAIT, HOW DO YOU KNOW THAT WE WERE TOGETHER?
I WAS WATCHING THE WHOLE TIME, YOU SEE.
Clearly!
I-I SEE.
SO YOU HEARD EVERYTHING, THEN?
LIKE...
THAT I'M A VESSEL OF FLESH, TOO.
......
TYPICAL SUFY, WARNING HER LIKE THAT.

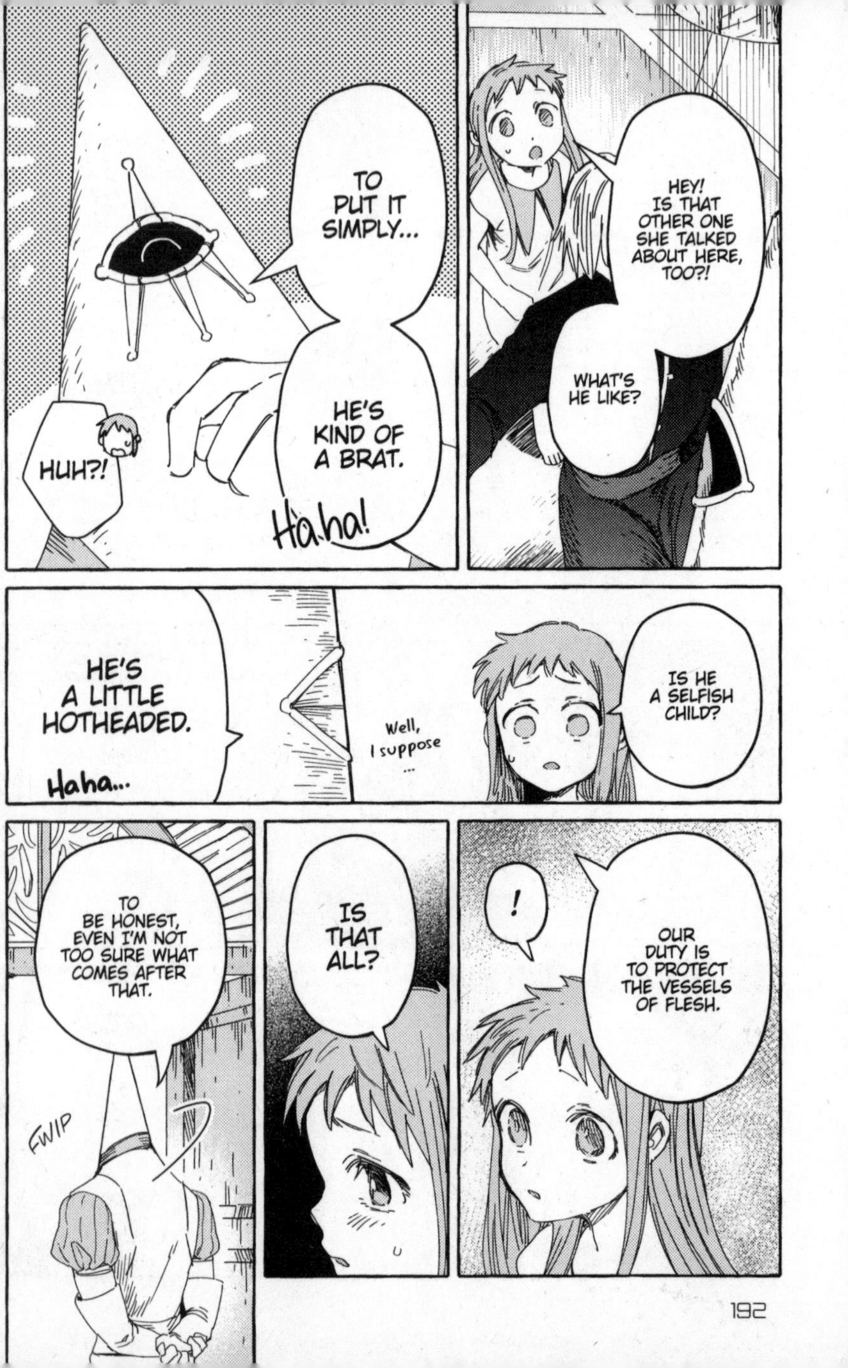
HEY! IS THAT OTHER ONE SHE TALKED ABOUT HERE, TOO?!
WHAT'S HE LIKE?
TO PUT IT SIMPLY...
HE'S KIND OF A BRAT.
Haha!
HUH?!
IS HE A SELFISH CHILD?
Well, I suppose ...
HE'S A LITTLE HOTHEADED.
Haha...
!
OUR DUTY IS TO PROTECT THE VESSELS OF FLESH.
IS THAT ALL?
TO BE HONEST, EVEN I'M NOT TOO SURE WHAT COMES AFTER THAT.
FWIP

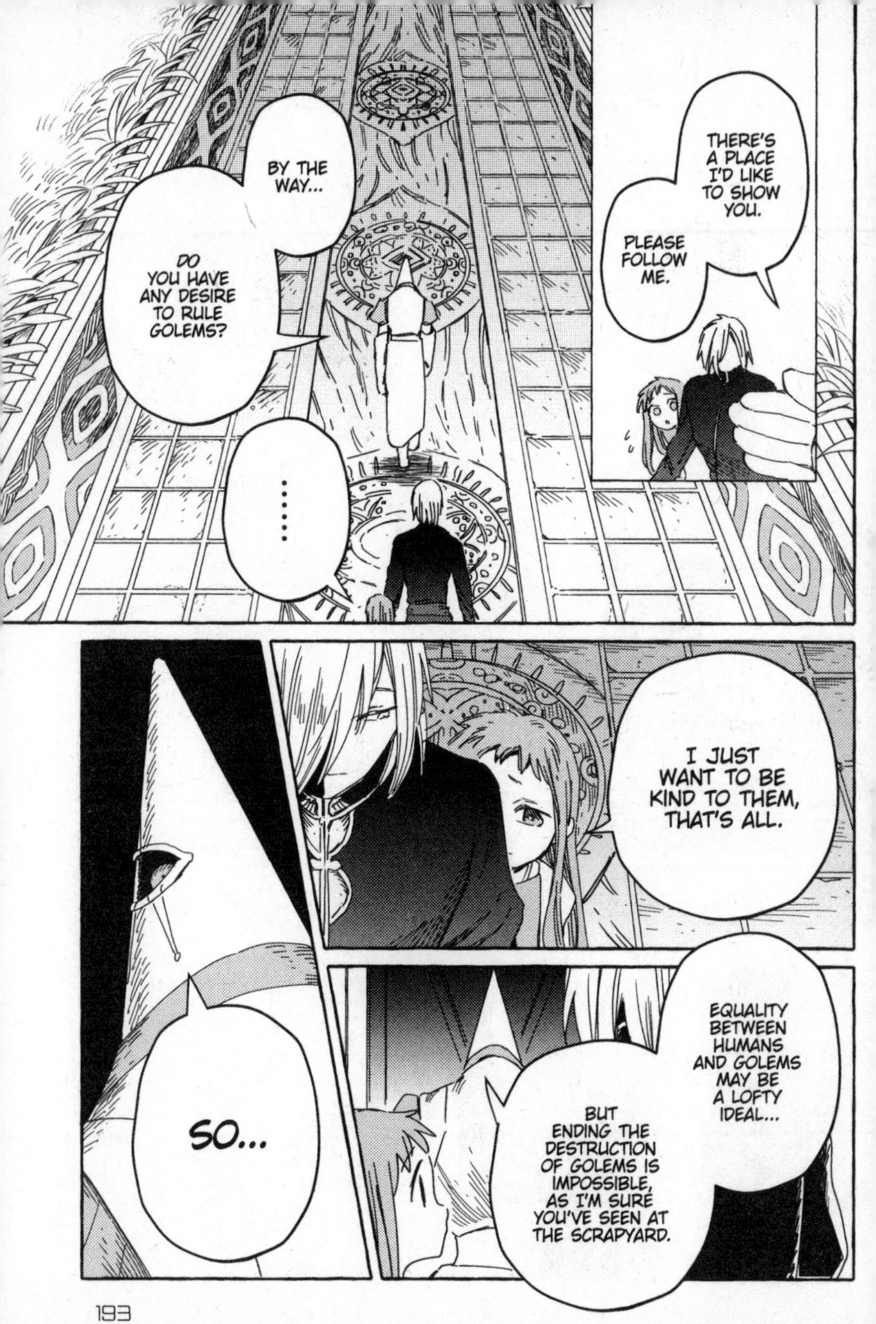
THERE'S A PLACE I'D LIKE TO SHOW YOU.
PLEASE FOLLOW ME.
BY THE WAY...
DO YOU HAVE ANY DESIRE TO RULE GOLEMS?
......
I JUST WANT TO BE KIND TO THEM, THAT'S ALL.
EQUALITY BETWEEN HUMANS AND GOLEMS MAY BE A LOFTY IDEAL...
BUT ENDING THE DESTRUCTION OF GOLEMS IS IMPOSSIBLE, AS I'M SURE YOU'VE SEEN AT THE SCRAPYARD.
SO...

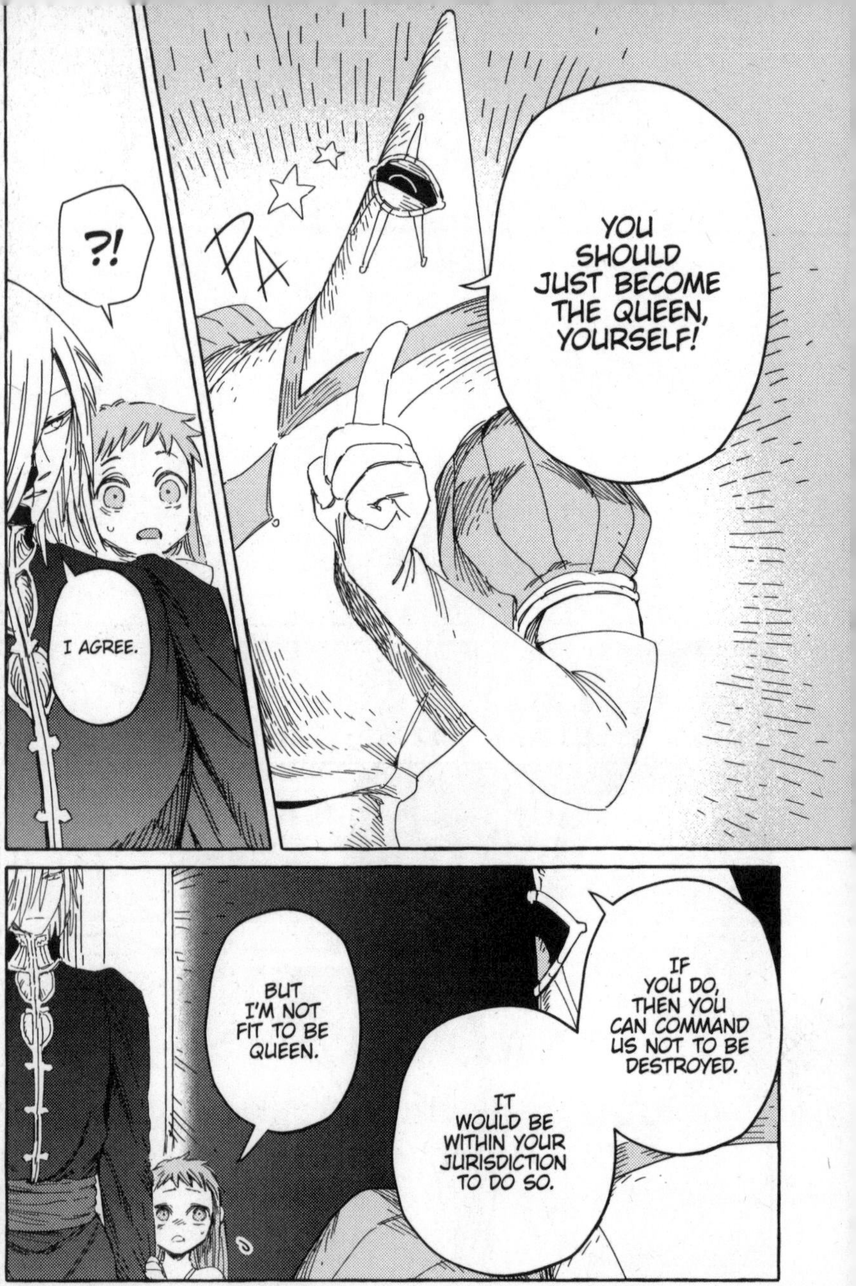
YOU SHOULD JUST BECOME THE QUEEN, YOURSELF!
PA
?!
I AGREE.
IF YOU DO, THEN YOU CAN COMMAND US NOT TO BE DESTROYED.
IT WOULD BE WITHIN YOUR JURISDICTION TO DO SO.
BUT I'M NOT FIT TO BE QUEEN.

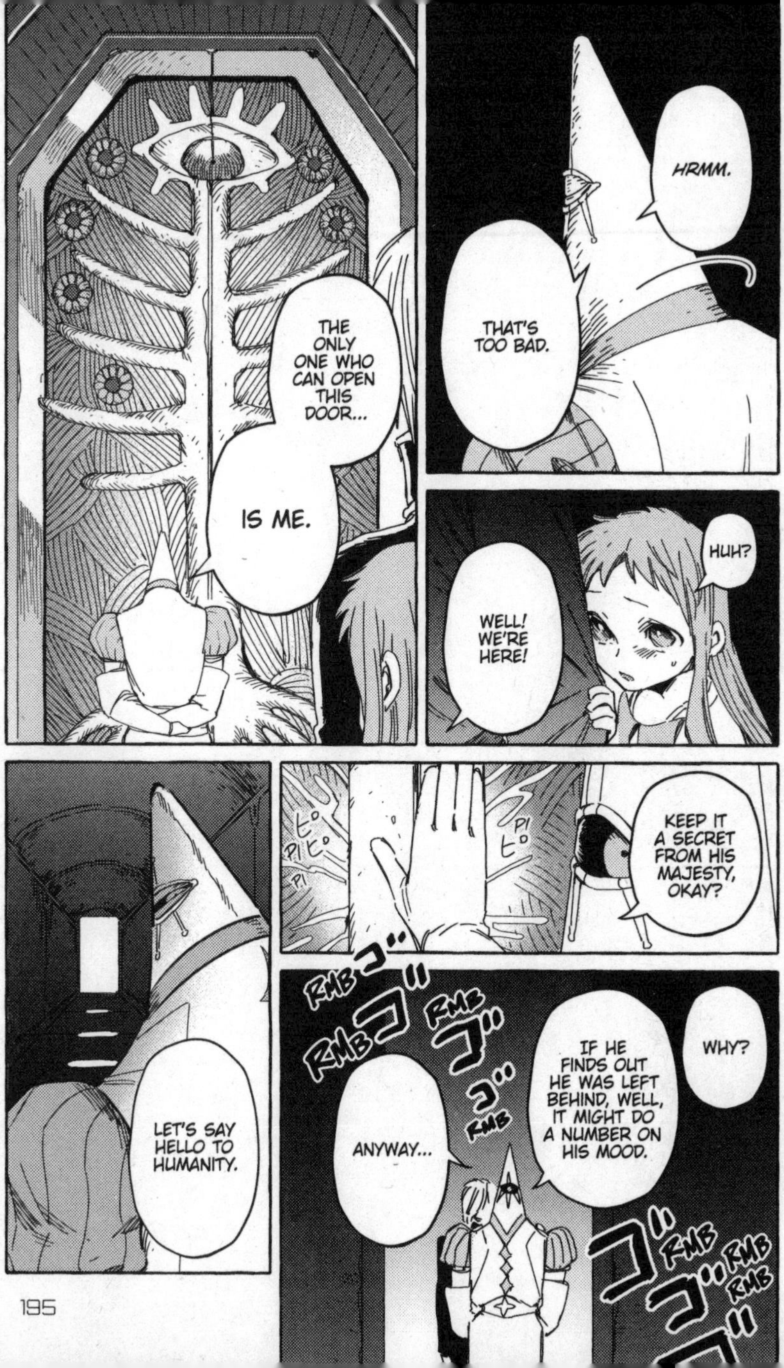
HRMM.
THAT'S TOO BAD.
HUH?
WELL! WE'RE HERE!
THE ONLY ONE WHO CAN OPEN THIS DOOR...
IS ME.
KEEP IT A SECRET FROM HIS MAJESTY, OKAY?
PI PI PI PI
WHY?
IF HE FINDS OUT HE WAS LEFT BEHIND, WELL, IT MIGHT DO A NUMBER ON HIS MOOD.
ANYWAY...
RMB RMB RMB RMB RMB RMB RMB
LET'S SAY HELLO TO HUMANITY.

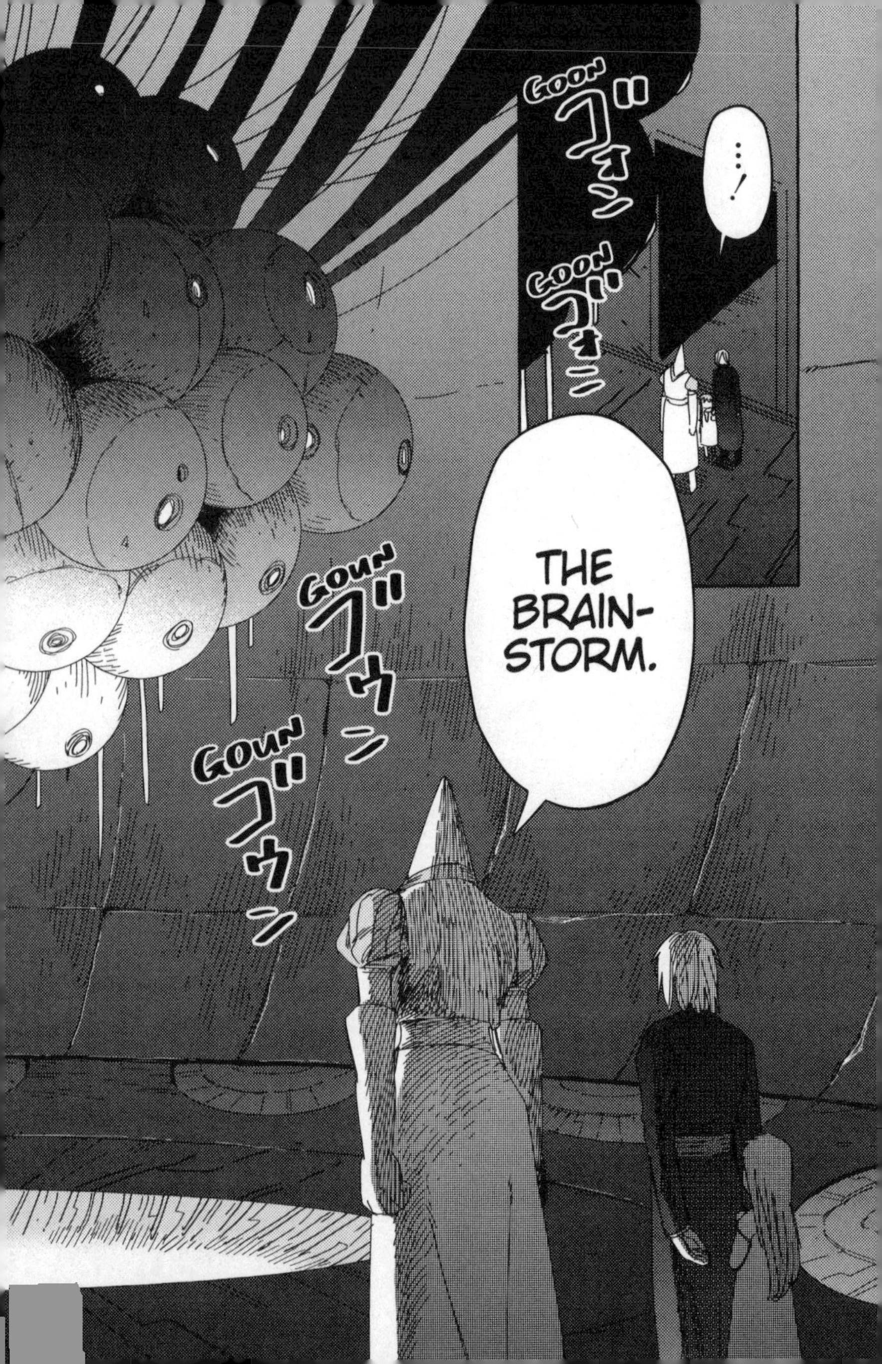
…!
GOON ゴォン
GOON ゴォン
THE BRAIN-STORM.
GOUN ゴウン
GOUN ゴウン

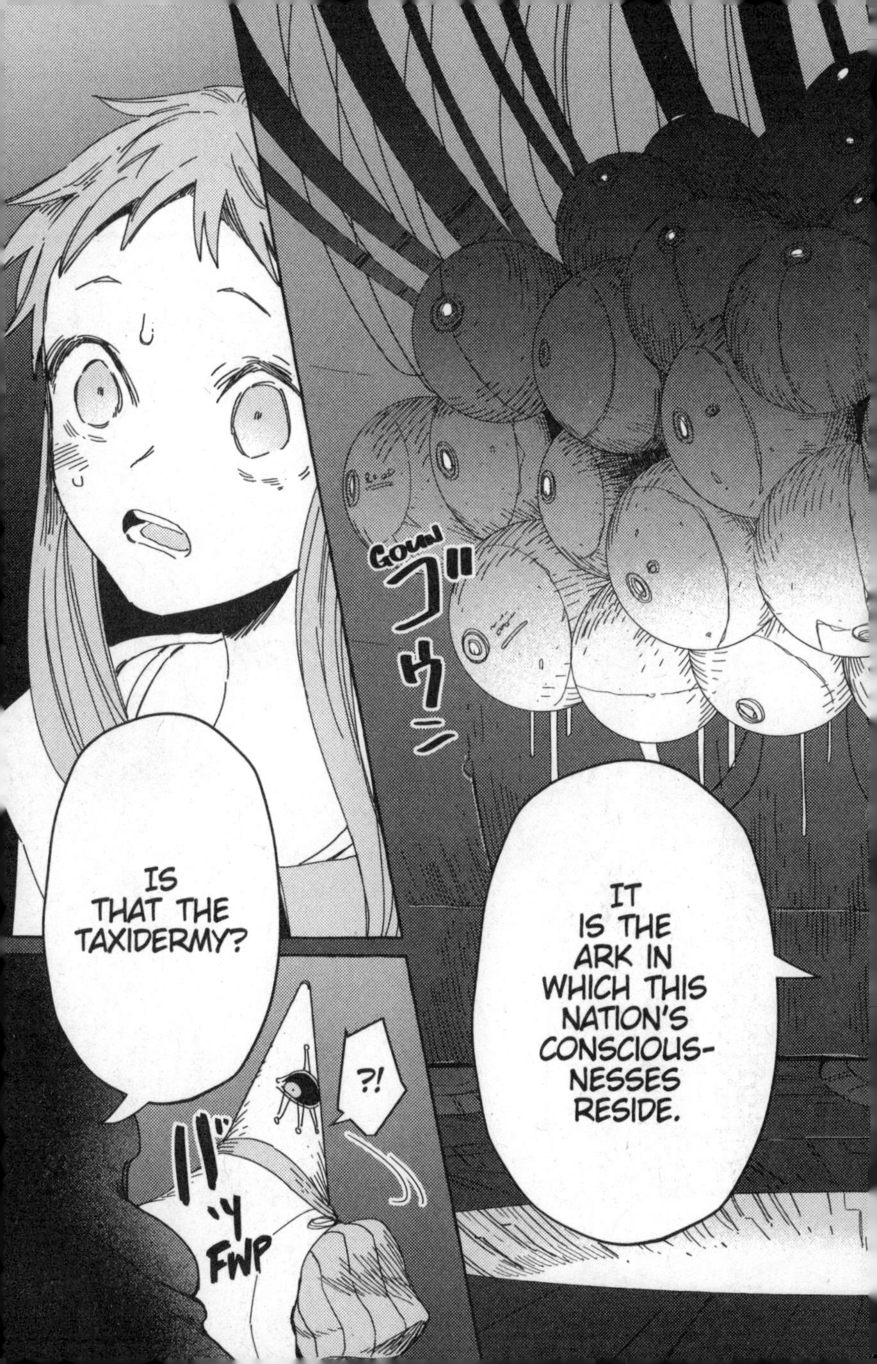
GOUN ゴウ～
IS THAT THE TAXIDERMY?
IT IS THE ARK IN WHICH THIS NATION'S CONSCIOUS-NESSES RESIDE.
?!
バッ FWP

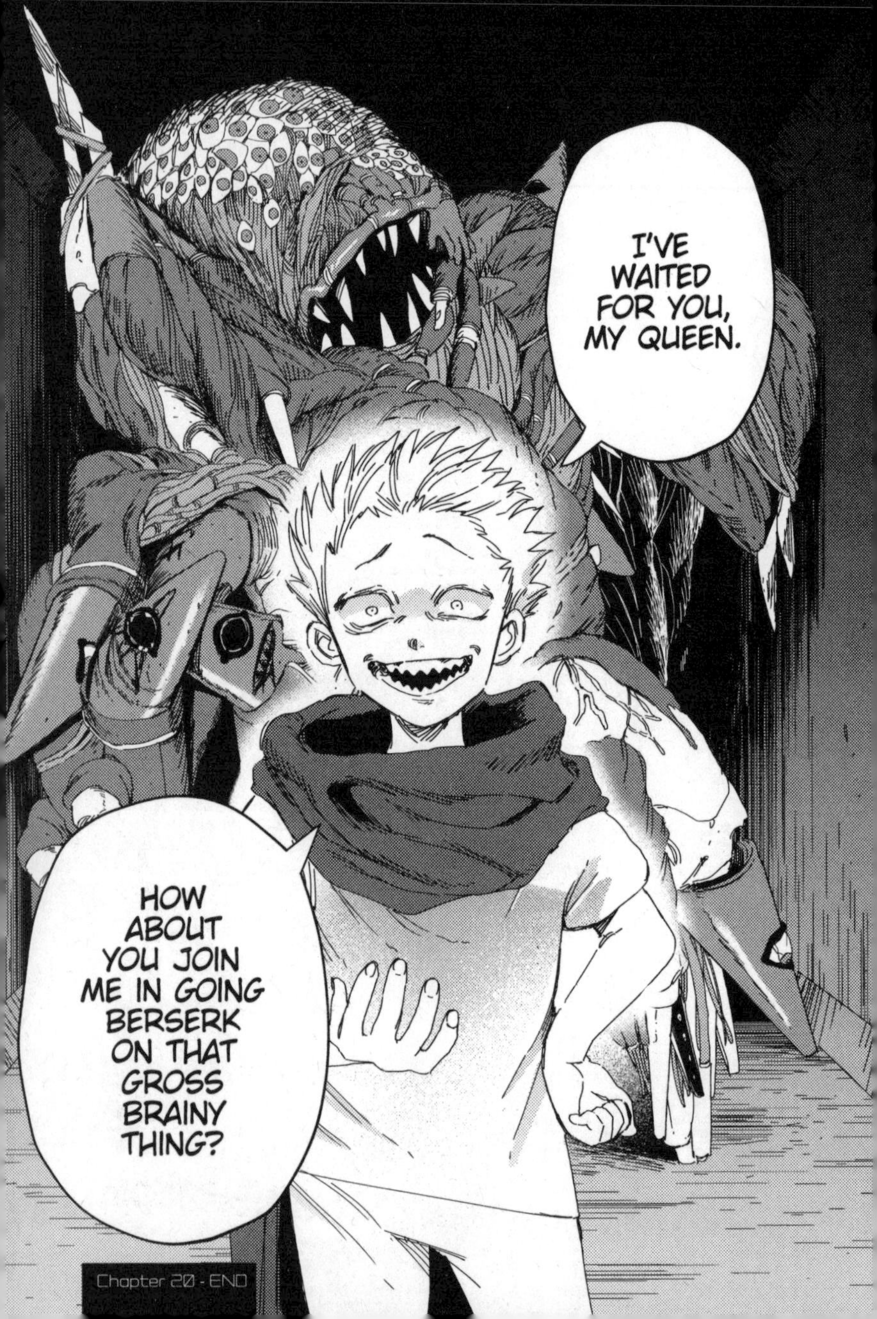
I'VE WAITED FOR YOU, MY QUEEN.
HOW ABOUT YOU JOIN ME IN GOING BERSERK ON THAT GROSS BRAINY THING?
Chapter 20 - END

SEVEN SEAS ENTERTAINMENT PRESENTS

The Country Without Humans

story and art by IWATOBINEKO　　VOLUME THREE

TRANSLATION
Deniz Amasya

ADAPTATION
Kim Kindya

LETTERING
Robert Harkins

PROOFREADER
Leighanna DeRouen

COPY EDITOR
B. Lillian Martin

SENIOR EDITOR
Jenn Grunigen

PRODUCTION DESIGNER
Christina McKenzie

PRODUCTION MANAGER
Lissa Pattillo

PREPRESS TECHNICIAN
Melanie Ujimori
Jules Valera

EDITOR-IN-CHIEF
Julie Davis

ASSOCIATE PUBLISHER
Adam Arnold

PUBLISHER
Jason DeAngelis

The Country Without Humans Vol. 3
©IWATOBINEKO 2019
All rights reserved.
First published by Futabasha Publishers Ltd., in 2021.
English version published by Seven Seas Entertainment, Inc.

Seven Seas press and purchase enquiries can be sent to Marketing Manager Lianne Sentar at press@gomanga.com. Information regarding the distribution and purchase of digital editions is available from Digital Manager CK Russell at digital@gomanga.com.

Seven Seas and the Seven Seas logo are trademarks of Seven Seas Entertainment, Inc. All rights reserved.

ISBN: 978-1-63858-360-8
Printed in Canada
First Printing: December 2022
10 9 8 7 6 5 4 3 2 1

▨▨▨ READING DIRECTIONS ▨▨▨

This book reads from *right to left*, Japanese style. If this is your first time reading manga, you start reading from the top right panel on each page and take it from there. If you get lost, just follow the numbered diagram here. It may seem backwards at first, but you'll get the hang of it! Have fun!!

Follow us online: www.SevenSeasEntertainment.com